Canon Pietro Casola's Pilgrimage to Jerusalem in the year 1494

Pietro Casola

Mary Margaret Newett

Alpha Editions

This edition published in 2020

ISBN : 9789354157035 (Hardback)
ISBN : 9789354156533 (Paperback)

Design and Setting By
Alpha Editions
www.alphaedis.com
email - alphaedis@gmail.com

As per information held with us this book is in Public Domain. This book is a reproduction of an important historical work. Alpha Editions uses the best technology to reproduce historical work in the same manner it was first published to preserve its original nature. Any marks or number seen are left intentionally to preserve its true form.

University of Manchester Publications
No. XXVI.

PREFACE.

I HOPE the following itinerary may prove nearly as interesting and attractive in the English Version as it is in the quaint medieval Italian, in which Canon Pietro Casola recorded the events of his momentous voyage, for the amusement and instruction of his Milanese friends, more than four hundred years ago.

Those who desire to know more about the writer and the friends with whom the chances of the journey brought him in contact, will find, in the Introduction and the Notes, what the dusty shelves of the Archives could furnish concerning them.

For those who care to learn more than Casola tells about the conditions in which medieval pilgrims carried out their pious purpose, I have traced, as far as possible, the legislation of the Venetian Republic with regard to the pilgrim traffic, from early times to the last law on the Statute Book. It has been a labour of love and yet disappointing. So few documents, comparatively speaking, have survived the destructive influences of time and the many great fires which devastated the Venetian State Records. Enough remains, however, to enable us to form a clear idea of the intentions of the legislators, and of the ceaseless war they had to wage, against the egoistical tendencies of human nature, in the effort to carry them into effect.

It only remains for me to thank heartily my many kind friends in the Record Offices and Libraries of Venice and Milan, and especially at the Archives of Venice, and at the Trivulzian Library and the Cathedral at Milan, for the help so willingly given me in the difficult work of translation and research. Also to express my thanks to Prof. T. F. Tout for the interest he has taken in and the time he has bestowed upon a publication which, unfortunately, involved a great deal of trouble owing to the distance which separates me from England; and to gratefully acknowledge the kindness of Mr. W. E. Rhodes, for his share in the work of proof-correcting.

M. MARGARET NEWETT.

VENICE, *April, 1907.*

CONTENTS

Fac-simile page from the Book of Prayers and Gospels for the Triduan Litanies ... *Frontispiece*
Map ... *At End of Introduction*

	PAGE
Preface	v
Historical Introduction	1

Chapter I. Casola determines to undertake a pilgrimage to Jerusalem, and after receiving the archiepiscopal benediction, leaves Milan on May 15th, arriving at Venice on May 20th ... 115

Chapter II. Description of Venice. He meets Fra Francesco Trivulzio ... 124

Chapter III. Visits to various monasteries and churches at Venice. The Arsenal. Glass Industry. Venetian Men and Women ... 134

Chapter IV. Festival of the Corpus Domini. Preparations for leaving Venice... 146

Chapter V. Casola embarks. Description of the galley, the Contarina. Voyage from Venice to Zara ... 155

Chapter VI. Voyage from Zara to Ragusa ... 168

Chapter VII. From Ragusa to Modone... 181

Chapter VIII. From Modone to Rhodes ... 195

Chapter IX. From Rhodes to Jaffa ... 212

Chapter X. The galley anchors at Jaffa. Casola lands after considerable delays caused by the Governor of Gaza ... 221

Chapter XI. Journey from Jaffa to Jerusalem ... 236

Chapter XII. Visits to the Holy Places at Jerusalem, Bethlehem, etc. ... 246

Chapter XIII. Visit to the River Jordan and Jericho. Description of the Church of the Holy Sepulchre. Visit to Bethany... 266

Chapter XIV. Return to Jaffa. Departure for the West after renewed difficulties with the Governor of Gaza ... 281

Chapter XV. Return voyage to Rhodes... 292

Chapter XVI. From Rhodes to Modone ... 309

Chapter XVII. From Modone to Parenzo ... 321

Chapter XVIII. Return of galley to Venice. Festival on All Saints' Day. Casola arrives back at Milan ... 336

Notes ... 349
Appendix ... 403
Index ... 413

INTRODUCTION

AMONGST the subjects which have attracted the attention of historical students during the last half century, not the least interesting is the story of the pilgrimages directed unceasingly to Palestine from the early centuries of the christian era—a story told in many cases by the pilgrims themselves who found their way by different routes to the common goal from all parts of christendom.

An immense impulse was given to the study of the pilgrim voyages by the publication, in 1868, of the *Bibliographia Geographica Palaestinae*, compiled by the late Professor Titus Tobler. This useful work was afterwards so enlarged and supplemented by his disciple, Professor Reinhold Röhricht, that the new edition, published in 1890, gives an almost exhaustive list of the pilgrimages—from the earliest down to modern times—undertaken by pilgrims who have left some account of their voyages; together with full details as to where those relations are to be found—and whether in manuscript or in print—or both.

Meanwhile Professor Röhricht, in collaboration with Dr. H. Meissner, was preparing the first edition of the *Deutsche Pilgerreisen nach dem Heiligen Lande*, which saw the light in 1880; a second, and enlarged edition, was published by Professor Röhricht alone in 1900. The bibliography of the German pilgrim voyages there completed, closes with a notice of the Pilgrimage of Heinrich Wilhelm Ludolph, who went to the Holy Land *viâ* Constantinople, in 1699, and returned by way of Leghorn. Röhricht notes that in 1494 Ludwig Freiherr von Greiffenstein, Reinhard von Bemmelberg, and Konrad von Parsberg went to Jerusalem.[1] They were fellow pilgrims with Casola, and left descriptions of their voyage, still preserved, which I have unfortunately not been able to consult. Judging, however, from the summaries given by Röhricht, the German pilgrims confirm the account given by Casola.

Much valuable work has been done in France by the *Société de l'Orient Latin*, especially by means of the Society's journal, to which M. N. Jorga contributed the *Notes et extraits pour servir à l'histoire des Croisades au XVe Siècle*—largely drawn from the Archives of Venice, and carried down to the fall of Constantinople in 1453. The geographical series published by the Society—the *Itinera Latina*, the *Itinéraires Français*, and the *Itinéraires Russes en Orient*,—the latter translated by Madame B. de Chitrow,—are of very high interest; and the publication of the Russian voyages is a testimony to the work done by the Russian Palestine Society. Two volumes of the *Receuil de voyages et de documents pour servir à l'histoire de la Géographie depuis le xiiie jusqu à la fin du xvie Siècle*, published under the direction of M.M. Charles Schefer and Henri Cordier, have been specially useful to me in illustrating the general history of the pilgrim voyages, namely, *Le voyage de la Saincte Cyté de Hierusalem avec la description des lieux, portz, villes, citez, et aultres passaiges, fait l'an mil quatre cens, quatre vingtz, étant le siège du Grant Turc à Rhodes, et regnant en France Loys unzièsme de ce nom*, and *Le voyage de la Terre Sainte composé par Maître Denis Possot, et achevé par Messire Charles Philippe Seigneur de Champarmoy et de Grand Champ, 1532.* The first of these was probably

---

1. Reinhold Röhricht, *Deutsche Pilgerreisen nach dem Heiligen Lande*, Innsbruck, 1890, p. 183.

written by a French clerk, whose name is unknown; it is of importance in relation to Casola's voyage, because the pilgrims of 1480 were conducted to Jerusalem and back by Agostino Contarini, who commanded the pilgrim galley also in 1494.

In England nearly three centuries ago, 'Purchas's *Pilgrims*,' and 'Hakluyt's *Voyages and Discoveries*,' stimulated popular interest in pilgrimages and voyages of discovery and commerce, etc. Amongst other accounts Hakluyt includes the Latin text and the English translation of the description of his voyage left by Odorico of Pordenone, in Friuli, who went to Palestine in the beginning of the fourteenth century. In recent years important contributions have been made to the subject by the *Palestine Pilgrims' Text Society*, created for the translation and publication of historical and geographical works relating to the Holy Land. I believe that collection was closed with the publication of the *Life of Saladin*, translated by Lieutenant Colonel Conder.

In Italy, in 1882, Count Pietro Amat di San Filippo published under the auspices of the Italian Geographical Society, biographical sketches of Italian voyagers to Palestine, somewhat on the lines of Tobler's and Röhricht's books,—to which the Count added an appendix in 1884. The enterprise of societies or of private individuals has also led to the publication of the text of many Italian voyages, such, for example, as *Il Viaggio in Terra Santa fatto e descritto per Roberto da Sanseverino*, included in the series of literary curiosities from the XIIIth to the XVIIth centuries, published in Bologna under the direction of the poet Giosuè Carducci; and the invaluable *Trattato di Terra Santa e dell' Oriente* of the Franciscan friar, Francesco Suriano, edited in 1900 by P. Girolamo Golubovich, a member of the same order.

All these and numberless other publications have revealed the pilgrim stream flowing in all ages steadily in the direction of the Eastern Mediterranean; at first by various channels, then concentrating its chief force on Italy, and finally choosing Venice almost exclusively as the common outlet—the port, that is, of embarcation—as long as she maintained her pre-eminent position on the sea.

Long before 1000 A.D. the busy little Italian Republics had acquired supreme commercial and maritime importance; and Venice, Amalfi, Pisa and Genoa, had concentrated in their own hands the world's commerce, which then and for long after had its centre in the Mediterranean.

As far back as the seventh century Amalfi, the first Italian city which is certainly known to have traded with the Levant, offered a formidable resistance to the advance of the Saracens; and the Tarì of Amalfi was universally accepted as current coin in the East, as later the Golden Ducat or Zecchino of Venice. The vessels of Amalfi went regularly to the ports of Beyrout and Alexandria with pilgrims and merchants. But the victories of the Normans and the hostility of Pisa were fatal to the enterprising little city, which was reduced to impotence at the beginning of the twelfth century.

Pisa had a powerful fleet, and was one of the chief commercial cities of Italy, between the tenth and the thirteen centuries. It had its share of Eastern commerce, and of the pilgrim transport, and the record of the Pisan establishments in Jerusalem was still preserved at the time of Casola's visit, in the " Pisan Castle " outside the city gate to which he several times refers. Pisa after completing the ruin of Amalfi fell in turn before the maritime power of its Genoese rival at the rock of Meloria in 1284, and the field was left clear for the duel between Genoa and Venice, for commercial supremacy and the control of the carrying trade in the Eastern Mediterranean.

The facilities given by the Venetian Republic to the Crusaders of 1201-4, and the establishment of the Latin Empire in Constantinople, resulted in converging the pilgrim stream more than ever on Venice; and this not only because of the size of her naval and mercantile fleet, but also on account of the guarantees she was able to offer to travellers for a safe and successful journey, owing to the chain of ports on the mainland and in the islands, which fell to her share when the spoil of the Byzantine Empire was divided. Genoa struggled hard, but in spite of the advantages she secured in the Black Sea over Venice, when the Greek Empire was re-established, her good fortune was shortlived, and after the great defeat at Chioggia in 1380, she ceased to be dangerous to her great rival of the Adriatic, and Venice was indeed mistress of the seas. From the second half of the fourteenth century, and especially after 1380—save for isolated cases of pilgrims who embarked for special reasons at Genoa, Gaeta, Naples, Brindisi, Ancona, etc.—the overwhelming majority went for two centuries on the sea voyage to Syria from Venice; and the pilgrim traffic gave rise there to a voluminous and special legislation, continued down to the middle of the sixteenth century—to the time, that is, when the sun of Venetian commercial and maritime importance was slowly and surely setting, and when she therefore ceased to be able to offer the special advantages which had drawn pilgrims from all parts of Europe to her port for so many centuries.

Among the Italian pilgrimages to Jerusalem there is a record of one completed in 570 by Saint Antonino of

Piacenza, whose account, *De Locis sanctis quæ perambulavit Antoninus Martyr*, is mentioned by Tobler.[1]

Between 1062 and 1066 Pantaleone, a rich citizen of Amalfi, accompanied by Bishop Alfano of Salerno and Bernardo of Praeneste, went to Constantinople, and thence to the Holy Land, where, through the generosity of his father Mauro, a hostel was established in Jerusalem for the citizens of Amalfi.[2]

A century and a half later, in 1219, Saint Francis of Assisi with a company of courageous missionaries, landed at Acre and visited the holy places. On his return by way of Damietta he entered the camp of the Saracens, who, astonished at his boldness, and probably not understanding what he said, let him preach the Gospel and condemn the Koran.[3]

The voyages of Italian pilgrims increased enormously in the fourteenth century, and the accounts which have come down to us include, in addition to the lists of the places visited and the enumeration of religious ceremonies and of the devout practices and beliefs of the pilgrims, some notices of Oriental manners and customs, fauna and flora, geography, commerce and industry. The chief are those written by three Tuscans—a friar, a noble and a merchant. The two latter were the Florentines, Leonardo Frescobaldi and Simone Sigoli, who went to Jerusalem in 1384–5.

The most interesting accounts, however, belong to the fifteenth century, and those written by Roberto da Sanseverino, the great Condottiere, whose father was a Neapolitan, and whose mother was a sister of Francesco Sforza; by Santo Brasca, a Milanese; by Gabriele

---

1. See Preface to *Biografia di Viaggiatori Italiani, &c.*, by P. Amat di S. Filippo Rome, 1882; and the *Bibl. Geog. Palæs.*, by Titus Tobler.
2. See preface to *Biografia di Viaggiatori Italiani*, by P. Amat di San Filippo. Rome, 1882.
3. *Idem*.

Capodilista, a noble Paduan; by Francesco Suriano, a Venetian; and by Girolamo Castiglione, Bernardino di Nali, and Pietro Casola, all three natives of Milan, stand out pre-eminently.

The number of Milanese pilgrims in preceding years might well make Casola feel disappointed that he was destined, in spite of all his efforts to the contrary, to go on his voyage alone in 1494. Nevertheless he could at least profit by the experiences of fellow countrymen who had undertaken the pilgrimage in previous years.

Roberto da Sanseverino, who settled definitely in Lombardy, when his uncle became duke of Milan, went on his pilgrimage in 1458. He was accompanied by several friends, one of whom, "The Magnificent Giovane Mateo Butigella, ducal courtier," wrote on his return a *History of the Holy Land*. Another passenger on board the same pilgrim galley with Sanseverino and his companions was "John, Earl of Exeter, a great lord and a relative of the King of England." Sanseverino's own description of the journey includes an acount of his visit to Mount Sinai, and his return to Jerusalem by way of Cairo. He was killed in 1487, while waging a frontier war for the Venetians against Sigismund, Count of Tyrol. Whether Casola ever met the great Condottiere we do not know; but he could certainly read his *Voyage to the Holy Land*,[1] of which copies were in circulation in Milan. There is one at the present time in the Trivulzian Library.

In 1486, Fra Girolamo Castiglione (or de Castellione) a native of Milan, travelled through Palestine, Arabia and Egypt. In his *Treatise on the Country beyond the Seas that is the Holy Land*, he says little about the countries he visited; but gives elaborate details with regard to the

---

1. *Viaggio in Terra Santa fatto e descritto per Roberto da Sanseverino*, published with preface and notes by Romagnoli dall' Acqua, Bologna, 1889.

pious beliefs of the pilgrims, and the devotions they usually performed.[1]

A Milanese merchant named Bernadino di Nali (or di Noli) went as a pilgrim to the Holy Land in 1492, and wrote a short account of his experiences, a copy of which is preserved in the National Library of Lucca. It commences, "In the name of the Father, Son and Holy Spirit, here begins the pilgrimage to Jerusalem made by me, Bernardino di Nali, Milanese merchant in Venice, in the year of the human salvation, 1492, on the Jaffa Galley.[2]

Casola must, however, have received more valuable help still from the written and verbal instructions of two fellow townsmen, both living in 1494—the Lord Guidantonio Arcimboldi, Archbishop of Milan, and the Cavalier Santo Brasca, who was twice quæstor of his city, and who was also ducal Chancellor under Lodovico Sforza.

Guidantonio Arcimboldi was a son of Nicolo Arcimboldi, president of the Senate, and of Ursina Countess of Canossa. He succeeded his brother Giovanni, as Archbishop of Milan, in 1488. But, before taking orders, he had been Senator and president of the Senate, like his father. Because of his culture, his oratorical gifts, his knowledge of law, and his remarkable prudence, he was frequently employed as Ducal Ambassador and plenipotentiary.[3] In this capacity Sanuto mentions his arrival in Venice, in April, 1496, adding that he had already been as ambassador to Spain. Later on Sanuto remarks that the Milanese Archbishop in "leaving and coming to the audiences observes the order of the hours given him by the duke according to astrology, which the duke follows greatly."[4] The Archbishop left Venice on the 14th of

---

1. P. Amat di San Filippo, *Biografia di Viaggiatori Italiani*, &c., p. 170; and Röhricht, *Bibl. Geog. Palaes.*, p. 139.
2. Idem. See Amat di San Filippo, p. 199, and Röhricht, p. 143.
3. Argelati, *Bibliotheca Scriptorum Mediolan.*, vol. i. part ii. cap. cxix.
4. *Diarii di Marino Sanuto*, vol. i. pp. 116, 120.

June, 1496, and returned to Milan, where he died in October, 1497.

As far back as 1476, Arcimboldi had gone with the celebrated Gian Giacomo Trivulzio, another condottiere, and Count Galeotto da Belgioioso on a pilgrimage to Jerusalem. Unfortunately all we know of their voyage is contained in the few letters sent home by the travellers themselves, and in the despatches of Leonardo Botta, Milanese Ambassador in Venice at that time, who mentions their arrival there on the outward and homeward voyages. On the 14th of October, 1476, Botta wrote that Trivulzio had arrived that day in Venice "all shaken to pieces by the sea," after a disastrous voyage.[1] He had separated from Arcimboldi at Jaffa, where the latter went on board the pilgrim galley because he could not endure the rolling of the sailing ship on which they had gone out from Venice. His vivid recollection of the sufferings and hardships endured on this pilgrimage no doubt accounts for the "no ordinary tears" with which the Archbishop bestowed his benediction on Casola on the eve of his departure, and the joy with which he welcomed him on his return.

The Cavalier Santo Brasca went to the Holy Sepulchre in 1480, on board the pilgrim galley, owned and commanded by the "magnificent miser, Augustino Contarini, a Venetian patrician, and a very upright man of good fame." Among Brasca's fellow pilgrims were the author of the *Voyage de la Saincte Cyté de Hierusalem* . . . . *fait l'an mil quatre cens quatre vingtz*, already cited; and the celebrated Felix Faber, author of the *Evagatorium*, who went on a second pilgrimage in 1483.

Brasca's description of his journey was deservedly popular at Milan, where it was printed for the first time

---

1. *Gian Giacomo Trivulzio in Terra Santa*, by Emilio Motta in the *Archivio Storico Lombardo*, Anno xiii., 1886, pp. 866—878.

in 1481, and republished in 1497. He carefully mentions the hymns, chants and prayers said and sung by the pilgrims on various occasions, and in all the sacred places, and enumerates the indulgences to be procured in the places they visited. This probably accounts for the fact that Casola, though a priest, gives little information on these points. He clearly saw no purpose in repeating what others in Milan—such as Castiglione and Santo Brasca—had recently written so fully. In conclusion, Brasca devotes a chapter to practical instructions for intending pilgrims, of which the following is a translation:—

"The instructions promised above to anyone who desires to undertake this most Holy Voyage are the following, to wit:—In the first place, a man should undertake this voyage solely with the intention of visiting, contemplating and adoring the most Holy Mysteries, with great effusion of tears, in order that Jesus may graciously pardon his sins; and not with the intention of seeing the world, or from ambition, or to be able to boast 'I have been there,' or 'I have seen that,' in order to be exalted by his fellowmen, as perhaps some do, who in this case from now have received their reward. Similarly, he should prepare himself to pardon the injuries done him; to restore everything belonging to others; and to live according to the law, because without this first and necessary disposition every hope and every fatigue is in vain.

"Secondly, he should put his affairs in order and make his will, so that whatever God wills to happen to him his heirs may not find themselves in difficulties.

"Thirdly, he should carry with him two bags—one right full of patience, the other containing two hundred Venetian ducats, or at least one hundred and fifty—namely, one hundred which each person needs for the voyage, and

INTRODUCTION

then nothing will be lacking to the man who loves his life and is accustomed to live delicately at home; the other fifty for illness or any other circumstances that may arise.

"Fourthly, let him take with him a warm long upper garment[1] to wear on the return journey, when it is cold; a good many shirts, so as to avoid lice and other unclean things as much as possible; and also tablecloths, towels, sheets, pillow cases and such like.

"Then he should go to Venice, because from there he can take his passage more conveniently than from any other city in the world. Every year one galley is deputed solely for this service; and although he may find it cheaper to go on a sailing ship,[2] he should on no account abandon the galley. He should make an agreement with the captain,[3] who usually requires from fifty to sixty ducats. For this price he is obliged to provide the passage there and back, supply all food (except on land); pay for the riding animals in the Holy Land, and also pay all duties and tribute.

"Next he should cause to be made an overcoat[4] reaching down to the ground to wear when sleeping in the open air, and buy a thin mattress[5] instead of a bed, a long chest, two barrels—to wit, one for water, the other for wine—and a night-stool[6] or covered pail.

"Further, let him take a supply of good Lombard cheese, and sausages and other salt meats of every sort, white biscuits, some loaves of sugar, and several kinds of preserved sweetmeats, but not a great quantity of these last because they soon go bad. Above all he should have with him a great deal of fruit syrup, because that is what

---

1. *Veste.*
2. *Nave* = one of the largest Venetian sailing ships—which made no use whatever of oars.
3. *Patrono* = Captain—Captain-owner or owner.
4. *Gabano* = a long mantle of coarse cloth with sleeves.
5. *Strapontino.*
6. *Zangola.*

keeps a man alive in the great heat; and also syrup of ginger to settle his stomach if it should be upset by excessive vomiting, but the ginger should be used sparingly, because it is very heating. Likewise he should take some quince without spice, some aromatics flavoured with rose and carnation and some good milk products.

"He should take care to arrange in good time—especially if given to suffering from the head on account of the movement of the sea—to have his lodging in the middle of the galley and near the middle door in order to have a little air.

"When he goes ashore in any place, he should furnish himself with eggs, fowls, bread, sweetmeats and fruit, and not count what he has paid the captain, because this is a voyage on which the purse must not be kept shut.

"On landing at Jaffa he should be humble in his behaviour and in his dress. At this place the chief officer[1] of the galley, the supercargo,[2] the pilot, the trumpeters, the drummers, the chief rowers,[3] the crossbow men, the stewards, the cooks and others all come forward, each with a cup in his hand, and it is advisable to give something to each of them. In the Holy Land carry a cushion, and never leave the caravan of the pilgrims, and do not venture to argue about the faith with those Saracens, because it is a waste of time and productive of trouble.

"As I do not desire to discourage poor men—whose substance is not sufficient to allow them to put together so much money—from undertaking this voyage, I can assure them for their consolation that, when a captain knows that certain pilgrims are poor he is ready to agree for thirty or thirty-two ducats, and for this sum to give them their passage, and pay for the riding animals, the

1. *Comito.*
2. *Scrivano.*
3. *Proveri.*

INTRODUCTION

duties and the tribute; while they themselves can provide their own food out of their own purses a little more economically than those who have large means; and such pilgrims are allowed access to the kitchen to cook their victuals like the others.

"Finally, it is necessary that the gold and silver money taken should be fresh from the Venetian mint, otherwise the Moors will not accept the coins, even if they were ten grains overweight; and the captain must be paid in the same money because he is obliged to pay the same to the Moors."

Santo Brasca died in the beginning of the sixteenth century, and was buried in the Church of Santa Eufemia.[1]

It is clear from what he tells us that Casola had carefully read and profited by Brasca's suggestions. To the two bags of money and patience he added, however, on his own account a bag of faith—an article of which a renaissance prelate who had spent much of his life in Rome, probably stood more in need than the average layman.

The nobility of the Casola family is proved by the simple fact that one of its members was canon of the Metropolitan Church in the fifteenth century, when only nobles were admitted. Moreover, a list of noble Milanese families, drawn up as early as 1277, includes the name of "Cazolis," or "Casola" as it came to be written later.[2] The author of this book, Pietro Casola, was born in 1427, and died on Saturday, the 6th of November, 1507, aged eighty, as is proved by the following extract from the series of *Registri Mortuarij*, preserved in the State Archives at Milan:—"*In the year 1507, on Saturday, the*

---

1. Argelati, *Bibl. Scriptorum Mediolanen.*, vol. i. part ii. p. 226.
2. Giulini, *Memorie Spettanti alla storia, &c., di Milano nei Secoli bassi*, part viii. pp. 369, 681.

6th of November, in the district of Porta Ticinese, and in the Parish of St. Victor of the Well—the Reverend Lord, the priest, Pietro Casola, aged eighty, of a suffocating catarrh. The malady was not suspicious in the opinion of Master Ambrogio Varese da Rosate."[1]

The suffocating catarrh which proved fatal to Casola was probably acute bronchitis, and the note that the malady was not suspicious indicates that there was no suspicion of the plague, that terrible epidemic disease which from time to time decimated mediæval cities, and was the terror of municipal governments. The Physician who attended Pietro Casola in his last illness, and granted the death certificate was a famous professor and astrologer and a celebrated Court physician. He died on 27th October, 1522.[2]

The most careful search has so far yielded only a very small harvest of documents relating to the author of this *Voyage to Jerusalem*, but the few which have been brought to light are certainly interesting; they will be found *in extenso* in the Appendix.

The first is a ducal rescript dated August 13th, 1467, from which it appears that Pietro Casola, then aged forty, had been nominated by the Papal See to the benefice of St. Victor at Corbetta, in the diocese of Milan, and that he had petitioned for a confirmation of this appointment from the Duchess Bianca. The latter gave him full authority to exercise his rights, and ordered all "our officers and subjects concerned" to give due and legitimate aid to the "aforesaid priest Pietro or his procurator."[3]

There is another petition—undated—addressed by Casola to the "Lords of Milan." The internal evidence

---

1. See Appendix, Document F.
2. Emilio Motta, *Morti in Milano dal 1452—1552*, in the *Archivio Storico Lombardo*, 1891, p. 254.
3. Appendix, Document A.

shows that it belongs to the period between the death of Galeazzo Sforza in 1476, and the domination of his brother Lodovico il Moro. Probably it was written shortly after the death of Galeazzo, because in the beginning Casola states that a few months earlier, he and other priests and clerks had been required to take the oath of allegiance to the Lords of Milan and their state—that is, to the Regents, Bona and Lodovico, who governed on behalf of the young duke Gian Galeazzo.

The petition in question was probably written by Casola himself: certainly the caligraphy resembles that of the manuscript of his journey in the Trivulzian Library, which Count Giulio Porro considered autograph. In it the petitioner styles himself "The Orator before God" for the "Illustrious Princes and most excellent Lords" of Milan; their "most faithful servant" and "Ordinary Canon of the Cathedral of Milan." He then entreats permission to establish and exercise his rights in the Canonries of St. Stephen, at Milan, and St. Victor, at Corbetta; which had been usurped by others. He supports his petition by three arguments:—firstly, that princes who intend to administer justice impartially, especially in ecclesiastical matters, need never be afraid of the consequences; because God will surely protect and perpetually preserve them, and "thus the said orator will ever pray that he may do in the masses which he says continually."

In the second place, he points out, with the spark of humour which enlivens his itinerary every now and then, that each of the two usurpers of the Canonries in question, is disqualified for holding such posts—that of Saint Stephen on account of his youth, because he is a boy, and "whoever is appointed to the said Canonry of St. Stephen's must be a priest"—and the occupant of the Canonry of

Corbetta, because "he is fit for everything else except being a priest"—and the duty of their Excellencies is to see that suitable persons are appointed to Church benefices.

Thirdly, Casola lays stress on his own personal merits and services, reminding the illustrious princes that "for sixteen years he has been at the Court of Rome in the service of this State," and that therefore it seems to him that when he asks for justice from his liege Lords, he should not be denied.[1]

There is no positive evidence as to the result of this petition; but the absence of any similar document in after years would seem to point to the fact that it had been favourably received. Indeed, the comfortable pecuniary circumstances—to which Casola himself alludes—enjoyed in the later years of his life, may be explained by the emoluments of a benefice and three Canonries, in addition to his income as secretary attached for many years to the Milanese Embassy at Rome, not to speak of any private means he may have had.

In many parts of his voyage Casola displays a close acquaintance with Rome and the neighbourhood. He draws comparisons between the Roman palaces and churches, and those seen elsewhere; he specially mentions the "Wood of Baccano," outside Rome, in connection with the decoration of Saint Mark's place for the festival of the Corpus Domini; and he refers to years spent in the Papal City. In the Petition he is more precise, and says definitely that at the time of writing—probably 1477—he had been already sixteen years at the Court of Rome. In a letter from the Milanese Ambassador there, dated August 14th, 1477, Casola is mentioned as being then in the service of the Embassy. In his letter the Ambassador

---

1. Appendix, Document B.

INTRODUCTION 17

relates that he has sent "Priest Pietro Casola" to warn and reprove a certain Giovanni Maria de la Mayrola, who had tried to obtain from the papal see the appointment to a certain Milanese benefice, without first seeking license from his own princes.[1]

In 1478, Casola was included among the ordinary Canons of the Metropolitan Church at Milan.[2] It is very likely that this marks the time when he returned from Rome, to settle in his native city. In the year 1502 he appears as the senior of the cardinal deacons of the Duomo.[3] Several times between 1481 and the year of his death, his name appears in official documents, with those of other Canons who were concerned with the execution of work of various kinds in connection with the Duomo.[4]

Two other documents relating to Casola belong to the years 1478 and 1479. From them we gather that a contest had arisen between "Pietro Casola" on the one part, and "Girolamo Casanigo and Ambrogio de Cepis" on the other, with regard to the possession of the Chapel of Santa Maria de Cepis. On August 3rd, 1478, the venerable doctor, Don Andrea de Fagnano, Canon of the Duomo, was ordered by the Regents to hear and settle the question. This injunction was repeated with emphasis on the 17th of February, 1479.[5]

Casola enjoyed a great reputation at Milan for works—requiring a large culture and much study—relating to the Ambrosian ritual, which were either compiled by him or printed under his direction—sometimes at his expense.

In 1490 he published the *Officium Ambrosianum* or the Ambrosian breviary in large quarto, an important and now rare book, dedicated to Guidantonio Arcimboldi,

1. Appendix, Document C.
2. *MS. Catalogue* in the Chapter Library, Milan Cathedral.
3. Document, dated 3rd March, 1502, in the Archives of the Archiepiscopal Court, Milan.
4. Appendix, Documents E.
5. Appendix, Document D.

C

Archbishop of Milan. In 1492 Casola published the Breviary in octavo for the use of priests in travelling. The print is clear and beautiful. Only two examples are known to exist, and both are now in the Ambrosian Library.

In 1494, Casola published, at his own expense, the *Librum Triduanarum Rogationum*, that is, the Book of the Triduan Litanies which belong exclusively to the Milanese Church. The Rubrics are given in Italian, and in the order in which they were observed in that age by the Ambrosian clergy.

The *Rationale Ceremoniarum Missae Ambrosianae*, compiled by Casola, was printed in 1499. In it he describes and explains the ceremonies then in use, and this is the more interesting now for the Milanese Church, because many of them have been abandoned or reformed at various times since, especially by St. Charles Borromeo. The book is the fruit of long, patient and careful study, and also of Casola's pilgrimage, for he notes the ceremonies which concord with the Greek rites from which the Ambrosian took their origin, and which he had ample opportunity for observing in different places on the voyage, especially in Candia and at the Holy Sepulchre itself.

Both in the Breviaries and in the *Rationale* there are readings which differ from those in earlier and later missals, and this has given rise to controversy from time to time. For example, as the *Confiteor* of the Ambrosian Mass in the *Rationale* is more prolix than that used at present, Muratori inferred that a great change had taken place in this respect in the Liturgy. But in the Milanese Missals of 1492 and 1499 the *Confiteor* is almost identical with that now used. The fact is that up to the time of St. Charles Borromeo, a very large discretion was left to individual priests in the matter of rites and ceremonies, and this is attested by Cardinal Federico in the preface to the Breviary of 1625.[1] The Liturgical works published by Casola, while of great interest and authority for the story of the Ambrosian ritual, must always therefore be accepted with reserve, and carefully compared with similar books of his own time, and also of the centuries which preceded and followed. A very fine copy of the *Rationale* in parchment, gilded and painted in miniature, and bearing the arms of the author, is preserved in the Library of the Lateran Canons of Santa Maria della Passione.[2]

In the Sacristy of the Milan Cathedral there are two volumes in parchment beautifully illustrated—two of the volumes published under the supervision of Casola. One contains the prayers and gospels chanted on the first day of the Triduan Litanies. The book has forty leaves in all, measuring 36 × 26 centimetres. The character is large Gothic in black and red, and the first page, painted in miniature, contains at the right side a small medallion portrait of Casola, with the letters " P.P.C.," *i.e.*, Presbyter Petrus Casola, and at the bottom the arms of the Casola family. This is the page chosen to illustrate the voyage, and from which Casola's likeness has been photographed separately.

The other volume contains the gospels used in the Masses chanted by the Archbishop. It was prepared by order of Canon Pietro Casola, and presented by him to the Sacristy of the Cathedral. It is also in parchment, and consists of 23 leaves, measuring 41 × 34 centimetres, in addition to two fly-leaves at the beginning and two at the end. There is an index and notes by Francesco Castelli, another ordinary of the Cathedral frequently mentioned in contemporary documents. Fourteen of the leaves are

---

1. Card. Federico wrote:—" Ante S. Caroli pontificatum unicuique ecclesiastico homini fere liberum fuerat componere Breviarium ex animi sui sententia, idque sive typis impressum sivi manuscriptum arbitratu suo divulgare."
2. Argelati. *Bibl. Scriptorum Mediolanen.*

painted in miniature, with rich borders, and each of the initial letters has figures relating to the mystery of the festival of the day. At the foot of each miniatured page are Casola's arms, surrounded on the first page by the legend in gold: "PRESBITER PETRUS DE CASOLIS, ORDINARIUS."

On his return from the Holy Land in 1494, Casola gave to his friends, though only in manuscript, his interesting description of what he had seen and heard—one of the most acute and comprehensive, one of the most modern-spirited and unprejudiced of the many itineraries written by pilgrims during the Middle Ages. The author, a keen observer, was not only a priest, but also a man of the world, widely read and largely travelled, with much experience of men and things, and possessed of a practical philosophy of life, and a saving sense of humour which carried him successfully through all difficulties.

Not the least interesting part of the narrative is that devoted to a description of the city of Venice, whose outward aspect at the close of the quattrocento is so graphically represented also in the Plan of Albert Dürer belonging to the year 1500, and in the wonderful pictures of Carpaccio, and Gentile Bellini. In 1494, the sun of the powerful and dreaded Republic was slowly but surely setting; though the artistic beauty of the unique metropolis, the splendour of its state pageants, the size and importance of its naval and mercantile fleet, and the activity on 'Change,—at the Rialto, that is,—and in the port, concealed the fact from observers as acute and practised as Pietro Casola and Philippe de Comines, the then French envoy to Venice, whom Casola met on his return at the house of the Milanese Ambassador. They had time to compare their impressions, and Casola tells us the effect on Comines of certain manifestations of

INTRODUCTION 21

Venetian luxury and magnificence. The fact that they expressed themselves afterwards on the subject, quite independently, in almost the same written words in their memoirs, seems to demonstrate that they agreed in their judgment with regard to the religious attitude of Venetian statesmen.

The only copy of Casola's MS. known to exist, is that in the Trivulzian Library at Milan. It was no doubt carefully preserved there, because it contains the only authentic account of the last days of a distinguished member of the Trivulzio family—Fra Francesco Trivulzio —who was buried at Rhodes on the homeward voyage. In the eighteenth century, the learned Carlo Trivulzio, who died in 1789, at the age of seventy-four, gave himself up with enthusiasm to archæological studies, and formed an interesting and valuable museum in the family palace. His attention was attracted by Casola's manuscript, which he annotated here and there, and in which he inserted a life of his ancestor, Fra Francesco, written on loose sheets of paper. In later times Casola's voyage had been completely forgotten; it was saved from oblivion by Count Giulio Porro, who had it transcribed, and then printed a hundred copies, with a short preface and notes, on the occasion of the marriage of Donna Evelina dei Marchesi Trivulzio with Count Antonio de Lumiarez, in the year 1855. Naturally, the printed edition is rare now. There are two copies in the Trivulzian Library at Milan, and one in the Correr Museum in Venice. I was fortunate enough to be able to procure a copy through the courtesy of a friend, who found it for sale in Milan. Suspecting the existence of some inadvertent errors of transcription in the printed Voyage—a suspicion which proved to be well founded—I went to Milan to consult the original, and received courteous permission from Prince Trivulzio to make the necessary corrections, so that the translation should be made from the original text—considered by Count Giulio Porro to be an autograph of Casola. This is very possible, though not absolutely certain: the corrections and changes of word or phrase are in the same handwriting as the body of the document, which renders it very probable that they were made by the author himself; and, as has been said, the caligraphy of the MS. of the Voyage, closely resembles, if it is not identical with, that of Casola's petition with reference to the Canonries of St. Stephen's and St. Victor's.

The first leaf of the manuscript—conceivably containing a preface, in which Casola probably determined the year of his Voyage—is unfortunately missing; and the missing sheet corresponds with another in the body of the MS., on which Casola completed his description of Candia; now left incomplete. In the text, however, as Porro observes, Casola "gives such indications as suffice for arriving at the precise date of his Voyage, which was the year 1494. He says he left Milan on Wednesday, the 14th of May, the third day of the Triduan Rogations. Now, these being six weeks after Easter, that solemnity must have fallen on the 30th of March; and Easter day in 1494 occurred exactly on March the 30th. If this proof were not sufficient, there is another in the expedition of Charles VIII. to Italy, which took place in 1494, about which Casola says he heard from a friar belonging to the Zorzi family, and also later from Bernardino Contarini, who came aboard the pilgrim galley at Modone to return to Venice."

In the account of his journey, Casola shows how certain Venetians, under government supervision and control, undertook what may be described as the work of a modern Cook's Agency, and conducted tours to the one special

INTRODUCTION

place beyond the seas which was still sought—though from very mixed motives—by pilgrims from all parts of Christendom. As has been said, the importance of the pilgrim traffic gave rise to an extensive special legislation in Venice, whose development will now be traced.

During the early middle ages those who were concerned in maritime enterprises in the Mediterranean used to watch personally over their own interests, and the shipowner and captain were confounded in one single person, the *Patronus*. The patronus shared in the venture with the merchants who owned the cargo, and who often accompanied their goods on the sea voyage.[1] In Casola's manuscript it is to be noted that the title invariably given to Agostino Contarini is that of "*Patrono*." Except in one instance I have translated this by the word "Captain," but captain must always be understood to mean captain-owner or captain-part-owner.

For several centuries legislation on maritime subjects seems to have been lacking in Venice, though its place was to some extent supplied by the contracts which preserve the usages of the time. But the increasing development of sea traffic, especially at the time of the Crusades, necessitated the transformation of immemorial custom into more formal law. The first Venetian maritime statutes belong to the first half of the thirteenth century, and legislated for the pilgrims who crowded year by year to Venice as well as for all others who under the protecting shadow of the Republic, went down to the sea in ships, and did their business in great waters.

The first of these statutes issued under the Doge Pietro Ziani, 1227, dealt exclusively with the disposition of the ballast and cargo, and ordered that no ship was to be

---

1. Preface to *Statuti Maritimi Veneziani*, edited by R. Predelli and A. Sacerdoti. Venice, 1903.

loaded more than two feet above the cross, that is, above a conventional sign on the side of a ship which indicated the limit of submersion.[1] In this way the old Venetians provided for the general safety at sea, and anticipated by many centuries the Plimsoll Mark.

This statute was followed two years later by the more comprehensive measure of the Doge Jacopo Tiepolo, 1229.[2] This provided for the caulking, painting and decorating of ships, for the storing of ballast and the due packing away of the cargo. Ships in general were not to be loaded more than two feet above the cross, and when they were over six years old, only a foot and a half above that mark. If any ship was hired to pilgrims, either in Venice or elsewhere, the captain-owner must come to terms with the pilgrims in question as to the amount of cargo to be taken on board. Ships of 200 *migliaia*[3] were to carry 20 mariners, not counting amongst these knights, pilgrims or cooks; and each mariner was to be armed with a helmet, shield and jacket, a sword and three lances. For every increase of 50 *migliaia* in a ship's tonnage, five mariners, equipped as above, were to be added. Every ship was to be duly furnished with ropes, anchors and other necessary tackle. The captain-owner of each ship was required to carry a scribe, whose duty was to write down in his book all details about the passengers and cargo, and give duplicates to the persons interested, report to the proper authorities if the ship was overloaded, etc.

Each merchant, mariner, knight or priest might have one chest on board in which to carry what he pleased—a privilege expressly withheld from servants. Each passenger and each sailor might have a mattress weighing

---

1. *Liber Plegiorum*, p. 105, Archives of Venice, printed in Romanin, *Storia Documentata di Venezia*, vol. ii. p. 441.
2. *Statuti Marittimi Veneziani*, edited by R. Predelli and A. Sacerdoti, Venezia, 1903.
3. A *Migliaio* or *Milliario* = 1000 lbs. = 476·998720 kilos.

not more than 10½ lbs. No merchant or sailor might bring on board more wood than was necessary for the voyage; any left over was to be the property of the captain-owner. Each person who went as far as Barbary might carry one barrel of wine and one of water; for longer voyages a double quantity of wine and water was allowed.

If an owner hired his ship to other persons, any damage done during the voyage to masts, anchors, sails, etc., was to be made good or paid for by the hirers, save in the case of pilgrims, who were not held responsible for damages.

The statute closed with the *Capitulum Peregrinorum*, which laid down that ships which took pilgrims on what was called the " Easter voyage " to Syria, that is, during the spring, were to sail for home by the 8th of May; and those which went on the " winter voyage," that is, in the autumn, were to leave Syria by the 8th of October, unless there was just cause for delay. The captain-owners were to present themselves to the Bailo of Acre or other Venetian representative there, and swear to conduct the pilgrims where they wanted to go, according to their agreements with them, and to safeguard their persons and goods. If a ship touched at any place in Greece or elsewhere and three-fourths of the pilgrims wished to land, while one-fourth desired to remain on board, the captain was obliged to continue his voyage with the remnant according to his contract; and if less than a fourth of the pilgrims remained, the captain was obliged nevertheless to take them to the port named in the agreement, or give back all the passage money he had received from them. Disobedient captains were liable to a heavy fine.

All contracts made between captain-owners, and merchants, the crews, passengers of all kinds, &c., were to be faithfully observed, and judges were appointed to settle disputes arising out of any particular voyage.

In 1255, the Maritime Statutes of the Doge Rainiero Zeno [1] repeated what had been enacted by his predecessors, but in fuller detail, and added some new provisions.

The first twenty-nine clauses refer to the caulking and decorating of ships and their equipment with anchors, sails, masts, ropes, and all necessary tackle; the disposition and quality of the ballast; the position of the quarters of the *Patrono*, and the number of sailors to be carried, which, as before, was in proportion to the tonnage.

Ships of 400 *milliarij* and over, that went beyond the Adriatic Sea were now to carry two trumpeters, who were to count among the sailors. Every sailor must be at least eighteen years of age; and, as before, no knight, pilgrim, or servant could count as a mariner. Each sailor was to be armed with a leather cap, or a helmet of leather or iron—a shield—a leather jerkin—a knife—a sword—and three lances. Those who received over forty pounds for their pay were to have a breast plate in addition. Before starting on any voyage, the sailors were required to take an oath to take care of the ship and its tackle; not to steal more than the value of five small *soldi;* and to remain for fifteen days to help in recovering ships and cargo in case of shipwreck.

Ships of 200 *milliarij* or more were to carry two scribes, and these were to take an oath to do their duty faithfully and act as a check on each other.

To prevent overloading, the Consuls of the Merchants in Venice, and the Governors of Venetian possessions elsewhere, were to examine each vessel just before its departure, and fine the *Patroni*, in case the law had

---

1. *Statuti Marittimi Veneziani*, edited by R. Predelli and A. Sacerdoti. Venice, 1903.

been violated. And captain-owners were to swear not to allow anything to be placed over the cross, so as to prevent the right measuring of a ship. For five years from the first day they set sail, ships of 200 *milliarij* and more might be loaded two and a quarter feet above the cross; from five years to seven years, two feet above the cross; and when they had been at sea over seven years, one and a half feet above the cross.

Any ship hired to pilgrims was to carry the amount of cargo agreed upon between the captain-owner and the pilgrims. If the captain violated his agreement he was liable to lose the extra cargo, and pay a penalty.

The provisions as to compensation due from the hirers of a ship, for damages done to the tackle, &c., were the same as those of the Tiepolo Statute; and, as before, pilgrims were not held liable.

The clauses with regard to chests, mattresses, wood, wine and water were unchanged. It was now added, however, that each person going to sea might carry $2\frac{1}{4}$ *staria*[1] of flour and biscuits, for the outward, and the same for the homeward, voyage.

As before, the last clause was the "*capitulum super peregrinis*"—which provided that ships which went to Syria with pilgrims must leave there at the time mentioned in the contracts made with the pilgrims before starting, unless there was just cause for further delay. This was a modification of the corresponding clause of the Tiepolo Statute requiring ships carrying pilgrims to leave Syria by a given day; and which had probably been found impracticable for obvious reasons. The rest of the clause relating to pilgrims in the Zeno Statute merely repeated the provisions already given of the Tiepolo Statute.

---

1. The *Staio* = 83·317200 litres or over 2 bushels.

In this way, in early times, the State sought to safeguard the lives and interests of the pilgrims, in common with those of all others who went to sea under the banner of St. Mark, by ordering, and trying to ensure that ships should be properly equipped; that they should not be overloaded, so as to run the risk of foundering, or of depriving pilgrims and other passengers of the space duly allotted to them; and that all contracts should be properly drawn up and observed.

Fifty years after the proclamation of the Zeno Maritime Statute in 1255, the Great Council decreed in 1303[1] that all laws and provisions relating to maritime affairs, &c., should be collected into one book, of which two copies were to be made and kept—one in the Ducal Chancery, and the other in the office of the *Provvisori* at the Rialto. Every new law passed, and every provision made was to be added to this book, and cancelled when, and if, revoked. Unfortunately, neither these books, nor later copies of them, are known to exist in the Archives; and we do not even know whether they were ever carefully kept. The discovery of such a collection of statutes would immensely facilitate research on maritime questions subsequent to 1255. Lacking such help careful investigation has not brought to light any special legislation for the pilgrim traffic until the beginning of the fourteenth century. The notices then are at first scanty; but, afterwards, for nearly a hundred years, almost overwhelming in number, and of the highest interest.

The sketch which follows of the legislation of the Republic on the pilgrim passenger transport, which was of immense importance to its interests materially, morally, and politically, throws much light on the conditions under

---

1. *Maggior Consig. Delib.*, Reg. Magnus, p. 40, 19th Jan., 1303 (modern style) 19th Jan., 1302, according to old Venetian reckoning—by which the year began with the 1st day of March.

which mediæval pilgrims performed their pilgrimages, and will enable us to put the Voyage of Casola in its right place,—midway between the high fever of pilgrim enthusiasm which marked the end of the fourteenth century, and its total decline towards the end of the sixteenth century.

In 1305, a decree of the Doge Pietro Gradenigo ordered all naval commanders, and all governors of Venetian possessions to permit any male and female pilgrims who desired to come to the abode of the blessed St. Mark, the approaching Ascension-tide, to do so freely.[1] This calls attention to the fact that the favourite time for undertaking pious pilgrimages was the spring, when land travelling was pleasantest—for the excessive cold of the winter was over and the roads were in the best condition; and when there was the hope of returning from the Holy Land before the storms of the late autumn added to the discomforts and the perils of the sea voyage. Although, in these early times, pilgrims went to Palestine at various times of the year, the greatest crowd always assembled in Venice between Easter and Ascension-tide, and the ships generally set sail after the festival of the Corpus Domini.

For the next fifty years the only notice relating to a pilgrimage which I came across in the Venetian registers belongs to the year 1337, when the Senate gave permission to the noble Andrea Mocenigo to undertake a voyage for the good of his soul, to the Holy Sepulchre as he had arranged.[2] During this half century it is to be assumed that the transport of pilgrims was regulated by the existing laws, and no doubt interrupted occasionally by difficulties with the Saracens, as happened between 1360 and 1368.

1. *Maggior Consig. Delib.*, Reg. xv. Magnus and Capricornus, p. 93*b*. The decree is not dated, but follows one issued Aug. 26th, 1305.
2. *Senato, Miste.*, Regis. xvii., p. 76, 2nd June, 1337.

At this time Pope Urban V. had formed the design of a new Crusade against the infidels, which was favourably received by the King of France, the Emperor, and others, including King Peter of Lusignan, King of Cyprus, then on very good terms with Venice, which also gave a certain amount of support to the project. The Christians as usual lacked the union necessary for a great common effort, but isolated attacks were made on the Turks and Saracens. The King of Cyprus, for example, sacked Alexandria, though he was immediately obliged to retire; and Venice, as his friend and ally, was immediately involved in difficulties with the Saracens. Venetian merchants in Alexandria were imprisoned and their goods sequestered. After representing the exigencies of the position to the Pope, Venice succeeded in coming to terms with the Sultan of Egypt;[1] but before matters were settled the Great Council had declared (May 1st, 1367) that no pilgrims or other passengers could go from Venice to Cyprus or Rhodes.[2]

Next year a number of persons arrived in Venice who desired to go to these places. They were:—" Two Friars Preachers to whom the province of Cyprus has been entrusted by their superior. A servant whom Ser Federico Corner wants to send to his brother in Cyprus. A servant whom the Prior of St. John of the Temple wants to send to the Grand Master of Rhodes. A Tuscan merchant. A native of Cyprus, who lately married a wife in Venice, and wishes to return home. A lame brother belonging to the Order of St. John, who wants to go to Rhodes. A young man who came from Cyprus to these parts to seek his brother whom he has not found; and a certain Jacobinus de Magagnis of Cremona (accompanied by his

---

1. Romanin, *Storia Documentata di Venezia*, vol. iii. pp. 213, &c., and 233.
2. *Maggior Consig. Delib.*, Regis. "Novella," p. 114.

INTRODUCTION

son), who came from Rhodes on the galley of Ser Franceschini Corner, and now wishes to return."[1]

It was doubtful whether, in view of the Act of May 1st, 1367, these persons could be allowed to embark; but the Maggior Consiglio decided by a majority to grant the permission, as they were neither pilgrims nor passengers in the sense of the Act; they were returning, that is, to their homes or official duties, and not merely stopping temporarily at Rhodes or Cyprus on their way to other places.

During the next few years a number of distinguished pilgrims sought the aid of the Republic in order to accomplish the voyage to the Holy Land.

In 1375 the Senate declared that as "the Illustrious Lords Otto and Stephen junior, Dukes of Bavaria, our intimate friends, have sent an ambassador to us asking in a friendly way that we would be pleased to allow the said Lord Duke Stephen—who wishes, out of reverence to God, to visit the Holy Sepulchre and the Holy Land—to equip a galley in Venice at his own expense. . . . We are very happy to oblige him by the loan of one of the galleys of our Commune furnished with arms, tackle and everything necessary, which he can equip in Venice at his good pleasure." The only condition made was that, *according to ancient custom* in such cases and for the honour and greater security of the said Lord Duke, a Venetian patrician was to be appointed to the command of the galley and its crew.[2] Similar favours were granted to the "Magnificent Lord Stephen, Count of Veglia[3] our dear friend and citizen," and to another noble described as "Dominus Duyni."[4] The first was allowed to choose

---
1. *Maggior Consiglio* Reg. Novella, p. 114. 14th March, 1368.
2. *Senato Miste*, Reg. xxxiv. p. 160 *b*, 13th Feb., 1375 (Mod. style—1374 more Veneto)
3. Island of Veglia in the Gulf of Fiume.
4. *Senato Miste*, Reg. xxxv., 17th and 27th April, 1375, p. 17 *b*.

between a galley and a *bucentauro*;[1] to the second a galley, the size of a *bucentauro*, was conceded.

In 1376 Stephen, Voyvode of Transylvania asked for a galley on which to make the voyage to the Holy Sepulchre and back, with about fourteen persons of his suite. As the Voyvode wished to visit the shrine of Saint Catherine on Mount Sinai, it was arranged that he and his companions should go on one of the galleys of the Beyrout fleet, commanded by Ser Andrea Dandolo, who had orders to land them at Jaffa if the Voyvode so desired; and they sailed for the East on September 7th, 1376. One of the galleys of the naval fleet of the Adriatic was ordered to go to Beyrout and bring the distinguished pilgrims home, as they would be too late to return with the Beyrout merchant fleet. The Senate decreed special honours to the Voyvode in Venice, and ordered the governors of all Venetian possessions at which the ship touched to receive him well.[2]

In 1382 the Bishop of Agram requested permission to equip a galley at his own expense to go to the Holy Sepulchre. The Senate granted the request, with the proviso that if instead, the Bishop preferred to take his passage on one of the unarmed sailing ships going to the East, instructions would be given to the Beyrout and Alexandria trading fleets—which always left Venice about August and returned towards Christmas—to bring him and his servants back to Sclavonia free of charge.[3] In 1384 the Bishop made the same request, and the Senate replied in the same terms.[4] The first voyage may have been deferred, or he may have made a second pilgrimage after two years.

1. The name *Bucentoro* is generally connected with the Doge's state barge; but in Venetian documents of the 14th century it is a general name for a very strong seagoing vessel with sails. See also *Venezia e le sue Lagune*, vol. i. p. 201, part ii.
2. *Senato Miste*, Reg. xxxv., pp. 122, 130 b, 132 b, 133.
3. *Idem*, Reg. xxxvii., p. 67 b, 10th April, 1382.
4. *Idem*, Reg. xxxviii., p. 111 b, 1st April, 1384.

INTRODUCTION

It may be noted here that the Voyvode of Transylvania, the Bishop of Agram and the Count of Veglia were actively engaged in the negotiations between Venice and Sigismund, son of Charles IV., and brother of the Emperor Wenceslas, at the time of Sigismund's accession to the Crown of Hungary.[1]

Amongst the pilgrims of 1392 the chief were a group of six French nobles, including Rudolph de Montfort, the Viscount of Dinan, Jean d'Estouteville, Philippe Berot and about eighty companions whom the Senate ordered to be transported across the seas on the galley *Arduina*; the famous Condottiere Jacopo del Verme; and Henry, Earl of Derby afterwards Henry IV.[2]

Jacopo del Verme was appointed in 1388 Captain General of the troops of the League formed by Venice and the Viscontis against the Carraras of Padua. As a recompense for his services he was inscribed amongst the Venetian patricians, and received the palace at San Polo, which formerly belonged to Francesca da Carrara.

When the Beyrout galleys were auctioned in 1392, it was provided that one of the four should be set apart to conduct the pilgrims to Jaffa. As there was cargo on board the galley would naturally go first to Beyrout to unload, and afterwards to Jaffa to land the pilgrims. Jacopo del Verme, described by the Senate as "Our devoted and dear friend," begged as a favour that the galley in question should first carry him and the other pilgrims to Jaffa, and go afterwards to Beyrout to discharge the cargo. The Senate consented, and ordered that when the ships arrived near Cyprus, one of the two galleys owned and commanded respectively by Ser Niccolo Soranzo and Ser Antonio Bragadin, should be chosen by agreement or by

---

1. Romanin, *Storia Documentata di Venezia*, vol. iii. pp. 311-14.
2. See for Derby's pilgrimage, Lucy Toulmin Smith's *Expedition of Henry, Earl of Derby, 1390-1, 1392-3*, Camden Society, 1894.

lot and take the said Lord Jacopo and the other pilgrims—who up to that moment were distributed over all the four galleys—directly to Jaffa, remain there two days only. and then proceed to Beyrout. The cargo carried from Venice by the galley selected was to be transferred to the other galleys when they separated off Cyprus.[1]

Later in the year 1392, on the 18th of November, the "Magnificent Lord Henry of Lancaster, Earl of Derby, Hereford and Northampton, Lord of Brabant and eldest son of the Duke of Aquitaine and Lancaster, through his noble ambassadors and knights, and also the Lord Duke of Austria on his behalf, through his letters," begged the Venetian Senate " to be pleased to grant him a galley, furnished with the necessary tackle, which he wishes to equip at his own expense in order to go and visit the Holy Land." [2]

Derby arrived in Venice on December the 1st, nearly a fortnight after his envoys had presented his request to the senate.[3] When he reached Venice he found everything in train for his departure. The Senate affirming ingenuously that it had always been the policy of the Republic to secure the favour of the great ones of the earth, had voted that the request for the galley should be immediately granted, "considering especially the advantages and favours which Venetian subjects, trading with or temporarily resident in England, would obtain and enjoy in the present and in the future." In communicating the acquiescence of the Senate to the Earl, no mention was to be made of the expenses incurred by the Venetian Government in fitting out the galley; though, in order that he might know the full extent of his indebtedness, the English Embassy was to be informed of the precise sum spent; and also that the Signoria did not wish it to be

---

1. *Senato Miste*, Reg. xlii., p. 75*b*, 24th August, 1392.
2. *Idem*, p. 88, 18th Nov., 1392.
3. Rawdon Brown, *Archivio di Venezia con riguardo alla Storia Inglese*, p. 173 &c. Cf however, *Expeditions of Henry, Earl of Derby*, pp. lx, and 211.

INTRODUCTION

refunded. Afterwards, according to the usual custom, the Great Council voted three hundred ducats to be spent in suitable presents.

Bolingbroke's sojourn at the Holy Sepulchre was brief, and on March the 20th, 1393, he was back in Venice, where another one hundred golden ducats were voted to honour him at the moment of his return.

The courtesy of the Republic was recompensed. Among the documents preserved in the *Commemoriali* there is a letter despatched by Henry IV. to the Doge Venier on the 6th October, 1399—four days after the deposition of Richard II.—announcing his accession to the throne; and in which he promises to treat all Venetians who should come to any part of his dominions with the same favour as his own proper subjects.[1]

In 1399, Henry of Derby's famous rival, Thomas Mowbray, Duke of Norfolk, desiring also to visit the Holy Sepulchre, sought and obtained the loan of a galley for the purpose from the Signoria.[2] He brought a letter from Richard II., which he presented in February, 1399. In the register of the Senate he is referred to as the "Magnificent Lord the Duke of Gilforth." Although it is not clear why he took this title, or how long he bore it, Mr. Rawdon Brown considered that there could be no reasonable doubt as to the identity of the Duke of Norfolk with the so-called Duke of Guildford. In two later Venetian documents belonging to 1403 and 1404, published by Sir Henry Ellis, he is called Duke of Norfolk. The documents contain the petitions of two nobles, a Zane and a Bembo, for the payment of a debt contracted by the Duke in 1399 to cover the expenses of his pilgrimage. He soon died in Venice, and more than a

1. Rawdon Brown, *Archivio di Venezia*, p. 180.
2. *Senato Miste*, Reg. xliv., p. 83, 18th Feb., 1399 (1398 more Veneto).

century later Marino Sanuto mentions a request made by Thomas Howard, Duke of Norfolk—uncle of Queen Anne Boleyn—that the bones of his ancestor should be transferred to England, to be buried amongst the Mowbrays and the Howards.[1]

Meanwhile the Venetian registers give some idea of the crowd of humbler pilgrims who took their passage from Venice, especially between 1380 and 1390.

After difficulties with the Sultan of Egypt which are alluded to but not explained in a decree of January 21st, 1382, permission was given to a number of ships to navigate to Alexandria and other parts subject to the Sultan.[2]

In March of this year the Venetian Senate licensed Zanino Tirapelle to carry forty or fifty German and Hungarian pilgrims—men and women—on his ship to visit the Holy Sepulchre.[3] In April, Ser Francesco de Canal was authorised to take on his galley 25 foreign pilgrims who wanted to go to Alexandria, Mount Sinai and other parts of Egypt.[4] The same day the Senate ordered that about 100 pilgrims, men and women, going to the Holy Sepulchre should be taken on the unarmed galley belonging to Ser Andrea Morosini.[5] In May, six French nobles and about 80 companions went on the galley *Arduina*.[6] In June it was arranged for 25 pilgrims to be conducted as far as Zante on the galley belonging to Ser Marino Malipiero.[7] In July Ser Zanino de Cha de Zara was licensed to carry on his ship about 10 pilgrims going to the Sepulchre.[8] At the same time permission was given

---

1. Rawdon Brown, *Archivio di Venezia*, pp. 176—179.
2. *Senato Miste*, xxxvii. p. 48, 21st Jan., 1382 (more Veneto 1381).
3. *Idem*, p. 62 b, 17th March, 1382.
4. *Idem*, p. 68 b, 18th April, 1382.
5. *Idem*, p. 69.
6. *Idem*, p. 81 b, 17th May, 1382.
7. *Idem*, p. 84 b, 8th June, 1382.
8. *Idem*, p. 97 b, 22 July, 1382.

INTRODUCTION

to the Noble Ser Giovanni Barbarigo, who was appointed Venetian Consul in Damascus, to go for fifteen days or so to Jerusalem. A few days later Ser Zanino de Cha de Zara was empowered to take on board about 25 additional pilgrims;[1] while in August, 17 pilgrims were to have passages as far as Candia on the ship belonging to Guglielmo Bono.[2] Over 300 pilgrims therefore sailed from Venice in 1382; and in July of that year, on account of news received there about certain Provençal galleys, probably belonging to pirates, special measures were taken to protect all Venetian ships in the Eastern Mediterranean.[3]

In 1383, the Senate decreed that 96 pilgrims were to be taken to Jaffa on the unarmed galley belonging to Pietro Fino;[4] 60 pilgrims to the same place on the large galley belonging to the Noble Ser Filippo Pisani;[5] 27 pilgrims were to be conducted to Syria on their way to Jerusalem on the large galley owned by Paulo de la Colla;[6] 60 pilgrims to Syria on the galley of the Noble Francesco Delfino;[7] 70 pilgrims on the galley of Lorenzo Dono;[8] finally Zanino de Zara was to take about 20 persons on his *nave* to Syria.[9] In all 330 pilgrims.

In 1384 the Senate permitted 90 pilgrims to be conducted to Jaffa on the galley of Ser Bernardo Nadal;[10] 70 or 71, between men and women, on Ser Dardi Morosini's galley;[11] about 80 on the large galley owned by Virgilio Rizo;[12] about 100, men and women, on the galley belonging to Ser Francesco Michael;[13] and 64 pilgrims, between

1. *Senato Miste*, R. xxxvii., p. 98 *b*, 28th July, 1382.
2. *Idem*, p. 102 *b*, 5th August, 1382.
3. *Idem*, p. 99, July 25th, 1382.
4. *Senato Miste*, Reg. xxxviii. p. 17 *b*, 2nd April, 1383.
5. *Idem*, p. 26 *b*, 5th May, 1383.
6. *Idem*, p. 27, 12th May, 1383.
7. *Idem*, p. 27, 12th May, 1383.
8. *Idem*, p. 48 *b*, 21st June, 1383.
9. *Idem*, p. 55 *b*, 12th July, 1383.
10. *Idem*, p. 102, 26th Feb., 1384 (more Veneto 1383).
11. *Idem*, p. 111 *b*, 14th April, 1384.
12. *Idem*, p. 119 *b*, 12th May, 1384.
13. *Idem*, p. 120, 12th May, 1384.

men and women, on Ser Andrea Morosini's galley.[1] Further, in June, Raphaeletto de Stella, the *Patrono* of an unarmed galley, was authorised to take on board about 100 Sclavonian pilgrims, men and women, and carry them beyond the seas to go to the Sepulchre.[2] Shortly after, Francesco Bachino, a Venetian citizen, received permission to pick up on the shore at Pesaro, and take to Jaffa and back, 20 men and 10 women from Urbino—and three Jews with their wives and two children—and to take also about 20 persons from Venice.[3] Finally, Nicoletto Bono was authorised to carry 70 pilgrims to Candia [4] on board his *Cocha*.[5] In this way the tale for the year 1384 rose to over 600.

In 1385 only three ships seem to have been licensed for the pilgrim voyage to Syria, but each carried over 100 pilgrims. Ser Francesco de Canal was authorised to take 110 pilgrims or other passengers;[6] Zanino Nicolai 120 pilgrims;[7] and Ser Francesco Michael 150 pilgrims or thereabouts;[8] in all 380 persons.

A new law at the beginning of the next year again forbad the overloading of ships. No cargo was to be placed above the prescribed sign, and the latter was to be renewed if necessary.[9]

In 1386 Pietro de Creta, described as "Our faithful subject, and *Patrono* of a *nave* about to go to Jaffa," was licensed to take 120 pilgrims to the Sepulchre;[10] Nicoletto Duracino, 100;[11] and the Noble Ser Francesco Michael, 120;[12] in all, 340.

1. *Senato Miste*, xxxviii. p. 134, 14th June, 1384.
2. *Idem*, p. 136, 20th June, 1384.
3. *Idem*, p. 140, 5th July, 1384.
4. *Idem*, p. 155 b, 14th August, 1384.
5. A *Cocca* or *Cocha*—one of the largest and strongest kind of sailing ships or *Navi rotonde* which made no use of oars.
6. *Senato Miste*, Reg. xxxix. p. 63, 18th April, 1385.
7. *Idem*, p. 65 b, 27th April, 1385.
8. *Idem*, p. 80 b, 25th May, 1385.
9. *Senato Miste*, Reg. xl. p. 12, Jan. 11th, 1386 (more Veneto 1385).
10. *Idem*, p. 22, 13th March, 1386.
11. *Idem*, p. 26, 1st May, 1386.
12. *Idem*, p. 29, 22nd May, 1386.

INTRODUCTION

In 1387 the Senate gave permission to Lorenzo Dono to carry 100 pilgrims to Syria;[1] to Marco de Roma to carry 123 pilgrims to Jaffa;[2] and to Martino Cortese to carry 100 more to the same place.[3]

In 1388 Ser Guglielmo Bono received permission from the Senate to take about 80 pilgrims;[4] Jacobello Buatello to take 150,[5] and Nicoletto Duracino to carry 160[6]— all going to Jaffa for the Holy Sepulchre.

In 1389 Antonio de Elia was empowered to take on board his galley 150 pilgrims bound for Jaffa;[7] and other pilgrims, whose number is not specified, went to Syria in the autumn on the Beyrout galleys. Each of the four galleys of the fleet had its own *Patrono*, while the direction of the entire convoy was given to a commodore nominated by the Venetian Government. When he arrived near Beyrout, if he saw he could do so with safety, the commodore had orders to detach one galley —to carry pilgrims to Jaffa—which was to start back to rejoin the others after landing the pilgrims. This implies that the galley must either have returned to Jaffa after a suitable interval, or that the pilgrims must have rejoined it at Acre or Beyrout.[8]

The result of this great concourse of pilgrims is to be traced in two important provisions; one tending to protect the interests of the pilgrims during the time they spent in Venice; the other to ensure their safe transport across the seas.

The first, dated March 22nd, 1387, was the *new* oath required from the Piazza Guides, or *Tholomarii*, who were

---

1. *Senato Miste*, R. xl. p. 60, 10th Feb., 1387 (more Veneto 1386).
2. *Idem*, 68 b, 14th May, 1387.
3. *Idem*, p. 69, 29th May, 1387.
4. *Idem*, p. 102, 8th Jan., 1388 (more Veneto 1387).
5. *Idem*, p. 112, 17th April, 1388.
6. *Idem*, p. 112 b, 26th April, 1388.
7. *Idem*, p. 167 b, 20th April, 1389.
8. *Senato Miste*, xli. p. 30 b, 21st August, 1389. See also *Senato Miste*, Reg. xlii. p. 71 b, 4th August, 1392.

licensed by the magistrates, called the *Cattaveri*, to conduct pilgrims about the city, find them lodgings, aid them in changing their money and making their purchases, introduce them to the shipowners with whom they made their agreements for the return voyage, and, in fact, help them in every possible way during the time they were obliged to spend in Venice. They met the pilgrims on their arrival at the Rialto or in the Piazza.

Each guide or *tholomarius* was required to swear not to accompany any merchant to make his purchase; but only to go about with pilgrims, priests or knights and advise them honestly, and see that they bought what they needed in the best market—accepting from them in payment for the services rendered, what they gave of their own free will and no more. Any stranger found buying with the evident intention of selling again, was to be sent to the *Missetae*—the agents or brokers, who had a legal claim to a percentage on every contract. The guide pledged himself not to enter the Fondaco dei Tedeschi[1] save with pilgrims for the purpose of sealing their goods; and as soon as this was done he was to retire. And he swore not to take a gratuity from any money changer for conducting pilgrims, priests, or knights to his shop; but to see that they received good money of the right Venetian stamp and weight in exchange for their own.

In order to supervise the guides better, their number was at this time limited to eight, nominated by the Consuls of the Merchants, and subject to the authority of the *Cattaveri;* and rules were laid down for the just division of their gains among the whole body, in order to obviate the quarrels and disputes so common in the past. These continued, however, in the future, and gave rise, as will be seen, to many other provisions.

1. *i.e.*, The German Warehouse.

INTRODUCTION

Finally, as differences frequently sprang up between the guides and shipowners as to the emoluments due to the former, it was now laid down that for each pilgrim who took his passage, through one of the guides, the latter was entitled to receive from the shipowner two-thirds of a ducat if the passage money paid amounted to over ten ducats; and half a ducat if below that sum.[1]

The second statute was more important still, and took the form of a decree of the Great Council passed in June, 1392. This stated that many Venetian shipowners were guilty of extortions at the expense of the pilgrims and defrauded them by showing them rotten old ships, freshly painted and decorated, which they passed off on them as new; and, further, that the said owners did not fulfil the terms of the agreements made with the pilgrims. As these enormities gave just cause for complaint, and might lead to reprisals on Venetian subjects trading in foreign countries, the Maggior Consiglio enacted:—

First, that anyone who wanted a licence to carry pilgrims was to write his name down in the office of the *Cattaveri;* and these three magistrates were to send three experts, accompanied by one of their number, to examine the ship or ships in question, and declare on oath whether it was, or they were seaworthy. If the verdict was in the affirmative then, and then only, the owners were empowered to make agreements with pilgrims.

Second, the scribes of the said ships were required to write down in the ships' books the details of every contract made with pilgrims, and give a copy to the Judges of the Foreigners, under penalty of a fine. Amongst other clauses, the date fixed for the depar-

---

1. *Cattaveri*, Busta II., Reg. iv. p. 84, 22 March, 1387. The office of the *Cattaveri* was instituted in 1280 to provide for the preservation and the recovery of the "Averi" or property of the Commune; later on, the supervision of the Pilots, of the Pilgrim traffic, and of the Jews, &c., was entrusted to them. Mutinelli, *Lessico Veneto*, p. 98.

ture of a ship was to be expressly specified in the contract; and a ship was to depart on that day, under a penalty of fifty ducats, saving just impediment. This was to ensure that the pilgrims *non stent ad consumendum suum in hospicijs*, that is, should not be kept lingering in Venice indefinitely, until they had spent all they possessed in the inns.

Third, as many unscrupulous *Patroni* had been in the habit of compelling pilgrims to make new pacts to their detriment after leaving Venice, it was decreed that all captain-owners were to conduct pilgrims from Venice and back again according to the terms of the agreements made in Venice, unless any pilgrims desired to make changes for their own convenience. In this case it was to be quite clear that the pilgrims had altered the original clauses of their own free will, and that the changes had not been imposed on them.

Fourth. Ships were not to stop at any place on the outward or homeward voyage to take cargo or for any other reason, more than six days.

The governors of the chief Venetian possessions in the Mediterranean—Candia, Modone, Corone, Corfu—and the admiral of the fleet in those waters, were to receive a copy of the decree and see that it was faithfully executed. Wherever he touched, or if he met the fleet at sea, a captain-owner was under obligation to show the contracts with the pilgrims made by him to the respective governors, or the admiral, in order that they might assure themselves that he was doing his duty, and that the pilgrims might have an opportunity of ventilating their grievances if they were dissatisfied with their treatment.

Fifth, to prevent the pilgrims being cheated by the *Missetae* or agents, who were employed in the drawing up and signing of the agreements, it was ordered that for the future all persons desiring to exercise this business must be registered in the office of the *Cattaveri* after being approved by a majority of the Council of the *Quarantia*;[1] and these registered pilgrim agents were forbidden to accept anything from *Patroni*, pilgrims or other persons save what was legally due to them for their services. Any unlicensed person who acted as agent was liable to a fine of fifty lire for each offence, and the contracts they had drawn up were null and void.[2]

From this time there is no further mention in the Registers of the Great Council and the Senate of the swarm of private individuals who, especially between 1380 and 1390, engaged in the transport of pilgrims. Probably the increased surveillance of the State rendered the business much less profitable than heretofore. In addition, as for some years the government still allowed pilgrims to be taken to Syria in autumn, by the Beyrout fleet, the number who chose to take their passage on one of those galleys, where they felt safer in every way, was on the increase. Unfortunately the books of the *Cattaveri* which registered the licenses granted to shipowners in accordance with the above decree—and also the " Pilgrims' Books " or Registers, kept in the same office and containing the contracts made between pilgrims and *Patroni* have all been lost.

In 1393 one of the four galleys which went to Beyrout was deputed to carry pilgrims to Jaffa, and ordered to wait for them there or at Acre, " as seemed best for the

---

1. This was the highest Court of Appeal for all matters not within the jurisdiction of the Council of Ten.

2. *Delib. Maggior Consiglio*, Reg. Leona, p. 56, June 4th, 1392; *Libro D'Oro del Maggior Consiglio*, part v. p. 200 b; *Cattaveri*, Reg. iv. pp. 85-88.

safety of the ship, for ten days, not including the day of arrival and departure[1]"

In 1394 the concourse of pilgrims was so great, many of them being also " notable persons," that the commodore of the Beyrout fleet was ordered to choose two galleys, by agreement or by lot, to convey them to Jaffa.[2]

In 1395, the Senate provided that all pilgrims who had taken their passage by the Beyrout fleet should be concentrated on two only of the five galleys that went that year. Up to this time they had been distributed over all the four or five galleys forming the fleet until these were not far from the Syrian coast, and had then been transferred to the one or two galleys deputed to land them at Jaffa or Acre as the case might be. The fleet was on the point of sailing, and the books of the *Cattaveri* already registered contracts made for the voyage with 208 pilgrims, many of them " persons of consequence," when news came of the imminent arrival in Venice of a large number of other pilgrims. In consequence the Senate prorogued the day of departure and ordered that if two galleys proved insufficient to carry the pilgrims to Jaffa or Acre, a third should be deputed to the same service.[3]

In 1396 and again in 1397 the Senate decreed—having regard to the interests of both merchants and pilgrims, " and in order to avoid scandal,"—that " all *foreign pilgrims, except Italian pilgrims*,"[4] about to go with the Beyrout fleet were to be carried on two only of the galleys, chosen, as usual, by agreement or by lot. When the commodore thought that a suitable place had been reached, *all the pilgrims* were to be concentrated on the two galleys in question, or on one only if one proved suffi-

---

1. *Senato Miste*, Reg. xlii. p. 114, 29th May, 1393, and p. 120 b, 5th August, 1393.
2. *Senato Miste*, Reg. xliii. p. 27 b, 29th August, 1394.
3. *Idem*, p. 63 b, 27th May, 1395; p. 70 b, 18th July, 1395; and p. 79, 20th Aug., 1395.
4. Italians, belonging to cities not subject to the Republic, were "foreigners" to the Venetians.

cient for the purpose, and landed at Jaffa. In 1396 it was provided that the galleys, or galley, were to wait for the pilgrims at Jaffa or Acre for ten days; but, in 1397, the Senate provided that "Since Jaffa, as is well known, is a bad place for the purpose, and not adapted for galleys or other vessels, which are in great peril as long as they remain there, the said two galleys, or one of them, if only one goes there, must go to Acre as soon as the pilgrims have landed, after informing them that they or it will wait for them at Acre twelve days, not including the day of arrival and the day of departure." As happened frequently, a special license was given to Ser Vito de Canal—one of the captain-owners, appointed by lot to take the pilgrims to Jaffa—to go also to the Holy Sepulchre, leaving a noble deputy, approved by the commodore, in command of his galley during his absence.[1]

The transport of large numbers of pilgrims on the trading galleys produced such complications that it was prohibited in 1398 in the case of foreign pilgrims. The pious travellers took up the space really required for merchants and cargo, and the numerous disputes and difficulties due to the crowding together of persons of different and often hostile nationalities, seem to have often seriously interfered with business—which was the *raison d'être* of the Beyrout and similar fleets.

The preamble of the Senatorial decree of 1398 states that—"as is well known, many scandalous errors have occurred in recent years on board the galleys whose destination is Beyrout and Alexandria, on account of the pilgrims who go by them to the Holy Sepulchre—*because the said pilgrims are of diverse tongues*"—"and that unless a remedy is provided greater scandals may occur

---

1. *Senato Miste*, Reg. xliii. p. 129 b, 25th May, 1396; p. 135, 8th June, 1396; and *Senato Miste*, Reg. xliv. p. 5, 14th June, 1397; p. 12, 5th July, 1397.

in the future." It then enacts that for the future no pilgrims belonging to any nation or country may be taken to the Holy Sepulchre on board the Beyrout or Alexandria galleys, unless Venetian pilgrims or other subjects of the Republic. For each pilgrim carried in contravention of the law, a captain-owner was liable to a fine of 100 ducats, and six months imprisonment in one of the lower prisons.[1]

An attempt made in the Maggior Consiglio to repeal this statute in 1400 failed.[2] Nevertheless, by a special vote of the Senate, exceptions were made from time to time in favour of some great prince, as the following examples show. Indeed, when the galleys of the Beyrout fleet were put up to auction that very same year 1398, it was stipulated that the Magnificent Lord of Mantua and thirty-five persons of his suite should be conducted to Jaffa free of charge, on whichever galley of the five he was pleased to select.[3]

In 1406 the privileged pilgrim was the son of the King of Portugal, who was already at Treviso on his way to the Holy Sepulchre, when his ambassadors arrived at Venice. In his name they requested the Senate to allow the Prince and his suite of about twenty-five persons to be conveyed on one of the Beyrout galleys. The Senate immediately granted the request, and the galley *Capella* was placed at the disposal of the Royal visitor. Special instructions were given to Ser Andrea Capello, the captain-owner, and also to the commodore of the whole fleet. When the latter was above Cyprus, all Venetian subjects on other galleys who wished to go to the Holy Sepulchre were to be transferred to the *Capella*, which was then to go to Jaffa; while the other galleys, as usual, went to Beyrout. As soon as the Prince and the other pilgrims had landed

---

[1] *Senato Miste*, Reg. xliv. p. 37 b, 14th April, 1398.
[2] *Delib. Mag. Consig.*, Leona, p. 106 b, 22nd July, 1400.
[3] *Senato Miste*, Reg. xliv. p. 47, 22nd June, 1398.

INTRODUCTION

and the cargo for Jaffa had been unloaded, Ser Andrea had orders to go and wait ten or twelve days "in the place which seemed to him most suitable for ensuring the safety of the galley entrusted to him"—and which, it must be remembered was State property, though Ser Andrea had hired it for that voyage. After the expiry of the ten or twelve days, he was to go to Jaffa, embark the pilgrims, and then rejoin the other galleys at Beyrout.[1]

The voyage was evidently very successful. For in 1410 a bishop was sent to Venice by King John to ask leave on his behalf to invest in some of the Venetian State loans. In granting the request the Council noted with evident satisfaction the friendly feeling of the Portugese King towards the Republic—"which was due to the great honour we did to his son, the illustrious Lord Anfosio" [*i.e.*, Alphonso] "when he came to Venice."[2]

The next royal pilgrim in whose favour an exception was made is vaguely described as "that English noble, a relative of the Lord the King, with his company." The year was 1408, and the Senate decreed that the Englishmen were to be taken to Jaffa on board one of the Beyrout galleys on which no merchant was to have a passage either going or returning. The amount of the passage money was to be agreed on between the *Patrono* and the heads of the *Quarantia* and the *Savij*. The space to be allotted to the distinguished pilgrims on the galley was expressly specified in the decree.[3]

In 1414 Nicolaus de Birsa, brother of the Burgomaster of Bruges, with four friends and thirteen servants, asked permission to go to the Sepulchre on board the merchant galleys—permission which the Senate promptly granted:

---

1. *Senato Miste*, xlvii. p. 75, 6th August, 1406; p. 65, 26th August, 1406; and p. 74 *b*, 6th August, 1406.
2. *Delib. Maggior Consiglio*, Leona, Reg. xxviii. p. 197 *b*, 5th October, 1410.
3. *Senato Miste*, Reg. xlviii. p. 27, 4th August, 1408—"Et deputentur pro statio suo scandolarium pupis et barcha, et etiam armarolus Comiti quia est contentus."

"As it is greatly to the interest of our Government and of our merchants to oblige the said nobles."[1] In acceding to a similar request made in 1423 by a "Great Lord of Flanders," who, with eight friends, had come to Venice with the intention of sailing thence to the Holy Sepulchre, the Senate declared that it was very advisable to favour Lords of such great power and reputation, "especially considering how much they can injure or aid those of our merchants and citizens who pass through their countries."[2]

The Decree of 1398 was also suspended in 1415 on behalf of the "Lord Ugolino de Pijs," Vicar of the Lord Pandolfo[3] and in 1425 in favour of four noble pilgrims, two of whom, strongly recommended to the Venetian Government by the Duke of Savoy, were taken to the Holy Sepulchre on the Beyrout galleys with their friends and servants.[4] The Lord Ugolino was carried free of charge. Similar concessions were also made in later years.

Meanwhile, in 1395, all questions and disputes which should arise between pilgrims to the Holy Land, Rome or elsewhere, and the captain-owners, or between these and the *missetæ* or others, had been placed under the jurisdiction of the magistrates of the *Cattaveri*, who were empowered to make provisions on all matters relating to the pilgrims whenever they thought necessary. They had also authority to appoint, suspend, dismiss and generally supervise the conduct of these agents. The measure was provoked, as the decree says, "pro multis novitatibus que quotidie fiunt dictis peregrinis."[5]

In consequence, in February, 1396, the three magistrates of the *Cattaveri*—Marcello Marcello, Lorenzo Bembo and

---

1. *Senato Miste*, Reg. l. p. 143 b, 20th August, 1414.
2. *Senato Miste*, Reg. liv. p. 140, 28th August, 1423.
3. *Senato Miste*, Reg. li. p. 29, 3rd June, 1415.
4. *Senato Miste*, Reg. lv. p. 157, 23rd August, 1425; p. 157 b, 29th August, 1425.
5. *Cattaveri*, Reg. iv. p. 88, 18th March, 1395.

Pietro Civrano, appointed by name ten agents, who were to give in the office of the *Cattaveri* all contracts made with pilgrims within four days after they were signed.[1]

Two days later the same magistrates ordered the scribes of four ships carrying pilgrims and all other scribes, in the future, to give in, in writing, to the clerks of the *Cattaveri* within four days after they were signed, all agreements made between pilgrims and the captain-owners or *Patroni* of their respective ships.[2]

These two provisions of 1396 were designed to give the *Cattaveri* a double check on the contracts named, and enable them to protect the interests of the pilgrims. The Venetian Government realised very clearly that if these were unjustly treated, reprisals might follow at the expense of the persons and goods of Venetian subjects abroad, and diplomatic difficulties might be created which would involve the State in serious complications. The whole matter was the more delicate and hedged with dangers, because many noble pilgrims, in sign of humility, or to fulfil a vow, or to protect themselves from Saracen extortion and even imprisonment, travelled in disguise, and their identity was not always revealed to the officers of the Serenissima before their departure from Venice. Lack of good faith in drawing up and carrying out an agreement, made with the humble-looking wearer of a pilgrim's cloak and scallop shell, might easily, shortly after he returned home, raise a hornet's nest for the Venetian Government, or cause the representatives of a great Venetian mercantile house in a foreign country to lose immense profits and have their business hampered for an indefinite period.

Patroni, agents and guides, however, careless of political and other consequences, and intent only on enriching themselves at the expense of the numerous

1. *Cattaveri*, Reg. iv. p. 88, 21st February, 1396 (more Veneto 1395).
2. *Idem*, p. 88 b, 23rd February, 1396 (more Veneto 1395).

strangers who passed through Venice on their pious errand, sought constantly to evade the law. Their attempts provoked fresh legislation, which, in 1401, attacked the shipowners who carried pilgrims without having a license to do so, reformed the Piazza guides, and dealt again with the contracts.

In May, 1401, "on account of great abuses," as the preamble declared, a decree of the Senate forbad any unlicensed ship to carry pilgrims to the Holy Sepulchre, under a penalty of 100 lire for each pilgrim taken in defiance of the law. The *Cattaveri* were, as usual, empowered to watch over the execution of the decree and levy the fines on the transgressors.[1]

Later in the same year, these magistrates once more dealt with the question of the Piazza guides. These latter were now twelve in number, divided into six couples, and each couple was obliged to remain for a week, in turn, in the Piazza, &c., from early morning until sunset every day, at the disposal of any pilgrims who might arrive. The profits were divided into two parts: half belonged to the guide or guides who had rendered a particular service, and the other half went to a general fund. All sums were to be given in as soon as received, and the gains were to be divided among the whole body of the guides every month. Many had, however, neglected to take their turn in the Piazza, and even absented themselves from the city without leave—evidently counting on their share of the monthly division of profits even if they failed to do their duty. Others had not given a faithful account of what they had received or handed in the money at the right time. The *Cattaveri* were naturally besieged with complaints of guides against guides, and of *Patroni* and pilgrims against the guides.

1. *Cattaveri*, Reg. iv. p. 89, 20th May, 1401, ("In Consilio Rogatorum").

INTRODUCTION

In September, 1401, therefore, the magistrates of the *Cattaveri* ordered:—First, that everything the guides received from anyone for their services was to be paid into their office within three days. Second, that if any guide wished to absent himself from the city he must first obtain a license from the *Cattaveri*. Third, that each *tholomarius* must take his weekly turn in the Piazza, and anyone who failed to do so was to be reported to the office of the *Cattaveri*, where he would have a bad mark, and for every such mark be fined twenty small soldi. A guide who reported a companion was to inform the latter within eight days. This was, no doubt, in order to give the accused a fair chance of defending himself, and prevent unjust or underhand dealing.[1]

In spite of the provisions of 1396, it appears that the pilgrims' contracts had not been always given in to the *Cattaveri* by the time the law required, and captains did not in consequence depart on the day fixed—to the great loss of the pilgrims, who were obliged to spend their money in maintaining themselves in Venice. Further, the office of the *Cattaveri* was daily annoyed and overburdened by complaints of the *Misseta* or agents, who declared that the *Patroni* did not pay them their due. It was therefore enacted in December, 1401:—

First, that *Patroni*, scribes and agents were to give in to the office of the *Cattaveri* all contracts, made in writing with pilgrims, within *three days* after they had been signed; and, *second*, that all captain-owners and their partners were to pay in to the same office, three days before the departure of their ships taking pilgrims, everything owing to the agents, who were to divide the amount amongst them.[2]

---

[1]. *Cattaveri*, Reg. iv. p. 99, 25th September, 1401.
[2]. *Cattaveri*, Reg. iv. p. 89, 10th December, 1401.

Continuing on these lines, the magistrates of the *Cattaveri* laid down, in January, 1402, that all contracts made with pilgrims should be null and void unless they were drawn up and signed in the presence of the captain-owners, pilgrims and agents concerned, and registered in the pilgrims' books, kept in the office of the *Cattaveri*. As usual, the law was evidently broken or evaded by certain individuals, and had to be repeated in 1422.[1]

At the beginning of the fifteenth century the innkeepers, tempted by their opportunities and by a desire to increase their gains, sometimes usurped the functions of the *missetæ* or agents; while these latter found it to their interest to arrange passages for pilgrims on foreign vessels when there were Venetian ships ready. On account of these "*inconvenientias, que sequebantur et quottidie multiplicabant*," as they said, the magistrates of the *Cattaveri* enacted in March, 1407:—That no innkeeper or other person should dare for the future to take the place of the agents in making arrangements between pilgrims and shipowners, under a penalty of 25 lire and a month in prison. They also forbad Andrea Ongaro (Andrew the Hungarian, who seems to have been the chief offender), and other *Missetæ* to engage foreign vessels until all Venetian vessels in port were full.[2]

The foreign vessels referred to were evidently those belonging to other Italian States, engaged chiefly, if not exclusively, in the Adriatic coasting trade, which carried pilgrims to Ancona and other ports on their way to Rome or to famous shrines at Loreto or elsewhere. The provision forbidding passages to be taken for pilgrims on foreign vessels as long as Venetian ones were available was re-enacted in 1423. At the same time, clauses were added

---

1. *Cattaveri*, Reg. iv., p. 89, 21st January, 1402 (more Veneto 1401); and p. 93 *b*, 27th February, 1422 (more Veneto 1421).
2. *Cattaveri*, Reg. iv. p. 91 *b*, 5th March, 1407.

INTRODUCTION

to protect pilgrims against unscrupulous agents and captains who, taking advantage of their ignorance, made them believe they were to be landed at one port, and took them instead to another. *Patroni* and *misseta* who deceived pilgrims in this respect were punished by a fine.[1]

In 1403 the voyages of Venetian ships to Syria were temporarily stopped by the Venetian Government owing to the threatening movements of the Genoese in the Eastern Mediterranean.[2] But in the summer, among other pilgrims awaiting a passage from Venice, there were the Duke of Burgundy, and many other knights and nobles of France and other countries, strongly recommended by the Kings and Lords whose subjects they were. These distinguished guests besieged the Government with requests to be allowed to go on their way to the Holy Land; and pointed out the pecuniary and moral damage they would suffer if they had to return home without attaining their object.

When the embargo was laid on the Eastern voyages, the intention of the Government was, if possible, to avoid a *casus belli* with Genoa, and in any case to prevent Venetian merchants and rich cargoes from falling into Genoese hands. It may be noted here that the effort to avoid a war failed; and on October 9th, 1403, the Genoese were defeated near Modone by Carlo Zeno. Peace was made between the two Republics in March, 1404.

Meanwhile, pressed by the foreign pilgrims, the Senate, on the 25th of August, 1403, gave authority to Venetian ships to take pilgrims to Syria on condition that they did not go beyond Jaffa and Acre, and that they did not carry any merchandise whatsoever or any merchants or other ordinary passengers save Venetian subjects returning home

---

1. *Cattaveri*, Reg. iv., p. 93, 18th May, 1423.
2. *Senato Miste*, Reg. xlvi. p. 83 b, 15th May, 1403; p. 92, 20th July, 1403.

from these two Syrian ports. No ship was to sail without at least 25 pilgrims, and the names of the latter were to be given in by the *Patroni* to the office of the *Cattaveri*.[1] A month later the enactment was modified. Permission was given to carry other passengers than pilgrims from Venice to Syria, but no merchandise; and on the return the pilgrim ships might take merchandise and ordinary passengers aboard at Jaffa, Acre, Rhodes, and even Beyrout, if there was a possibility of going to the latter place in reasonable security.[2] When hostilities broke out the Genoese had seized the goods belonging to their Venetian rivals in Cyprus, Rhodes, and Beyrout, and threatened the shipping in the Levant.

In February, 1405, there were a number of pilgrims assembled in Venice who desired to go from there to the Holy Land if they could find a ship; but who were determined to sail from Ancona if they could not get a passage from Venice, as they seem to have found some difficulty in doing—perhaps because it was early in the season. The Senate felt that in the interest of the shipowners and for the honour of the city, steps must be taken to provide the pilgrims with what they needed, and gave them license to engage a sailing ship or galley of 300 *botte*[3] or less for the voyage, with the proviso that no merchandise of any kind was to be carried either going or returning from Syria.[4] The pilgrims, however, could not find any vessel of the tonnage prescribed, and appealed again to the Senate, which empowered them to hire any sailing ship over six years old. It is to be presumed that they found what they wanted this time.[5]

We now reach one of the epoch-making statutes in the

1. *Cattaveri*, Register iv. p. 90, 25th August, 1403, "in Rogatis."
2. *Senato Miste*, Register xlvi. p. 103 b, 25th September, 1403.
3. About 150 tons burden.
4. *Senato Miste*, Reg. xlvi. p. 167 b, 27th February, 1405 (more Veneto 1404).
5. *Senato Miste*, Reg. xlvii. p. 1, 24th March, 1405.

pilgrim legislation. Since the thirteenth century and the General Maritime Statutes of the doges Tiepolo and Zeno there is no mention in the many laws relating to pilgrim ships of the arms to be carried for the protection of a vessel and its passengers.

But, in 1408, Ser Andrea Quirini's galley, returning to Venice with pilgrims from the Holy Sepulchre, was attacked in the Gulf of Satalia, on the south of Asia Minor, by a Turkish ship. In the combat there were many killed and wounded on board the *Quirina*. The Senate declared that this deplorable occurrence was due to the fact that the *patroni* of the pilgrim ships did not take care to carry the cross-bows and other arms necessary for defence, and that if it had not been for the foreign pilgrims aboard the *Quirina*, who made a courageous defence, the galley would certainly have fallen into the hands of the Turks. In consequence the *patroni* of the said pilgrim galleys were ordered to carry a fixed number of crossbows, arrows, lances and other arms, and eight crossbow men.[1]

Another important statute was that of December 30th, 1410, which offers the first example of a proposal to put up a State galley to auction for the pilgrim traffic. This was due to the fact that the Beyrout galleys had been unable to bring back in the autumn all the cargo waiting in that port, and an extra ship had to be sent for the purpose. The proposal was rejected, and other arrangements made for the transport of the spices and other merchandise left behind at Beyrout.[2]

---

1. The Patroni were ordered to have:—"Corratias lxxx. cum suis brazalibus et todidem bazinetos, triginta lanceas longas, ballistas xx. cum suis manetis et crochis, et arma pro sua persona. Item capsas veretonorum xv. a ducentis veretonis pro capsa, et clipearia lx. Et ultra hoc Nauclerij et Scribani, Marangoni et Calefati Galee predictarum teneantur portare arma et ballistas suas sicut tenentur. Teneantur insuper quilibet dictorum patronorum, conducere secum ballistarios octo qui accipiantur per solutores armamenti secundum accipiuntur alii ballistarij Galearum nostrarum a mercato."—*Cattaveri*. Reg. iv. p. 92. 28th September, 1408, and *Senato Miste*, Reg. xlviii. p. 33 b.

2. *Senato Miste*, Reg. xlviii. p. 199 b, 30th December, 1410, and p. 203, 20th January, 1411 (more Veneto 1410).

When the Beyrout galleys (four in number) were put up to auction in 1413, it was provided that the cargo they were obliged to leave behind for want of space, was to be warehoused and sealed; and as occasion presented itself the Consul at Damascus and the Council of twelve merchants there were to send the goods so stored to Venice by any ship they thought fit, including the pilgrim galleys. Goods carried by the latter paid three-fourths of the usual charges for freight.[1] It was soon thought necessary to take additional precautions to ensure the safety of the merchandise carried by these pilgrim galleys—merchandise often of great value: *Quia pro maiori parte rata galearum Baruti conducitur cum ipsis Venetis*. And the Senate decreed, on the 1st of March, 1414, that each pilgrim galley was to be equipped with two rowers or *Galeotti* to each bench, and carry twenty crossbow men, including among the latter two Venetian Patricians.[2]

It is to be noted that the Venetian galleys were described as *Biremi* or *Triremi*, according to the number of men—each with an oar—rowing at each bench, and all on the same level.[3] The above-mentioned statute would therefore imply that the galleys which carried pilgrims were *Biremi*. There are reasons, however, for believing that the pilgrim galleys, at least in the second half of the fifteenth century, and including that of Agostino Contarini, were Triremes, and would in other circumstances have been equipped with three oarsmen to each bench.

In 1417 Ser Zaccaria da Ponte and Ser Donato Erizzo carried pilgrims to the Holy Sepulchre on board their galley the *Erizza*, and on the return voyage brought spices and other merchandise from Beyrout.[4] When the *Erizza*

---

1. *Senato Miste*, Reg. 1. p. 4 b, 7th July, 1413.
2. *Idem*, p. 80 b, 1st March, 1414, and p. 150, 4th September, 1414.
3. L. Fincati, *Le Triremi*, p. 6, &c.
4. *Senato Miste*, Reg lil. p. 43, 23rd August, 1417.

INTRODUCTION

reached Venice strong complaints were made of the way in which these joint *Patroni* had treated the pilgrims. One specific charge was that the latter had been half-starved, and another that cargo had been placed in the space allotted to them by contract. Many " Great Lords " had in consequence refused to continue the voyage, and remained behind at Beyrout, Rhodes and other ports. A certain number had taken passages on Genoese ships, threatening to take revenge later for the extortions, innovations and injuries of which they had been the victims. Many of those who came back on the *Erizza* to Venice departed immediately in a very hostile frame of mind, and with the intention of indemnifying themselves for all they had suffered.

The Government was alarmed, especially—as the decree dealing with the matter declared—" Considering that the said pilgrims who remained behind in Beyrout, Rhodes and other places, are great Lords, and could greatly injure our merchants and citizens, since, as is well known, most of our relations and trade are with the countries of the West." In consequence the Senate ordered the galley to be sequestered, and also all the money received either from the pilgrims or for freight; and out of the latter just and reasonable compensation to be given to the pilgrims. Further, for the honour of the Republic, the advocates of the Commune were ordered to initiate proceedings against Ser Zaccaria da Ponte and Ser Donato Erizzo.[1] These proceedings, however, seem to have been quashed next year, though no reason is given for this.

In February, 1418, however, the Senate, in order to prevent the pilgrims from being crowded out of the very limited space allotted to them, voted a decree which forbad the *Patroni* of the pilgrim galleys, under a penalty

1. *Senato Miste*, Reg. lii. p. 61, 6th December, 1417.

of 500 ducats and perpetual exclusion from this traffic, to carry for the future any merchandise whatever abroad except *havere capselle*.[1]

A few months later people interested, complained to the Government that whereas the pilgrim galleys carrying *havere capse* and letters from merchants in Venice to others in Syria, used to go first to Beyrout; they now went straight to land the pilgrims at Jaffa. In the interests of trade the Senate ordered that these galleys—if they had such letters or merchandise aboard—were to go first to Beyrout, and then to Jaffa, and that the pilgrims before signing the agreements, were to be fully informed of the order in which these ports would be touched at.[2]

The officers, *galeotti*,[3] and other sailors on board Venetian galleys and other vessels, had the right of carrying merchandise on their own account in their sea-chests; and added to their salaries by doing a little private trading in the places visited. A doubt was raised as to whether—in spite of the clause in the Act of February, 1418, which expressly permitted *havere capselle* to be carried on board the pilgrim galleys—the officers and men of those galleys could carry merchandise in their chests; and it was represented to the Government that "with the pay they had they could not maintain themselves and their families otherwise." The Senate declared by a large majority that the officers and men of the pilgrim galleys were to have the same privileges in this respect as those of the merchant galleys.[4] Casola frequently speaks of them trading at the ports.

---

1. *Senato Miste*, Reg. lii. p. 77 b, 16th February, 1418 (more Veneto 1417). The "havere capsella" or "havere capse" appears to have been merchandise in boxes or cases.
2. *Senato Miste*, Reg. lii. p. 110 b, 16th July, 1418.
3. Galeotti = oarsmen. See Note 43.
4. *Senato Miste*, Reg. lii. p. 86 b, 7th April, 1418.

INTRODUCTION

In June of this year, 1418, the Senate licensed Francesco Cavallo to go on his voyage with his galley, and the pilgrims who had taken their passage by it.[1] In November the pilgrims who returned to Venice on board the *Priola*, had each brought a certain quantity of sugar which was seized at the Custom House. The Senate, however, ordered it to be restored to the owners free of duty.[2]

Every year a certain number of galleys were equipped in the Venetian arsenal for the merchant service. Divided into squadrons—usually of three, four or five ships—they were put up to auction for the voyage to Beyrout, Alexandria, the Black Sea, Barbary or Flanders, on certain conditions and knocked down to the highest bidders. These latter then set up benches—with banners bearing their arms at the side—in the Piazzo San Marco, and there enrolled the crew and did other business. But before being authorised to set up these benches or *ponere bancum*, as it was called, these *Patroni*, who were always patricians, were required to present themselves before the Senate or the Maggior Consiglio, and be approved by a majority of votes. This rule had not been strictly observed in the case of the *Patroni* of the pilgrim and other galleys not forming part of the merchant fleets named. In September, 1423, therefore the Senate decreed: "That all *Patroni* of galleys going to Jaffa for the Holy Sepulchre or elsewhere must be at least 30 years of age, and be approved by the Senate before setting up their benches in the Piazza."[3] Another statute of 1428 laid down that each *Patrono* was to furnish clear proofs that he had attained the required age of 30.[4]

1. *Senato Miste*, Reg. lii. p. 104, 23rd June, 1418.
2. *Idem*, p. 133, 29th November, 1418.
3. *Senato Miste*, Reg. liv. p. 145, 4th September. 1423.
4. *Senato Miste*, Reg. lvi. p. 162, 19th February, 1428 (more Veneto 1427).

Between 1422 and 1426 there was danger of war breaking out between Venice and the Turks, who besieged Constantinople in 1422 for the fourth time. This explains why, in July, 1424, the Senate decreed that an additional large galley, subsidised with 1,000 ducats by the State, should be deputed to protect the Beyrout and Alexandria fleets. This galley was put up to auction and knocked down to Ser Andrea Mudacio, who was authorised to carry pilgrims, but not either merchants or merchandise.[1]

In 1425, owing to outrages inflicted on Venetian merchants in Egypt and Syria, the *Patroni* of all ships going to Jaffa and other ports belonging to the Sultan of Egypt, were forbidden to carry any kind of merchandise.[2] During the war with the Turks, marked, in February, 1430, by the Turkish siege and capture of Salonicco—which was defended by Lorenzo Contarini, the Venetian Governor—and closed by the Treaty of Adrianople, September, 1430, the *Patroni* of galleys going to the Holy Sepulchre were forbidden to carry any kind of merchandise for the whole of that year.[3]

New difficulties with the *Tholomarij* or Piazza Guides provoked new measures on the part of the *Cattaveri* in 1428 and 1429. There were quarrels amongst the guides about the division of profits and work. One of their number, Andrew the Hungarian, claimed that he alone was entitled to act as guide for the Hungarian pilgrims, and not John Sartor, from Bohemia. After due consideration and in the interests of peace the *Cattaveri* ordered :—

(1) That within fifteen days the *Tholomarij* were to have a box made with two keys—one to be kept by their representative or *Gastaldo*, and the other by one of the notaries of the office of the *Cattaveri*. The box was to be

---

[1]. *Senato Miste*, Reg. lv. p. 46, 28th July, 1424.
[2]. *Idem*, p. 81 b, 22nd January, 1425 (more Veneto 1424), and p. 112 b, 11th May, 1425.
[3]. *Senato Miste*, Reg. lvii. p. 207, 4th April, 1430.

placed in the office of the latter, and the gains of each week—after being registered by one of the clerks of the *Cattaveri*—were to be placed in it. Any money earned by guides out of their turn was to be handed to those whose turn it was.

(2) That each two of the guides were to attend in the Piazza for a week at a time, and no one was to usurp the turn of another.

Further, John of Bohemia was recognised as an authorised guide.[1]

A very few months later, in March, 1429, the Lords of the *Cattaveri* were called upon to deal with the same questions, and others in addition, which they did in a very comprehensive measure. Amongst other things complaints had been made that the two guides whose turn it was to wait in the Piazza sometimes only knew one language, while the pilgrims who arrived belonged to different countries, and spoke various languages; and that pilgrims who wanted to go to Rome were often deceived by the owners of the small coasting vessels, who agreed to take them to Rimini, and instead landed them at other places more convenient to themselves. Further, some *Patroni* agreed to take pilgrims for a certain price, and then, when they arrived at the places named in the contracts, they found pretexts for exacting much larger sums. And all this in spite of numerous laws checking such abuses.

The magistrates of the *Cattaveri* therefore enacted:—

(1) That the twelve *Tholomarii* should meet together under the presidency of their *Gastaldo* and form themselves into six couples, each couple speaking at least two different languages.

(2) Each couple, in turn, was to remain daily during a whole week in St. Mark's Place, and honestly serve the

---

1. *Cattaveri*, Reg. iv. p. 93 *b*, 16th December, 1428.

pilgrims. When one guide went to dinner, the other was to wait in the Piazza till his companion returned; then, having also dined himself, they were both to remain until the usual hour. If a guide failed to appear, or to do his duty, he was (save for illness or other just cause) to lose his share of the monthly profits; and for a third offence be suspended for two years.

(3) The other *Tholomarii* were forbidden to interfere with the two on duty, or to accept any money, or arrange any contracts.

(4) The two guides whose weekly turn it was were to give in all money received, to the office of the *Cattaveri*, where it was to be registered and placed in the proper box; the whole sum being divided at the end of each month.

(5) The *Tholomarii* were to find passages for pilgrims going to Rome and elsewhere with Venetian *Patroni*, and, failing these, with honest persons who would not deceive them. At the time of signing the agreements the *Tholomarii* were to tell the pilgrims the whole amount of their passage money.

(6) *Patroni* of coasting vessels who failed to land pilgrims where they had promised, were liable to a fine of fifty small lire and a month's imprisonment in one of the lower prisons.[1]

Next year, however, the *Cattaveri* were obliged to order the guides once more, to remain two and two in the Piazza for a week in turn, under a penalty of losing all share in the profits and being dismissed, if they failed to do their duty; and to carry all the money received from pilgrims and others, *immediately* to their office, on pain of a fine in case of disobedience.[2]

1. *Cattaveri*, Reg. iv. p. 94, 9th March, 1429.
2. *Cattaveri*, Reg. iv. p. 97 b. 26 July, 1430.

INTRODUCTION

At the end of 1430 hostilities broke out with Filippo Maria Visconti, Duke of Milan, and continued until 1433. Genoa was at that time under the domination of the Visconti; and the Venetian Republic had, therefore, to protect its commerce from the attacks of the Genoese fleet in the Mediterranean, as well as wage war against the Milanese and their allies on the mainland. In the spring of the next year, it was felt to be unsafe for the two galleys, the *Canala* and the *Vallaressa*, then preparing to go with pilgrims to the Holy Sepulchre, to undertake the voyage separately; and so, while each galley had its own captain-owner as usual, the Senate appointed Ser Giorgio Malipiero to the supreme command.[1]

In the Commission given to the commodore, he was ordered to govern both galleys and administer justice in civil and criminal matters to those on board. He was not to land during the voyage save at places belonging to Venice. He was to see that each galley had its full complement of two oarsmen to each bench, and twenty crossbow men, including two patricians. He was not to allow merchants or merchandise (not even *havere capse*) to be carried. The captain-owners were to pay him 150 ducats for the whole voyage, out of which sum he was to pay two servants; while he was to have two trumpeters at the expense of the two galleys.[2]

A similar arrangement was made in April, 1432, when the supreme command of the same two pilgrim galleys was given by the Senate to Ser Nicolo Arimondo.[3] The *Vallaressa* had on board certain Savoyard nobles, who had taken their passage for Cyprus; while on the *Canala* there were some nobles from Burgundy, recommended to the

---

1. *Senato Miste*, Reg. lviii. p. 48 b, 13th April, 1431, p. 49 b, 17th April, 1431.
2. *Idem*, p. 50 b, 23rd April, 1431.
3. *Idem*, p. 110 b, 26th April, 1432, and p. 113 b, 9th May, 1432.

courtesy of the Signoria by their Duke. It was to be decided by agreement or by lot, which of the two galleys was to carry the commodore; and that galley had orders to sail on the Sunday following, May the 9th; its companion was to follow next day, Monday. Special permission was given to Ser Giovanni Cornaro to send 2,500 ducats by these pilgrim galleys to his business at Episcopia, in Cyprus.[1] Casola gives interesting details about his visit to these famous sugar plantations belonging to the Cornaro family.

The instructions given to Ser Nicolo in his Commission resembled those given to his predecessor, save that he was to see that each galley carried twenty-five, instead of 20 crossbow men; and he was not to allow any ordinary passenger or servant to be written down either as an oarsman or as a crossbow man. He was expressly forbidden to trade on his own account, even in pearls or jewels, under a penalty of 1,000 ducats. On the outward voyage he was to stay only two days at Cyprus, and on the homeward voyage he was not to touch at Rhodes, and he was to remain the shortest time possible in any port of Cyprus. Pilgrims and other passengers taken on board at other ports than Venice were to be charged in proportion to the length of their voyage.[2]

In engaging the crews for the galleys, &c., the old custom was to engage and pay them by the month. But not long before the year 1434, the *Patroni* of ships going to the Sepulchre began to make their bargains with the men for the voyage, which naturally led to discontent when, for any reason, this was prolonged beyond the time anticipated. In March, 1434, therefore, when Ser Giralamo de Canali, Knight, was approved in the Senate

---

1. *Senato Miste*, Reg. lviii. p. 114, 9th May, 1432, and p. 114 *b* 11th May, 1432.
2. *Idem*, p. 114.

as *Patrono* of a galley going to the Holy Sepulchre, he was empowered to *ponere banchum* and engage as many men as necessary to equip the galley, with the proviso that he and all other *Patroni* in the future, were to pay the crew by the month, and for two months in advance. A disobedient *Patrono* was liable to a fine of 500 golden ducats.[1]

In the autumn of 1437, as there was more merchandise at Beyrout than could be brought to Venice by the regular fleet, the law of February, 1418, was suspended, and the pilgrim galley was licensed to take on board the surplus at Beyrout and also at Rhodes; but was forbidden to take any other merchandise, or give a passage to any merchant.[2]

The next year the question of the pilgrim traffic seriously occupied the Senate, which was betrayed into a piece of hasty legislation, soon repealed.

On the 11th of March, three Senators proposed that permission should be given to Ser Lorenzo Tiepolo, Ser Nicolo Grimani, Ser Stefano Trevisano and Ser Lorenzo Loredano (son of Ser Bartolomeo) to build and equip a galley each in Venice for carrying pilgrims to the Sepulchre; and that Ser Marino Contarini should have license to adapt his galley for the same purpose. Further, that each *Patrono* should be approved, not only before departure, but also within fifteen days after his return, so that the Government might know how the pilgrims had been treated.

But the Government had evidently been much harassed by complaints of the conduct of the *Patroni*, and the proposal found few supporters. Instead, when one of the Councillors, Ser Luca Trono, invited the Senate to pro-

---

[1] *Senato Miste*, Reg. lix. p. 37 b, 13th March, 1434.
[2] *Senato Miste*, Reg. lx. p. 35 b, 13th September, 1437.

hibit the building and equipment of any pilgrim galley for the next five years, he carried the whole body with him. He justified his drastic measure by saying: "That everyone knew that the pilgrim galleys had given great worry and annoyance to the Government, and had caused great harm to our citizens on account of the abominable way in which princes, counts and other foreign noblemen who went disguised as pilgrims, to the Holy Sepulchre, on board our galleys, had been and were actually treated."[1]

A few days later, when the Senators had had time to consider the effect of this decree, which punished the innocent as well as the guilty, and put an end, at least for five years, to a lucrative branch of trade, it was repealed as *"useless."* At the same time the Senate voted that several galleys in the Arsenal, which were not needed, should be sold the next Saturday by auction to private persons, and that if any purchaser wished to equip any one of these galleys for going with pilgrims, he was at liberty to do so, provided that the *Patrono* had attained the age of thirty, and was approved by the Senate.[2]

This year, because of attacks made by the Sultan of Egypt on Venetian merchants in his dominions, the pilgrim galleys were forbidden to load *havere capselle* or any other merchandise for or in those parts.[3] But in the autumn Ser Lorenzo Loredano, son of the late Ser Bartolomeo, was preparing to start for the Holy Sepulchre, and having only twenty pilgrims, he sought license to carry some cargo as well. The pilgrims themselves went more than once to the Senate to support the request, representing that they were so few that the cargo would

---

1. *Senato Miste*, Reg. lx, p. 66 b, 11th March, 1438.
2. *Idem*, p. 68 b, 24th March, 1438.
3. *Senato Miste*, Registro lx. p. 78 b, 8th May, 1438, and *Cattaveri*, Reg. iv. p. 27 b, and *Senato Miste*, Reg. lx, p. 83 b, 20th May, 1438.

INTRODUCTION 67

not interfere with their comfort; and that if permission were refused, the galley could not depart with only twenty passengers. In consequence, and "as a concession to the pilgrims," Ser Lorenzo was authorised to take certain goods on board in ports which were specified.[1] He went again with pilgrims next year, and was allowed to carry a certain quantity of copper from Modone to Syria on his galley, the *Loredana*; the rest was loaded on another galley called the *Gritta*.[2] Soon after, the decree of May 8th, 1438, forbidding the pilgrim galleys to carry any merchandise to and from Syria was repealed; so that they were henceforth subject to the laws passed previously.[3]

In 1439, the noble Antonio Loredano, son of Ser Daniele, and the noble Stefano Trevisano, were empowered by the Senate to build and equip two galleys for the transport of pilgrims to the Holy Sepulchre.[4] In October, 1439, however, about sixteen noble foreigners, who came to Venice on their way there, could not find a pilgrim galley willing to sail with such a small number; and the Senate was obliged to permit them to take their passages by the Beyrout trading fleet.[5]

In the spring of 1440, Ser Andrea Gritti (son of the late Ser Marino), Ser Lorenzo Loredano (son of the late Ser Bartolomeo), and Ser Antonio Loredano (son of Ser Daniele), were approved in the Senate as *Patroni* of three pilgrim galleys.[6] The month after, several foreign pilgrims of "notable condition," who had taken their passage with Ser Antonio Loredano, went to the Senate and, representing that they were few, asked that their *Patrono* might have license to carry certain mer-

---

1. *Senato Miste*, Reg. lx. pp. 105 b and 106, 14th October, 1438; p. 106 b, 16th Oct., 1438, and 20th October, 1438; pp. 107 and 108, 23rd and 30th October, 1438.
2. *Idem*, p. 133, 23rd March, 1439; p. 143 b, 9th May, 1439.
3. *Idem*, p. 146, 9th May 1439.
4. *Idem*, p. 150, 8th June, 1439; p. 154 b, 25th June, 1439.
5. *Idem*, p. 174, 17th October, 1439.
6. *Idem*, p. 208 b, 12th April, 1440.

chandise prohibited by the laws in force. The request was granted after much discussion, on condition that Ser Antonio did not take any cheese on board, and that he gave to the State the fourth part of the money received for the freight. The money was to be handed to the heads of the Arsenal. The Senate also stipulated that certain parts of the galley were to be give up entirely to the pilgrims, so that their comfort should not be interfered with.[1]

In June, 1440, license was given by the Senate to the noble Francesco Venier (son of the late Ser Santo, Knight) to build a galley for conducting pilgrims to the Sepulchre on the usual conditions.;[2] and, in August, Ser Lorenzo Loredano (son of the late Ser Bartolomeo) was approved as *Patrono* of a pilgrim galley. As he had previously been approved in April, this is rather curious, and seems to indicate that he had either made an unusually rapid and successful Easter voyage, and was preparing to go again, or that he had deferred the spring voyage for lack of sufficient passengers.[3]

Another member of the Loredano family desired to engage in the transport of pilgrims, and, in April, 1441, the Senate authorised Ser Pietro Loredano, brother of Ser Lorenzo, who had been occupied with this branch of the passenger trade for several years, to build in Venice, but outside the Arsenal, a galley designed for the pilgrim voyages.[4]

As has been seen, in more than one case, pilgrims anxious to hasten their departure from Venice, had begged the authorities to suspend the law dealing with

---

1. *Senato Miste*, Reg. lx. p. 212, 10th May, 1440, and 11th May, 1440.—" Intelligendo etiam quod dictus patronus debeat dimettere pizolum et Scandolarium et glavam, ita et taliter disoccupatum quod peregrinj possint commodissime stare."
2. *Idem*, p. 223, 14th June, 1440.
3. *Idem*, p. 242, 19th August, 1440.
4. *Senato Mar.*, Reg. i. p. 31 *b*, 22nd April, 1441.

the transport of merchandise on pilgrim vessels, in favour of their *Patroni*, and permit the latter to take a general cargo. But the Government was not satisfied with the results of these temporary returns to the old system. There was, no doubt, always the temptation and the tendency to let the cargo encroach on the space assigned to the passengers; and the loading and unloading kept the galleys in various ports beyond the specified time. Consequently, in October, 1440, the statutes already mentioned, of February, 1418, and May 8th, 1438, were re-enacted. The pilgrim ships were not to become merchant galleys, and might not carry anything save what was permitted by the laws named. A disobedient *Patrono* was liable to a fine of 1,000 ducats, and lost what he had carried in contravention of the statutes.[1] From this time the merchandise on board a pilgrim galley was practically limited to what officers and men might take on their own account for private trading.

At this time the pilgrim transport trade was so lucrative, that the Government determined to claim a share in the profits and assume the direct control as far as the galleys were concerned—leaving the sailing ships still free, subject only to the supervision and license of the *Cattaveri*. On the 19th of May, 1441, therefore, the Senate voted the first *Incantus Galearum Peregrinorum*—that is, an auction of licenses for galleys destined for the pilgrim service—and thus initiated a change of policy, which lasted ten years; after which the pilgrim traffic was again thrown open freely to private enterprise.

The decree enacted that licenses to carry pilgrims in galleys to the Holy Sepulchre for the next five years—(*a*) on the Easter voyage, and (*b*) on the August voyage—

---

1. *Senato Mar.*, Reg. i. p. 5, 29th October, 1440. See also *Senato Mar.*, iii. p. 21 *b*, 19th June, 1447, when, owing to difficulties with the Sultan of Egypt, even the officers and crew of the Jaffa Galley that year were forbidden to carry any merchandise to the Levant.

were to be sold by public auction to the highest bidders on certain conditions, of which the following is a summary:—

(1) The *Patroni* who received the licenses were to sail at the time fixed, on the prescribed voyage to Jaffa, with the pilgrims who had taken passages on their respective galleys; and were liable to a fine of 1,000 ducats if they did not do so.

(2) The *Patroni* were not to receive from any pilgrim for passage money and other expenses, more than fifty ducats. (This is the first definite limitation of the expenses met with in the documents; former provisions on the matter are vague.)

(3) The *Patroni* were to equip their galleys in accordance with the requirements of the statutes relating to the pilgrim galleys.

(4) Before setting sail each year, the *Patroni* were to pay a fifth part of the whole sum they had offered at the auction.

(5) The *Patroni* must be approved each year by the Senate before setting up their benches in the Piazza. If rejected on any of these occasions, a *Patrono* might nominate a substitute, who must, however, be approved in his turn by the same Council.

(6) All previous legislation with reference to pilgrim ships which had not been repealed was now confirmed.

(7) In order that *Patroni* who bought these licenses might be sure of not being exposed to competition, it was provided that no other galley might be built or equipped for the purpose, or carry pilgrims during the five years for which the concession lasted. The Government, however, reserved to itself the right to concede a State or other galley to "any magnificent lord" who should ask for one, as such requests on the part of "friends and

INTRODUCTION

potentates could not well be denied." In such a case, however, the *Patrono* of a pilgrim galley was not obliged to pay the quota due of his auction money, or go on that voyage if he did not wish to do so; but, if he went, he was to pay a fifth of the money as usual.

(9) The Easter voyage was to be understood to mean from the first of January to the last of June; and the August voyage was to be understood to mean from the first of July to the 31st of December.

(10) As at the time there were three pilgrim galleys belonging to Venetian citizens, who had received license to build them for this trade, it was enacted that the *Patroni* who now purchased the monopoly for five years should, if the owners desired to sell, be obliged to buy the three galleys in question, with their tackle, at a price fixed by the estimate of friends of both parties to the bargain.

(11) The money paid for the new licenses was to be given to the Arsenal, and used for buying wood with which to build some new large galleys. The licenses were to be auctioned the next day at Vespers, and they were to date from the 1st of January, 1442,[1] modern style.

The licenses were duly auctioned on May 20th, 1441, with the result that the monopoly for what was now described as the March voyage was granted to Ser Lorenzo Mauro, son of the late Ser Antonio, for 802 lire, 16 soldi; and that for the August voyage to Ser Zaccaria Contarini, son of the late Ser Hector, for 150 lire. The immense difference between these two amounts shows clearly that the majority of pilgrims chose to go to the Holy Sepulchre in the spring and return in the autumn.[2] In July, 1441, the license for the autumn voyage was

---

1. *Senato Mar.*, Reg. i. p. 35 b. *Incantus Galearum Peregrinorum*, May 19th, 1441.
2. *Senato Mar.*, Reg. i. p. 36, 20th May, 1441.

again put up to auction at the expense of Ser Zaccaria Contarini, the first purchaser, and knocked down to Ser Antonio Loredano, son of Ser Daniele, for 64 lire, 13 soldi.[1]

The statute embodying the conditions of the monopoly, obliged the *Patroni* to depart on the date fixed, irrespective of the number of pilgrims on board. This clause was soon modified, and the Senate decreed that if a *Patrono* had thirty-five pilgrims or more he must set sail, under a penalty of 1,000 ducats; but, if he had not as many as thirty-five, he need not undertake that voyage, though he must pay the quota due of the auction money all the same.[2]

About this time it appears that unauthorised persons had been taking on themselves to go about to the hostels and taverns and treat directly with the pilgrims about their passages. The guides and agents were thus defrauded of their profits, and Government supervision being evaded, the interests of the pilgrims could not be safeguarded.

The Senate dealt with the abuse in January, 1443, and forbad and *Patrono* of a barque, any sailor, or any other persons save the licensed *Tholomarii* to treat with pilgrims to Rome or elsewhere about passages; and once more ordered the *Tholomarii* to arrange passages for their clients with *Patroni* belonging to Venice and living there, or, if there were not any such available, with the best foreign *Patroni* to be found.[3]

Some other provisions relating to the *Tholomarii* passed within a few years may be noted here. As much trouble had arisen because they would not obey their head or *Gastaldo*, in 1447 the magistrates of the *Cattaveri*

---

1. *Senato Mar.*, Reg. i., p. 36, 11th July, 1441.
2. *Idem*, p. 42 b, 19th June, 1441.
3. *Cattaveri*, Reg. iv. p. 100, 22nd January, 1443 (more Veneto 1442), "In Rogatis."

INTRODUCTION

inflicted a bad mark on any guide who refused to obey an order given by the *gastaldo*. The first such mark carried with it a fine of six grossi *ad aurum*; the second, of eight grossi *ad aurum;* the third, twelve grossi *ad aurum*; for the fourth offence a guide was to be dismissed.[1] As they still quarrelled about the division of profits and worried the *Cattaveri* with their disputes, these magistrates laid down once more and with greater emphasis, in 1448, that all such profits were to be divided equally.[2] Not many years later, as the guides failed to observe certain regulations relating to the pilgrims, the then magistrates of the *Cattaveri* enacted, in January, 1455:—First, that the *Tholomarii* were to obey all existing orders relating to them. Second, that two guides, chosen by lot, were to be on duty every week, at St. Mark's Quay, in St. Mark's Place, and at the Rialto, each morning up to the dinner hour, and afterwards from the ninth to the twenty-fourth hour, under an additional penalty of 25 lire, besides those prescribed in former ordinances. Third, that under the same penalty, the guides were to hand in every Saturday to their *gastaldo* everything they had earned during the week. The *gastaldo*, either that day or the following Monday, was to carry the money to the office of the *Cattaveri* and place it in the box kept for the purpose; and every month the money was to be divided according to the orders previously issued.[3]

In consequence of news received in Venice in the spring of 1444, to the effect that the Sultan of Egypt was preparing an armada against the Knights of Rhodes, the Senate issued an order to the armed pilgrim galley—then on the point of starting—not to touch at Rhodes, unless

---

1. *Cattaveri*, Reg. iv. p. 100, 13th November, 1447.
2. *Idem*, p. 100 b, 28th June, 1448.
3. *Idem*, p. 101, &c., 14th January, 1455 (more Veneto 1454).

at Crete it was found that the armada had not set out, or that hostilities had been abandoned.[1]

In August, 1445, six or eight pilgrims, who came to Venice "from various and distant parts," to go to the Sepulchre, found that the noble Bernardo Contarini, *Patrono* of the galley due to go there on that voyage, refused to depart with such a small number. They therefore begged the Senate to let them go by the Beyrout fleet, and their request was granted, with the consent of Ser Bernardo, who was, however, required to pay the usual fifth part of the auction money, although he did not go on the voyage.[2]

Many noble pilgrims of notable condition arrived in Venice in April, 1446, with letters from the Duke of Burgundy strongly recommending them to the good offices of the Venetian Government for help in carrying out their purpose. It will be remembered that the Senate, in granting the monopolies in 1441, had reserved to itself the right of dealing with special cases, concerning persons of importance. On this occasion the Senate desired to give the preference to the monopolists, and authorised the two *Patroni* in question to take these distinguished pilgrims on their galleys, at a price for passage money and all expenses not exceeding fifty ducats. Each *Patrono* before setting sail was to pay 600 ducats to the Government to be given to the Arsenal. The *Patrono* or *Patroni* who accepted these conditions must be ready to depart on the 6th of June. A clause was expressly added to the effect that the foregoing did not revoke any arrangements made for passages on board *navi* (or sailing ships); but that all pilgrims and sailing ships were in the enjoyment of the

---

1. *Senato Mar.*, i. p. 229, 8th April, 1444.
2. *Senato Mar.*, Reg. ii. p. 106, 31st August, 1445.

INTRODUCTION

usual liberty.[1] This last provision clearly meant that all pilgrims were perfectly free to choose between taking their passage on the monopolists' galleys or on any sailing ship which was licensed by the *Cattaveri* for the voyage to the Holy Sepulchre. The monopoly granted in 1441 prevented any other galleys from competing for the transport of pilgrims, but did not interfere with any sailing ships which might engage in the trade. The relative advantages and disadvantages of the two kinds of vessels were explained by the Senate in June, 1441, to the Count of Nassau, who was sent by the Duke of Burgundy to help the knights of Rhodes, and who asked advice as to the advisability of also going to the Holy Sepulchre. The Count was told that he would go more safely and more quickly in a galley, but that it would cost him more than if he went on a *nave*.[2]

As the five years' monopoly would expire in January, 1447, there was a new *Incantus Galearum Peregrinorum* in the previous September. The conditions were in general those of the former auction, so that the modifications only will be noticed. For example, one galley having gone with pilgrims to Jaffa, it was provided that when it came back—if the *Patrono* wished to sell it—it must be bought by the new monopolists. A second galley, one of the three then engaged on a voyage to Greece, was to be sold to them by the heads of the Arsenal. An amicable agreement or the chance of the lot was to decide which of these two galleys was to be assigned to each of the new *Patroni*.[3]

The monopoly for the Easter voyage was granted to

---

1. *Senato Mar.*, Reg. ii. p. 141, 22nd April, 1446.
2. "Sua magnificencia ibit molto securius et citius cum una galea quam cum una navj. Sed ibit cum multo maiori expensa quam iret cum navj."—*Senato Mar.*, i. p. 43 b, 19th June, 1441.
3. *Senato Mar.*, Reg. ii. p. 175, 12th September, 1446. "*Incantus Galearum Peregrinorum.*"

Ser Domenico Trevisano, son of the late Ser Zaccaria, for 510 lire and 2 ducats. Next day the same patrician bought the monopoly for the August voyage also.[1] Experience had evidently proved that it was more profitable for both to be in the hands of one shipowner, who might or might not command one of the galleys himself, but who could easily find captains for them.

In June, 1448, as many important persons were awaiting the departure of the pilgrim galley, the Senate issued an order that the *Patrono* of the Jaffa galley was to set sail the following Sunday, as he had promised the pilgrims to do, and if he was not ready he would be fined 200 golden ducats.[2]

Owing to complications with the Sultan of Egypt in 1449, the *Patrono* of the pilgrim galley was forbidden to go on the spring or autumn voyage to the Sepulchre, and he was exempted from the payment of the quota due of the auction money. At the same time he was informed that at the end of the five years—if he wished—the monopoly would be extended to him for two extra voyages.[3] In May, however, as there were a good many pilgrims already gathered in Venice, the Senate modified its decision and licensed Ser Antonio Loredano to treat with the pilgrims then in Venice, on the understanding that, if on the return of the Venetian Ambassadors to the Sultan, matters had been satisfactorily arranged, then the pilgrim galley might go on its voyage.[4]

The mission of the Ambassadors Lorenzo Tiepolo and Marino Priuli was successful, and the Sultan Melech-el-Daher addressed a letter to the Doge in which he declared that he had given orders for the removal of the abuses

---

1. *Senato Mar.*, Reg. ii., p. 176, 15th and 16th September, 1446.
2. *Senato Mar.*, Reg. iii. p. 66, 7th June, 1448.
3. *Idem*, p. 108, 28th March, 1449.
4. *Idem*, p. 118, 16th May, 1449.

INTRODUCTION

complained of by the Venetians.[1] These orders were really issued.

Meanwhile many intending pilgrims, tired of waiting for the pilgrim galley, had taken their passages on various sailing ships as far as Cyprus, where they hoped to find vessels ready and willing to undertake the short voyage thence to Beyrout or Jaffa. In the circumstances the Senate removed the embargo on the departure of the galley, and, while still forbidding the *Patrono* (Ser Antonio Loredano) to go to Syria under a heavy penalty, authorised him also to carry pilgrims as far as Rhodes or Cyprus.[2]

Eight pilgrims from Burgundy, who brought letters of recommendation from their Duke, came to Venice in October, 1449. As they were unable, owing to the smallness of their number, to find a passage either on a galley or sailing ship of those which usually went to Jaffa, they asked and obtained permission from the Senate to go by the Beyrout fleet, and two were assigned to each of the four galleys put up to auction and sold that year.[3]

During the disturbances which followed the death of Filippo Maria Visconti, Alfonso of Naples declared war against Venice in 1449, and began to harass the shipping of the Republic. Peace was made in July, 1450, and Venice and Naples were allies in the war ended by the peace of Lodi. But when the Duke of Cleves, nephew of the Duke of Burgundy, came to Venice in May, 1450, and asked for permission to go to the Holy Sepulchre on a Venetian galley, the Senate, while assuring him of its desire to satisfy him in every way, pointed out that, owing to the war with the King of Naples and the presence of a

---

1. *Commemoriati*, Libro 14, p. 83, 21st May, 1449; pp. 87 and 83, see *Regesti*, by R. Predelli.
2. *Senato Mar.*, Reg. iii. p. 120 b, 1st June, 1449.
3. *Idem*, p. 147, 10th October, 1449.

hostile fleet at sea, it was not advisable that any Venetian ship should set sail, and begged the Duke to have patience.[1]

As he insisted, however, the Senate gave way. At the same time the Government wrote to the Duke of Burgundy explaining the circumstances, and declining all responsibility.[2] Instead of making arrangements with a galley, it seems that the Duke, who had brought a suite of twenty persons, took his passage on the *nave Mantella*, and it was reported to the Senate that he wanted to conduct with him on board the said ship sixty persons who, for the most part, had already made their agreements with the pilgrim galley. The Senate therefore interfered, and enacted that the Duke might take with him on board the *Mantella* forty pilgrims and two friars, paying 100 ducats as compensation to the *Patrono* of the pilgrim galley.[3]

In September, 1450, a French noble, subject of King René, who had arrived in Venice with eight or ten companions, ten days after the pilgrim galley sailed, and who had vainly waited several months in the hope of finding a passage on another ship, asked permission to go on board the Beyrout galleys. The request was granted then,[4] and also the similar one made next autumn (1451) by several notable Ultramontanes.[5] This probably marks the time when the voyage to the Holy Land at this season, having proved unprofitable, owing to the small number of pilgrims who gathered in Venice in the autumn, was abandoned by the pilgrim galley or galleys. For the future one or two galleys, according to circumstances, went just after the Feast of the Corpus Domini only, to Jaffa, as was the case in the time of Casola.

1. *Senato Mar.*, iii. p. 185 b, 16th May, 1450.
2. *Idem*, pp. 186 and 187 b, 18th May, 1450.
3. *Idem*, p. 186 b, 22nd May, 1450, and p. 187, 25th May, 1450.
4. *Senato Mar.*, iv. p. 3 b, 21st September, 1450.
5. *Idem*, p. 84, 31st August, 1451.

INTRODUCTION

When the period of the five years' monopoly again expired a new statute, passed by the Senate in May, 1552, threw the pilgrim traffic open to galleys as well as sailing ships; and it remained so for over half a century. It was now enacted:—

(1) That all Venetian nobles who desired to do so, might build large galleys outside the Arsenal at their own expense for conducting pilgrims to the Holy Sepulchre; but that before equipping them or setting up their benches in the Piazza, they must prove that they had reached the age of thirty, and be approved by the Senate.

(2) That on every voyage the *Patroni* were to carry the number of rowers (galeotti) and crossbow men (balestrieri) prescribed by the law, including among the *balestrieri* two patricians.

(3) The said galleys were not to carry merchants, money, or merchandise of any sort.

(4) That in order to prevent disputes between the *Patroni* and the pilgrims, the former were to hand in to the office of the *Cattaveri* the agreements made for the passage money and all other expenses, in the presence of the pilgrims concerned, to whom the contracts were to be read by the clerks of the office. If this were not done, or if any *Patrono* failed to register contracts made with pilgrims at the office of the *Cattaveri*, and any question arose between him and them, the simple word of the pilgrims would be accepted.

(5) That once an agreement was signed and registered in the office of the *Cattaveri*—having been duly read in the presence of both parties—the *Patrono* and pilgrim or pilgrims concerned were required to undertake the voyage under penalty of paying compensation for damages, unless prevented from going by sickness, death, or any other valid reason.

(6) Each *Patrono*, before undertaking his first voyage with pilgrims, was required to pay 100 golden ducats to the Government.

(7) Each *Patrono* on his return from every voyage was under obligation to give 200 pounds of white wax to the Procurators of Saint Mark's, as in the case of the merchant galleys.

Finally, the Senate declared that "all other orders and decrees voted in this Council and dealing with this free way of conducting pilgrims—which are not in opposition to the above clauses—are to be understood to be included in this statute."[1]

In September, 1452, as there was no pilgrim galley ready for the voyage, the Senate permitted several notable pilgrims to go on the Beyrout galleys to Syria, and declared that it was not only advisable to grant the request of these pilgrims *for this voyage only*, because they were persons of importance, but especially because the Senate had lately made the concession that pilgrims could go to the Sepulchre by any ship whatever.[2]

Casola relates that once during a great storm a collection was made and certain pilgrims volunteered to undertake pilgrimages to certain shrines as soon as they landed safely in Venice again. This was a very common way at that time of seeking to propitiate the Deity, and imploring the intercession of the Madonna and saints. It appears, however, that the *Patroni* frequently pocketed the money so collected instead of giving it to the pilgrims who went to fulfil the vow. The Senate, in order to remove this abuse, laid down, in July, 1454, that for the future, whenever a pilgrim was elected for this purpose on a galley or other ship, the *Patrono* was to account for the

---

1. *Senato Mar.*, Reg. iv. pp. 122 *b*, 123, 16th May, 1452.
2. *Idem*, p. 151 *b*, 26th September, 1452.

money collected, within three days after his arrival in Venice, to the Government authorities, by whom it was to be handed to the pilgrim or pilgrims in question. A *Patrono* who failed to do this was liable to a fine equal to the sum collected, which he was also to refund.[1]

In June, 1455, the Senate was informed that the pilgrim galley, the *Contarina*, was about to depart insufficiently equipped—that is, without the full crew. The *Patrono*, Ser Andrea Contarini, was immediately forbidden to set sail "without a license from this Council."[2] Naturally, the pilgrims who had taken their passages were disturbed by this embargo, and went to the Signoria every day, begging insistently that the Government would either give the galley leave to go on its way, or order the money they had paid to be restored to them, so that they could make other arrangements for pursuing their journey. Finally, the Senate ordered Ser Andrea either to equip his galley for the voyage to Jaffa as the law required, and be ready to sail at latest on July 6th, or to give back their money to the pilgrims.[3]

Amongst those who went to the Sepulchre in the spring of 1458 there were the celebrated Condottiere Roberto da Sanseverino and the English John, Earl of Exeter.[4] They made the voyage on the galley *Loredana*, and as the *Patrono*, Ser Antonio Loredano, was a man of much experience and intelligence, the Earl asked the Senate to permit Ser Antonio to accompany him everywhere in his visits to the Holy places. The Senate acquiesced, and in order to free Ser Antonio from the responsibility of command, approved as *Patrono* of the galley the noble Baldesar Diedo, *qui est affinis ipsius Antonij Lauredano, ac sufficiens et practicus ad rem istam*.[5]

1. *Senato Mar.*, Reg. v. p. 42 b, 1st July, 1454.
2. *Idem*, p. 98 b, 17th June, 1455.
3. *Idem*, p. 98 b, 26th June, 1455.
4. See Roberto da Sanseverino's *Voyage to the Holy Land*.
5. *Senato Mar.*, Reg. vi. p. 68, 14th May, 1458. In the decree of the Senate the Earl of Exeter is described as "quidam dominus Anglicus beni status et reputationis in partibus suis, qui sacrum sepulcrum dominicum visitare statuit."

G

The *Loredana* went again to the Sepulchre in June, 1459, as we learn from a petition addressed to the Senate by the magnificent orators of the Duke of Savoy, who had taken their passages on this galley and asked to be landed at Rhodes. At this time the galleys had orders not to touch there. The knights were continually engaged in hostilities with the Turks, with whom the Republic, which had so much to lose, desired to keep on good terms. The *Patrono* of the *Loredana* was ordered to put the Savoyard Ambassadors ashore at Rhodes, but not to land there himself nor let any of his officers or crew do so.[1]

The son of the Duke of Savoy, who was either then in Venice or arrived soon after, wanted to go to Rhodes on board one of the Beyrout or Cyprus galleys. The Senate replied that that would disorganise trade, but gave him the choice between going on board one of those galleys and landing at some other port than Rhodes, or equipping two galleys at his own expense by which he could go direct to Rhodes.[2]

An example of the way in which pilgrims were liable to be delayed on their journey is afforded by a statute of September, 1463. For some time Pope Pius the Second had been trying to unite Christian Europe in a Crusade against the Turks. Venice, while approving the general scheme, had been anxious to avoid beginning the war alone, but an accident precipitated matters, and war broke out in the middle of this year between the Turks and the Venetians, which lasted for sixteen years. Naturally reinforcements were sent to Venetian possessions in the Mediterranean, and their fortifications were strengthened. When the *Contarina* and the *Morosina*, the two pilgrim galleys which had made the Easter voyage to the Holy

---

1. *Senato Mar.*, Reg. vi. p. 130, 3rd June, 1459.
2. *Idem*, p. 133 *b*, 8th June, 1459.

INTRODUCTION 83

Sepulchre, reached Crete on the way home, they were requisitioned by the Governor there to carry soldiers to the island of Amorea (probably Amorgo, one of the Cyclades). The *Patroni*, Ser Andrea Contarini and Ser Andrea Morosini, claimed compensation, and the Senate awarded them 15 large lire each.[1]

Early in 1464, Venice, already fighting the Turks, was nearly involved in hostilities with the knights of Rhodes. Three Venetian galleys, loaded with goods and having several Moors as passengers on board, were compelled by a violent storm to take refuge in the port of Rhodes, where they were seized and plundered. As soon as the news reached Venice the admiral Jacopo Loredano was ordered to go to Rhodes, and his action was so energetic that the Grand Master gave up the Moors and all the merchandise.[2] While the matter was still unsettled, the Senate was informed that Ser Andrea Morosini was preparing to go to the Levant and loading timber, arrows and other things for Rhodes. In view of the late incident he was forbidden to go there or to any other place belonging to the knights of St. John.[3]

In the spring of 1465, the Senate had to deal with a serious accusation brought by Flemish and German pilgrims against the noble Lodovico Pasqualigo, on whose *Trireme* they had been to the Holy Sepulchre. They declared that beside the sum agreed upon before starting, he had extorted 600 ducats from them in one way or another, and asked for the money to be returned to them. The Senate, after premising that the dignity of the State required that justice should be done to everyone, and especially to these pilgrims whose countries were frequented by Venetian citizens, merchants and triremes,

1. *Senato Mar.*, Reg. vii. p. 131, 26th September, 1463.
2. Romanin, *Storia Documentata di Venezia*, vol. iv. pp. 321, 322.
3. *Senato Mar.*, Reg. vii. pp. 192 *b* and 193, 28th September, 1464.

ordered the Savij of the Council and of the Terrafirma to hear the complaints of the pilgrims and the defence of the *Patroni*, and to pronounce judgment according to justice and equity without delay.[1] Perhaps some details of the inquiry, or at least the result, might be traced in the account of some German pilgrim who was interested.

A short decree of May, 1466, informs us that the galley *Contarina* was destined for the Jaffa voyage that year.[2]

Since 1463 Venice had been at war with the Turks. In February, 1468, news came of the death of the Albanian hero Scanderbeg, and soon after, alarming tidings of the great armament, which was being prepared at Pera, and which it was feared would be sent against Negropont. The suspicion was well founded. Negropont was taken by the Turks, July, 1476. Extraordinary efforts were made in Venice to raise large sums of money and build and equip new ships.[3] Amongst other expedients, in May, 1469, the Senate ordered the two *Patroni* of the pilgrim galleys to raise, before leaving Venice, 5,000 ducats each to be given to the Lord High Admiral.[4]

The galley which was preparing to sail to Jaffa in June, 1472, was the *Contarina*. As navigation in the Levant was dangerous on account of the Turkish war, the Senate issued a special order that the *Contarina* was to be equipped in accordance with the Statute of 1414, that is, with two rowers to each bench and 20 crossbow men, including two patricians.[5]

The *Patrono*, Ser Andrea Contarini, appealed against this order, and represented to the Senate that he could

---

1. *Senato Mar.*, Reg. viii. p. 21 *b*, 16th April, 1465. The Statute begins : " Comparverunt his diebus coram nostro dominio aliqui nobiles, et nonnulli alij peregrini qui fuerunt cum triremi nobilis viri Lodovici Pasqualigi, graviter de eo querentes ac dicentes eum ultra pecunias sibi datas juxta formam nabulizati sui, et mutus et aliter habuisse ultra duc : sexcentos, supplicantes eius modi pecunias sibi restitui, &c."
2. *Senato Mar.*, Reg. viii. p. 75 *b*, 16th May, 1466.
3. Romanin, *Storia Documentata di Venezia*, vol. iv. p. 350, &c.
4. *Senato Mar.*, Reg. ix. p. 8, 16th May, 1469.
5. *Idem*, p. 135, 1st June, 1472.

not, without great loss, equip the galley in this way, as he had only 32 pilgrims in all, who had paid some 25, some 26, and some 30 ducats, and having put their things on board the galley were pressing him to leave without delay. The galley was ready, and he asked for licence to sail with a crew of 110 all told. The pilgrims besieged the Government with requests for permission to go on their pilgrimage, and after several days the Senate reluctantly voted that for this time only Ser Andrea might leave with 110 men, including 18 crossbow men.[1]

The same question arose in 1473, and it looked as if Ser Andrea had purposely delayed his departure in order to force the Senate to yield. On July the 1st, the noble pilgrims who had taken their passage on the *Contarina* went to the Signoria, and begged vehemently that licence should be given to the galley to depart. As a concession to the pilgrims the Senate consented, on condition that Ser Andrea went himself on the voyage, that he had a crew of 110, including the *Ballistarij* and that he sailed the next Monday. At the same time, the Senate declared that no other exception whatever would be made, and that every Venetian noble or other who went in the future as *Patrono* of a pilgrim galley, must have two men to each bench according to the requirements of the law.[2]

Ser Andrea Contarini and his galley, the *Contarina* are first mentioned in connection with the pilgrim traffic in 1455, and though there are lacunæ in the sequence of documents, in the absence of evidence to the contrary, it may be assumed that the galley went to Jaffa every year from that time, even if Ser Andrea sometimes proposed a substitute as commander, as is implied in the statute of 1473. After nearly twenty years' service, the

1. *Senato Mar.*, Reg. ix., p. 136, 12th June, 1472 ; 137 *b*, 17th June, 1472.
2. *Idem*, p. 174, 1st July, 1473.

Contarina was the worse for wear, and in the spring of 1474 the Government appointed three experts from the Arsenal to examine the vessel. Their report, presented to the Senate, is a quaint specimen of fifteenth century Venetian. In it they declared, that if it were a question of changing owners, no *Patrono* would buy the galley, nor could they recommend her to anyone as seaworthy. Nevertheless, if the repairs they suggested were executed, and the galley left at Ascension-tide and returned in September, perhaps she might be allowed to make the voyage. If, however, nothing more was done than was being done at present, and the galley came back in the winter, they thought she would run a great risk.[1] On the strength of this report the Senate ordered that the *Contarina* must not go any more "on the usual voyage" to Jaffa either with pilgrims or with merchandise.[2] Ser Andrea asked for a loan of 400 ducats to put the galley thoroughly in order; but the Senate preferred to give him permission to buy a certain galley made in Ancona, and suitable for the transport of pilgrims, which was in the Arsenal, and which did not serve the purposes of the Government. The price was to be fixed by experts in the presence of the heads of the Arsenal, and paid down before the galley was handed over to the new owner.[3]

It seems to have taken a long time to get this galley into sea-going trim, for a year after, a number of distinguished pilgrims went to the Signoria, and declaring that they could not wait for the galley conceded to Ser Andrea Contarini, asked permission to go to the Holy Sepulchre on the sailing ship belonging to Pietro Franco. The Senate granted the license requested on condition that

---

1. *Senato Mar.*, Reg. x. p. 6 b, 6th May, 1474.
2. *Idem.*
3. *Idem*, p. 7 b, 10th May, 1474.

going and returning, the *Patrono* called at Modone and placed himself at the disposition of the Lord High Admiral of the Fleet if he happened to be there, or of the Governor in his absence; and that he carried out such a quantity of biscuits and ammunition as would not cause inconvenience to the pilgrims.[1] A month later, when the new *Contarina* was preparing to sail, Ser Andrea was ordered by the Senate to present the *Patrono* for approval to that Council, to engage the full complement of crossbow men and carry the noble apprentices required by the law. In addition, under a penalty of 500 ducats in case of refusal, he was to give a free passage to Ser Francesco Giustiniani—who had been elected Provvisore of Cyprus—and his company as far as Modone.[2]

This year, "in order to obviate difficulties which might arise between *Patroni* taking pilgrims to the Holy Land," the *Cattaveri* decreed, that when any pilgrim had been written down in the books of that office to go with any captain to the Holy Sepulchre, he could not change to another ship unless the compact made with the first captain was annulled.[3]

In the second part of the fifteenth century these magistrates were several times obliged to make new provisions with regard to the guides.

In 1463, owing to frequent disputes between the *Tholomarij* and the *Patroni* of the pilgrim galleys, caused by the fact that these latter did not always pay the guides their commission, or did not pay at the right time, the *Cattaveri* laid down that as soon as a pilgrim was written down in the pilgrims' book in their office, by the *Tholomarij*, the *Patrono* concerned must pay the

---

1. *Senato Mar.*, Reg. x. p. 45, 6th May, 1475.
2. *Idem*, p. 47 b, 5th June, 1475, and 7th June, 1475.
3. *Cattaveri*, Reg. iv. p. 101, 9th May, 1475.

latter the commission due for each pilgrim going to the Holy Sepulchre.[1]

The *Patroni* now began to try to dispense with the intervention of the guides, and often arranged contracts with pilgrims through persons to whom they could give what they pleased, while the *Tholomarij* were entitled to a fixed sum—a percentage on the passage money paid. The contracts irregularly drawn up and signed were naturally not given in to the office of the *Cattaveri* as the law required. The abuse had become so common that in 1476, when they were obliged to deal with the matter, the *Cattaveri* declared that *every day Patroni* of galleys and sailing ships defrauded the *Tholomarij* in this way; therefore, after solemnly confirming previous legislation, they unanimously decreed:—

(1) That when any *Patrono* wanted to register his galley, or large sailing ship, or vessel of any kind for the voyage to the Holy Sepulchre, he must first give in to the office of the *Cattaveri* satisfactory security to pay—three days before leaving Venice—everything due to the *Tholomarij* for each pilgrim. The *Tholomarij*, on the other hand, must do their duty faithfully and diligently.

(2) That, as the *Patroni* had been in the habit of coming to terms privately with the pilgrims, and concealing from the *Tholomarij* the real number sailing with any given ship; if the latter could prove that any pilgrim or pilgrims had been taken on board a ship, over and above the number registered on the Pilgrims' Book at the *Cattaveri*, they were entitled to adequate compensation from the sureties offered by the *Patrono* when his ship was written down for the voyage to the Holy Land.[2]

1. *Cattaveri*, Reg. iv. p. 101 b, 14th March, 1463.
2. *Idem*, p. 102, 6th June, 1476.

INTRODUCTION

Nevertheless the law was still evaded with the aid of the innkeepers, who, in collusion with the *Patroni*, prevented the *Tholomarij* from verifying the number of pilgrims staying in a given inn. The pilgrims no doubt lent themselves to irregular practices owing to ignorance of the language and the law, or because they also found it to their interest not to employ the licensed guides, who from time to time are shown by the documents which survive, in anything but a favourable light.

To protect the rights of the guides more effectively, the magistrates of the *Cattaveri*, acting on an order received from the Government in 1488, after emphatically ratifying the provisions just noted of 1476, now enacted:

(1) That all innkeepers and others who gave hospitality to pilgrims going to the Holy Sepulchre, must, within three days after the arrival of a pilgrim or pilgrims at an inn or private house, give in the name or names of their guests to the office of the *Cattaveri*, under a penalty of 25 lire for each pilgrim whose name was not given in duly.

(2) That under the same penalty in case of refusal, innkeepers and others having pilgrims staying in their houses, must give the licensed guides free access to treat with the said pilgrims about their passages, and must not place any obstacle in the way of arranging the contracts between the pilgrims and the *Patroni* of galleys and sailing ships going to the Holy Sepulchre.[1]

According to the itineraries of numerous German pilgrims, the following were the chief clauses usually included in the contracts:—The *Patrono* was to take the pilgrims to Jaffa and back, and be ready to sail on a given day. He was to receive the passage money agreed upon, half in Venice and half at Jaffa. The vessel was to be equipped with the prescribed arms and crew, and carry

---

1. *Cattaveri*, Reg. iv. p. 102 b, 16th May, 1488.

a barber and a doctor. It was only to stop at the usual ports, and not remain more than three days in any port of Cyprus on account of the malaria. Each pilgrim, who did not cater for himself, was to receive his meals and drinking water every day, and these were to be as fresh and good as possible. At each meal he was to have a glass of malmsey. Wherever the ship touched, the pilgrims were to have an opportunity of renewing their supplies of provisions; and if that was impossible the captain was to let them have what they needed from his own stores. Each pilgrim was to have a place on the ship for keeping fowls and for doing his cooking. A pilgrim might leave the ship where he liked for any valid reason. The *Patrono* bound himself to protect the pilgrims from injustice in every possible form, to conduct them personally about the Holy Land, and go with them as far as the River Jordan, and pay the necessary duties and tribute with the exception of small gratuities. Each sick person was to have a better place assigned to him. If a pilgrim died on the voyage the *Patrono* was not to seize his property, and must give back part of the passage money. The dead were only to be buried on the high seas if no land was near; otherwise the *Patrono* must carry any corpse to the nearest port.[1]

As has been said, all these contracts were signed by the *Patroni* and the pilgrims, and the law required that they should be countersigned by the appointed officers of the Republic and duly registered in the office of the *Cattaveri*.

But, in spite of continuous legislation and of Government surveillance, the law was often evaded, and the accounts of the foreign pilgrims especially are full of complaints—that ships were unseaworthy, or overloaded, or

---

1. Röhricht, Preface to *Deutsche Pilgerreisen nach dem Heiligen Lande.*

insufficiently equipped; that they stayed too long in the ports, and that the food was bad or insufficient or both. Indeed, through the unaccustomed and bad nourishment and sea-sickness the pilgrims were often very ill. In addition, the itineraries give graphic descriptions of the inconveniences attending the agglomeration of people of all classes on the same small ship and the frequent friction between the different nationalities; of how they all suffered from excessive heat owing to the large number of passengers crowded into a small space, and from vermin of every size and kind.

Hans von Mergenthal, who accompanied Duke Albert of Saxony to the Holy Land in 1476—the year that Arcimboldi and Gian Giacomo Trivulzio went there—recounts that the sleeping place allotted to each pilgrim was so narrow, that the passengers almost lay one on the other, tormented by the great heat, by swarms of insects, and even by great rats which raced over their bodies in the dark. If a luckless pilgrim succeeded in dozing in spite of the general discomfort, he was soon awakened by the stamping of the animals penned up on deck, or by the talking, singing and shouting of his neighbours.

Most of those who fell sick died. "God be gracious to them!"

In the daytime the pilgrims were ruthlessly ordered to move from their appointed places, if this was necessary for manœuvring the sails—even though the sea was rough, and their heads were aching and swimming.

At meals the *Patrono* gave them soup, salad, meat, and greens. But nothing was good. The meat was bad, the bread hard and full of worms, the water often stinking, the wine hot and tasteless. They had often to eat in the blazing sun. The crew was dishonest. Several times the pilgrim galley was chased by Turks and pirates. On the return journey in the autumn there was much bad weather, and the pilgrims suffered greatly from the wet and the cold. "In short," the writer concludes, "we had little rest, and I know not what else to do on the ship than have patience." [1]

The pilgrim who wrote the voyage to the *Saincte cyté de Hierusalem,* undertaken in 1480, dwells specially on the hardships endured in the Holy Land. He says that on the homeward voyage, "When we landed at Cyprus there were several sick pilgrims on our galley. Their illness began in the Holy Land, where the pilgrims were badly treated, for during the time we were in the Holy Land we had always to sleep on the hard ground and often out of doors. And we fared badly there, for there is no wine in the city of Jerusalem or in any other city of those parts, for the Moors drink nothing save water. And the bread is bad, for it is not properly baked, and is as soft as dough. And moreover the pilgrims suffer much in visiting the Holy Places by reason of the great heat of the country, and because they are forced to hasten overmuch. Now these are the causes of the maladies of many of the pilgrims." [2]

When Felix Faber asked the advice of Eberhard, Count of Würtemburg, who had been to Jerusalem, about undertaking his first voyage, in 1480, the Count replied that there were three things which can neither be recommended nor discouraged: marriage, war, and the voyage to the Holy Sepulchre—"they may begin very well and end very badly." [3] Faber, like so many others, determined to take his chance. Afterwards he expressed himself thus:—" People without experience say that the

---

1. Röhricht, *Deutsche Pilgerreisen, &c.*, preface.
2. *Voyage de la Saincte Cyté de Hierusalem . . . fait l'an 1480*, p. 104. Edited by MM. Chas. Schefer and Henri Cordier, Paris, 1882.
3. *Idem,* preface.

INTRODUCTION

voyage from Venice to Jaffa is a promenade, and that he who undertakes it runs little or no risk. Oh! heavens! what a melancholy amusement, what a wearisome promenade! With how many miseries is it not strewn! I have seen many young men who could not endure them, and who succumbed. I claim for the Pilgrims to the Holy Land the sympathy and the compassion they deserve."[1]

Casola describes the hardships endured in the Holy Land by himself and his fellow pilgrims in much the same way as they are summed up by the French clerk; and he frequently mentions their sufferings at sea from heat and cold, and the risks they ran from bad weather and piratical attacks. As to the life on shipboard, Canon Pietro does not disguise the fact that he was one of the privileged passengers and fared in every way better than most of his companions, because, as he says, he paid more than the rest; but, no doubt, partly also because he was an Italian, belonging to a noble family, subject of a near neighbour of Venice, and a Church dignitary. He does not, unfortunately, give many details as to the way in which the other pilgrims were treated; but he relates that the foreigners were often rightly dissatisfied with the food. In short, even if things had improved since the days of Hans von Mergenthal, a sea voyage in 1494, was still a dreary holiday for the majority.

As to the expenses incurred by the pilgrims who went by sea from Venice to Jaffa, and thence to the Holy Sepulchre, Santo Brasca's "Instructions" are confirmed and supplemented by Fra Francesco Suriano.[2] Fra Francesco was a noble Venetian, who twice undertook the voyage to the East, and who was Prior of the Convent of Mount Sion[3] at the time of Casola's visit. There can

1. *Voyage de la Saincte Cyté*, Preface, p. 33.
2. See Note 76.
3. See Note 75.

be no doubt, therefore, that he was perfectly well informed.[1] He says:—

"Although the Venetians appoint two galleys for the service and transport of pilgrims, they do not, however, carry them free, nor for the love of God; but according to the quality and condition of the persons, they make them pay some fifty, some sixty, others forty, and others, again, thirty ducats—some more some less, according to the contract. The *Patrono* of a galley is obliged, in addition to the simple transport, to give the pilgrims food and drink while they are at sea, and also when they go to places where the pilgrims cannot buy victuals. He is also obliged to pay all the ordinary and extraordinary taxes for them in the Holy Land.

"The ordinary expenses of pilgrims to Jerusalem are as follows:—First, for the tribute to be paid to the Sultan, 7 ducats and 17 grossi; for the Sultan's interpreter, 1 ducat; to the custodians of the door of the Holy Sepulchre for each pilgrim, $23\frac{1}{2}$ grossi; for the animals for riding, in all, 3 ducats; for six places: Bethlehem, Bethany, the Mountain of Judea, the Mount of Olives, the Sepulchre of the Madonna, and the Pools, 1 grosso for each place; for the custodians who guard the roads in eight places, 1 grosso for each place; for the house at Rama, 4 grossi; for the custodians at the sea, 1 grosso; for the Governor of Rama, 3 grossi; for the Governor of St. George, 1 grosso. In all there are 13 ducats and a half, and this is the tariff of expenses up to the year 1500." [2]

Merchants, sailors and servants paid $3\frac{1}{2}$ ducats each as tribute to the Sultan. The other charges were the same for them as for the pilgrims.

---
1. The text from which the extract is taken was compiled by Fra. Francesco Suriano, first in 1485, and revised in Mount Sion in 1514.
2. *Il Trattato di Terra Santa e dell' Oriente di Frate Francesco Suriano*, edited by Padre Girolamo Golubovich. Milano, 1900.

INTRODUCTION

Elsewhere Suriano notes that although the friars are poor, "all of us who go on the voyage to the Holy Land simply from motives of devotion, are charged from 15 to 20 ducats on the pilgrim ships. But of those who are going to one of the monasteries in the Holy Land, two are taken free on each of the pilgrim galleys, and the others pay 10 ducats each. On the merchant galleys and sailing ships, however, all the friars are carried for the love of God, with all their goods."[1]

Between 1455 and 1475, one of the chief *Patroni* engaged in the transport of pilgrims was Ser Andrea Contarini, whose name appears in the documents in the Archives of Venice for the last time in 1475; and it is probable that he retired then or soon after. A younger member of the Contarini family, Ser Agostino, Casola's captain in 1494, was certainly patron of a pilgrim galley as early as 1479.

Agostino Contarini, known as "Agostino dal Zaffo" (Agostino of Jaffa), was son of Benedetto Contarini, grandson of Luca Contarini, "the doctor," and great-grandson of Zaccaria Contarini, since whose time, at least, this branch of the family had been established in the parish of San Cassiano, in the Sestiere of San Polo, on the far side of the Grand Canal.[2]

I have not found any record of Agostino's birth, but the date can be calculated very nearly. In the Register known as the *Balla d'oro*,[3] we find that on the 29th of November, 1447, Benedetto Contarini, son of the late Luca, and husband of Giustiniana Giustinian, presented his two elder sons, Girolamo and Ambrogio, to the Great Council as having completed eighteen years of age. For

---
1. *Il Trattato di Terra Santa di F. Suriano.*
2. See Marco Barbaro, *Genealogie delle famiglie patrizie Venete.* Venice, St. Mark's Library.
3. *Archives.* Venice.

the same reason, on November 19th, 1449, he presented his younger son, Agostino, to the same Council; so that Agostino was probably born in 1430 or 1431, and he died either in 1500 or 1503.[1]

Soon after his presentation to the Council he must have chosen the sea as his profession. In 1494 he told Casola that he had been at sea forty-two years. In 1455 he married the daughter of Ser Francesco Giustinian,[2] by whom he had one son Luigi or Alvise, who does not appear to have left any mark on his country's history.

In 1471 Agostino Contarini was *Comito* of the galley which conducted Giosafatte Barbaro on his mission to the East. Two years later, in September, 1473, he took command at Cyprus of the galley of his brother Ambrogio, who had been recalled to Venice to receive his commission as Ambassador to the King of Persia, with whom the Venetians desired to strengthen their relations in order to stir up a powerful enemy in the rear of the Turks.[3]

When J. Tucher of Nuremberg—whose description of his voyage was printed in 1482 at Nuremberg and Augsburg—went to Palestine in 1479, Ser Agostino was captain of the pilgrim galley for Jaffa. Next year, 1480, the writer of the *Voyage de la Saincte Cyté de Hierusalem* says that in that year the *Patrono* of the Jerusalem galley was a Venetian gentleman, named *Agostin Contorin qui avoit faict l'année passée le voyage*. This is confirmed by Felix Faber and Santo Brasca. Indeed, Santo Brasca was singled out from the other passengers by Contarini, who offered to use in his favour the privilege he then had of taking a pilgrim to lodge with him at the Monastery of Mount Sion. With regard to this privilege, it is interesting to note that on their arrival at Jerusalem Casola

---
1. See Barbaro, *Genealogie delle famiglie patrizie Venete*.
2. See Marco Barbaro, *Nozze Veneziane*. St. Mark's Library, Venice.
3. *Le Voyage de la Saincte Cyté de Hierusalem*, p. 24, Note A.

INTRODUCTION

wrote in his journal:—" The Magnificent Patrono was in the habit of lodging with two persons in Mount Sion, which is a good way outside the city; but this Prior, however, in order to appear wiser than his predecessors, had taken him a house within the city."

Casola might have criticised the Prior differently, if he had known—as it may be assumed he did not—of the following decree, passed by the Venetian Senate July 12th, 1493,[1] and of the abuses of hospitality which had provoked it.

The decree runs:—" In the petition just now read to this Council the inconveniences therein enumerated, and principally due to the residence taken up by the *Patroni* of our pilgrim galleys in the venerable Monastery of Mount Sion, in contempt of the divine worship and to the no small detriment of that Holy Place, are of such a nature that it is absolutely necessary that such errors and inconveniences should be opportunely dealt with and prevented by our most Christian Government.

" It is therefore enacted that henceforth, none of our *Patroni* of the pilgrim galleys, for the whole time of their sojourn, shall in any way or under any pretext reside in the aforesaid monastery under a penalty of 200 ducats to be paid out of their own possessions. And, further, the galley of a disobedient captain shall never more go on that voyage.

" And in order that from time to time it may be known how this most pious order is observed, the Prior of the said monastery shall be required and obliged every year, on the departure of the said galleys, to write letters to our Government and report therein as to the observance or the contravention of this order. And as soon as they know the truth the Advocates of the Commune shall be obliged,

1. *Senato Mar.*, Reg. xiv. p. 16.

H

without waiting for another Council, to carry into execution the provisions contained above. The half of the said pecuniary penalty shall go to said Advocates, and the other half to our Arsenal."

Letters patent containing this decree were re-issued on July 12th, 1512, *ob ammissionem illarum*.

It is unfortunate that the "errors and inconveniences" which caused such pious horror on the part of the Government were not enumerated in detail. Whatever they were, there is little doubt that Agostino Contarini was one of the chief sinners, and he was irritated when the new law came into force in 1494. Casola reflects his feeling, for he naturally took the captain's point of view, and accepted his version of the facts.

To return to 1480. One of the few documents belonging to the last years of the 15th century, in which the pilgrim galleys are mentioned records that in May, 1480, the Great Council granted the request of Ser Ambrogio Contarini, then Councillor in Cyprus, and on the ground of ill-health gave him leave to return to Venice on board the Jaffa galley, "whose Patrono is the Noble Ser Agostino Contarini, his brother." [1]

When Felix Faber made his second pilgrimage in 1483, he found Agostino Contarini in command of one of the *two* galleys which went to Jaffa that year.

In August, 1484, Fra Francesco Suriano returned to Venice on the pilgrim galley commanded by the same *Patrono*, and his account of the terrible storms they experienced, in which he—the Franciscan Friar—navigated the ship, does more credit to Contarini's generosity of sentiment than to his seamanship. Perhaps he was less jealous of Suriano than he would have been of another man, not a Venetian patrician like himself;

1. *Maggior Consig. Delib. Stella*, p. 2 b, 23rd May, 1480.

INTRODUCTION

Suriano was an old sailor too, and a humble follower of St. Francis.[1]

Although for many years documentary evidence is lacking, it may be safely assumed that from 1479 for the next seventeen years Captain Contarini took his galley the *Contarini* to Jaffa each year, with the pilgrims who never failed to assemble in Venice about Ascensiontide. In 1496 Malipiero noted in his famous diary that, "On the 21st of December the galley from Jaffa, Patrono Agostino Contarini, reached Venice in a bad state with all the pilgrims."[2] The weather had presumably been worse than that experienced by Casola, and the *Contarina* was two years older. The "bad state" may also have referred to the moral conditions on board, judging by a Senatorial decree of April, 1497, which will be noted in its place. This was Agostino Contarini's last voyage, and the reason for this may be divined from two decrees passed by the Senate in 1497.

The first, dated January 14th, 1497 (M.V. 1496) ran thus:—

"The frequent inconveniences which result from the bad faith of the Jaffa *Patroni* and which give rise to outcries, lamentations, and formal complaints on the part of the Signori pilgrims tortured by them, compel our Government to make due provision in this matter, not only for its own honour, but also in order to avoid the enmity of many provinces and places, which are stirred up against our Government, through no fault of its own, but solely on account of the bad behaviour of the aforesaid Patroni.

"It is therefore decreed that henceforth, whoever wishes to go as *Patrono* of a galley or any other ship whatsoever on the voyage to Jaffa, must, in the first place, and before everything else, offer to our Advocates of the Commune

---

1. See Note 76, pp. 384-386.
2. *Chronicle of Domenico Malipiero*, part ii. p. 635. *Archivio Storico Italiano*, vol. vii.

four sureties in 250 ducats each (which sureties must be ballotted for and approved in our College), for the observation of the terms and contracts made with the pilgrims in the office of the *Cattaveri*, and these shall be guarantees that the said *Patroni* will not do, or cause to be done, any injuries or acts of violence or outrage to the said pilgrims, but that they will treat them well and take care that they are well treated wherever they go.

"If, however, the said *Patroni* violate the said contracts, the said Advocates must, without delay, compel the said sureties to provide for the satisfaction of the said pilgrims, in so far as the majority of the said Advocates are convinced that the pilgrims have been defrauded, or that the contracts made with them have not been duly observed.

"Further, the office of each of the said Advocates is empowered to inflict a severe punishment on the said *Patroni* who have broken their contracts.

"And it is declared that the aforesaid persons who desire to go as *Patroni* must—before they set up their benches—be approved in this Council, as the *Patroni* of the trading galleys are approved; and in the same way they must be approved on their return. And any *Patrono* who is not approved on his return shall forfeit 200 ducats, to be given to the Advocates of the Commune, and shall not be allowed to go any more as *Patrono* on the said voyage." [1]

From a second decree, passed in the Senate on the 1st April, 1497,[2] we learn that certain of the pilgrims who went to the Sepulchre the previous year, 1496, on the galley of the Noble Ser Agostino Contarini, had made accusations against the said Ser Agostino to the Advocates of the Commune as soon as they got back to Venice.

1. *Senato Mar.*, Reg. xiv. p. 112 *b*.
2. *Idem*, p. 118.

INTRODUCTION 101

Unfortunately no clue is given to the nature of the complaints made, though from what Casola and other pilgrims relate, the principal ones at least may be safely inferred. Even Casola, who always tries to make out a good case for the *Patrono*, implies that in certain respects the pilgrims had reason to be dissatisfied.

Although he was not expressly named in the decrees of January, 1497, and July, 1493, as he was in that of April, 1497, they were all evidently directed chiefly against Agostino Contarini, who had been oftener to Jaffa than any other *Patrono* since at least 1479. The outcome of the legal proceedings cannot be traced in the documents. Was it unfavourable to the *Patrono* or did he now decide that at his age—well over sixty as he was—it was wise to retire from a business which brought much fatigue and worry in its train? At any rate, Contarini did not go any more to the Holy Land, and in June, 1497, Sanuto wrote: "The Jaffa galley left this city commanded by the new Patrono, Ser Alvise Zorzi, and went to Jaffa with the pilgrims."[1]

Before he left, however, there was a curious incident which showed that the new *Patrono*, like the old, had a keen eye to business.

In June, 1497, many noble pilgrims of various nations appeared before the *Cattaveri* and complained that the berths assigned to them by the Noble Lord Alvise Zorzi, *Patrono* of the trireme on which they were to sail, were so small that it was impossible to lie in them without extreme discomfort. Ser Alvise, on the other hand, declared that he was prepared to give them the same accommodation as had been given to all pilgrims in times past. The magistrates went on board the trireme, inspected the berths and heard the opinion of the officers and of

1. Sanuto, *Diarii*, vol. i, p. 645.

the experts appointed to examine the pilgrim ships before they were licensed. Then, " in order that in the future all should know what sized berths they were entitled to have on the triremes going to Jerusalem, and especially considering that notable persons and powerful lords go on this voyage, who, although they may go incognito, deserve to be well treated in every way," they ordered that the berth allotted to each pilgrim was to be precisely a foot and a half wide and long enough for him to lie at full length; and that all the old signs of division were to be removed from the galley, and the new signs placed there a foot and a half apart.[1]

Hans von Mergenthal evidently did not exaggerate when he complained of the heat and the crowding in 1476, although things were better even then in this respect than in the old Crusading days. On the vessel of Saint Louis of France it was stipulated, for example, that two should sleep in the place of one only, " each with the feet towards the head of the other."

The voyage of the *Zorza* was an eventful one, and I hope to give the details on another occasion. Suffice it to say here, that, although Venice was at peace with the Sultan, the galley was attacked on the outward voyage not far from Modone, by a Turkish squadron of nine sail, commanded by the famous Arigi or Erichi, ex-Corsair, who, although the *Patrono* hoisted the banners of the Holy Sepulchre and St. Mark, pretended not to recognise the pilgrim ship. After a hot fight, in which the *Zorza* was damaged and had many killed and wounded on board,

---

1. *Cattaveri*, Reg. iv. p. 104, 26th June, 1497. The enactment begins: "Comparverunt coram spect. et. generos. Dominis Cathavere complures Domini peregrini diversorum nationum profecturi ad loca sancta se condolentes, *de Patrono Triremis*, qui eis dare intendit modicum quod stationis pro quolibet in qua non est possibile quemmo posse permanere nisi cum maxima incomoditate." The magistrates therefore ordered "quod omnis statio cuiusque peregrini proficiscientis et de cetero profecturi ad viagium Hierusalem *cum Triremi*, sit et intelligatur per Latitudinem pedis unius cum dimidio integre et precise, et per Longitudinem quantum est usque stantes . . . . et removeri ex Galea omnia signa stationum vetera: et fieri nova signa cum hac mensura pedis unius cum dimidio inter quelibet signa."

INTRODUCTION

the Turkish ships were obliged to retire. Erichi tried hard to make Alvise Zorzi take on himself the responsibility of the so-called " error," and failing, excused himself after a fashion[1]

The Duke of Pomerania, one of the pilgrims, and the *Patrono* specially recommended nine of the crew to the Senate for having bravely defended the galley at the risk of their lives, and as a reward each of the nine received the appointment to two posts as crossbow men, one a year, for any voyage they chose, " in order that they may enjoy the fruit of their good deeds," and "inspire others in similar circumstances to bear themselves valorously." [2]

It is probable that Captain Zorzi undertook the voyage to the Sepulchre next year also; for in May, 1498, Sanuto noted that several German nobles had arrived in Venice, amongst them a nephew of the Duke of Saxony, Lord George "da Torre," and other pilgrims going to Jerusalem; and that Alvise Zorzi, who owned the Jaffa galley, having been appointed Governor of Gradisca, did not want to undertake the voyage. But the pilgrims, in order to induce him to do so, offered 70 ducats a head, while he said he would resign his position and go if they gave him 80 ducats each.[3] Sanuto promised to give the result of the negotiations later one, but he forgot. However, as a new Venetian representative was sent to Gradisca in June, it may be inferred that Alvise Zorzi had come to terms with the pilgrims, and was then on his way eastward."[4]

In 1499 war was renewed between Venice and the Turks, and continued up to the peace of October, 1503. In 1500 the Republic lost Corone, Modone, and other important

---

1. Sanuto, *Diarij*, vol. i. pp. 702, 728, and Malipiero, *Diario* in the *Archivio Storico Italiano*, Tome vii. part i. p. 154.
2. *Senato Mar.*, Reg. xiv. p. 150, 31st March, 1498.
3. Sanuto, *Diarii*, Vol. i. p. 959, May, 1498.
4. *Idem*, p. 985, June, 1498.

places in the Morea. The diarist Priuli wrote at this time: "The City of Venice is in great trouble for fear of losing the maritime supremacy upon which the riches and prestige of the Venetian State depend. For its fame and glory have been built up by the voyages and by its reputation at sea. Therefore there can be no doubt that if the Venetians should lose their shipping and their maritime supremacy, they would also lose their reputation and their glory, and little by little in a very few years they would be consumed." [1]

On account of the disturbed state of affairs in the Levant, there was apparently no galley for Jaffa in 1499. Indeed the Doge advised many pilgrims to turn back on account of the danger from the Turkish fleet. Nevertheless, in June, Ser Marco, the owner of the Nave *Malipiera e Giustiniana*, offered four sureties who were ballotted for and accepted by the Senate, and two days later the *Patrono* Francesco Vasallo was approved in the same Council.[2] They were ready to take the risk of carrying pilgrims to Syria.

In March, 1500, Sanuto mentions that a beautiful galley was being built for the Jaffa voyage by Ser Bernardo Boldù, aided by other persons, because Ser Bernardo was poor, and he added: "What will happen I do not know." In June, when some important French pilgrims arrived, the galley was not ready, and the Senate solemnly reproved Ser Bernardo. On account of the war between the Republic and the Turks, the Doge advised the pilgrims to give up their project. In August many French pilgrims complained to the Government that Ser Bernardo Boldù refused, either to go to Jaffa or give back the 700 ducats they had paid him. A month later the galley was sold to

1. Romanin, *Storia Documentata di Venezia*, vol. v. p. 150.
2. Sanuto, *Diarij*, vol. ii. p. 688 (7th May, 1500); 779—81 (3rd June, 1499); and p. 792 (5th June, 1499).

Ser Jacopo Michiel for 1,010 ducats. Eight hundred ducats were returned to the pilgrims, and out of the rest the Advocates of the Commune were ordered to pay those who had worked on the galley, and who, " cried out every day " for their salaries. Sanuto's doubt as to the success of the enterprise was justified.[1]

Whether there was peace or war with the Turks the danger from pirates in the Mediterranean was a constant one. Having heard that there were Corsairs at sea, the Venetian citizen Bernardo di Marconi and the patrician Marcantonio Dandolo, joint owners of the galley licensed to go to Jaffa in 1515, asked the Government in June for the loan of two pieces of artillery, " which throw stones, to place at the prow . . . . . for the security and ornament of the galley and for the satisfaction of the pilgrims on board," and offered to give security for the value. The Senate consented, and required, in addition to the offered security, that the partners should lend 50 ducats to the Arsenal, to be returned to them when the pieces of artillery were given back at the end of the voyage.[2]

Next year the noble Marcantonio Dandolo, " *Patrono* of the pilgrim galley," asked the same favour once more. But while some Senators were willing to consent on the same terms as before, others thought he ought to buy the cannon outright.[3] Ser Marco then asked the Government to deign to sell him the two pieces of artillery for the price of the metal, and offered 200 ducats down and the rest on his return. The Senate thereupon ordered the heads of the Arsenal to sell them for the price of the metal plus the expenses of casting, and to accept 200 ducats

---

1. *Diarij di Sanuto*, vol. iii. pp. 139, 140 (3rd March, 1500); pp. 367, 368 (2nd June, 1500); p. 546 (26th July, 1500); p. 596 (10th August, 1500); p. 790 (17th September, 1500).
2. *Senato Mar.*, Reg. xviii. p. 70 b, 22nd June, 1515.
3. *Idem*, p. 111, 7th June, 1516.

down and sureties for the payment of the remainder when the galley came back. The money was to be used for casting two new cannon.[1]

From a decree of the Senate, June, 1517, we learn that two *navi* were then on the point of sailing with pilgrims. The *Patroni* had offered to carry to Cyprus free of charge a quantity of artillery and ammunition, and the ships were to leave as soon as the cargo was stowed away. For greater security the Senate ordered the *navi* to sail together under the supreme command of Ser Fantin Michiel, whom the *Patroni* were required to obey. But it appears that for some reason not given the order was revoked.[2]

An important statute of 1518 marks a return to the policy of 1441—1552. The preamble runs thus:—

"For the spiritual commodity of faithful Christians, and for the honour and profit of our State, our forebears have always arranged that a galley should sail from our city every year on the pilgrim voyage. Since, therefore, the galley engaged in the said navigation has been dismantled it is convenient to replace it, for the honour of our Government, and for the greater satisfaction of Christian princes who desire that their subjects may be able to go on their pilgrimage in all security." It was then enacted:—

(1) That the heads of the Arsenal were to put up to public auction at the Rialto and sell to the highest bidder, *whether citizen or patrician,* the licence to build, outside the Arsenal, a large galley at the expense of the purchaser of the licence, for the transport of pilgrims. The money was to be paid in to the Arsenal within a month, and the galley ready to sail by Ascensiontide 1519, otherwise the

---
1. *Senato Mar.*, Reg. xviii., p. 111 *b*, 11th June, 1516.
2. *Senato Mar.*, Reg. xix. p. 13, 9th June, 1517.

owner would be liable to a fine of 500 ducats. The *Patrono* was to present himself for approval in the first meeting of the Senate after the auction, and also every voyage afterwards.

(2) That until the galley to which the monopoly was now granted had made twelve voyages, no other galley was to be built for or engage in this trade. At the same time, pilgrims were free to go either on the licensed galley, or on a *nave*, or on any other vessel they pleased.

(3) The *Patrono* who bought the monopoly was to equip his galley according to the requirements of the existing laws, and treat the pilgrims according to the regulations preserved in the office of the *Cattaveri*.

Ser Luca Trono, one of the Councillors, proposed as an amendment that, considering the immense importance of this measure, which needed mature consideration, a decision had better be deferred, and the matter brought up again in another meeting of the Senate. But the majority of the Senators were against him, and the proposal to renew the monopoly for twelve voyages was approved by a large majority.[1]

Unfortunately I have not been able to find any documents which record who bought the new monopoly, or if it was bought at all. Two things are very noticeable, however, in the decree just summarised—first, that the monopoly was to be sold to the highest bidder, "whether citizen or patrician." In the fifteenth century the *Patroni* of the galleys were always Venetian patricians. The new concession, together with the contemporary difficulty in disposing of the merchant galleys which were often now put up to auction several times before finding a purchaser, whereas in earlier times they were taken as soon as offered, is symptomatic of the change coming over the Venetian

1. *Senato Mar.*, Reg. xix. p. 61, 13th July, 1518.

spirit. From a variety of causes—the advance of the Turks, the loss of Venetian possessions in the Mediterranean, the discovery of the sea route to India and the transfer of the spice trade to Portuguese hands, the acquisition of territory on the mainland, and many others—the patricians were beginning to withdraw their energies from trade and the sea traffic which had made their fathers rich and glorious, and which Venetian legislators, in the preambles to innumerable statutes, had always declared to be "the chief foundation of the greatness of their city." Less than fifty years before, when Malipiero commented on the election as Doge of the wealthy Ser Andrea Vendramin, he said: "He was a great merchant in his youth, and when he was in partnership with Luca, they used to load a galley and a half between them for Alexandria, and he has had many agents who have become rich in managing his business, and, amongst others, Giacomo Malipiero, son of the late Tommaso of Santa Maria Formosa, and Piero Morosini, son of the late Giovanni of San Cassiano."[1] Such notices abound. In the sixteenth and seventeenth centuries the best and wisest spirits deplored the abandonment of the old ways.

The other significant point is that in former auctions three, or at least two, galleys were provided for the pilgrim transport, in addition to any *navi* or other vessels which were licensed by the *Cattaveri*. Now, however, one galley was considered sufficient, and this shows that the number of pilgrims who came to Venice was decreasing. The decline was no doubt due in part to the cooling of this particular form of religious enthusiasm, but it was also due to the fact that Venice had begun to lose her possessions

---

1. *Diario di Malipiero. Archivio Storico Italiano*, vol. vii. part ii. p. 666, 6th March, 1476.

INTRODUCTION 109

in the Mediterranean, and her commercial and naval supremacy there, and was continually threatened by the advance of the Turks. The fears Priuli had expressed were being realised.

In May, 1520, the Government needed two ships to carry soldiers, artillery, ammunition and wood to Corfu and Cyprus, and could not find any *nave* to hire for the purpose. Some were not ready, and others were already engaged for the pilgrim service.

At this time the Turks, who had conquered the Mamelukes of Egypt in 1517, were preparing the great armament which attacked and took Rhodes in 1522, and Venice was obliged to limit her efforts to the defence of her most important remaining possessions.

Three *Patroni* of pilgrim *navi*—Ser Marco Dandolo, *Patrono* of the *Coressa;* Bartolomeo Boza, *Patrono* of the *Cornera;* and Gabriel da Monte, *Patrono* of the *Dolfina*, made an offer to the Senate in which, after declaring that it was necessary to place public affairs of the present importance before any others whatsoever, they proposed that the Doge should cast lots to decide which of the three should abandon the transport of pilgrims to serve the State. The *nave* chosen—the *Dolfina*—was to receive compensation from the other two. At the same time, arrangements were made with a certain Ser Galeazzo Simiteculo, to provide the second *nave* needed for the transport of troops and military stores. On this occasion the Senate expressly declared that no pilgrim was to be charged over fifty ducats for his passage, food and other expenses.[1]

Maitre Denis Possot, with Messire Charles Philippe, Seigneur de Champarmoy et de Grandchamp and others, went on a pilgrimage to the Holy Land in 1532. They

1. *Senato Mar.*, Reg. xix. p. 128 *b*, 1st May, 1520.

left Venice on the 14th of May, on the *Santa Maria*, the largest ship sailing under the flag of St. Mark, owned by two patricians whose names are not given. The captain was Paulo Bianco, and the destination Cyprus. At Cyprus the pilgrims arranged with a certain Constantin de Fyo to take them to Jaffa, and thence to the Holy places and back for 45 ducats, half to be paid down immediately and the other half on the return. When they got back to Jaffa after visiting the Holy Sepulchre, instead of entering the *Grippo*[1] of Constantin de Fyo, they made—for reasons not given—a new arrangement with George of Naples, who took them on his galley for a ducat and a half to Candia. The writer does not mention the sum paid for the return voyage from Candia to Venice.[2]

After a long interval, in which the registers are silent, the last document I have been able to find which legislates for pilgrim traffic is an enactment of the *Cattaveri*, who had for so long been charged with the supervision of all matters relating to the trade. It is dated June 6th, 1546.

From it we learn that for some time past many unpleasant incidents and even disasters had happened to pilgrims who went to Jerusalem on Venetian ships, and notably the last year (1545) when, "determined to have their own way," they had hired an unsuitable ship, with the result that on the voyage back the ship went down and all the pilgrims were drowned. "It was therefore necessary," the magistrates said, "for the honour and glory of God, for the credit of this our city, and for the comfort and advantage of the pilgrims themselves, to regulate that voyage in order to encourage many more persons to go on that holy and blessed pilgrimage." And so, after confirming all previous legislation, they enacted :

1. See Note p. 188.
2. *Le Voyage de la Terre Sainte composé par Maître Denis Possot et achevé par Messire Charles Philippe seigneur de Champarmoy et de Grandchamp.* Published by M. Charles Schefer, Paris, 1890.

INTRODUCTION

That no pilgrim could be taken on board any Venetian *nave* or *navilio*, in Venice or elsewhere, and passed off as an ordinary passenger or as a merchant, and carried to Candia, Cyprus, Jaffa or any other place. But that in future, "at the time when pilgrims usually come to this city, that is, about Ascensiontide," the pilgrims, immediately on arrival, were to give in their names at the office of the *Cattaveri*. When forty names had been received, the magistrates were to invite the *Patroni* of *navilii* of 400 tons or more, prepared to go to Jaffa, to send their names to the same office, and after the vessels offered had been carefully examined, if they fulfilled the requirements of the law, as many as necessary were to be licensed for the voyage—one at a time. The best was to be chosen first, and the one whose *Patrono* offered the cheapest and most advantageous terms to the pilgrims.

The *Patrono* was then to give adequate bail for the fulfilment of his obligations, and if he broke a contract and the pilgrims exercised their right of complaint on their return to Venice, the *Cattaveri* were to administer summary justice and compel the sureties to compensate the pilgrims. A *Patrono* who once offered to convey pilgrims and had been accepted, must go on the voyage, and if he refused for any reason whatever, he must compensate the pilgrims for damages. Poor pilgrims were to be charged less than the others.

No other ship could sail from Venice with pilgrims until eight days after the departure of the first selected.

Finally, under a severe penalty, the *Tholomarij* or guides and the agents or *missetæ* were forbidden to negotiate for passages with the *Patrono* of any ship not entered in the books of the *Cattaveri*.

1. *Cattaveri*, Reg. iv. p. 105, 6th June, 1546.

It is clear from the above that the disasters deplored were largely due to the fact that passages had been given to pilgrims, not as pilgrims, but as ordinary or merchant passengers. In this way the legislation which protected their interests and sought to ensure their safety had been evaded, and they had been conveyed to the Levant on unlicensed ships. Probably on these the passage cost less, and the pilgrims who had " determined to have their own way" thought it worth while running the risk. So far as I know there is no record of the loss of a whole shipload of pilgrims before 1545.

It is noticeable that the statute does not mention galleys or triremes, but only *navi* (the largest kind of sailing ship) and *navilii*. In this period of declining trade with the East, it is clear that the galleys did not compete any more for the pilgrim transport.

In spite of this last attempt to so regulate the voyage to the Holy Land that many persons might be induced to undertake that blessed pilgrimage for the good of their own souls and the pecuniary benefit of the subjects of the Serenissima, the numbers of pious travellers so diminished, that towards the end of the sixteenth century the annual voyage was abandoned; no pilgrim ship sailed any more from Venice after the Corpus Domini, and the Prior of Mount Sion gave up going to Jaffa to meet the pilgrims and conduct them to Jerusalem, as had been the custom from time almost immemorial.

Friedrich Eckher and Karl von Grimming, two German pilgrims, who arrived in Venice on the 26th of March, 1625, found that the pilgrim ships which used to sail about the Corpus Domini, had not gone for over twenty years, and they and three Capucin friars took their passage to the Holy Land on a Dutch ship.[1]

1. Rohricht, *Deutsche Pilgerreisen nach dem Heiligen Lande*, p. 294.

INTRODUCTION

Pilgrimages did not go quite out of fashion even with the opening of the seventeenth century, but they changed their character, and pilgrims reached the common goal by various routes. Some went overland by way of Constantinople now that the Turk had a firm footing in Europe; and though Venice was not entirely abandoned, she had to divide the ever decreasing profits of what had once been such a lucrative branch of trade with many other ports in Italy and the Western Mediterranean—Marseilles amongst the number.

A record of what had once been, was preserved to the downfall of the Republic in the Corpus Domini procession, when in later times, the Senators no longer paired with the pilgrims, each walked with a poor man on his right hand in sign of humility.

NOTE.—*In the translation of Casola's Voyage, the division into chapters each preceded by a summary of the contents, has been adopted for convenience in reading. It does not exist in Casola's MS. which is continuous from beginning to end.*

BLACK SEA

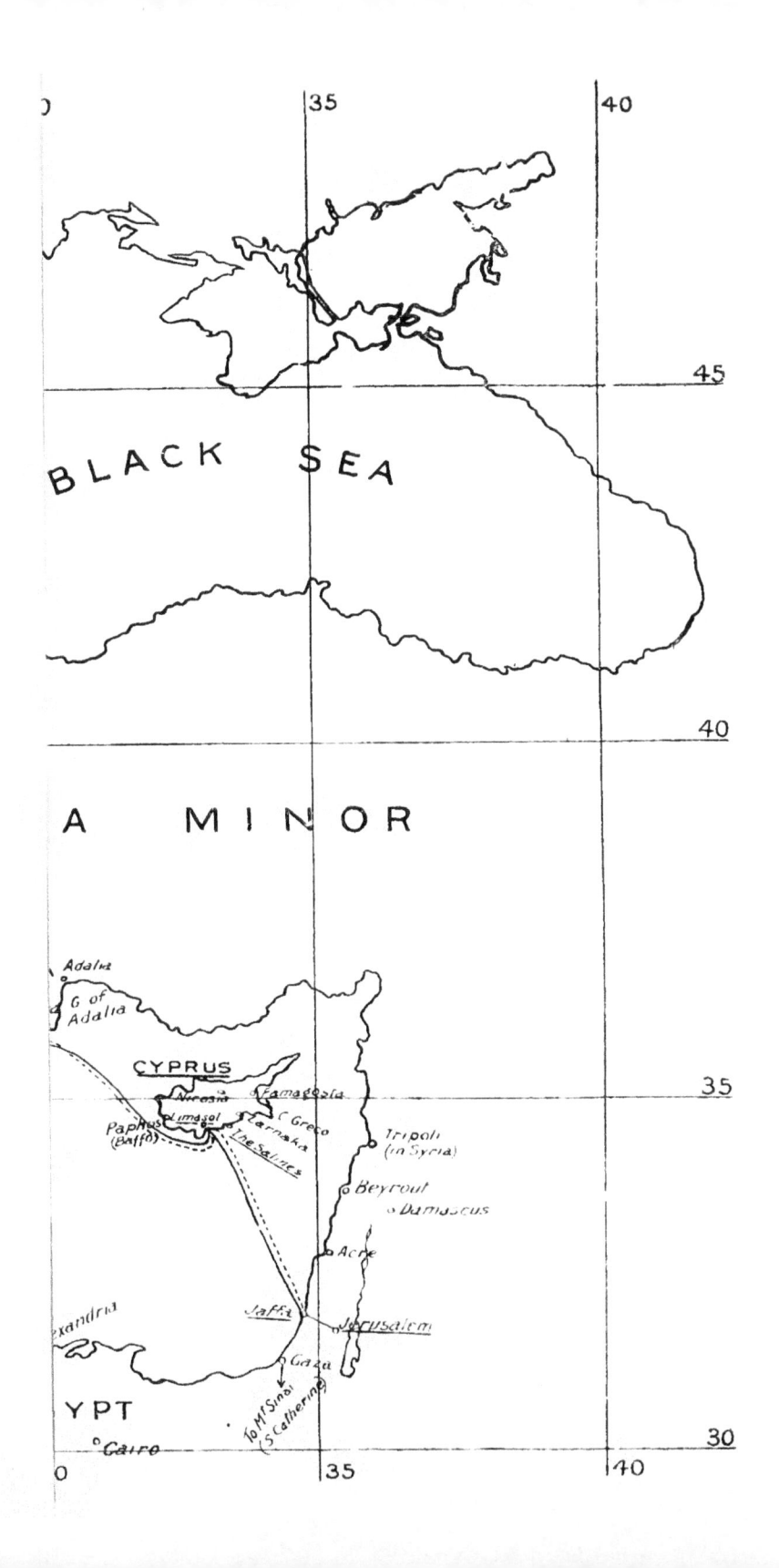

A MINOR

Adalia
G of Adalia
CYPRUS
Nicosia
Famagosta
Paphos (Baffo)
Limasol
Larnaka
C Greco
The Salines
Tripoli (in Syria)
Beyrout
Damascus
Acre
Alexandria
Jaffa
Jerusalem
Gaza
to Mt Sinai (S Catherine)
EGYPT
Cairo

CHAPTER I.

Determination to undertake a Pilgrimage to Jerusalem.—Casola receives the Benediction from Archbishop Arcimboldi in the Cathedral at Milan, May 14th, 1494.—Leaves Milan, May 15th, and travels by Caravaggio, Calci, Brescia, Lonato, Peschiera, Verona, Vicenza, Padua to Venice, where he arrives May 20th.

MANY years ago, as I was invited by a citizen of Milan to accompany him at his expense on this holy voyage, I accepted very gladly. But afterwards the citizen named changed his mind, and gave up the idea of accomplishing what he had proposed; so I remained very doubtful in my mind, as my purse could not satisfy my new-born desire. Nevertheless a great longing always remained with me to visit those holy places beyond the sea, although in my youth I was unable to satisfy it, being continually hindered by some cause or other. Since, however, the most high God by His Grace, freed me in my old age from every impediment and provided me with all I needed, it seemed good to me to renew the determination to go on this holy voyage. And in order that I should have no opportunity of becoming lukewarm any more, I bound myself by a vow, two years ago, to go at all costs, although I was then between sixty and seventy years of age.

I began therefore to arrange to undertake the journey together with certain monks and fellow countrymen, so that I thought to have both a large and agreeable company. And as I always had fair words from them, I set about putting my affairs in order, so that if anything happened to me, they would not be left in confusion. But as the time of departure drew near, all my companions became indifferent as regards our project, so that at the beginning of this year I found that I must start alone, and I felt troubled. Nevertheless I turned again to the Most High God and prayed that He would not let me lose courage, and—although I was frustrated by the company—that He would not let me lack the company given to Tobias when he wanted to go to Rages of the Medes.

As God sustained me in the resolution to accomplish this journey, I spoke much every day about my departure (although, because of my age, I was not believed); and all this I did to stir up some company if it were possible. But this time not a single Milanese could be found. I was not alarmed, however, on this account, and in order that I should be bound more straitly, and that I should not let myself be conquered by the enemy of human nature, not only did I preach the pilgrimage constantly throughout the city, but on Easter Day, when the people—given into my care for the administration of the Sacraments—were gathered together to receive the Holy Communion according to the general Commandment, I declared publicly that, God willing, after the Feast of the Ascension of Our Lord Jesus Christ, I intended to go to the Holy Sepulchre. At the same time, by means of friends in Venice, I informed myself as to the time of the departure of the galley, which usually goes on the voyage to the Holy Land, and prepared everything necessary for the journey, according to the instructions given me by those who had been there in previous years. Then, still finding myself alone, I resolved, as is the duty of all pilgrims, to furnish myself with spiritual weapons for my protection on the journey by land and by sea.

On the 14th of the month of May of the present year,

THE ARCHBISHOP'S BENEDICTION

which was a Wednesday, and the third day of the Rogations or Litanies, according to the Ambrosian ritual *(Note 1)*, when the service was ended in the Cathedral Church of Milan *(Note 2)*, in the presence of the people not a few, I went up to the high altar, where the most Reverend Lord, Don Guidantonio Arcimboldi, the most worthy Archbishop of Milan, stood, according to custom, to bless the people. And I begged his most Reverend Lordship to bless the emblems of my pilgrimage—that is, the cross, the stick or pilgrim's staff, and the wallet—and to bestow his blessing on me, according to the order and the ancient institution to be found written in the pastoral. Notwithstanding that he was very weary, because of the long office of the said Litanies, the said most Reverend Lord blessed me very graciously and with great solemnity in the sight of all the people, and gave me the emblems of my pilgrimage.

When the benediction was over, his Lordship embraced me with no ordinary tears, and kissing me most affectionately, left me with the peace of God, surrounded by a great crowd, from which I had some difficulty in separating myself, for everyone wanted to shake hands with me and kiss me. Nevertheless, as well as I could, I got away from the multitude, and shut myself in the Sacristy, where the Venerable Chapter of my Reverend brethren the Lord Canons was gathered together, of whom I took the most tender and loving farewell. Then I went home as secretly as I could, for at every step I had to stop, shake hands and kiss the company.

On Thursday, the 15th of May, after saying Mass at the altar of St. Ambrose *(Note 3)*, our most glorious patron—where lies not only his sacred body, but also the bodies of the most glorious martyrs Protasius and Gervasius *(Note 4)*, I returned home, that is, to *Sancto Victore al*

Pozzo,[1] and took the necessary refection with certain of my dear friends. Then, leaving all the company, by the grace of God I began my journey on foot as a pilgrim, and visited on the way our principal Church.

From there I went to St. Dionysius',[2] where I found certain friends, who, contrary to my wish, were waiting for me. There I mounted on horseback, and thus we rode together as far as a village called Pioltella, where the greater number, yielding to my entreaties, saying " God keep you," turned back. With the rest I went that day to Caravaggio, a very fruitful place, though not indeed beautiful considering the number of gentlemen who live there, where I was lodged very honourably by the Magnificent Don Fermo dei Sichi.[3]

On Friday, the 16th of May, I remained in the said place, as I had been warned that on account of the rain during the night, the passage of a neighbouring torrent named the *Cerro*,[4] was not safe. In the morning, I went to the Chapel of our Lady of the Fountain, and there said Mass in honour of the aforesaid blessed Virgin.

On Saturday, the 17th of May, I continued my journey, and stopped to rest at a place called Calci, as I had been invited to do by the aforesaid Magnificent Don Fermo, who has large farms in the said place. After dinner was over I rode into Brescia, an ancient city built near a hill.

Amongst those who have written about its origin, I find a great variety of opinion, and therefore I leave the subject alone. I can say, however, with reason, that it is a very beautiful city, and strongly walled. It has a fine strong

---

1. M. S. Casola, "Sancto Victore al Pozo." This was one of two churches in Milan dedicated to St. Victor, both of which have been demolished. It stood not far from Saint George's Church (in via Torino), in the district of Porta Ticinese.
2. In Casola's time the church of St. Dionysius was outside the city near Porta Orientale. According to popular tradition it was built by St. Ambrose, on the spot where St. Barnabas first preached Christianity to the Milanese. It has been destroyed.
3. Don Fermo dei Secchi.
4. *i.e.*, The Serio.

castle, situated on the summit of the said hill. In the city there are beautiful houses for the citizens, and so many artificers[1] of every kind that I almost seemed to see Milan. There is a beautiful palace elaborately adorned, where the Governors of the city live. It is well supplied with munition, and especially with land weapons of every kind; it is a thing worth seeing. The Loggia, begun in front of the Piazza, will be a beautiful sight when it is finished. There are many beautiful piazzas in the said city.

I visited the Cathedral Church, which, in comparison with the city, is not beautiful. As to the other churches, I saw nothing worthy of notice. In this city, however, I saw something very praiseworthy—that is, a large, long and ample space, very clean and well ordered, where the butchers are gathered together. The cleanliness and order gave me great pleasure, and there is an abundance of meat of every kind. The said place astounded me, because I had never seen the like anywhere else. Further on I saw a piazza full of fish of every sort. I used to think that only in the market at Milan could fish be found in such a great quantity.

I refrain from describing the fortifications which adorn the said city, beecause there are too many of them. Everything good can be said of the said city; and I must not pass over in silence the many pleasant fountains there—public ones in the piazzas and private ones in the houses. In truth I used to think that in Italy, Viterbo had the greatest number of fountains; now I have changed my opinion. He who called this city "Brixia Magnipotens" made no mistake, because it is so opulent. It was formerly

---

1. Casola writes: "In la citade belle caxe per citadini, e spessa de ogni artificio, ita che me pariva veder quasi Milano." He may therefore have meant that the houses were beautiful, numerous, and of every style; but I have preferred the reading given in the text.

held, together with the surrounding country, by whoever obtained the dominion of Milan; now it is subject to the Signoria of Venice.

On Sunday, the 18th of May, the day of Pentecost, called *Pascha Roxata*,[1] after hearing Mass, I took the road again, with two good rests—first at Lonato, and then at Peschiera. These are prosperous and beautiful places, little less than cities. They were formerly subject to the Lords of Gonzaga, as appears still from certain arms I saw on a tower at the entrance to the place. Finally, in the evening, I arrived at Verona.

To be brief, this is a large and long city, and beautiful considering that it is ancient. There are various opinions as to who built it, but in a few words it may be said that it has been the delightful habitation of remarkable men, because in it I saw many tall, beautiful and ornate palaces, and these seemed numberless to me, for it takes such a long time to pass through the said city that I became confused. At the present time, in building palaces and even ordinary houses, they delight in adding numerous balconies to the façades—some of iron, and some with little columns of white and delicate marble.

I also saw the Colosseum, now called the Arena, which is built, in my opinion, in the likeness of that at Rome, though it is in a better state of preservation. It is held in little honour, however, to judge by the filth it is deputed to receive.

It must be said that this has been, and now is, a magnificent city. I went to see some of the churches. It seems to me that, beginning with that of the mendicant friars, they are more sumptuous than our Milanese churches in every respect. I leave aside the one which

---

1. In Italy the Feast of Pentecost is also called "Pasqua delle rose," or Pasqua Rosata," that is, "Easter of the roses," because the roses generally come into bloom about that time.

never will be finished—that is, the Cathedral—and I speak of all the others. Another thing I must not omit to mention is the great magnificence of their funeral monuments—the ancient as well as the modern—so that it seems to me there is nothing to add.

I had better say nothing about the beauty given to the said city by the great river called the Adige, which passes through the centre, and is crossed by so many and such fine bridges, lest I should err in overpraising. There is a great abundance in the said city, though less than at Brescia. Formerly it was subject to various Lords, but now it is ruled by Governors, sent by the Signoria of Venice,[1] who have two beautiful palaces for their habitation. As I did not frequent the society of the inhabitants of Verona, I have nothing more to say. As I was there on a holiday, I saw many beautiful women, very handsomely dressed and adorned.

On Monday, the 19th of May, after hearing Mass at Verona, I directed my steps towards Vicenza, and arrived there early. According to the opinion of many people this city was first built by the Franks.[2] It is very fine, but not equal to Verona. I saw nothing very notable there except a palace opposite the inn where I lodged, which, however, is a fine building.

The said city has a great trade in silk. As I rode through the country I was shown the whole process of making the silk, which is very interesting. Very few other trees are to be found there save mulberry trees, which are stripped of their leaves to feed the worms that make the silk. I saw many women looking after the said worms, and they explained to me the great care they needed by day and by night. It was a very pleasant

---

1. *i.e.*, the Government of Venice.
2. The word used in the MS. is "Franzosi," commonly employed in medieval documents to describe the inhabitants of France. Casola may have meant the *Gauls*.

thing to me to see such a great quantity and in so many places.

On Tuesday, the 20th of May, I left Vicenza, and set out towards Padua. The road was disagreeable on account of heavy rain the night before; but at length I reached Padua, a very ancient city, which, according to the common belief, was built by the Trojan Antenor after the destruction of Troy.

The city is not only large, it is immense. I do not know why, but it pleased me less than the other places I had seen. I went about here and there to see what I could of it; but I did not find either palaces or houses worthy of its size or of the great reputation it has among Christian people. It seems to me that there are three cities, and when a man thinks he is outside, nevertheless he is then inside, and *vice versâ*.

I saw the Cathedral. It did not appear to me worthy of the large income enjoyed by the Bishop and Canons of the said church. I saw the Church of Saint Anthony. It is a wonderful building, and very ornate, especially in the chapel, where the body of the said saint is honoured. There is a beautiful choir furnished with very beautiful stalls. There is a large convent of Franciscan friars who administer the said church. In front of the church there is a large piazza, in which the Signoria of Venice has placed a statue of Gattamelata of Narni on horseback *(Note 5)*. He was formerly a good captain for the Venetians. I saw also the monument of the said Antenor, the builder of Padua *(Note 6)*. It is impossible not to praise the said city, considering that, in the University maintained there, so many great and good men of so many nations have been educated. The city is abundantly supplied with victuals, from what I could learn.

After dinner I recommended my horse to the care of

the innkeeper, as is the custom *(Note 7)*, and entered the boat to go to Venice, where I arrived at the twenty-third hour.[1] I was taken by a courier to the house of the Master Courier of the Milanese merchants, and went at once to rest, being too weary to seek the friends to whom I had letters of introduction. In truth, I was somewhat agitated—so much so indeed that, fearing I could not endure the sea, and yielding to the enemy of well-doing, I thought of turning back. Nevertheless God willed to lend me grace to accomplish this holy voyage in spite of my unworthiness. I was lodged very courteously by the said master of the couriers, and well treated by him. He understood my needs so well that in the morning I felt quite restored.

---

1. The first hour of the day began an hour before sunrise. The third hour or *Ora di Terza* was two hours after sunrise. This was the time when the Magistrates usually assembled. *Vespers* was always two hours after midday. The twenty-fourth hour marked the sunset and the close of the day.

CHAPTER II.

May 21st, Casola Introduced to Agostino Contarini.—Visit to the Milanese Ambassador.—Situation of Venice.—The Ducal Palace and Plans for the Restoration.—The Sforza Palace.—Piazzas.—Merchandise and Warehouses. — Provisions. — Flour Market and Bread Shops.—Meat.—Fowls.—Fish.—Fruit and Vegetables.—Wine.—Drinking Water.—Splendour of Venetian Edifices.—Casola's Meeting with Fra Francesco Trivulzio and his Friends.

ON Wednesday, the 21st of May, I took one of the Milanese couriers to guide me about Venice, and went to the houses of the merchants for whom I had letters, and to each one I gave his own. Then, as I was afraid of not finding a place in the galley, I was immediately introduced to the Magnificent Don Agostino Contarini,[1] a Venetian patrician and captain of the Jaffa galley—thus the galley is named which carries the pilgrims going to Jerusalem—and he ordered my name to be written in the Pilgrims' Book.[2] At this time I found that I had been in too great a hurry to leave home, and that I must wait several days before the departure of the said galley.

In order that the tediousness of waiting should not make me desire to turn back and do as the children of Israel did when they went into the Promised Land, I determined to examine carefully the city of Venice, about which so much has been said and written, not only by

---
1. See Introduction, pp. 95-101.
2. The Pilgrims' Book was the Register of the Contracts, between Patroni and Pilgrims, kept in the office of the Cattaveri.

learned men, but also by great scholars, that it appears to me there is nothing left to say. And I did this solely to amuse myself during the time I had to spend in such a great port. I wanted to see everything it was possible for me to see; and I was aided continually by the company given me by the Magnificent Doctor and Cavalier, the Lord Tadiolo de Vicomercato *(Note 8)*, Ambassador to the aforesaid Signoria of Venice for our most illustrious Lord the Duke of Milan. I paid him a visit, as was my duty, as soon as I arrived, and from him, although I did not merit it, I received more than common attention.

Before going further, I must make my excuses to the readers of this my itinerary, if it should seem to them that I have overpraised this city of Venice. What I write is not written to win the goodwill of the Venetians, but to set down the truth. And I declare that it is impossible to tell or write fully of the beauty, the magnificence or the wealth of the city of Venice. Something indeed can be told and written to pass the time as I do, but it will be incredible to anyone who has not seen the city.

I do not think there is any city to which Venice, the city founded on the sea, can be compared; nevertheless I appeal always to the judgment of every person who has been there some time. Although this city is built entirely in the water and the marshes, yet it appears to me that whoever desires to do so can go everywhere on foot, as it is well kept and clean. Anyone, however, who does not want to endure the fatigue can go by water, and will be entreated to do so, and it will cost him less than he would spend elsewhere for the hire of a horse. As to the size of the city, I may say that it is so large, that, after being there so many days as I was, I made but little acquaintance with the streets. I cannot give the dimensions of this city, for it appears to me not one city alone but several cities placed together *(Note 9)*.

I saw many beautiful palaces, beginning with the Palace of St. Mark, which is always inhabited by the Doge and his family *(Note 10)*. The façade of the said palace has been renovated in part with a great display of gold; and a new flight of steps is being built there—a stupendous and costly work—by which to ascend to the said palace from the side of the Church of St. Mark. The lower portico on the ground floor is so well arranged that no more can be said; it is true, however, that it is spoiled by the prisons, which are not well placed there *(Note 11)*. The portico, which goes round above, looks partly over the piazza, partly over the Grand Canal, partly over a small canal, and one part towards the Church of St. Mark, and all this portico has its columns of marble and other beautiful ornaments. In these porticos many Courts are established with their benches, and at every bench there are at least three assessors or hearers all together. At the time of the hearings many cries are heard there, as also happens at Milan at the Broletto *(Note 12)* at the time of the trials. Among the said tribunals there is that of the Lords of the Night *(Note 13)*, who employ in their hearings the torment, called in our tongue *the Curlo*.[1]

Besides the other notable things in the said palace, I saw a very long hall whose walls are painted very ornately. And there is painted the story how Frederick Barbarossa drove away Pope Alexander the Fourth,[2] who fled in disguise to Venice, and was recognised in a monastery called the Monastery della Carità *(Note 14)*. The whole story is represented with such richness and naturalness in the figures that I think little could be

---

1. The Curlo is the axis of a well, round which the cord is wound; on this account the word was applied to the torture of the cord or rack.
2. Barbarossa's opponent was Pope *Alexander III*.

VENICE—THE DUCAL PALACE

added. The ceiling of the said hall is decorated with great gilded pictures. Seats are placed round the said hall, and in addition there are three rows of double seats, in the body of the hall, placed back to back. There are two magnificent gilded seats, one at each end of the said hall; I was told they were for seating the Doge, one for the winter, and the other for the summer. In this hall the Great Council is held—that is, the Council of all the gentlemen, who, it is said, are two thousand five hundred in number.

The Council called the Council of the Pregadi *(Note 15)* is held in another hall. I will say little about it because it is not adorned like the others. The hall where the Doge and his Councillors hold audience constantly is not very large, but it is magnificently decorated, with its gilded ceiling and its painted and storied walls. The throne on which sits the Doge, also called by the Venetians the "Prince," is all gilded and much higher than the others.

With regard to the magnificence and decoration of the habitation of the aforesaid Doge—as I have seen many other princely palaces in this our time both in Italy and abroad, beginning at Rome—I venture to say that it is the most beautiful in Italy. It is so rich in carved work and everything gilded, that it is a marvel. One of the pages of the aforesaid Doge showed me everything, beginning with the bed in which he sleeps, and proceeding even to the kitchen, and in my opinion nothing could be added. The decorations are not movable, but fixed. There is no lack of marble and porphyry and woodwork subtly carved, and all is of such a nature that one is never weary of looking.

The said palace is being renovated, and in the new part the arms of the immediate predecessors of the present prince are to be seen. But after seeing the said palace several times, and especially after looking at the plan for the renovation, I hope the aforesaid Venetian gentlemen (who want to have the reputation of never sparing expense in carrying out their will), who have commenced the restoration of the said palace will pardon me if I say, that they have done ill in not enlarging it beyond the minor canal, for they will spend a great sum and nevertheless, because it is not extended on the side I name, they will never be able to build courtyards worthy of the said palace. And the only reason for this is that they have not wanted to spend enough. Several gentlemen with whom I discussed the matter as we stood on the balcony of the said palace agreed with me.

I will not attempt to describe the number of large and beautiful palaces splendidly decorated and furnished, worth, some a hundred, some fifty, some thirty thousand ducats, and the owners of the same, because it would be too hard an undertaking for me, and better suited to someone who had to remain a long time in the said city of Venice. On the Grand Canal there is the most remarkable beginning of a palace for the Sforza family, and for the honour of the Milanese I am very sorry it has not been finished *(Note 16)*. For after seeing the said foundations, I am sure that the palace would be very magnificent if it were completed.

The said city, although it is in the water, as I said, has so many beautiful piazzas, beginning with that of St. Mark, that they would suffice for any great city placed on the mainland. It is a marvel to see how long and spacious they are. I have observed that the said city is so well ordered and arranged, that however much it rains, there is never any mud.

Something may be said about the quantity of

VENICE—THE WAREHOUSES

merchandise in the said city *(Note 17)*, although not nearly the whole truth, because it is inestimable. Indeed it seems as if all the world flocks there, and that human beings have concentrated there all their force for trading. I was taken to see various warehouses, beginning with that of the Germans *(Note 18)*—which it appears to me would suffice alone to supply all Italy with the goods that come and go—and so many others that it can be said they are innumerable. I see that the special products for which other cities are famous are all to be found there, and that what is sold elsewhere by the pound and the ounce is sold there by *canthari*[1] and sacks of a *moggio*[2] each. And who could count the many shops so well furnished that they also seem warehouses, with so many cloths of every make—tapestry, brocades and hangings of every design, carpets of every sort, camlets of every colour and texture, silks of every kind; and so many warehouses full of spices, groceries and drugs, and so much beautiful white wax! These things stupefy the beholder, and cannot be fully described to those who have not seen them. Though I wished to see everything, I saw only a part, and even that by forcing myself to see all I could.

As to the abundance of the victuals, I can testify that I do not believe there is a city in Italy better supplied than this with every kind of victuals. This time my own city, which I used to think the most abundant, must forgive me, and so too all the other cities in Italy and also abroad where I have been, because, whether it is due to the good order or other cause I do not know, but I never saw such a quantity of provisions elsewhere.

---

1. The *Cantarium* was a weight varying in different parts of Italy. At Naples it equalled 25 lbs., at Genoa 150 lbs., and elsewhere even a quintale (200 lbs.) or nearly two hundredweight. Du Cange. Glossarium.
2. According to Martini (Manuele di Metrologia) the *Moggio* in Medieval Venice contained 333·268 &c. litres. That is about 1¼ English quarters. The Milanese *Moggio* contained 146·234 &c. litres or about ½ an English quarter.

J

I went to the place where the flour is sold wholesale;[1] the world at present does not contain such a remarkable thing. When I saw such abundance and beauty around me I was confused. The bakers' shops,[2] which are to be found in one place specially, namely, the piazza of St. Mark, and also throughout the city, are countless and of incredible beauty; there is bread the sight of which tempts even a man who is surfeited to eat again. In my judgment Venice has not its equal for this.

With the meat they give a great piece of bone. When I saw the place where the meat[3] is sold, I thought I had never seen such a miserable place in any city, or more wretched meat to look at. It drives away the wish to buy. I do not know the reason for this, unless it be that the Venetians are so occupied with their merchandise, that, they do not trouble much about what they eat. It is enough to say that in that place you could not have a good and fine-looking piece of meat whatever you were willing to pay, or at least in the quantity to be had at Milan.

For the time of year I was there, there seemed to be a great abundance of fowls and other kinds of eatable birds, though they were somewhat dear. There was a great abundance of cheese or *caxi*,[4] and butter—more, I can assure you, than at Milan, which ought to be the great centre for these things, and which used to be.

It is superfluous to try and recount the daily abundance of fish, especially in two places—at St. Mark's and at the

---

1. The Fondaco della Farina or public flour warehouse was erected 1493, and restored in 1584 and 1717. It stands close to the present steamer landing stage at Calle Vallaresso (San Marco). In the 18th century the upper rooms were used as a picture gallery. Since 1810 the building has been the seat of the Capitaneria di Porto (Harbour Master's Office).
2. Besides the bakers' shops distributed over the city, two places were specially set apart for the sale of bread; one at St. Mark's close to the Campanile, the other at the Rialto. In the former place there were 19, in the latter 25 shops. As the bread sold here was chiefly of the coarser kind, the rolls were large, which was what the people desired.
3. The meat market was transferred to the Rialto in 1339 and located in the Palace, confiscated from those of the Querini family, who had taken part in the famous conspiracy of Baiamonte Tiepolo, 1310.
4. *Cacio*, which Casola writes Caxi, means cheese in Italian, from the Latin, Caseus.

VENICE—THE PROVISION MARKETS

Rialto, as it is commonly called. There is never a dearth of fish, though in truth, as to the excellence of the quality, it is not on a level with that of certain other cities. All the time I was there I never saw a fine fish and never ate a good one, although my hosts took great trouble to procure good fish.

As to the fruit. During the time I was awaiting the departure of the galley—not having anything else to do—I went several times very early in the morning to St. Mark's, and also to the Rialto, to watch the unloading of the boats which arrived from time to time. There were so many boats full of big beans, peas and cherries—not indeed of every kind as at Milan, but every day in such quantity, that is seemed as if all the gardens of the world must be there. The number was so great that I declare that after seeing them, when I turned my back I hardly believed my eyes. There is an abundant supply of good vegetables of every kind—*verdure*, as we say—and they are cheaper than in any place I ever visited. I heard that they come from a distance of twenty-five miles.[1] I went several times in the morning to watch the unloading of the boats, and the vegetables looked as if just taken from the gardens and very fresh. I know it is difficult for anyone who has not seen these things to believe what I say, because I have fallen into the same error myself—that is, I used not to believe what was told me about them.

I may recount the abundance of wine of every sort—so much malmsey, so many muscatel wines, Greek wines, white wines of every kind and also red wines,—but it is almost incredible. Although they are not so perfect as ours, nevertheless they are good—I speak of the red wines —and owing to the heavy duties they are dear. I wanted to count the wine shops of every kind, but the more I

1. That is from Chioggia and the neighbourhood.

counted the more I became confused, for they are indeed innumerable.

One thing only appears to me hard in this city; that is, that although the people are placed in the water up to the mouth they often suffer from thirst, and they have to beg good water for drinking and for cooking, especially in the summer time. It is true that there are many cisterns[1] for collecting the rain water *(Note 19)*, and also water is sold in large boatloads—water from the river called the Brenta, which flows near Padua. In this way indeed they provide for their needs, but with difficulty and expense, and the people cannot make such a business of washing clothes with fresh water as is done elsewhere.

The splendour of the edifices, especially the public buildings, may be described by one who has examined them carefully, but it is hard of belief for anyone who has not seen such a quantity of marble of every kind and colour, and so well carved that it is a marvel. They carve wood of all kinds so well and produce such natural figures, that a man passing by without considering what they are will mistake them for living persons.

While I was thus anxiously waiting for the time of departure, which was put off from day to day, I heard of the arrival, a few days before me, of the venerable religious and most remarkable evangelist of the Word of God, Don Frate Francesco Trivulzio *(Note 20)*, belonging to the order of the observants of St. Francis, and of Frate Michele of Como, who came with him. They had been joined in Ferrara by Giovanni Simone Fornaro of Pavia *(Note 21)*, and Giovanni Luchino of Castelnuovo, and I hoped to be added to the company. So, in order to discharge my duty to the fatherland, and also to his

---

1. That is the wells or Pozzi,

exceptional virtues, I paid him a visit and gave him to understand that, like him, I intended to go on the voyage to the Holy Land. We became good friends at once, and to while away the tedious time of waiting for the day of departure, we arranged to visit certain monasteries much talked about in Venice.

CHAPTER III.

Visits to Various Monasteries, &c.—Sant' Elena.—Sant' Antonio.—San Cristoforo.—San Giorgio Maggiore.—Sant' Andrea.—San Francesco delle Vigne.—Frari and Milanese Chapel.—Santa Maria dei Servi and the Chapel of the Lucchese.—La Carità.—San Salvatore.—Carmine.—San Nicolo del Lido.—San Giorgio in Alga.—Madonna dell' Orto.—Convents.—San Zaccaria.—Virgini.—Zelestre.—Churches.—San Pietro.—San Marco.—Parish Churches.—San Giovanni e Paolo.—Scuola di San Marco.—San Domenico.—Miracoli.—Arsenal.—Ships.—Gondolas.—Murano.—Glass Industry.—Gardens.—Venetian Gentlemen.—Their Dress.—Venetian Women.

THE first visit we paid was to the Monastery of Sant'Elena, belonging to the Camaldolese Order *(Note 22)*. As far as we could learn it was first built and endowed by a certain Alessandro Borromeo, who has a splendid tomb in a chapel at the side of the church. The body of Saint Helena was shown to us and many other relics. The church is beautiful, and has a choir adorned with very magnificent stalls, in which pictures are inlaid representing all the cities under the dominion of the Venetians; it is a most beautiful piece of work. The monastery is as beautiful as could be described.

I visited the monastery of Sant 'Antonio of the Order of Monte Oliveto *(Note 23);* it is so beautiful that it lacks nothing. The church is beautiful, and in the said church there is a very wonderful thing—a Christ taken down from the Cross and placed in the lap of our Lady, with the Maries at the side, St. John, Joseph of Arimathea and Nicodemus. It is sculptured with such art and genius that, setting aside the figure of Christ, all the others seem more alive the nearer you approach them. Then I saw the Monastery of San Cristoforo of the Order of the Eremitani *(Note 24)*. I did not see there anything much worth mentioning except the process of making white wax in one of the gardens; indeed, there was such a quantity that it seemed to me it ought to suffice for all the world.

I saw the Monastery of San Giorgio Maggiore *(Note 25)* of the Order of Santa Justina, which is too beautiful to be in the place where it is. It appears to me that the monks have begun a most stupendous thing. I visited the Monastery of Sant 'Andrea *(Note 26)* of the Carthusian Order, which is beautiful and well ordered. The monks are re-building their church, which will be very fine when it is finished. I saw the Monastery of San Francesco delle Vigne *(Note 27)*, where the aforesaid Don Frate Francesco was lodged; it is a most notable place.

The Monastery of the Conventual friars of Saint Francis is beautiful *(Note 28)*. Their church is very ornate in the choir and everywhere else. In the principal chapel there are two very splendid tombs, one opposite the other, to two Doges, Foscari[1] and Trono.[2] In the said church there is also a chapel dedicated to Saint Ambrose, set apart for the use of the Milanese, who hold their congregation or school at the side of the said church.

I visited the Church and Monastery of Santa Maria dei Servi *(Note 29)*, a most remarkable place. The natives of Lucca have their chapel at the side, and they make a great festival on the day of the Corpus Domini. I visited

1. Francesco Foscari. Doge, 1423–1457.
2. Nicolo Tron. Doge, 1471–73.

the Monastery della Carità *(Note 14)*, belonging to the Order of the regular Canons of Saint Augustine, and also another belonging to the said Order called San Salvatore.[1] In the said Monastery della Carità, Pope Alexander the Fourth was discovered and recognised when he fled in disguise before Frederick Barbarossa, and he bestowed many privileges on the said Monastery. I visited the Monastery of Santa Maria,[2] belonging to the Carmelites, and also so many others that it would take too long to write about them all:—San Nicolo del Lido *(Note 30)*, San Giorgio in Alga *(Note 31)*, Santa Maria dell 'Orto *(Note 32)*,—the last two are both of the same Order.

As I had heard a great deal about certain Monasteries for women, I went—also in company—to visit a few of them, especially the Convent of San Zaccaria *(Note 33)*. There are many women there, both young and old, and they let themselves be seen very willingly. They have a beautiful new church and many relics in the altar. I think it is their first church, because they have their choir there. They are said to be very rich, and they do not trouble much about being seen. Another is called the Convent of the Virgins *(Note 34)*. There are many women there, and they are rich. It is said that only Venetian women are received as nuns there. They have a beautiful church with the choir in a prominent position. There is another Convent of the "Donne Zelestre" *(Note 35)*. I went to see it, and found that the nuns dress in white. In addition to these there are many other convents[3] in which there are women who are secluded

---

1. Casola saw the old church of San Salvatore or St. Saviour; the new church was begun early in the 16th century, and completed 1534; the present façade was added after 1663.
2. That is the church commonly known as the *Carmine*.
3. Probably Casola had in mind here the distinction between the "Conventuals" and the "Observants." The expression he uses "Monasteri pure de done serrate et ánche da serrare" (Convents also in which are women who are secluded and to be secluded)—might therefore be translated more fully—Convents in which there are women who are secluded, that is the observants; and who *ought* to be secluded, but are not, that is the Conventuals.

and to be secluded *(Note 36)*. I will leave them to attend to another matter, because I must descend to most special praise of these Venetian gentlemen.

I have been to Rome, the chief city of the world, and I have travelled in Italy, and also very much outside of Italy, and I must say—though I do not say it to disparage anyone, but only to tell the truth—that I have not found in any city so many beautiful and ornate churches as there are in Venice. It would take too long to name them all; nevertheless I will mention one or two, especially of those I saw.

The patriarchal Church or Cathedral is called the Church of San Pietro.[1] It has not many ornaments. I think that Saint Mark, who was his disciple, must have stolen them. The Church of Saint Mark, who was the disciple of Saint Peter, at first sight seems a small thing, but the man who examines and considers everything about it carefully, will find that it is a grand church. I think it has no equal, adorned as it is within and without with so many beatiful and subtle mosaics. It would take too long to describe the beauty of the façade and the doors— beginning with the four horses in metal which are over the great door,—and so many rows of columns on every side. Suffice it to say that for its size it is one of the most beautiful Christian churches. The campanile is separate from the said church, and the piazza is in front of it. I cannot estimate the value of the great treasure in relics, and of the pala of the altar; it seems to me infinite. The church is adorned with two large and beautiful organs, one on the right side and the other on the left of the high altar. It is excellently served by singers and priests furnished with beautiful vestments, as is becoming to

---

1. St. Peter's was the Cathedral Church until 1807, when the title was transferred to St. Mark's.

the city and the place. They say it is the chapel of the Prince, and therefore cannot be too rich or too ornate.

I am afraid in particular to speak of the beauty and decorations of the parochial churches, otherwise called in the Venetian speech " Plebanie," because I could not give the details without offending someone, especially at Milan. I will only say, speaking generally, that the poorest parish church of Venice is more ornate than the finest at Milan. Almost all the Venetian churches—the parish churches I mean—have a beautiful choir and an organ, and no expense is spared to decorate them; everything is gilded, and they are well served. This makes me think strongly that the Venetians must be greatly aided by God in all their affairs, because they are very solicitous with regard to divine worship in all their churches *(Note 37)*.

As I said above, there are all sorts of monks and nuns in the city who have beautiful churches and monasteries. The Order of Saint Dominic, which I have not mentioned above, has a church called San Giovanni e Paolo *(Note 38)*. It appears to me so beautiful that nothing could be added. It is large and lofty, its pavement is all in white and red squares; it has a beautiful organ, and the choir has stalls on which neither gold nor carving has been spared. In that church, in splendid tombs, many princes or Doges of Venice and other remarkable persons belonging to various families have been buried. At the side of the said church there is a school of laymen, called the Scuola di San Marco. The façade is very beautiful and richly adorned with marbles and gold, and the decoration inside is worthy of the outside. I will explain what the said school is another time. The monastery, being ancient, has not the pleasing aspect of the modern ones. There is also a church dedicated to Saint Dominic *(Note 39)* where the observant friars are established. The monastery is beautiful and adorned with all it needs.

It appears to me that I should now make an end of praising the city as regards its churches, and leave the rest for another. As, however, I several times visited a church called Our Lady of the Miracles *(Note 40)*, which is a handsome building, especially outside, I will say a little about it. The said church is a great object of devotion in Venice, and was built with the daily offerings, which are administered by certain gentlemen. There is a convent there for nuns belonging to the Order of St. Clara. I heard from several men worthy of credence that since the said church was begun only a few years ago, the offerings have amounted to over forty thousand ducats.

I saw many other things worthy of record, but I will omit them for fear of wearying my readers too much. Nevertheless, having been several times to the Arsenal, as it is called *(Note 41)*, which is an almost incredible thing to one who has not seen it, I will say a few words about it.

I may mention briefly that it is a large place surrounded by walls as if it were a fortress, where so much water enters that every galley, large and small, can go in and out. In the first place, it is a marvel to see so many long halls arranged with perfect order and full of munition for the equipment of the galleys and the *navi*—covered and uncovered cuirasses,[1] swords, *ranghoni, (sic)* crossbows, bows, large and small arrows, headpieces, arquebuses, and other artillery suitable for the purpose. In short, it appears as if all the munition of the world for furnishing galleys and *navi*[2] were collected there. Then there are three large sheds, *Cassine*,[3] as we say— and one much bigger than the others—where the galleys

---

1. The cuirasses were sometimes of metal, sometimes of leather; and some were covered to conceal them, with damask, &c.
2. By "Navi" Casola probably meant all other vessels not galleys; but as "Nave" was also the term applied to a ship of a special form—the largest kind of sailing ship—I have preferred to leave the exact word he uses.
3. In the Milanese dialect the term *Cascine* is applied to the various outbuildings of a farm, sometimes also to the farm proper and outbuildings, &c., all taken together.

are placed all together to preserve them when they are lifted out of the water, and also when they are new. One of these *Cassine* has eighteen divisions, which are so large that under each one of them there was a large galley and a small one. Under another *cassina* of twenty compartments there was one galley only, but a large one, in each compartment; and under the other cassine there were other ships[1] of different kinds, and both large and small.

In one part of the Arsenal there was a great crowd of masters and workmen who do nothing but build galleys or other ships of every kind. There are also masters continually occupied in making crossbows, bows and large and small arrows; and all by order of the Signoria.[2] In one great covered place there are twelve masters each one with his own workmen and his forge apart; and they labour continually making anchors and every other kind of iron-work necessary for the galleys and other ships. There seems to be there all the iron that could be dug out of all the mountains of the world. Then there is a large and spacious room where there are many women who do nothing but make sails.

Within the walls of the said Arsenal, above the water which enters, there is a most beautiful contrivance for lifting any large galley or other ship out of the water, with little fatigue, and also if necessary for putting it back again. Outside the said Arsenal, but near the walls, there is a place where they make all the ropes used at sea on the galleys and all the other ships—that is, the cables which the Venetians call "gomene" and every sort of rope. It is a place all covered below, and so long that I could hardly see from one end to the other. The number

---

1. Casola here uses the word "Navilii"—and the phrase runs in the text:—"E sotto le altre cassine, stavano de altri diversi navilii, grandi e picoli."
2. The Venetian Government, also called the *Serenissima*.

VENICE—THE SHIPPING

of masters and workmen who are constantly employed there is amazing. No one would buy any ropes of importance, especially those for casting the anchors, anywhere else than there, because there are certain officers whose duty it is to give guarantees of their quality. And there are certain persons who sort the hemp when it is brought in.

This Arsenal has many officials, and two gentlemen are at the head. These principals told me that every Saturday the Signoria [1] paid out at the least one thousand two hundred ducats, and sometimes more, for the labour and work done in the said Arsenal. They have already built the main walls of another Arsenal which will be a fine place when it is finished.

I fatigued myself very much by trying to find out if possible—and with the aid of people very familiar with Venice and the surrounding places—the number of all the ships, both large and small, to be found in Venice, beginning with the boats otherwise called gondolas, up to the largest *nave* and galley in the Grand Canal. I commenced the work; but, although the days were long, because it was the month of May, I found it was no task for me any more than for Saint Augustine—as they recount—to write about the Trinity *(Note 42)*, for the number is infinite. I find also that it is a great expense for the inhabitants of Venice, because almost every citizen keeps at least one gondola, which costs at the lowest fifteen ducats, and is a greater expense to maintain than a horse. I leave alone those who keep large and small boats for gain, by crossing the ferries or letting them out on hire. I leave out also the galleys and *navi* for navigating long distances because they are numberless. When I inquired of experienced persons who have seen many maritime cities which are great seaports, they told

1. *i.e.*, The Venetian Government.

me that there is no city equal to Venice as regards the number of the ships and the grandeur of the port, and this I can fully believe.

Having abandoned the business of counting the ships, I accompanied the Venerable Don Frate Francesco Trivulzio to Murano, a place situated in the sea by itself, although it is a part of Venice. There are many furnaces there for making glass, and work in glass of every colour is carried on there constantly. All the beautiful glass vases which are taken throughout the world are made there. I stood to watch the work at the various furnaces, and I saw, above everything else a glass chalice, the price of which was ten ducats. It was noble and very subtly worked, but I would not touch it, fearing it might fall out of my hand.

In the said Murano there are seven convents for women, and amongst them, one, where building is continually going on by order of the present Doge the Lord Agostino Barbarigo, who has two of his daughters in the said convent.[1] Much more might be said about the said place and its beauty and pleasantness and how it is situated in the water and has beautiful gardens, but I will leave something for another to say. I cannot refrain from repeating, however, that there is nothing which astonished me more in this city built on the water, than the sight of the many beautiful gardens there are there, especially in the monasteries of every Order.

As the day of our departure was drawing near, I determined to leave everything else and study the owners of the many beautiful things I have noted—that is, the Venetian gentlemen, who give themselves this title. I have considered the qualities of these Venetian gentlemen. For the most part they are tall, handsome men, astute and

---

1. Santa Maria degli Angeli, or Saint Mary of the Angels.

very subtle in their dealings, and whoever has to do business with them must keep his eyes and ears well open. They are proud—I think this is on account of their great dominions—and when a son is born to a Venetian gentleman they say themselves, " A Lord is born into the world." [1] They are frugal and very modest in their manner of living at home; outside the house they are very liberal.

The city of Venice preserves its ancient fashion of dress—which never changes—that is, a long garment of any colour that is preferred. No one would leave the house by day if he were not dressed in this long garment, and for the most part in black. They have so observed this custom, that the individuals of every nation in the world—which has a settlement in Venice—all adopt this style, from the greatest to the least, beginning with the gentlemen, down to the sailors and *galeotti (Note 43)*. Certainly it is a dress which inspires confidence, and is very dignified.[2] The wearers all seem to be doctors in law, and if a man should appear out of the house without his toga, he would be thought mad. The Milanese do the same, except, that if a lark, from one hour to the other, should come from the ends of the earth and bring some new fashion in dress, all, or the majority, both of those who can afford it and those who cannot, would want to follow the fashion; so that a Milanese cannot be distinguished from a Spaniard. I need say no more.

When the Venetian gentlemen take office or go on some embassy, they wear very splendid garments; in truth, they could not be more magnificent. They are of scarlet, of velvet, of brocade, if the wearers hold high office; and all the linings of every kind are very costly. In order not to

---

1. " E le nato un Signore al Mondo " (Casola MS.)
2. " Habito certo pieno de fede e de gravitá." (Casola MS.)

praise the Venetian gentlemen at too great length, I want to mention one thing more which pleased me very much, and that is, that they keep all their offices and profits for themselves, and do not give them to strangers except in the case of the first Secretary *(Note 44)*, who is not a Venetian.[1] The other offices they distribute among themselves.

Their women appear to me to be small for the most part, because if they were not, they would not wear their shoes—otherwise called *pianelle*—as high as they do For in truth I saw some pairs of them sold, and also for sale, that were at least half a Milanese braccio[2] in height. They were so high indeed that when they wear them, some women appear giants; and certain also are not safe from falling as they walk, unless they are well supported by their slaves. As to the adornment of their heads, they wear their hair so much curled over their eyes that, at first sight, they appear rather men than women.[3] The greater part is false hair; and this I know for certain because I saw quantities of it on poles, sold by peasants in the Piazza San Marco. Further, I inquired about it, pretending to wish to buy some, although I had a beard both long and white.[4]

These Venetian women, especially the pretty ones, try as much as possible in public to show their chests—I mean the breasts and shoulders—so much so, that several times when I saw them I marvelled that their clothes did not fall off their backs. Those who can afford it, and also those who cannot, dress very splendidly, and have magnificent jewels and pearls in the trimming round their

---

1. Casola means evidently not a Venetian Patrician.
2. The Milanese braccio = ·594936 metres, or just over half a metre.
3. A glance at the pictures of Carpaccio and Gentile Bellini shows that it was the fashion then for the men to wear their hair cut over their foreheads, while the women wore theirs smoothed back and knotted behind.
4. In his portrait Casola is represented as clean shaven. He had allowed his beard to grow, as was the custom for obvious reasons, before starting on his pilgrimage.

collars. They wear many rings on their fingers with great balass rubies,[1] rubies and diamonds. I said also those who cannot afford it, because I was told that many of them hire these things. They paint their faces a great deal, and also the other parts they show, in order to appear more beautiful. The general run of the women who go out of the house,[2] and who are not amongst the number of the pretty girls, go out well covered up and dressed for the most part in black even up to the head, especially in church. At first I thought they were all widows, and sometimes on entering a church at the service time I seemed to see so many nuns of the Benedictine Order. The marriageable girls dress in the same way, but one cannot see their faces for all the world. They go about so completely covered up, that I do not know how they can see to go along the streets. Above all—at least indoors— these Venetian women, both high and low, have pleasure in being seen and looked at; they are not afraid of the flies biting them, and therefore they are in no great hurry to cover themselves if a man comes upon them unexpectedly. I observed that they do not spend too much in shawls to cover their shoulders. Perhaps this custom pleases others; it does not please me. I am a priest in the way of the saints, and I had no wish to inquire further into their lives. I thought it my duty, as I said above, to seek out the churches and monasteries and go and see the relics which are very numerous; and this seemed to me a meritorious work for a pilgrim who was awaiting the departure of the galley to go to the Holy Sepulchre—thus finishing the time as well as I could.

1. The balass ruby is becoming now more and more rare. It was much used and appreciated in medieval Venice, and is frequently mentioned in inventories, wills, &c. In value it ranks after the oriental ruby, and before the Spinel and the Siamese ruby.
2. That is women belonging to the class of the "Popolo."

K

CHAPTER IV.

Festival of the Corpus Domini.—Service in Saint Mark's.—The Five Great Schools.—Procession Round the Piazza.—New Contract with Agostino Contarini.—Preparations for the Departure.

On Thursday, the 29th of May, there was the great festival of the Corpus Domini *(Note 45)*. I had heard from those who knew, that all the pilgrims were expected to assemble in the Church of St. Mark to join the procession. In order therefore, not to neglect my duty, and fearing lest otherwise I might not find a place, I went early in the morning to the palace of St. Mark, thinking to be among the first. There I found the royal and ducal ambassadors already congregated, and several bells were ringing continually in the bell-tower of St. Mark's. About the eleventh hour the most illustrious Doge descended from the palace to go into the Church of St. Mark. His name is the Lord Agostino Barbarigo *(Note 46)*. He is a handsome old man, with a fine white beard, and wore his tiara on his head and a mantle made in the ducal fashion, as he always does when he appears in public. He was accompanied by the Reverend Father, the Lord Nicolo Francho, Bishop of Treviso (said to be the Papal legate), by the magnificent ambassadors aforesaid, and by a great number of Venetian gentlemen. These were dressed, one better than the other, in cloth of gold—each more beautiful than the other—crimson velvet, damask and scarlet; and each had his stole over his shoulder. As they entered the Church of St. Mark all the noises of the bells and every other noise ceased.

FESTIVAL OF THE CORPUS DOMINI

The aforesaid Doge was conducted to his seat *(Note 47)*, which seemed to me very much in the background; that is to say, it was behind the choir; however, it was draped with cloth of gold. He was accompanied by the Ambassadors only. I was told that that is not his usual place, but only for that day in order to see the whole of the procession. The other gentlemen were all seated in the choir.

The musical Mass began, and was chanted by the most Reverend Lord the Patriarch of Aquileia, named the Lord Nicolo Donato *(Note 48)*, because the Patriarch of Venice, whose name is the Lord Tommaso Donato *(Note 49)*, and who belongs to the Order of the Preachers, was infirm. The aforesaid Lord of Aquileia was assisted by a large number of deacons and sub-deacons. A great silence was maintained—more than I have ever observed on similar occasions—even in seating so many Venetian gentlemen; every sound could be heard. One single person appeared to me to direct everything, and he was obeyed by every man without a protest. This filled me with astonishment, because I had never seen such perfect obedience at similar spectacles elsewhere.

The ceremonies of the Mass seemed to me much less solemn and impressive than the Milanese or Ambrosian, when the Mass is sung by our most Reverend Lord of Milan; nor did I see anything worth noting except that when the Gospel was ended, after the Patriarch had kissed the place of the Gospel, two deacons and as many sub-deacons went to the Excellent Doge and offered to him also the place of the Gospel to kiss. I did not notice any other unusual ceremony, save that when the Gloria in Excelsis, the Patrem Omnipotentem, the Sanctus and the Agnus Dei are said, four of the priests of St. Mark in their surplices and hoods go and stand before the Doge and there they repeat everything with him, as the Ordinaries of the Cathedral of Milan do before the Most Reverend Lord the Archbishop or some Papal Legate.

The Mass closed with the benediction, and after the declaration of the Indulgence, which was for forty-two days, the procession was set in movement by the organisers and directors in the following way:—It entered by the great door of the said church, and mounting upwards into the choir, went close to the high altar, on which the body of Christ was placed in a transparent pix shaped like a golden throne. It stood upon a chalice, the largest I ever saw; they said it was of gold; it was very beautiful. Then the said procession turned to the right of the altar to leave the choir, and passed in front of the Doge and the Ambassadors, so that they saw it all without impediment.

The first to set out was the Scuola della Misericordia.[1] The brethren were all dressed in long white over garments, which had a small red sign on one side containing the name of the Misericordia. Certain of them, to the number of fifty-six, went in front, each carrying a beautiful gilded wooden candlestick; I mean like the long ones commonly used by the friars when they go in procession at home. They were so beautiful that I do not think anything could be added. For every candlestick there was a *doppiero*[2] of at least two pounds weight each, of green wax, and all lighted. Behind these walked a man who carried a very ornate cross—with a certain little painted banderole—on which the gold had not been spared to make it beautiful. Many boys followed after him, and I think there were some girls as well, to judge by their heads, arranged as they arrange the little angels. Each

---

1. The Schools or "Scuole" were pious confraternaties and mutual aid societies. The most important were known as the "Scuole Grandi dei Battuti." These were *five* in number, as Casola relates, until the year 1552, when the School of St. Theodore (founded in 1268) was declared by the Council of Ten to be the sixth and last of the great schools

2. A Doppiero is a torch formed of several wax candles fastened together.

one of them carried in the hand a *confectera* or bowl of silver or some other vase such as they could carry, full of flowers and of rose leaves, and when they came where the aforesaid Doge was seated with the Ambassadors and the other gentlemen, they scattered the flowers over all of them, and there was a very sweet smell. After these children walked as many as five hundred brethren, all belonging to the said school, all dressed in white garments, as I said above, all in pairs, and each one of them carried a large lighted candle of green wax weighing six ounces. But before these brethren passed after their cross, there were certain singers who sang many praises by the way, and who—when they came to the altar opposite the Sacrament of the body of Christ—knelt down, and there they continued to sing praises until the said brethren had all passed; then they got up and followed the said school.

Next came the brethren of Our Lady of Charity,[1] as they are called, in the order aforesaid, and wearing a similar dress, except that the red sign was different. In front, there were forty brethren with candlesticks as beautiful as the first. Their *doppieri* were of the same weight, but they were red. Behind them was their cross with its banner, and behind the cross many children arranged and adorned like the first; and they scattered flowers like the first. Then followed the singers, who did as was said of the first. After them walked five hundred brethren, each carrying a large candle, six ounces in weight, of green wax.

The Scuola di San Marco went next. All the brethren were dressed as has been said above—that is, in white garments—and the sign they wore on their breasts was a small St. Mark in red. Before their cross walked at least thirty-six brethren with their candlesticks, made as was

---

1. Scuola Grande della Carità.

said above, and the *doppieri* they held were of the same weight, but they were of white wax. There followed a great company of children adorned as I said above, and throwing flowers in the manner above mentioned. Then came their singers, who observed the order observed by the first. Behind them, there were at least five hundred brethren, each with his big lighted candle of white wax weighing also six ounces.

Behind these walked the brethren of the Scuola di San Giovanni, preceded by twenty-eight of their number dressed, as is said, in white, and having a red mark different from the others. Their candlesticks were made like those above, and their *doppieri* were similar in weight, but of yellow wax, that is, the natural colour. Next to these came their cross with its banner, and behind the cross there was a great company of little angels, who threw flowers in the way described above. They were followed by at least two hundred brethren in white garments also, each carrying his great candle of six ounces, which was also of the natural colour. They were preceded by singers like the foregoing schools.

Finally, behind these walked the brethren of the Scuola di San Rocco, dressed like the others, though the red sign they wore was different from the others. Before their cross there were at least thirty-four of the brethren with magnificent candlesticks like the others, and as far as I could see their *doppieri* were grey, other people said they were black; be that as it may, they were of the same weight as the others. Then came their cross, as was said of the other schools; then many little boys dressed as little angels, who threw flowers as described above; then the singers, who did as the other singers did; and behind them at least two hundred brethren dressed as was said above, and each of them with his great candle of black or grey wax, also lighted.

THE CORPUS DOMINI PROCESSION   151

After these schools there followed every kind of observant and conventual friars; from the Gesuati *(Note 50)* to those of the congregation of Santa Justina [1] there was not one lacking. Their number was counted up to eight hundred; really there were a few more, but not many. All, or the greater part of them, carried white *doppieri* or at least lighted candles in their hands, and they all wore the most beautiful vestments they possess. So beautiful were they that we cannot come even after them. For I saw certain pluvials that between the border [2] and the cape had so many and such large and beautiful pearls that they appeared to me worth all the vestments in our city. I cannot describe the abundance of the brocades of every kind, because there were so many that my eyes became confused, and I lost count. After the friars all the clergy followed in good order with their crosses well adorned, but their vestments were not rich; indeed, they seemed to me very old-fashioned and of small value. The only other observation I will make about the Venetian clergy is, that they are few in number compared with our clergy; for, comparing them with the clergy of Milan, even the *Stradioti* [3]—who are those without benefices—are more numerous than all the clergy of Venice.

The clergy were followed by sixty men in togas—twelve for each of the above-named schools, which are five in number—and each one of them had in his hand a large and heavy *doppiero*. I think the weight of each must have been not less than thirty-six or forty pounds, and there were twelve of every colour used by the said schools,

---

1. Santa Justina or Giustina was a Paduan of Royal birth, martyred as a Christian under Maximian. She was a Saint of the Benedictine Order.
2. That is the border which goes round the neck and down the front.
3. The light cavalry, formed of Albanese, Dalmatians, Greeks, &c., and employed by the Venetians in their wars were known as "Stradioti." Perhaps from a certain quaint analogy Casola applied the term to the unbeneficed clergy, who were frequently to be seen hurrying along the streets (Strade) from one church to another to say mass.

as I said above. When I asked what order they belonged to, I was told that they were twelve brethren of each of the said schools, and all Venetian gentlemen, and they went thus in procession two by two.

When all these had passed by, the aforenamed most Reverend Lord the Patriarch, who had chanted the Mass, took up the Sacrament of the body of Christ arranged as I said, and followed after them. He was accompanied only by those who had assisted him at Mass, and the canopy was carried by priests only. Thus he commenced to walk after the procession, which, proceeding as I said, went out by the door which led to the palace of St. Mark, and passed through the court of the palace. Behind him, the aforesaid Doge took his place, together with the Ambassadors, and after them the Lord Councillors and the other gentlemen. The pilgrims who were there, being very courteously invited to do so, followed, and were paired with the aforesaid gentlemen as long as there were any pilgrims unaccompanied. At the said door of Saint Mark's, by which the procession went out, there were two priests, one on the right side and the other on the left, who offered a white lighted candle of six ounces and more to each person, beginning with the aforesaid Doge down to the end, and to the pilgrims as well as the others. And so they went in procession.

It must be noted that the said procession did not go further than out of the door of Saint Mark's, as I said, and all round the piazza, which was covered the whole way it went with white cloths. At the side of the course taken by the procession many oak trees—otherwise called *rovere* [1]—and other kinds of trees were planted in such numbers that it would have sufficed if they had had all

---

1. A very hard kind of wood (*lat.* Robur).

CASOLA PAYS HIS PASSAGE MONEY 153

the woods of Bachano[1] over the doors. And another magnificent thing; beside the said trees many large candlesticks of every kind stood, which contained lighted *doppieri*. Thus the procession returned to St. Mark's Church.

When the Sacrament of the body of Christ had been restored to its place, the Doge was accompanied by every man to the palace, where he placed himself at the head of the staircase until all the gentlemen had mounted with the pilgrims; and then, saluting all the company, he went into the palace to his own apartments, and each one returned to his own house or hostel, for it was dinner time.

On Friday, which was the 30th of May, as I was assured that the Magnificent Captain of the galley did not intend to depart for four days, I employed the time in visiting the sights of Venice until the following Sunday, which was the 1st of June. I still hoped that some Lombard would arrive with whom I could join for the living on the galley, but no one appeared. I had the benefit of the advice of a certain Don Giovanni Toretino, a merchant of Lucca, settled, however, in Venice, who, by reason of the letters of Don Jacobo Rotuli, of Fra Ghiringhelo, and of Don Francesco di Roma, had received me into his house, and treated me very hospitably.

On Monday, the 2nd of the month of June, I went with the aforenamed Don Giovanni to see Don Agostino Contarini, *Patrono* of the pilgrim galley, and, although I had previously arranged to pay him forty-five ducats, I gave up that bargain, and agreed to pay sixty gold ducats of the Mint of Venice. For this he undertook to keep me by sea and by land and take me as far as the

---

1. The forest of Baccano, 27 kilometres north-west from Rome, served in the middle ages as an asylum for numerous bands of brigands.

River Jordan if I wished to go there, and give me a place at his own table. I paid down, then and there, thirty ducats in advance.

On Tuesday, the 3rd of June, I bought a chest and a mattress and sent them and also my other things aboard the galley, which was being loaded for the departure. That evening, out of regard for me, the aforementioned Don Giovanni invited the Venerable Don Frate Francesco Trivulzio to supper, and I did the cooking Milanese fashion, especially a pasty.

CHAPTER V.

Casola and the other Pilgrims go on Board the Jaffa Galley.—Description of the Galley.—The Officers and Crew.—The Number of Pilgrims.— First Day at Sea.—Parenzo.—The Cathedral.— Absenteeism of the Clergy. — The Franciscan Monastery.—Church of St. Nicholas.—Voyage to Zara—Cathedral.—Franciscan Monastery.—Church of St. Simeon.— Relic of that Saint.—Sermon Preached in the Cathedral at Zara by Fra. F. Trivulzio.—Departure from Zara.

ON Wednesday, the 4th of June, at sunset, having taken leave first of the Magnificent Don Tadiolo Vicomercato, the ducal Ambassador, and also of the other friends, I entered a boat in the company of the aforesaid Fra Francesco and certain other pilgrims and non-pilgrims to go to the galley. This had gone outside the port to a place called "Above the Two Castles,"[1] five miles distant from Venice they say, and there we went on board the galley, which was called the Jaffa Galley.

Outside it has the shape of the other Venetian galleys. It is eighty *braccia*[2] long, and where it is widest it is only twenty *braccia*. There is a platform all round outside, projecting from the body of the galley, more than a *braccio* wide, which is supported by numerous brackets attached to the body of the galley. On this platform many bales of merchandise and also many barrels and

---
1. Beyond the two Castles of Sant' Andrea and San Nicoletto at the entrance to the Lido Channel.
2. The Venetian *Braccio* (for measuring wool) = ·683396 metres.
,, ,, (for measuring silk) = ·638721 ,,
The Milanese ,, ... = ·594936 ,,

casks of wine are packed. Towards the bottom the galley is almost round, and diminishes from the middle downwards. From the middle, where it begins to diminish downwards, three out of the four parts are full of sand and gravel in order that the galley may draw enough water and stand firm, and in the sand many barrels and casks of wine were stored for the majority of the pilgrims.

Over the said sand there was a floor of boards which could be taken up if necessary, and on the said floor there was built a kind of hall almost sixty *braccia* long, which stretched from the mizzen mast to the prow. The ceiling of this hall, between one extremity and the other, was supported by strong columns, and it formed the deck of the galley. The said deck was made of strong planks and well tarred, so that the rainwater and the seawater could not penetrate into the room below.

The fourth part of the galley—that is, from the mizzen mast backwards—was divided, first, into a place called the poop, which has three divisions. The lower is called the *pizolo*—a place conceded to distinguished men for sleeping, and also reserved for the storage of munition and of merchandise belonging to the captain and others at the discretion of the captain. In the middle region, which is called the poop proper, the tables are spread for meals, and there is also a small altar where Dry Mass *(Note 51)* was said for the captain; and at night many mattresses were spread here for sleeping, according to the distribution of the places amongst the pilgrims or other passengers. Many weapons, too, are attached to the roof of the said place—crossbows, bows, swords and other kinds of weapons—for the defence of the galley in case of need; and in that place all the tackle of the galley is made. Above the said poop proper there is a place called the Castle, where, for the most part, the captain lived, and also

DESCRIPTION OF THE "CONTARINA"

any great persons, if such there happened to be aboard. It is floored with tarred planks, so that however much it rains, no water can enter the poop. The navigating compass was kept in the castle, and on the voyage this castle was covered, first with canvas and then with a curtain of red cloth on which the ensign of the Sepulchre and also the arms of the Contarini family were embroidered.

Behind the aforesaid castle a place is arranged for managing the rudder of the galley, which is moved by the force of men's arms alone. Several times, when there was a great storm at sea, more than two men were needed to manage it, and it is moved by means of a thick rope. Further behind, there was a place where two terra-cotta vessels full of water were kept, and also a place necessary for purging the body: and these all projected outside the body of the galley, on timbers well tarred and well joined together. I cannot well describe the great size and weight of that rudder, but I may say that when we were in the port of Rhodes and it was in need of repair, several men were required to drag it ashore, and it was a grand instrument to look at.

About ten *braccia* outside the poop there was a fixed mast—that is, one which is never moved—about as large as could be embraced by a tall man; the sail-yard was fixed to it with the sail called the *Mezzana*,[1] and there were cords on both sides which were always pulled on the side away from the sail according to the direction of the wind. After passing the said mast, on the right side, there was the captain's canteen, where not only water, but every kind of wine was kept; and in that same place there was a store of cheese and sausages of every kind—that is, of meat and also of fish.[2] Opposite the door of the said

1. The mizzen sail.
2. Fish sausages are still made in Milan.

canteen there was the kitchen, called the *Foghone*,[1] which extended towards the side of the galley and contained many utensils and necessaries for cooking. There were numbers of large and small cauldrons, frying-pans and soup-pots—not only of copper, but also of earthenware—spits for roasting and other kitchen utensils. Further along that side there were two places, one over the other, where the live animals were kept which were killed in case of need when fresh meat could not be obtained on land. They were fed on barley, but very sparingly, so that at the end of the voyage there was more skin than flesh. From here to the end of the galley many benches were fixed, called *balestriere*,[2] and between one bench and another there was space for two oars which after all were very little used.

After passing down the centre of the galley, going towards the prow, there was a large mast fixed, which in its lower part could only be embraced by three men, and it reached to the bottom of the galley. I was told by the master who had bought it, that it was more than sixty *braccia* long. There was a cage at the top, and below the cage the yards, made in three pieces, hung down. A great sail called the *artimone*,[3] made entirely of white canvas, was usually hoisted there. Many cords hung from the said mast, and on each side there were twelve ropes fastened to the side of the galley which were drawn on the side opposite the sail according to the weather and the winds. The said mast had also another very long rope hanging down, and still another, called the *angel*, that was often used to hoist something up to the top of the mast. There was another sail called the *cochina*. The

---

1. *i.e.*, The "big fire."
2. Strictly speaking the "Balestriere" were openings in the bulwarks—between the benches at which the Galleotti sat to row—for the "Balestre" or crossbows.
3. The main sail.

DESCRIPTION OF THE "CONTARINA"

artimone and the *mezzana* were pointed; this was square, and was only used in a great storm. At the head of the galley—that is, at the prow—there was a small mast with a square sail; it was called the *trinchetto*,[1] and was often hoisted and often taken down.

On the said galley there were so many heavy cables called *gomene* used for various purposes, and also others of medium thickness, that they were worth a thousand ducats, according to what I was told. I could easily believe it, because when I was talking to the captain he told me that he had paid a hundred and fifty ducats for one cable alone for casting the anchor into the sea, and he had two others. It was enormously thick and six hundred and twenty-five feet[2] long. I doubt whether two Milanese waggons with two pair of oxen to each waggon could have carried all the ropes there were on the said galley.

On the left side of the said galley, beginning at the poop and proceeding towards the prow—on deck I mean—there was no other impediment except the benches called *balestriere* with the oars as I said above—and this as far as the prow.

On the deck of the said galley, beginning at the poop, as far as the main mast of the galley, there were a row of large cases *(Note 52)* down the centre, each of which was two *braccia* wide, over two *braccia* long and two *braccia* high, and all were tarred outside so that the water might not damage them. They were so well arranged one after the other that they made a raised platform down the centre of the galley called the *corsia*. There were other similar cases from the said mast as far as the prow; but these last were always covered with the heavy cables

---

1. The fore sail.
2. A Venetian foot = ·347735 metres.

for casting the anchors. Around the said mast some of the cases were disposed so as to form a small platform called the *extimaria;* and there, the officers appointed for that purpose administered justice to the *galeotti.*

There were six anchors on the said galley, and the lightest weighed one thousand two hundred pounds. For the defence of the said galley there were thirty-six pieces of artillery and good provision for them—that is, powder and stones. There were also many stones amongst the munition above and below deck.

On the said galley there was the aforenamed Magnificent Don Agostino Contarini, a Venetian patrician, the principal *Patrono,* who had four young men to serve him. There were with him two Venetian gentlemen,[1] assigned to him by the Signoria *(Note 53);* but Don Agostino gave them so much a month and maintained them at his own table. The said captain had an officer called the *comito,* who, after the captain, was obeyed by all, in what concerned the government of the galley. There was another officer called the *parono,* who looked after the provisionment of the galley, and was usually the first to leave the galley when anything had to be done. Then there were other eight companions,[2] to whom more than to the others the management of the galley was entrusted; and these, together with several others, were called *balestrieri (Note 54).* Finally, there were many other men called *galeotti,* and altogether for the management and defence of the galley there were a hundred and forty persons. Amongst these were men of every existing trade and craft, and when the sea was not stormy they followed their trades. The majority of them, and especially

---

1. These were apprentices to the sea. Each galley was obliged by law to take a certain number in proportion to its size.
2. *i.e.*, The Patrician Balestrieri—as distinguished from their non-noble fellow crossbow-men.

of the experienced sailors, were Sclavonians and Albanians; there were also a few Lombards, but not many. There was not a single man of them who had not some kind of merchandise on the galley, according to the terms of the agreement made when they were engaged; and when the galley entered a port they took the said merchandise ashore and established a sort of fair. There were more than three thousand pieces of cloth alone on board, and so much other merchandise besides, that, unless he saw it, no man could believe that the galley was capable of carrying so much cargo in addition to the passengers and crew. Nor without seeing them could anyone believe that the *galeotti* were so obedient as they were, for at a whistle from the *comito* all the men raised their heads and asked, "What's your will?" There were three trumpets and good trumpeters, and besides the aforesaid persons there were one hundred and seventy pilgrims, counting men and women,[1] friars, priests and hermits, Ultramontanes and Italians; and all had places assigned for their chests on which they slept if there was room enough. Much more might be said about the said galley, but I will leave something for another time and return to when I went on board the galley for the first time.

The greater number of us, both pilgrims and also the friends who accompanied us, were already upset by the sea, and I more so than the others because I had never been to sea before. I was therefore obliged to make up my mind to go and take possession immediately of the place assigned to me below deck; and God willed that I should find myself neighbour to a Lombard, called Bernardino Scotto *(Note 55)*, who, although we were not otherwise intimate, was nevertheless a good neighbour to

---

1. The Germans, Bemmelberg and Parsberg, who went on the same pilgrimage, mention that amongst the company there were "24 monks and 20 women." *Deutsche Pilgerreisen*, Rohricht, p. 183.

L

me. Behind us, so they said, was the place of the magnificent captain.

On Thursday, the 5th of June, having passed through my share of the tribulation due to the sea, I went on deck at the second hour of the day, leaving my companions below; and I stood to watch the spreading of all the sails of the galley to the sound of the trumpets and the chanting of several friars and other pilgrims. It was a very interesting sight, especially for a person who had never seen the like. At first we had a favourable wind, so that at the eighteenth hour the mariners said we had made as much as sixty miles going towards the city of Parenzo. This particular part of the sea is called the Gulf of Trieste. After the said hour, however, there was a calm at sea which so fixed the galley that it remained quite still until night. Then a slight wind sprang up accompanied by rain, and the mariners, thinking it might favour us, spread all three sails, hoping to reach Parenzo at least by the morning. But they were disappointed, for the wind changed, and there was nothing to do but await a change in the weather, and meanwhile let the galley go as it would, thus drifting out of the path and drawing nearer the coast.

On Friday, the 6th of June, at the sixteenth hour, we arrived opposite Parenzo *(Note 56)*, and had it not been necessary to procure a supply of mutton for the galley the captain would have passed by without stopping. However, he made the port, but he refused to allow any of the pilgrims to go on land; nevertheless, yielding at last to the entreaties of many, especially of the preacher, Father Francesco Trivulzio, he gave them license for an hour. Those who wanted to go had to hire the boats from the fishermen and pay them well. In order to see as much as possible I joined the aforesaid preacher very gladly, because in truth he was treated with great respect, and everything was shown to him without much difficulty. I did the same all the voyage as long as he was well, and his Reverence also liked to have my company. Thus we entered the city of Parenzo, situated in Istria, which they say is a hundred miles from Venice.

It is an ancient city; it appears to me to be a citadel situated in the plain, which has been re-built. I do not know to what I can compare it for size; if I say to the city of Corbetta [1] it is too little, if I say Abbiategrasso [2] it is too much; it is collected there what little there is.

We went to the Cathedral. It is an ancient church, and I think it must have been very beautiful, judging by the mosaics of the tribune and by the pavement which shows some signs still of having been worked in mosaic. Now, owing I think to the absenteeism of the pastors, the church has a neglected appearance. Amongst others, I saw one thing which showed me that there are very honest people in that city—more so than at home—for in the choir of the said church there was not a stall (it is true there were not many of them) which had not the surplice of a priest thrown over the back. I asked who they belonged to, and was told they belonged to the Canons. I am certain that if I left one of mine at our Cathedral or at the Church of St. Ambrose I should find either two or none when I got back. The said church has a little atrium in front, as the churches at Rome have and also our Saint Ambrose—and the baptistery is at the end. I think few persons go there because everywhere the grass is long.

Amongst others, I saw the Convent of St. Francis.

---

1. *Corbetta*, a small place 18 kilometres west of Milan, near the road to Magenta and Novara.
2. *Abbiategrasso*, on the Ticino, south of Magenta, and south-west of Milan. It was famous for the Castle of Filippo Maria Visconti, Duke of Milan.

It is a miserable place; I did not see a single friar there. Suffice it to say that the aforesaid Don Frate Francesco said it would be better if there were none. From what I could see, hear and also taste, the said city has red wines which are good and pleasant to look at; there seems to be a dearth of all other victuals except mutton.

We went to visit a church dedicated to Saint Nicholas, built on a rock in the sea opposite the said city. It is very beautiful, and was built with the offerings of sailors, to whom it is a great object of devotion. It is administered by two monks and two lay brothers of the Order of the Observants of Saint Benedict, who have a beautiful olive grove on the said rock, said to be their only source of income. The said city is subject to the Signoria of Venice.

We stayed there until the twenty-second hour, and then, notwithstanding that the sea had calmed down, all the sails were spread and turned, now to this side, now to that, to catch the different winds that sprang up—now *bonanza*,[1] now *provenza*,[2] now *garbino*,[3] now *scirocco*.[4] And thus we went, turning now to the right and now to the left through the sea called the Sino Fanatico, and passed many towns and villages on both sides. Anciently the people of these parts were called Liburnians. Continuing thus as I said, we came to a certain gulf called the Quarnero,[5] very difficult to navigate.

As we had not a favourable wind that night or on Saturday, the 7th of June, we did not make much progress, in spite of the efforts made to hasten, now with the sails and now with the oars, though not much with the oars because they were of little use with that galley.[6] All on

---

1. A calm at sea.
2. West wind.
3. South-west wind, otherwise called Libeccio or Africano.
4. South-east wind.
5. *i.e.*, The Gulf of Fiume.
6. There were only two oars to each bench. If, as seems probable, the galley was a Trireme, it would have had three oars to each bench, when it was of more importance to increase speed than to keep down expenses.

board were anxious to reach Zara, and as many of us were new to the sea it was more disagreeable to us than even to the sailors.

On Sunday, the 8th of June, by the grace of God, we arrived at Zara *(Note 57)*, the right name of which is Jadra, at the ninth hour of the day. As many small boats came alongside we all landed with great joy, and went to hear Mass and afterwards to dinner. And as the captain had landed to furnish the galley with certain things, I set about seeing the said city, having nothing else to do. It is in a plain, and not very large, but it is bright and clean, and has some beautiful buildings. It has no moat round it nor any drawbridges; but it is surrounded by fine high walls. There is a castle at one angle which has very much the appearance of a fortress as far as can be seen. All the city is paved with little hard pebbles in such a way that many of our Milanese (I mean those who have gouty feet) could not walk about there very comfortably. I did not see a single fine palace, but only humble houses, and as I said fine walls. There is a small square piazza before the place where the Governors sent by the Signoria administer justice;[1] I did not see any other piazza.

I went to the Cathedral of the city, which is dedicated to Saint Anastasia. The body of the church is very fine. The centre is high and in the shape of a galley, and there is a long, round, vaulted roof made of wood on which the Old Testament story has been painted by good masters. There is a choir well adorned with stalls after our fashion; they are beautiful, and rightly so, for it is the archiepiscopal church. There are no vaulted chapels in the body of the church, but there are altars at the sides, well

---

1. The Count or Governor of Zara, in 1494, was Ser Paolo Erizzo, son of the late Ser Antonio. The captain was Ser Michael Salomono. See "Segretario alle Voci," Reg. vi.

adorned with altar pieces—*majestate* [1] as we call them—in relief and well gilded. Over the choir, high up between one wall and the other, besides the crucifix, which is in the middle and very ornate, there is a beam which supports fourteen very large figures all covered with gold; they are beautiful and very natural.

I saw the Franciscan Monastery belonging to the Observant friars; it is very beautiful, and so also is the church. Being in the city, the friars have not a large garden in which to take their recreation as they have in many other places.

I went with the other pilgrims according to arrangement to the Church of Saint Simeon, where after Vespers were sung the body of Saint Simeon was shown—a very remarkable relic—certainly the most beautiful I ever saw, either at Rome or elsewhere. The body is perfectly preserved, there is nothing in the world lacking, either in the face or in the hands or in the feet. The mouth is open, and in the upper jaw there are no teeth; I was not surprised at that, because he was very old when he died. He it was to whom the Holy Spirit declared that he should not see death until he had seen the Son of God, and he it was who took our Lord Jesus Christ in his arms when he was presented in the Temple by our Lady, and who said: "Nunc dimittis servum tuum Domine, secundum verbum tuum in pace, etc." [2] I went several times to see the relic because there was a great crowd of pilgrims and also of people belonging to the city and country round who came there because it was a holiday. And the more I looked the more it seemed to me a stupendous thing, most of all when I remembered the time of his death which could not be less than one thousand four hundred and ninety-

---

1. See Note, p. 173.
2. "Lord now lettest Thou Thy servant depart in peace according to Thy word."—Luke, ii. 29.

three years ago. The body was very carefully guarded; the Governors of the city—Venetians as I said—keep the keys. The church is very beautiful. In the choir there are as many as ten very handsome stalls. The choir is only finished in one part. I calculated that they will finish the rest in time because what is already finished is new. High above the place where the said most holy relic is kept there is an arch, all of silver-gilt, on which the presentation of Christ in the Temple is sculptured. In the middle of the said arch there is an inscription in Latin which records how a Queen of Hungary caused it to be made. The pilgrims offered many oblations there, and touched the said relic with rosaries, rings, etc.

In the said city there is a good abbey belonging to the Order of Saint Benedict, dedicated to Saint Chrysogonus the Martyr. It is held in commendam and goes like the others. There are also several other churches in the same circumstances.

On Monday, the 9th of June, I heard Mass and also the sermon preached by the above-mentioned Don Fra Francesco in the Cathedral. It was very beautiful— concerning the conversion of sinners. He took for his text "Gaudium Magnum erit, etc." [1]

After dinner the order was given to the pilgrims by a trumpeter, who went throughout the city sounding and saying that every man must return to the galley, because a wind called *scirocco*—which had kept us all the preceding night and up to the eighteenth hour of the above-named day—had dropped. When all had come aboard, the galley sailed away at the nineteenth hour. It is said to be over three hundred miles from Zara to Venice.

---

1. "Great joy shall be in heaven over one sinner that repenteth."—Luke, xv. 7.

CHAPTER VI.

Voyage continued among the Rocks of Sclavonia.—Pilot runs the Galley on to a Sandbank.—Alarm on Board but no Damage done.—Island of Lissa.—Trau. — Spalato. — Lesina. — Curzola. — Melita. — Arrival at Ragusa.—Description of that City.—The Cathedral.—The Patron Saint Blaise.—Franciscan Convent and Church.—Dominican and Benedictine houses.—Palace of the Governor.—The Arsenal.—Water Supply of the City.—Fortifications.—Productions.—The People and Customs.—The Government.—Sermon Preached by Fra. F. Trivulzio in the Cathedral.—The Galley leaves Ragusa.

AFTER navigating slowly, with only a little *garbino*,[1] it was found that—amongst those rocks of Sclavonia, which are numberless and very arid and stony—we had gone seventy miles from Zara up to the following Tuesday, which was the 10th of June. Then the sea—or one might rather say among those rocks, the canal, because it did not appear to me wider than the River Po in Lombardy—settled into a calm.

On Tuesday, at the third hour of the day, the *scirocco*[2] rose again, and drove the galley backwards. All the sails were hauled down, and the anchors had to be cast, to the great perturbation of the captain, who wished as much as the pilgrims did to continue the voyage. Thus we remained until Wednesday morning.

---

1. The south-west wind—otherwise called Libeccio or Africano.
2. The south-east wind.

On Wednesday, the 11th of June, at sunrise, he ordered the sails to be spread, as he thought that a favourable wind had arisen; but the weather suddenly changed, and all the sails being again furled he ordered the anchors to be cast once more. It was found that only one mile had been made all that morning, and the captain and also his councillors thought of returning to Zara because the bread began to run short, and already it was necessary to begin on the biscuits; and although there is a dwelling here and there amongst those rocks, nevertheless there is no bread to be had; nothing in fact but a little mutton and also a few goats. Further, seeing that he could not proceed on the voyage because the adverse wind continued, the captain thought it would cost less to turn back and put into Zara, for there was no other place in which he could take refuge. We were very near the city of Sebenico, but he could not go there because the galley was so large, as I said, that it could not be propelled by the oars. So we remained thus with great inconvenience to the pilgrims, great loss for the captain, who had all the expense and could not proceed on the voyage, and extreme fatigue for the *galeotti*, who had to spread the sails and furl them so often and throw the anchors and heave them again. It excited one's compassion to see so much weary work, hardly to be believed by one who has not seen it; nevertheless things remained thus.

On Thursday, the 12th of June, at sunrise or shortly after, a favourable wind arose. The main sail and also the mizzen sail were spread, and, thanking God with words and also with the sound of the trumpets, we set out on our journey, passing still among those rocks of Sebenico in Sclavonia.

At dinner time when the greater part of the pilgrims were at table, some above and some below, there was a great uproar on board the galley. All the sails were lowered at once, and it seemed as if we were about to founder. Everybody was terribly alarmed, and no one understood what had really happened save the sailors; nevertheless those who understood and those who did not, left their dinner. Those who were below deck, as they did not understand what had occurred, had no further fear. I was amongst those who were afraid, because I was at the captain's table with others assigned to the same table, and the peril was only realised by those above. It was of such a nature that we thought we should all be drowned. This is what had happened. It is the rule for this galley to take a guide—a person with much experience of the sea—who begins at Venice and goes as far as Parenzo. At Parenzo, another is taken as far as Modone. At Modone another is taken as far as Jaffa. It appears that the guide or pilot, as they call him, taken at Parenzo had lost his way among those Dalmatian rocks, and had allowed the galley to drift on to a shallow, so that the helm bounced three times out of the helmsman's hand, and it was thought that a hole had been made in the bottom of the galley. But God had mercy on the many souls who were on the said galley, and especially on so many religious of all kinds as there were aboard; and on examination it was found that whereas it had been thought that the ship had struck on a rock, it had only touched mud or sand. Thus we passed the danger, and although we were in great peril, no damage was done.

When the mariners breathed freely again they put up the sails once more, as we had the wind in our favour, and thus pursuing the way, we passed many islands on our right hand, amongst which was the island called the island of Sant' Andrea, barren and uninhabited. After this came the island of Lissa, which is fertile and excellently supplied with good wines and other fruit, and has also a great trade in sardines. I think they are those fish they sometimes sell for anchovies to those who do not know the difference. On the left side of our course after leaving Sebenico we passed the city of Trau, and also the city of Spalato, as it is called, which is a very flourishing city; and all are subject to the Signoria of the Venetians. At length, by the grace of God, at the third hour of the night, we arrived at the city of Lesina, otherwise called Fara *(Note 95)*. As it was night the pilgrims were not allowed to land, nor were the requests of the *galeotti*—who wanted some provision for the galley —granted. Nothing was taken on board but a little water.

On Friday, the 13th of June, we left the canal of Lesina after sunrise and made sail with a very slight wind; but as the day advanced the wind improved and we came opposite the citadel of Curzola *(Note 58)*, which is beautiful to look at from the outside. The captain did not wish to stop there for fear of losing the favourable wind, and thus we passed by, and could only admire the place from the outside; it is said to be sixty miles from Lesina. The captain related that a few years ago King Ferdinand, the former King of Naples, sent his fleet there to try and steal it from the Venetians, but he failed completely because the people of Curzola were valiant, and defended themselves from that attack without additional help from the Signoria of Venice, to whom they are subject.

On the morning of Saturday, the 14th of June, we found ourselves opposite an island of the Ragusans, on the right hand, called Melita, having passed the other islands of Curzola during the preceding night. On the left hand, on the mountains also belonging to the Ragusans, there was a very large place called Stagno, they said. From the galley nothing could be seen save the top of one belltower, on account of the various mountains. The aforesaid captain, whom I often questioned as to the things we saw, told me that the said place was as large as Ragusa, but not so populous. Salt is made there, and they said that the Ragusans gain every year over forty thousand ducats from the salt, besides the salt they use themselves; it is beautiful and white.

Thus pursuing our course with a good wind we came to Ragusa *(Note 59)*, a city of Dalmatia, at the twentieth hour, and entered the port with a great display of banners and signals from the mortars and trumpets. Many Ragusans flocked on to the quay of the port, and many boats came to the galley to take off the pilgrims and also the *galeotti*, who carried away their merchandise to do their business as they desired in the market of Ragusa. All the pilgrims went ashore, especially those who were well enough to move; and with a great longing to refresh themselves, they entered the said city of Ragusa, in Dalmatia or Sclavonia.

For its size the city is beautiful in every respect. It is on the seashore, and has very strong walls, especially on the land side. The said walls are twenty-four feet [1] thick, so I was told. I measured them in several places, and they did not exceed twenty feet; perhaps that was due to the fact that the measure I used was larger than the others. There are many towers on the walls, and one at an angle towards the mainland is larger than the others. I climbed the said walls with the aforesaid Don Fra Francesco, who was accompanied by many friars of his

---

1. The Venetian foot equalled ·347735 metres. The Milanese foot equalled ·435185 metres. Casola, no doubt being a Milanese, used the Milanese measures.

Order. From that tower the plan of the said city can be seen very well. The said city appears to me to be triangular. On two sides it is washed by the sea; on the other, which is the land side, there is a high mountain. One street begins at the gate, which is entered from the port, and goes the length of the city to the gate where stands the Franciscan Convent; and on both sides of the said street there are shops of all kinds. The said city is flat in the centre, and all the rest seems to me to ascend. The houses are beautiful in appearance, and they are numerous and close together, so that nothing could be added.

The chief church, dedicated to Our Lady, is small for an archiepiscopal church. Nevertheless it is very beautiful, and more beautiful outside than inside. Outside it is built of stones white like marble, and there is a beautiful arcade—with beautiful little columns—by which one can walk all round the exterior of the church. One can go round inside as well, and even the women go there above the side naves of the said church. The choir of the said church is small, but it has a beautiful *majestà*,[1] after our fashion, with several figures in silver gilded over. I did not see any other handsome object in the said church. The patron saint of the Ragusans is Saint Blaise,[2] and I think he is greatly venerated because many of the said Ragusans and also many Sclavonians outside of Ragusa are called Blaise. The Ragusans have another church near the Cathedral and also near the piazza. For its size it is very ornate, and built of beautiful marble within and without.

---

1. *i.e.*, An altar-piece of wood or metal with figures of the saints, &c., in relief.
2. St. Blaise was Bishop of Sebaste in Cappadocia. He is the Patron Saint of Wool Combers, and of all who suffer from diseases of the throat, and also the patron saint of wild animals. He was martyred in 289. As the patron saint of Ragusa, he was represented in his episcopal robes on the coins of the city, holding in one hand a crosier, and in the other an iron comb such as wool combers use. See Mrs. Jameson, Sac. and Leg., Art ii. 696.

In the said city there is a Franciscan Convent. The friars live in good observance, and Frate Francesco Trivulzio lodged there with his companions. Considering it is in this city of Ragusa, it is, in my opinion, the most beautiful I have seen on this journey—I mean outside of Venice. It has a beautiful church. The altar has a *majestà* in silver gilt containing two rows of large figures with twelve figures in each row. In the upper row, in the centre, there is a God the Father; in the centre of the lower row there is Our Lady with her Son in her arms; and, as I said, everything is of silver. For greater ornament there are many jewels of every colour, and they are so large that I doubt strongly that they can be genuine, because if they were genuine, there would be a great treasure there, little guarded. I did not find anyone who could remove that doubt from my mind. On the left side of the said church there is a little chapel which was also a beautiful *majestà* with several figures in silver gilded over. The said church has a large and beautiful choir, and it has a beautiful sacristy very well furnished with certain relics covered with silver. Amongst other notable things, I saw five volumes of books which contain the Psalter; I think there are none more beautiful among Christian peoples.

The convent could not be improved. It has a beautiful cloister and a chapter house which contains three very ornate altars, and also refectories, dormitories, etc. Everything belonging to such a place is ornate. Amongst other things there are three gardens—each one higher than the other by at least eight steps—planted with oranges, pomegranates and other notable things; these gardens dominate all the buildings. Then all the friars are the most warm-hearted and hospitable I ever met, for, besides the affectionate attention they showed to the aforesaid Fra Francesco and his companions, they showed the same also to me; and I hear that they constantly offer hospitality, especially to foreigners and Italians.

The said city has a beautiful priory belonging to the observants of Saint Dominic. It has also several convents for women observants. Outside the city, on a rock in the sea, there is a monastery of the Order of Saint Benedict, belonging to the congregation of Santa Justina. Certainly it is a place adapted for monks, and full of every charm—they are remote from all society, they are surrounded by the sea, and they have beautiful gardens. If the building is finished as it has been begun it will be a most beautiful place; the work is continually going on there.

For its size the said city has a beautiful palace constantly inhabited by the Governor, called the Captain. Inside, amongst other things, there is a beautiful hall, built in the likeness of the hall at Venice, where the Venetian gentlemen hold their Great Council, and with similar benches. It is true that the seats are not gilded, as they are at Venice, for seating the Great Council; the ceiling, however, is adorned with gold and fine blue. Then there is a certain very ornate hall, where the aforesaid Governor holds audience together with the ten wise men. In the said palace there is an armoury, where, among other things, they showed a certain quantity of arms sent as a present by the Most Illustrious Lord the Duke of Milan.[1] The said Ragusans have, moreover, like the Venetian gentlemen, a place built towards the port, which they call the Arsenal, where they also construct galleys and sailing ships. At that time there were four there partly finished and partly unfinished.

---

1. Probably the present was sent during the war between Venice and Ferrara, 1482-84, when Milan took the side of the latter against the Venetian Republic.

The Ragusans have an aqueduct of fresh water which comes from a long distance, and by means of that aqueduct they turn nine mills in various places outside the city; then entering the city it supplies many places, especially two where there are two public fountains—one which has many mouths at the gate of the Franciscan Convent, and the other near the piazza, also with several mouths. The people flock there to draw the water. The said aqueduct also supplies the Franciscan friars. In the said city there are many cisterns for collecting the rain water which is better for drinking purposes than the water of the said aqueduct.

On the land side the Ragusans have a great many beautiful gardens, in which they have very ornate houses, and they go there for amusement. They have a quantity of vines, and they make good malmseys and many other wines, according to the locality.

They have a castle outside the city on a certain small hill near the sea. I do not know what use it could be to them, nor do I understand how it could receive succour from the city if by misfortune it were taken by assault. When I asked a Ragusan what good it would be to the city if an army were there and no succour could be given, he said that help could be given from a certain tower in the city by means of a cord. It appeared to me a very absurd answer, and I gave the matter up. I will only add that they change the Governor of the castle every day, not by the popular voice but solely at the will of the Governor for the time being. A guard is also posted on a hill which dominates the city on the land side.

From what I could hear they do not produce enough grain for their needs, and they import what is lacking from Apulia. As I said, they make good red wines and excellent malmseys; they say they are better than those of Candia, but I have not been able to pronounce this judgment. The Ragusans produce a great quantity of wax, and also much fruit. Owing to the poverty of the country round, the peasants flock to the city on Saturdays and Sundays, and with what they bring earn a few *bagattini*.[1] I think that the concourse of people on this occasion was also due to the arrival of the galley full of pilgrims who bought a quantity of things, especially for eating and drinking. Nevertheless I could not see or taste good bread. The bread appears to me to be unleavened, made without raising material such as we use.

The men of this city are generally handsome, and the younger they are the taller they seem to be; all, both old and young, and even the boys, wear togas in the Venetian fashion. There were crowds of them. Perhaps they made a special effort to show themselves to so many foreigners while the galley was there. In truth, they are very polite and pleasant to foreigners, at least in words. As far as I could judge from seeing their churches, they are very devout, and they give large subsidies to the monks, especially to the observants and amongst the observants, especially to the Franciscan friars.

They are content with their Government or Signoria. This seems natural to me, because they are free, and do not pay tribute to other than the Turk. It is twenty thousand ducats, and before the end of the year it becomes twenty-five thousand, and this is every year—in truth, they are near neighbours. Every year also they send a present of five hundred ducats to the King of Hungary, by whom they are protected. I could not discover that they have any other charges at present. They are occupied in building a port, which they intend to fortify,

---

1. The "Bagattino," otherwise called the "danaro" or "piccolo," was a small piece of copper money, first coined in Venice, according to Sanudo, in 1282. Its value depended on that of the "Soldo," of which it was a twelfth part. Twenty Soldi formed a Lira.

M

and in enlarging the moat of the said city on the land side. It will be a beautiful fortress when it is finished.

The women of Ragusa look very strange, because for the most part they wear a strange dress. I do not know how to describe it, but I can assure you that their dress is more than decent. For not only do they wear their dresses very high and cover themselves to the neck, but they have a certain thing which looks like the tail of a fat ram, which goes in front right under the chin and well over the hair behind. Considering the importance of the city, I saw, specially on the holiday, some beautiful women, though not many, but those I saw were very beautiful and well adorned with jewels. They were dressed in the fashion aforesaid and resplendent with gold and silver and pearls. They are pleased to be looked at even by foreigners; they go about, however, with the greatest modesty out of doors. From what I could hear they are not very fond of work or of gaining their living.

In truth, when I heard of the customs of the Ragusans, they all pleased me, except this, that not a man can keep wine in his house even though it is produced on his own property. When they want some, they must send for it to the tavern; and their women and servants, if they want it, must secretly do the same, and on that account also they are more lukewarm about working. Probably the Ragusans maintain this custom for some reason I could not divine, and perhaps if this custom were observed at Milan there would be fewer gouty people than there are there, both men and women.

The Signoria or free government of the Ragusans is administered thus:—Every month they nominate a Governor, who lives in the palace, like the Doge at Venice. He does not go out of the palace during the said month save for urgent reasons; if, however, he is obliged to do so, he goes with eight pairs of pages before him and the other officials behind. There are ten Councillors who are always present when the aforesaid Governor holds audience, and what is decreed by the said ten is law. These ten hold office two years, and they have a secretary who writes down everything pertaining to the State; he is a Cremonese by birth, and enjoys great credit. It is a pleasing thing.

On Sunday, the 15th of June, I landed with the magnificent captain (because even if we were in port I always returned to sleep on the galley), and accompanied him first to hear Mass in the Church of St. Francis. After Mass I went a short walk outside the city, and then I turned back to go on board the galley, but finding a great company I left them and went to the Cathedral Church to hear the sermon already begun by the Venerable Don Fra Francesco, who gave great satisfaction to the people by preaching that sermon, and they showed him so in fact by sending him a great quantity of presents. The sermon was very useful to those who understood it, because they are Sclavonians and I do not think that all understood the language. They know Latin well, but I do not think the women understood much; nevertheless the church was full. He took his subject from the Gospel of the day according to the use of the Court of Rome, which mentions how Jesus Christ entered the ship of Simon and prayed him " Ut reduceret eum a terra pusillum." [1] There he compared our faith and life to a ship, and spoke of what was needed in a ship, referring always to our galley, and he concluded by saying that whoever wished to be saved must enter with Christ in this ship. It was a beautiful discourse. I took away my part of it, for, amongst other things, he explained the reason why in the

---

1. "That he would thrust out a little from the land."—Luke, v. 3.

seven canonical hours, at the first hour and at compline, the shorter creed is said softly, and at the Mass it is said aloud—and many other noteworthy things. When the sermon was over I went with him to the Franciscan Convent, and there I stayed with his companions to dinner; then I went back to the galley to write some letters home.

On Monday, the 16th of June, I said Mass in the sacristy of the said Franciscan Convent out of consideration for the aforesaid Don Fra Francesco, who felt rather fatigued. After the Mass—while the magnificent captain sent the trumpet round to give notice to the pilgrims and *galeotti* that after dinner everyone must return to the galley because he intended to set sail—I dined at the Franciscan Convent with the companions of the preacher. The dinner was very well prepared and with great hospitality by the friars. After dinner, with the permission of the aforesaid preacher, I entered a boat together with his companions and went to the Monastery of Santa Maria, belonging to the Order of Saint Benedict, which is built on a rock, as described above. On the way back I stopped at the galley, and his companions went to fetch the preacher and certain other friars who wished to come to Jerusalem. When every man had entered the galley we set sail at the seventeenth hour with little wind.

CHAPTER VII.

Great Storm which Drives the Galley near the Coast of Apulia, and back towards Ragusa.—Voyage to Corfu.—Casola meets there Andrea Lanza, who shows him about the City.—Description of Corfu. —Cochineal and other Products.—Additional Passengers go on Board the Galley.—Amongst others a Spanish Prince, and Edward de Camardino, a Knight of the Order of St. John.—Departure from Corfu.—Vigil of St. John Baptist.— Sermon from Fra. F. Trivulzio.—Illuminations.— St. John's Day.—Fra. Francesco finishes his Sermon. — Zante.—Galley reaches Modone.—Silk Industry there.—Franciscan Friary.—Wines, &c., of Modone.—Government.

On Tuesday, the 17th of June, we found ourselves only twenty miles from Ragusa, and a terrible *scirocco* began to rise, very unfavourable for our journey. Nevertheless the captain wished to follow the course against the will of the winds, and was thereupon carried towards Apulia, at least two hundred miles out of the course, in a raging sea. The storm continued until night, and increased.

On Wednesday, the 18th of June, the storm began to show all its grandeur, and so upset, first the pilgrims who were not used to the sea, and also many of the experienced sailors, that it was pitiful to see them. On this occasion great restitutions were made, both of what had been well taken, as well as of what had been ill taken, and without any intermission. There was also one of the number who during his life had preached restitution hundreds of times, and yet this time he did not want to follow his own precept—that is, the venerable preacher. I was exempt that time also, although I saw the restitutions made by the others; but I must confess that as this day was the vigil of the Saints Protasius and Gervasius, the first patrons of Milan, I fasted as well as the aforesaid preacher, and in the Moorish fashion *(Note 60);* I did not taste a thing in the world all that day, for I had neither stomach nor head for eating.

The storm constantly increased with great tossing of the sea up to the following night, and it had increased so much that owing to the great blows given by the sea, the water was beaten under the decks where the pilgrims lay, and the galley, twisted by the fury of the storm, made a noise so that it seemed as if she would break up. Such were the cries of the pilgrims below deck, because of the great mass of water which came through the hatches that, being inexperienced, I thought I had finished my voyage that time, nor did I expect to celebrate the feast of Saint Protasius then, nor on any other occasion. Many vows were made publicly and secretly by every man, including the sailors. And who would not have done and believed what I did and believed, hearing the creaking of the galley, and the water coming in during the night, and the great cries of men and women (of whom there were several belonging to various nations) who cried aloud for mercy? Although I did not cry out, nevertheless I stayed with my mind turned to God with all my might, for I believed surely, that I had done, what I had often talked publicly of doing and laughed at the idea—that is, chosen a fish for my sepulchre. The storm was very terrible, and the terror of those who had never been out on such a holiday was beyond all description. When I was talking with the captain about this calamity he told me that, although he had been to sea forty-two years, he had never experienced such a storm at this season, or one which lasted so long, and that where he thought to advance, relying on his past experiences, he only lost ground.

On Thursday, the 19th of June, the day of Saint Protasius, as the said weather continued, he turned back towards Ragusa, and sailed back again the two hundred miles from there to Apulia. He desired to make a port out of compassion for the pilgrims, who suffered greatly, and he wanted to make the port at a fortified place called Budua, near another called Antivari. But when the sails were already furled and the anchor prepared for casting, the weather suddenly changed—and this was indicated by certain small flags hung over the castle of the poop—and a most remarkable *provenza*[1] sprang up. So amidst the loud shouts of the mariners and others thanking God, all the sails were spread and we went on our way at a great rate. This feast of Saint Protasius was very sad for me and also for many others, both pilgrims and *galeotti*, we were so much shaken by the storm.

On Friday, the 20th of June, we sailed at the rate of over twelve miles an hour, and from what I heard we could have made over eighteen, but the captain ordered the mizzen sail and the fore sail, which were both spread, to be lowered. On the left hand we passed several fortified places subject to the Signoria of Venice, and entering the Adriatic Gulf we passed many cities of Albania. When we reached Corfu the officers of the galley and the captain calculated that after leaving Ragusa we had made over seven hundred miles; they said it was three hundred miles from Ragusa to Corfu.

On Saturday, the 21st of June, before sunrise, we arrived at Corfu *(Note 61)*, the capital of the island and

---

1. West or north-west wind.

the beginning of Greece. It was anciently called Corcyra, and is a city subject to the Signoria of Venice. We arrived there to the great joy of the pilgrims, who had suffered more than I can say from the storm above mentioned. It was necessary to provide the galley with fresh water, which already began to run short, and the company also hoped to get some good wines that would put the disordered stomachs in order.

The magnificent captain entered the port, giving license to the pilgrims until mid-day, and the greater part landed as they could, for there was a dearth of boats to carry the company ashore. For the most part the pilgrims were disappointed in their expectations, because there was no good wine to be found at the taverns, no good water, no fruit. The water had to be fetched from a place two miles away called the "Cardaro,"[1] and it was very hot there, and besides, on one side of the port, there is a large suburb, a good distance away, where the market is held on appointed days, and where there are all the inns and taverns; in truth, it was better to stay on board the galley—I mean for the majority.

Against my will I was very fortunate this time,[2] for when I left Milan the very Reverend Lord the present Bishop of Piacenza[3] gave me certain letters to present to a certain Andrea Lanza, whom I sought out in order to please the aforesaid Lord. I found he was the son of the Venerable Doctor Don Pietro Lanza, Archdeacon of the Cathedral of Corfu, and Vicar of the Archbishop of Corfu. When he had read the letters of the aforesaid Lord Bishop he gave me such a welcome as I did not merit, nor could he have done more, I think, had I been the aforesaid

---

1. Probably a corruption of the word "Caldaio," that is the boiler.
2. Probably Casola meant that he would willingly have avoided consigning the letter on account of the heat.
3. The Bishop of Piacenza then was Fabrizio Marliani, a Milanese who was transferred from the See of Tortona to that of Piacenza in 1476. He died at Milan, 1508, but his body was taken to Piacenza and buried in the Cathedral.—Porro.

Lord Bishop in person—so much good wine, fruit and other good things did he offer us. My good fortune was shared by another pilgrim, a native of Friuli, who happened to be with me when I presented the letters. And because the aforesaid Don Pietro Lanza is greatly esteemed by the Venetian gentlemen, many important undertakings, temporal as well as spiritual, are entrusted to him, and the said Andrea his son has also great undertakings in his hands, and he is a very experienced person.

After dinner he showed me the position of the city and also the customs. This city of Corfu is placed on a hill, and has a large suburb in the plain, as I said. It has two very strong castles, situated a bowshot one from the other, and the one which is furthest west is higher than the other. They are built on two rocks, the one loftier than the other; indeed, the whole city is built on the rock. There are few inhabitants in the said castles which dominate the city and the suburb very notably. They have a good store of provisions, especially of water, which is collected in large cisterns dug out of the rock. There is also a mill very cunningly contrived. I was told it can grind three Venetian *staia*[1] of grain every hour, and it is worked by two horses and three men. It is a beautiful contrivance to look at.

The buildings of the said city are very numerous, and so close together that the roof of one touches the roof of the next, and the sun does not give too much annoyance to the people. There is a dense population of men and women, both in the city and in the suburb; but for the most part they are of a low class, although there are some of gentle birth. The said city, together with the suburb, used to be like a small island. Now the Signoria has separated the city from the suburb by a very thick wall

---

1. A Venetian Staio=83·317200 litres; a Milanese Staio=18·279287 litres.

made of square blocks, and the said city will be an island by itself, and by means of a moat which is being constructed to strengthen the said city it will be possible to circumnavigate it, though not with large ships. The work is constantly going on under the direction of the aforesaid Don Pietro.

I went into the Cathedral, but I will not write more about it because I did not find anything there worthy of record, for there is no single vestige of a choir in the said church, nor sign of its being a collegiate church. In the said church, as I was told, the body of Saint Arsenius reposes under the altar. I saw two bells in a window; I think that must be the bell-tower, because there is no other. The archiepiscopal dwelling does not seem to me worthy of such dignity, nor even of the merits of the person who lives there—that is, of the aforesaid Don Pietro, the Vicar. The deficiencies must be attributed to the person who enjoys the revenues and does not provide what is necessary.

The streets of the said city are so very narrow and dark that, exploring them alone, as I did, I was afraid at first. The said city is governed by an official called the *Bailo*,[1] aided by two councillors and treasurers sent by the Signoria of Venice every three years. The Governors of the two castles are changed every sixteen months. From what I could hear, the men of the said city are very skilful sailors, and there are always a great many away at sea.

This city has an island a hundred miles long, and the said island produces grain, wines in perfection—such as malmsey—and every kind of fruit. The chief product is *grana*,[2] of which a great quantity is gathered—I mean for dyeing cloths, and while we were in port it was being

---

1. At the time of Casola's visit, the Bailo and Captain of Corfu was Ser. Alvise Venerio. The two councillors for the first half of 1494 were Ser. Alvise de Canali and Ser. Girolamo Diedo, who were superseded by Ser. Domenico Vallaresso and Ser. Quintino Tagliapietra. Segretario alle Voci, Register vi., Venice Archives.

2. Cochineal.

collected. The said *grana* is made with great care. I watched how they extract, first, the fine powder, then the second and the third, and how there then remains what is sold as *grana*. I wanted to understand how it is collected, what the plants are like, which are not higher than the *brugh (Note 62)* at home, what the leaves are like which resemble those of the oak, and by whom it is gathered— that is, by poor men. What is gathered looks like the grains of buckwheat at home. After it is carried with great care (for in a moment the sun would spoil it) by the women to the buyers, the first powder is extracted, et cetera, and each kind as I said, and without great care the said seeds would become worms. The said island produces cotton and silk, and there is also a great quantity of a seed called *valania*[1] used for tanning leather, and there is a great trade in that.

In the said city I saw a great many ugly faces, and also some pretty ones, as in Venice. As I had no more time because the trumpet was sounding and hurrying the pilgrims aboard, I did not learn any more about the said city, but I hoped on the return to see it better. And as all were being hastened on board the galley, the aforesaid Don Pietro, or rather his son Andrea, who had never left me, and who had shown me all he could, took a boat on his own account with certain slaves, and loaded it with much fruit and young geese—he wanted also to put in wine and oxen, but I would not let him—and he took me to the galley and bestowed the very generous present on the captain of the galley—for thus I wished. Then embracing me many times, he recommended me to the aforesaid captain, who promised to go to his house on our return.

Several additional passengers came on board, who had been waiting for the galley. Amongst these there was

1. Valania = nut gall.

one said to be a nephew of the King of Spain. He was very young and magnificent, and said that he also wished to come to Jerusalem and then return to Rhodes to take the habit of the Jerusalem friars, for he was expecting a very large and rich benefice in Spain. He had been in Naples, and King Alfonso had given him some horses and certain falcons, and he had everything in a *greppo*[1] brought from Ancona, which followed at the side of the galley. With him there was another Lord called the Lord of Longo[2] (an island near Rhodes), whose name was Eduardus de Camardino *(Note 63)*. He is a Genoese, and has a commendam called the Commendam of Longo, worth, it was said, eight thousand ducats. He is a person of importance on sea and land, and is held in repute by the Order of Saint John. As I had formerly made his acquaintance at the Court of Rome, I made myself known to him, and he showed me many attentions both on sea and on land. These two Lords had left Rome together to join the pilgrim galley for greater security. Because of waiting for these two Lords we stayed longer at Corfu than we expected; nevertheless at the twenty-third hour we set sail.

By Sunday, the 22nd of June, at sunrise, we had made little progress. The island of Corfu was continually on our left hand, and on the right hand the island of Cephalonia,[3] belonging to the Turk, and other islands, belonging to the Signoria of Venice. We sailed through the Ionian Sea, leaving Arcadia on the one side and the Morea on the other; and we suffered greatly from the heat,[4] because

---

1. A *Greppo* or *Grippo* was a fast sailing trading vessel. It had one mast, and was sometimes of fifty tons burden.

2. *Longo* or *Lango* was the *Cos* of the ancient Greeks. It lies north-west of Rhodes.

3. In 1484 the Sultan restored Zante to the Venetian Republic, but kept Cephalonia.

4. An old Venetian chronicler quoted by Gallicciolli (Bk. i. p. 796) wrote: "In the year 1494, on the 26th of June, it was so hot that the fish died in the water."

there was a great calm at sea, and the galley could not be moved with the oars because it was too heavy.

On Monday, the 23rd of June, the Vigil of Saint John the Baptist, we found in the morning that we were opposite a mountain called the Capo del Ducato *(Note 64)*, in Turkey; and there was still a great calm very contrary to our purpose. As the pilgrims and also the sailors were very discontented because the barrels of fresh water were beginning to run short, and many other things also, and we were all very weary, the Venerable Father Don Frate Francesco Trivulzio, who in truth was a holy man, and had a wonderful library in his breast, at the seventeenth hour, by means of the *comito* of the galley, invited the company to a sermon in order to cheer the discontented on the occasion of the said vigil.

His Reverence went to the castle of the galley, where lived the magnificent captain and other distinguished men on the galley, both pilgrims and also passengers. All were congregated there, even the *galeotti*, who had nothing else to do because the galley was so becalmed. And beginning the said sermon in a way he had perhaps never done before—that is, sitting down—he took his text from the Gospel for Saint John's day, that is, "quis putas hic puer erit, etc."[1] Thereupon he began to show the company that he had in his mind some remarkable things to offer in praise of Saint John, and divided his sermon into nine meditations to be made on the Saint. As all, however, were not suitable before the day of the nativity, he said a great deal suitable for the vigil, that is, of the prophecies of the said Saint made by the prophets and of the annunciation of him made by the Angel, and in what place. With his charming words he comforted all the galley there until sundown, and promised to give the rest

---

1. "What manner of child shall this be?"—Luke i. 66.

of the sermon he had prepared, the following day, if the weather did not prevent him.

That evening the sailors made a great festival in honour of Saint John; they sounded the trumpets, let off many fireworks, fired off the mortars and made great illuminations. More than forty lamps lighted in honour of Saint John were hung up on the main mast of the galley.

On Tuesday, the 24th of June, the day of the nativity of Saint John, the calm continued, and the galley made little progress. When the company therefore had risen and several dry Masses had been said, as is the custom at sea, the preacher above mentioned went to the place he had chosen the day before and proceeded to give the promised sermon. He continued to treat the meditations to be made on Saint John, and preaching from the same text, "Quid putas erit puer iste, etc.," he finished the exposition of the nine meditations he had laid down in the preceding sermon on Saint John. He preached for two hours, to the great satisfaction of every nation, and especially of the learned persons. Many who had never heard him before, although he had preached on land in the course of the journey, came to ask me afterwards who that venerable father was, and I—not only for the honour of the fatherland, but also that the truth should not remain hidden—told all I could about him. And the company, satisfied with this spiritual food, went to refresh the body to the sound of the trumpet.

While the galley was so becalmed that she made hardly a mile an hour, we came opposite the island of Zante, which belongs to the Venetians. At nightfall we were still without a favourable wind, and every man went to sleep with a great longing to reach Modone. All complained of the extreme heat except the Germans and certain other nations, who—said the Venerable Don Fra

Francesco in his sermon—ate and drank from morning till night and then went supperless to bed. These individuals did not feel the heat; the rest of us did unfortunately. And thus ended the day of St. John the Baptist.

On Wednesday, the 25th of June, we thought to have reached Modone by the morning, but when the company arose we found ourselves still in the Sea of Arcadia on the left hand, and near the rock of Prodano, eighteen miles from Modone. On the right side there was the Ionian Sea, and Sicily opposite, according to what the sailors said, and that is the way to go to Barbary. We were still sailing past a part of the Morea. On a rock seven miles from Modone there is a castle called Gionchio, on the borders of the Turk, which belongs to the Signoria of Venice.

At length, by the grace of God, we arrived at Modone *(Note 65)* at the twentieth hour, and all landed in great haste, without waiting for the casting of the anchor, so great was the desire to go on land. Although, in truth, there was not much comfort in the way of lodgings to be found there for the pilgrims, beginning with the venerable father, who on leaving the galley went to the Franciscan Friary, and I followed him thinking to better my condition. But there was little to be had; it was as much as we could do to find a few eggs. I did the cooking as well as I could to restore the father preacher; anything was good enough for me.

On Thursday, the 26th of June, we remained at Modone, the *galeotti* having landed with their merchandise to hold a fair, as is usual when a port is made. And because I never stayed to sleep on land, but always returned to the galley, I accompanied the captain in the morning to a certain small church outside the city, which is being restored with the offerings of sailors. After hearing Mass he performed his devotions, and returned to the galley without entering Modone.

After dinner, seeing that he did not intend to set sail for that day, I went with certain companions to see the aforesaid city of Modone a little better. The said city is in a plain. The sea washes the walls, and it has a port capable of receiving the largest ships. It has strong walls with drawbridges at every gate, which are four according to my reckoning. It is well furnished with towers, and on the towers and the walls there are large pieces of artillery of every size. Towards the mainland it is very strong, and is being continually strengthened. The Signoria is adding there a large moat and a double line of thick walls, and it will be a stupendous thing and well placed when it is finished.

There is a large suburb, also walled. It seems to me that the greater part of the silk industry is carried on in the said suburb; certainly many Jews, both men and women, live there, who work in silk. They are very dirty people in every way and full of very bad smells. Their society did not please me; I speak, however, of those outside the city. Turning back, I entered the city, where I did not see either houses or palaces worthy of description; for its size it has many houses, and they are close together. I think there are few inhabitants, for in the finest and widest street there, the houses appeared to be shut up for the most part, and when I stood in the market place I did not see many people. Those I saw, besides that they are Greeks—for they also belong to the Morea—are thin and ugly to look at. The majority of their houses, whether they are large or small—at least from the middle upwards and on the side facing the public streets—are built of timbers. In short, I did not see any other beauty there.

The Cathedral, which is an episcopal church, can join the company of the other miserable churches, being badly kept in every way. I did not indeed see the Bishop, but they said he was in the city. His palace, such as it is, stands in front of the church, and the entrance to the said palace is a flight of steps of hard stone in the piazza. Certain of the pilgrims asked to see the relics—I mean those of the aforesaid church. Beginning with the caretaker—who seemed to me a cobbler, though he had a large tonsure—and then all the rest, it seemed to me a very wretched affair. At length the relics were shown us with a very poor light. We were shown the head of Saint Athanasius, Bishop of Alexandria (I mean the greater) [1] who composed the creed "quicumque vult salvus esse, etc.," [2] and then the body of Saint Leo. I wanted to know who he was, and was told that he was a pilgrim who came from the Sepulchre and died on the galley, and was buried on the seashore. Afterwards he was revealed to the Bishop, who caused him to be brought into the church where he worked many miracles; this is what I could find out about him. To tell the truth, the said body was kept in a wooden chest which was in a very bad condition.

I do not mention the other churches, because I saw nothing there worthy of remark. As I said before, I accompanied the Venerable Father Don Frate Francesco to the Franciscan Friary, which follows the rule of Saint Francis. It is poor and even more than poor, because when I sought firewood to make a little supper it was not possible to find any, and I had to make a fire with what material I could get. The said convent has no cloister and no refectory; the dormitory consists of four rooms made of planks; in short, the friars are indeed poor.

1. Alexandria in Egypt as distinguished from Alessandria in Piedmont, the "city of straw."
2. "Whoever will be saved, &c."

The said city has an abundance of wines and also of grain, and the wines are made strong by the addition of resin during the fermentation, which leaves a very strange odour. They say that the wines would not keep otherwise *(Note 66)*. That odour does not please me. The wines are always dear on account of the many ships which come there for supplies of bread and wine. I did not see much good fruit—a fig or two, but not many. The people prize greatly certain plums that at home with us are given to the pigs, and I made the captain laugh when I told him this. There are many long green water melons. There is a good meat market, especially for veal, beef and mutton. The meat is good, and so also are the fowls, but those are dear. There is a dearth of fish, although the people are in the midst of the sea.

This city is governed by a Captain [1] and a Governor of the castle, who are sent by the Signoria, and they are changed every two years. Good malmsey, muscatel wines and Roumanian wines are also to be found there.

---

1. In 1494 the Governor of Modone was Ser. Antonio Venier, and the Captain of the Suburb Ser. Pietro Gradenigo. See Segretario alle Voci, Register vi. in the Archives at Venice.

CHAPTER VIII.

Galley leaves Modone. — Corone Sighted. — Islands of Cerigo, Cerigotto, Paros.—Great Storm.—Arrival in Candia. — Great Earthquake. —Procession. — Greek Rites and Ceremonies.—Description of the City of Candia.—Cathedral of St. Titus.—Franciscan Convent and Church. — Bad Smells. — Wines.—Cheeses. — Galley Sails from Candia.— Death of a Priest at Sea.—Arrival at Rhodes.— Turkish Pirates. — Description of Rhodes.—The Great Siege of 1480.—Palace of the Grand Master and of the Governor of Longo.—Stories about some of the Islands belonging to the Knights of St. John.—Casola Visits the Grand Master.— Great Heat Experienced.—Relics Seen.—Departure from Rhodes.

On Friday, the 27th of June, about the twelfth hour, the magnificent captain, seeing that the weather was changing for the better, sent a trumpeter on shore to hasten everywhere and tell the pilgrims and *galeotti* that they must return at once to the galley because he intended to set sail. And about the fourteenth hour he did so, though not with the wind he hoped for, and the galley sailed very slowly. By the evening we found ourselves only opposite Corone, also a city belonging to the Signoria. It seems to be situated in a plain, and the position is not less beautiful than that of Modone—I repeat what I heard. The distance between them is not more than twenty miles. We left Corone behind on the left hand.

On Saturday, the 28th of June, the vigil of Saint Peter's

day, we had made very little progress, and so at the sixteenth hour we came opposite an island called Cerigo [1] on the left hand. Not far from there we passed a rock called Cape Malea, where the Ægean Sea, otherwise called the Archipelago, begins. When we entered the said sea we passed another island called Cicerigo,[2] which is very unfruitful, and also another called the island of Paros, from whence the whitest marble in the world is obtained. There, various winds arose which drove the galley into the open sea, to the great perturbation of the stomachs of the pilgrims and sailors. It was very pitiful to see them, and especially the Venerable Fra Francesco, who about the twentieth hour had come to the magnificent captain and given him to understand that, being a feast day, he wished to preach a sermon on St. Peter at supper time. As soon as the said weather began he was obliged to go and hide himself away like the rest. It was very sad to see a man like him so quickly placed in peril of his life, together with many others. For my part, reassured as I was by the magnificent captain, I had no more fear of the sea as regards seeing the storms, nor indeed as regards the stomach either. The said storm continued all the following night, and it seemed as if we must inevitably all go to the bottom, so terrible were the blows given by the sea and the great mass of water dashed over the galley.

On Sunday, the 29th of June, which was the feast of St. Peter and St. Paul the Apostles, many of the seasick got up, thinking the sea had calmed down a little. They found it raging more furiously than ever, so that, notwithstanding that they had fasted on the vigil, many were also obliged to fast on the festival. Suddenly the wind changed and began to blow with such force in the

---

1. *Cerigo*, the ancient Cythera, belonged to Venice from 1204; and every two years a noble was sent there as governor of the Castle.
2. *Cicerigo* or *Cerigotto* was the ancient Aegilia. It lies between Cerigo and Candia.

direction of our route that, had it not been for the merchandise of the captain and of several other merchants who had business in Candia, we should have gone as far in two days as we had previously gone in fifteen; but it was decided at all costs to enter the port of Candia. And as the wind was contrary, it was necessary to lower the sails and stop some distance from the city of Candia, twelve miles out of our course. We were at the mercy of the sea, because when the anchor was cast with the largest cable on board called the *gomena*, which was six hundred feet long, it did not reach to the bottom of the sea.

Thus, after we arrived at the said place, everyone was very dissatisfied, not only because of the disturbance due to the preceding storm, but also because we were disappointed in our great desire to go to the said city, which we saw, but which we could not enter. Certain of our company were courageous enough to face the stormy sea, and entered a small boat to go ashore, but several times, when I saw the waves wash over the boat, I thought they had foundered. And the fury of the sea continued, and the galley was struck by the waves with such force that at times it seemed as if she must break up.

On Monday, the last day of June, the sea had not yet calmed down, and the weather continued as on the previous day. But several eager or rather rash spirits went ashore in that small boat. I chose to stay with the majority on the galley, fearing to make shipwreck otherwise—from what the magnificent captain said, with whom I passed most of my time.

On Tuesday, the first day of July, at dawn, as the sea had somewhat calmed down, the necessary sails were spread—that is, the mizzen sail and the fore sail—with loud shouts from the sailors, who sweated terribly in pulling those cords, for it was difficult work, and great care on the part of the officers—that is, the *comito, parono*, companion of the *parono*, and councillors. We finally entered the desired port of Candia *(Note 67)*, which, because of the great fury of the sea, the large size of the galley and the narrow entrance to the port, could not be entered without peril.

Although it was very early, there were so many people of every kind on the quay—some come to see the galley, which was adorned with many flags, and some to help—that it was a marvellous sight. When the galley was fastened in the port, everyone who wished to do so went ashore. There was not one of the pilgrims who was well who did not go on land. We found that those who had left on chance the day before, because of their desire to go on land, had not yet arrived in Candia.

I accompanied the venerable preacher to his friary called San Francesco, where he was received by the friars with great cordiality, and we dined there together. After dinner—when the aforesaid preacher had gone to lie down, because he had suffered greatly from the sea, and I was enjoying the cool in a certain passage also in the convent—about the sixteenth hour, there was an earthquake of such a nature, that I was almost thrown from the seat on which I was sitting, to the ground. The friary seemed on the point of falling, the beams were seen to come out of their places, and made a great dust; and the friars cried aloud "Misericordia," as did the others who were in the convent. I desired to flee with the rest, but it was impossible; on one side were the convent and the church, from which came clouds of dust, and on the other side were the walls of the city, from which we could fall headlong and break our necks. There were dangers on every side, and we thought to have escaped the sea only to perish on land. What terrible experiences! At last we got out of the friary, and heard all the city crying "Misericordia," some in Greek, some in Latin, and all the people were running to the open country. It was a pitiful thing to hear and to see.

The said earthquake did much damage in the city to the bell-towers, the churches and also the private houses. A procession was at once formed to go through the city. It was joined by the priests, both Greek and Latin, and also by the friars of every kind, though there were only a few of them. Behind them went many men and women, who beat their breasts with their fists most miserably. It was said that there had been other earthquakes, but they had not lasted long or been so terrible as this one. All the people were terrified, the foreigners as much as the natives. And when I returned to the galley, because I was afraid, I found another thing which greatly alarmed the company. For the sea was stormier than when we had landed, and the great waves were dashing all the ships in the port one against another, so that it seemed as if they would all be broken to pieces; and the water was of various colours, so that the company was stupified at the sight. The captain told me that he had never seen the like.

This earthquake so frightened the company that many pilgrims who had decided to sleep in the city returned on board the galley to sleep; and then, whoever desired a stronger dose, drank another cup. For about the third hour of the night the earthquake was renewed with such violence, that people arose out of bed and fled to the open country. It was said that letters were brought to the Governors of the city from several places in the island which were destroyed by this earthquake.

On Wednesday, the 2nd of July, I left the galley to go and see the city of Candia, and I happened to see the beginning of the procession made in consequence of the earthquake. It was a very pitiful thing to see and to hear. For in front of the great company of Greek boys without any order, who cried with a loud voice "Kyrie Elieson," and nothing else, those Greeks carried in the said procession many very large figures, painted on wood. There were crucifixes, and figures of Our Lady and other saints. There was a great display of handsome vestments on the part of the Greek priests. They all wear on their heads certain hats, of which some are white, some black. Those who have their wives living wear a white hat, the widowers wear a black one. The cords hang down like those of the cardinals' hats. The higher in rank the priests are the more beautiful is the hat.

I was greatly astonished at the chanting of the said Greeks, because it appeared to me that they chanted with great discords. Nevertheless I think this was due to the motive of the said procession, which was the general sadness. And I think so the more, because of the custom of the Ambrosian Church, which takes its origin from the Greek, for in the service for the vigil of the saints or in the service for the dead they use many of these discords. At the end of the said procession walked the priests of the Cathedral, with the Archbishop's Vicar.

When the said procession, which I wanted to see entirely, was over, I set about seeing the city and learning its customs, especially with the aid of Don Nicolo de Domo a doctor and a good Milanese citizen, who, in order to earn a good income amongst those Greeks, exercises the profession of procurator and advocate. He has plenty to do.

The city of Candia is in the Island of Crete, which, so they say, measures not less than eight hundred miles in circumference. In the said island there are several cities which have a bishop. Candia is the capital, and the seat of an archbishop. Anciently the said island was more thickly populated than it is at present, and the part which was most beautiful and most thickly populated is now destroyed. The true histories tell a great deal about this, and poets also have invented much; but it has nothing to do with our journey. I only want to speak about Candia because I was ten days there on the outward and homeward journey.

Candia is a very large, strongly walled city, situated in a plain. It has beautiful houses, although they have flat roofs in the Eastern fashion. It has a fine port, which is very narrow and somewhat dangerous at the entrance, especially for large ships.

The Cathedral Church, dedicated to Saint Titus, is very beautiful. He is the Titus to whom Saint Paul wrote, and who was ordained bishop by Timotheus, a disciple of Saint Paul. There are many other smaller churches served by very ignorant Greek priests. The most beautiful is the Church of San Francesco, belonging to the observant friars. It is more beautiful than the Cathedral, and has a most beautiful choir with three rows of stalls beautifully carved and a beautiful convent. It is above the city wall. There are also two other Orders, but their churches and monasteries have not much dignity.

The said city has a suburb on the land side which everyone would consider more beautiful than the city. It contains beautiful palaces, beautiful gardens and beautiful streets; and there is the place of the markets, especially of the provision markets. On account of its importance the Signoria of Venice, to whom the city as well as the whole island is subject, has begun to enclose the said suburb with a strong and thick wall. When it is finished it will be more beautiful than the city. Just outside the gate which leads to the said suburb there is a beautiful chapel of Our Lady governed by the Greek priests, whom they call "calogeri"; but the Masses are also said there in Latin.

However beautiful their palaces and houses are, as I said before, they appear nevertheless houses begun and not finished, because they have flat roofs, and they have not the necessary place for purging the human body; and this is a general want. In the houses the people have portable vessels which they employ during the day, then in the evening, at the sound of a bell in the tower of Saint Mark's, they all empty the vessels from the windows or the doors without taking any precaution. And once the said signal has been given, though the contents should fall on a person's head, no penalty is incurred; and there is a great stink. I can testify to this fact from what I saw. When I remember that the city is called Candia, with this horrible smell, I think the name must have been applied for antiphrase. Perhaps they trust the good odours they have, such as that of the cypress, to confound those stinks.

There is an abundance of most excellent wines—malmseys and muscatels—in the said city, and not only in the city but also in the whole island, especially in a city called Rethemo. When a man asks for rough wine they give him malmsey. In the season there are good melons, grapes and other good fruit. The vines are left trailing on the ground as we leave the melons and water-melons; and when they gather the grapes to make the malmseys and muscatels they crush them on chalk, because otherwise they could not extract the wine nor even preserve it; and that chalk gives them the great odour and perfume they have. A great quantity of

DEPARTURE FROM CANDIA

every kind of wine is made all over the island, and all is brought to this city to be sold to the merchants. I inquired from experienced persons as to the quantity sold, and they told me that not less than sixty thousand *botte*[1] of malmsey and muscatel are sold every year. And they said that the whole island produces at least as much milk as wine—I mean ewe's milk.

They make a great many cheeses; but it is a pity they are so salted. I saw great warehouses full of them, and some in which the brine or "salmoria," as we say, was a *braccio*[2] deep, and the large cheeses were floating within. Those in charge told me that the cheeses could not be preserved otherwise, because they are so rich. They do not know how to extract the butter. They sell a great quantity to the ships that call there. It was astonishing to see the number of cheeses taken by our galley.

As there are so many sheep there I asked if wool and cloths are made, and was told no, that there is no wool industry either in the city of Candia or in the island. I can well believe it. Several times I saw some of their sheep, and they had

[a leaf is here missing from the MSS.]

through the city telling all the pilgrims that they must be on board the galley by the eighteenth hour; and this was done—the company supplying themselves with what was needed for the voyage to Jerusalem.

On Friday, the 4th of July, at dawn, with great difficulty we left the port of Candia and entered the open sea. All three sails were spread, but the wind was *garbino*[3] and rather contrary than otherwise, and in consequence many of the pilgrims were seasick. Never-

---

1, A Venetian "Botte" = 751·170 litres.
2. The Venetian "braccio" = ·683396 metres; the Milanese "braccio" = ·594936 metres.
3. South-west wind.

theless the galley made good progress, though with great fastings. Perhaps they were necessary because of the life we had led in Candia.

The following night, towards Saturday, after even I had been upset by the sea, another trouble befell me. For a priest called Giovanni, belonging to the diocese of Lausanne, whose lodging was next to mine, and who was ill when he came on board the galley, died, and there was great distress and agitation until day broke. His fellow countrymen begged the captain to permit them to place the body in a case and keep it thus until the evening, because, being then, as was hoped, at Rhodes, they wished to bury him on land. He consented, and thus sailing we passed on the left the island of Longo,[1] which belongs to the Rhodians—that is to say, it is held by a Commander of the Jerusalem Order, and, as I mentioned, the Commander of the said island was on board the galley. We also passed many other rocks, about which I will say something on the return.

On Saturday, the 5th of July, at sunrise, we had made two hundred miles, and having now a stern wind we sailed smoothly, so that at the twenty-second hour we reached the port of Rhodes.

There, we heard at once that certain ships of Turkish pirates, one of whom was named Arigi, the other Camalio *(Note 68)*, had seized a *nave* and a caravel, loaded with merchandise to the value of sixty thousand ducats, which were coming from Cyprus to Rhodes. The news caused great alarm, especially amongst those not used to travelling by sea, and on this account the usual demonstrations with trumpets, mortars and flying banners were not made as we entered the port. When the galley was fastened in the port with the cables, the pilgrims, or at

1. *i.e.,* Cos.

least the majority of them, went on land to refresh their bodies and visit friends, because at Rhodes, amongst the brethren of St. John of Jerusalem there are natives of many countries, and especially of Spain and of France. It was found that we had made three hundred miles since we left Candia until now.

On Sunday, the 6th of July, I left the galley in company with the magnificent captain, and we went to hear Mass at Saint Augustine's. Then, as he joined the Prior or Commander of the island of Longo, who, as I said, had come on board the galley at Corfu to come to Rhodes, I left his magnificence and set about certain commissions I had to do for friends in Rhodes. After dinner I went to see Rhodes, especially what was said to be best worth seeing.

The site of the city of Rhodes is very ancient, and it is the city to which Paul formerly wrote the Epistle to the Colossians. There are several reasons why it is now called Rhodes, but I omit them in order not to be too lengthy, and also because they are related by persons incomparably more learned than I am. It has always been very strong, and proved it a few years ago when it offered such a strenuous resistance to the Grand Turk in the year 1480.

Many traces of the siege remain which stupefy the beholder; it is an incredible thing to anyone who has not seen it. And, hearing the account, as I heard it, from those who were there during that war, one can more readily say and believe that it was a miracle than due to the power of man. For while the Rhodians believed they were going to their death, they gained the victory over the thousands of Turks who were besieging the city of Rhodes. I think the signs will remain until the day of the last Judgment. One cannot go about Rhodes without finding stones, and terrible ones, which were fired from the mortars. Some of them are so enormous that it seems incredible that they were thrown from the cannon. It is also an incredible thing that so many having been fired as have left their traces—that is, the stones I mentioned, which are of every size—the city still exists; and yet there it is, and it does not ever appear to have been besieged. It was said by those who were present at the siege that not less than five thousand were fired, between large and small.

I went to see the palace of the Grand Master, who is a Cardinal Deacon, with the title of Saint Adrian; his name is the Lord Peter Daubusson. I saw also the rest of the city from a height towards the land; it looked to me like a piece of Rome. There is no order, either in the palaces or in the circle of the walls. The city cannot be described as long or square or triangular. It is very strong, and is being continually strengthened; work is constantly going on around the walls, especially towards the sea, at a tower called the tower of St. Nicholas. The palace of the Grand Master, together with the Church of Saint John, appears to ascend somewhat, yet everything is in the plain. I did not see any other palace worthy of remark. There are a few beautiful façades, especially going towards the palace of the Grand Master, but inside there is nothing very rich.

The palace of the aforesaid Governor of Longo is handsome, though not more so than its neighbours, and it adjoins the city wall which looks towards the sea. I saw this palace all through, for the aforesaid Lord of Longo being, as I said before, a native of Genoa,[1] where

---

1. In the 14th and 15th centuries Genoa had to struggle against the ambition of the ruling families of Milan and other enemies, and was not always strong enough to maintain its independence. From 1315-35 Genoa was under the protection of Robert of Anjou: from 1353-56 and from 1421-35 it was subject to the Viscontis of Milan: from 1396—1413 and from 1458-61 it was subject to the King of France: and from 1464-78 and from 1487-98 it was subject to the Sforzas of Milan. In 1494, therefore, Casola belonged to the dominant, and the Governor of Longo to the subject State.

a very rich brother of his still lives, and I a Milanese, and I having made friends with him on the galley, he was pleased to invite me to dinner with him together with the Magnificent Don Agostino Contarini. At dinner, although we were the only guests, there was such a display of silver, such diversity of viands, and everything was so well decorated and served that it would have sufficed for any great lord, in spite of the fact that everything there is dear.

After dinner he showed me the said palace very thoroughly and all the decorations, which were worthy of such a potent Lord. From what I could hear afterwards, he is the most esteemed Knight and Commander in Rhodes. Because I was a subject of the Most Illustrious Lord the Duke of Milan, he made me great offers, beginning with money, and pressed me to go to his house on my return. He did the same to the Venerable Fra Francesco Trivulzio, hearing that he was a Milanese and of such a noble family, and as the said Fra Francesco was lodged at the Monastery, he paid him a visit and made him a beautiful present. I went to his hospital. It is beautiful in appearance, and where the infirmary was, there was a great display of tapestry, and there are large offices also and other arrangements. When I saw it, there were very few sick people, and for that reason I think they spend little.

The port of Rhodes seems to me the largest and strongest between Venice and Jaffa. It can be entered without danger because it is very deep. The said city has many windmills on the walls and also outside. I went to see these mills, which seemed to me beautiful contrivances. When I asked how much they ground, I was told a quantity which I could not believe, because when I saw the result it did not appear to me to be likely. There is a way of regulating the amount of wind by enlarging and reducing certain sails which catch the wind. I counted sixteen of the said mills on the walls of the port; the others, placed here and there, were more numerous.

Rhodes is an island which has, they say, a circumference of a hundred miles. It is very sterile, and everything is dear; more so than at any other place visited on this journey. If, indeed, there is some merchandise there, everything is brought either from Turkey, as are carpets, or from Italy, as are cloths.

The inhabitants of the said city are for the most part foreign Knights of the Order of St. John of Jerusalem or merchants of every nation under the sun. The Rhodians are Greeks. I saw some very beautiful women there of every nation. There are many and rich Jews, and they carry on the silk industry. The Rhodians live very long; it may be, either because the air is excellent, or because they eat very sparingly. Men are to be found there aged a hundred years, a hundred and ten and a hundred and twenty, in excellent health and spirits; and I was told by persons worthy of credence that the air of Rhodes is so good that anyone who knew how to regulate his manner of living would have difficulty in dying.

Besides the island of Rhodes, the Grand Master and his order have under their government several other islands, which, on account of their peculiarities, I must not omit to mention. I heard, from people who had seen it, that there is an island called the island of the *Symie*[1] where the air is so good, they say, that amongst the inhabitants there are men of a hundred, a hundred and ten, a hundred and twenty, and even a hundred and forty years of age. Another island is called the island of

---

1. The island of *Symi*, north-west of Rhodes, situated in the Gulf of Symi.

ISLANDS BELONGING TO RHODES

San Nicola de Carichi,[1] where they say that when the inhabitants marry their daughters, they do not give them in dowry anything but a spade and a hoe, and that these tools never wear out however much they are used. In the said island, tools of this kind are to be found in constant use, which are so old that no one can remember when they were made. The people of this island have another favour from Saint Nicholas—that is, if a foreigner should go to the said island and wish to steal, secretly, or with violence the value of a penny, he could never depart from the island without the leave of the person from whom he had stolen, or without immediately restoring to the owner what he had taken. To prove that this is true, I was told that a few days before, a caravel of pirates went to this island and stole some sheep and other animals. Before leaving, they ate some of them; but as soon as ever they had eaten, they vomited everything, which is contrary to the nature of pirates; and, further, they were not able to depart, and they never could depart, until they had given satisfaction to the owners for what they had stolen, even to a hair. There is another island called Nissari, which produces many figs and also good wine. Another island is called Episcopia,[2] and there, a great quantity of excellent honey is made. Each of the said islands used to be governed by one who was called King, but a few days before, the Knights of Rhodes had put an end to this name of King there. I have written this short account of the Rhodians because I had nothing else to do.

The same day, I went with the captain to visit the Grand Master, and presented several letters to him. He paid me many attentions; I think that was partly because I brought him, from Milan, some money, which he is

---

1. This is evidently the island of *Kherki*, a very few miles to the west of Rhodes.
2. The island of Tilos or Piskopi is one of the Sporades, and lies between Rhodes and Cos or Longo.

always glad to see. It was said in Rhodes that he did nothing else but accumulate, and that he was the chief merchant. While we were in the presence of his most Reverend Lordship, there came a messenger sent by his captain of the fleet, whose name is Frate Furiano, and who had gone to recover the *nave* and caravel stolen by the Turkish pirates, as I said above. The said messenger brought letters which related how he had recovered everything, but that he had not been able to take a single prisoner save Arigi's boy, whom he had cut in pieces *(Note 70)*. The reason why he had not been able to seize any other persons was that the Turkish ships had entered a certain torrent where the ships of the Rhodians, which were larger, could not follow them quickly enough. However, everything had gone well; he had recovered all that had been stolen, and had also taken the Turkish ships without the crews. This news completely reassured the captain, and the pilgrims also, when it was made known, because we had been very perplexed about going further on account of what had happened.

On Monday, the 7th of July, we remained at Rhodes because the captain and also the *galeotti* had much business to do. The pilgrims who had no other occupation went about to see the place. They avoided the heat—which was in truth very great—as much as possible, and they drove away their thirst with those malmseys, watered as much as possible. I do not say anything about the relics shown to us, because they are ordinary; there is that thorn which blossoms on Good Friday *(Note 71)*.

On Thursday, the 8th of July, after dinner, the magnificent captain, by means of the trumpet, sent to warn the pilgrims to be on board the galley by the evening, as he intended to depart. The pilgrims were obedient, and the galley was already outside the port with a favourable wind, and we were on the point of setting sail, when it was discovered that one of the noble deputies, whom I mentioned before,[1] called Don Alvise Morosini, was missing. As it was hoped he would come, the galley was left all night without the sails, thus drifting at the mercy of the water until the morning. We lost more than a hundred miles of the course, and on this account every man on board said Litanies, but they were in truth Spanish ones.[2]

---

[1]. One of the two Venetian gentlemen apprentices appointed to the galley by the Signoria. (See Note 53.)
[2]. To say Spanish Litanies = to blaspheme.

CHAPTER IX.

Voyage through the Gulf of Satalia.—Encounter with Seven Venetian Ships at Paphos.—Supply of Wood and of Water taken at Limasol.—Description of the Ruins there.—Plague Raging at Famagosta and Nicosia.—Casola Visits the Famous Cornaro Sugar Plantations at Episcopia in Cyprus.—Cotton Growing.—Carob Beans.—Fresh News of Turkish Pirates.—Alarm of the Captain and His Efforts to Ensure the Safety of the Pilgrim Galley.—Voyage continued to Jaffa.

ON Wednesday, the 9th of July, at sunrise, we set sail with what little wind remained, and made good progress in that Euxine Sea, now called the Sea of Natalia, from a city held by the Turks, which is called Natalia.[1] When the sun was somewhat up, however, the sea so settled into a calm that every man feared to die of heat, and this continued until night; then a fair *provenza* arose and good progress was made that night.

On Thursday, the 10th of July, as the *provenza* continued, we sailed through that gulf, and at midday discovered the point of the island of Cyprus *(Note 72)*, and came over against a fortified place called Paphos. There, seven Venetian ships, coming from Syria loaded with goods, had stopped, and because they had heard of the capture made by the Turkish pirates, of whom I spoke

---

1. *i.e.*, Sadalia or *Adalia*, a city on the south coast of Asia Minor at the head of the Gulf of Adalia. The Pilgrim who wrote the "Voyage de la Saincte Cyté de Hierusalem" (1480), relates, p. 54, that when they were passing through this gulf, Agostino Contarini, the Captain-owner, "nous conta que ung foys en passant par devant ledict gouffre il fut en si grant danger et eut si grant paour que tout soubdainement sa barbe et chevenlx lui devindrent blancs et encoires à present sont tous gris."

above, they were afraid of going further. When the captains of the said ships saw our galley a long way off, they sent the scribe or secretary off in a small boat. As we were not sailing fast and as he had good *galeotti*, he came up with us and, being aided by a rope, as is usual in similar cases, he climbed on to the galley and gave the messages of his captains to our magnificent captain. The latter encouraged them to continue their voyage, sending them back word of what had happened while we were at Rhodes—that is, of the good provision made by the Grand Master for what had occurred and of the victory gained by Frate Furiano.

On Friday, the 11th of July, we arrived near Limasol at sundown, and the sails being lowered, we approached a certain place where preparations were made for taking a supply of wood and of fresh water. This water is obtained almost from the impossible. That night the men dug several large trenches some distance from the seashore. In the morning they were so many beautiful springs flowing into the sea, and all the galley was furnished with that water: I say all, because, besides the captain, many others kept a supply in barrels.

On Saturday, the 12th of July, when the sun had risen, the magnificent captain made the port, and ordered the anchor to be cast off the shore of Limasol—an ancient city of the island of Cyprus—because there is no harbour there. All the pilgrims left the galley, thinking to refresh themselves with something good, for they were excessively afflicted by the heat which they had endured on the galley during the preceding days. But they were all disappointed in their expectations, not having found on the journey so far, a more arid place than Limasol. I can assure you that everything was lacking there, so that it was necessary for those who wished to dine on land, to get supplies at once from the galley. As both the magnificent captain and the Venerable Fra Francesco went ashore, I determined to go with them, fearing I should remain hungry if I went elsewhere, as in truth would have been the case.

When we landed from the galley we went immediately, as was fitting, to the Cathedral, which is indeed still upright, but which is on the point of tumbling down. It is enough to say, that it has a good revenue, from what I could hear. For the service of the said church there is no one but a certain priest from Mantua who has learnt to speak Greek.

After Mass and after dinner, taken in a certain house near the quay facing the sea, which appeared to me a warehouse—a storehouse for merchandise, because there were many bales of cotton and boxes of sugar there, which also served the company in the lack of other beds—I went to see this city or remains of a city. I saw from the ruins and beautiful walls, that it must have been a large and beautiful place, but there is not a single good house in the whole city. I saw the said church reposefully, because in all Limasol there was not a place so suited for repose on account of the shade there. I saw nothing worth mentioning except the high altar. There is a beautiful altar-piece with certain figures in gilded wood, and the tomb of one of our Milanese named Fra de Corte, which has a Pietà painted above. All the other churches are in ruins.

I saw that in the said city the inhabitants do not spend very much money in covering their dwellings, because they are covered with green boughs or with straw. If it rained there as often as it does in Lombardy perhaps they would adopt another system of roofing. It never rains there. I went to the castle, which is guarded by a soldier.

Certainly it must have been a fine strong place; nevertheless it is also tumbling down, and nothing is being done to repair it. What little remains standing is a notable sight, and within, there is the best water to be found in that country. I drank some of it, albeit in a shoe, and it revived my spirits which were dried up in my body.

When I asked the cause of the destruction of such a great city, I received various explanations. Some said it was due to the earthquakes, others attributed it to the many incursions of the Moors. The captain told me, when I spoke to him on the subject, that it had been thus destroyed by a King of England *(Note 73)* to avenge a niece who was oppressed by a King of Cyprus on the way from the Sepulchre. When I asked why the Signoria did not seek to repopulate it, standing as it does on the sea, he told me that people do not care to settle there on account of the earthquakes, and also because it is a very unhealthy place. The inhabitants have in truth an unhealthy appearance. They all appear to be ill. True there are only a few of them.

I do not write about the size and wealth of the island of Cyprus, in which the city of Limasol is situated, because I could not get any reliable information; however, it is commonly said to be five hundred miles in circumference. I heard much about the abundance and delicacy of the sugar, cotton and other good things. I can say little about what I saw of the island. The captain would not give anyone leave to go to Nicosia or to Famagosta, the principal cities of the island of Cyprus, because a guard at Limasol told him that the people were dying[1] there, and there was no prospect of improvement. Certain merchants who had come with us, went to Nicosia with their woollen cloths and proved the truth of what

---

1. *i.e.*, Dying of the plague.

the guard said, for when we returned we found they were dead.

I can only speak of a great farm not far from Limasol, which belongs to a certain Don Federico Cornaro, a patrician of Venice, and is called Episcopia *(Note 74)*, where they make so much sugar, that, in my judgment, it should suffice for all the world. Indeed it is said to be the best which goes to Venice, and the quantity sold is always increasing. It seems to me that no one ought ever to die there. It was very interesting to see how they make the sugar—both the fine and the coarse—and so many people at work. There were not less than four hundred persons there, all employed—some in one way, some in another. It was interesting too, to see such a number of utensils; it was like another world to me. There were cauldrons of such a size that if I described them no one would believe me. One of the factors of the aforesaid Don Federico told me that every man was paid every Saturday. The said factor was an Italian, but he knew Greek. There was also a great quantity of cotton in the fields, but it was not yet ripe for gathering. It was also a great pleasure to see so many trees in the woods, loaded with carob-beans, *bazane ultramarine*, as we call them. They were still green, and the taste was bitter; when they are ripe they are sweet. Everything in that island pleased me, except that they make their wine with resin, and I could not drink it.

I did not see any other people of the said island save certain peasants living in the neighbourhood of Limasol, who came to sell their fruits, which, however, were few, and to buy some of the things which the *galeotti* had brought to sell—cloths and other goods. They speak Greek. I know little about the island, because I was afraid of endangering my life.

While the captain was on shore, as I said, there came

a messenger from the Captain of the island,[1] who showed him a letter received from the Vice-Consul of Tripoli in Syria (a city belonging to the Sultan), which informed the said Captain of the island that there were four armed light galleys belonging to Camalio, a Turkish pirate, in the river of Tripoli, and that he was expecting two others which were at Lisso, and that they were hourly waiting to go in chase of and plunder, anyone less strong than themselves, and that he (the Vice-Consul) had heard, amongst other things, that they were waiting for news of the arrival of the pilgrim galley in order to plunder it if possible. This letter made our captain very anxious and also many of the pilgrims who heard the news; they were few, however, because the rest were dispersed here and there among the ruins in order to remain in the shade.

After taking counsel with those who were present, our captain wrote back to the aforesaid Captain of the island at Famagosta, asking him to send word whether the galleys of the Signoria of Venice had been sent, as they ought to have been, to make the sea secure, in order that Venetian ships could go on their way in safety; and to reply at once so that he might know what to do. When the letter had been despatched, by the same messenger, our captain thought of another plan—that is, to re-write the letters and say to the Captain of the island that if the said galleys had not yet started, that he must despatch them at all costs, and that he himself would not depart until he received his reply. But it appeared to him that, without laying himself open to blame, he could not take such a course without the consent of the pilgrims, because four or five days would thus be lost and this was very

---

1. In 1494, the Captain of Cyprus was Ser Cosmo Pasqualigo, son of the late Ser Paolo (v. Segretario alle Voci, Reg. vi.). The official residence of the Captain was at Famagosta.

inconvenient on account of the dearth in the place and the lack of victuals.

On Sunday, the 13th of July, having heard Mass in the chief church because there were no others, our magnificent captain, through the interpreter whom he had taken at Rhodes, as was the custom, summoned all the pilgrims before the door of the church and told them what he thought, and asked their opinion. When he had made his proposal—whether, because they did not understand, or for other reasons—the magnificent captain remained almost alone or at least with very few supporters. The rest of the company departed one by one, thinking some evil of the captain, and the only conclusion come to was, that he must do as he thought best, and this he did. For when he returned to his lodging, he wrote again to the Captain of the island, asking him at all costs to send the armed galleys for the protection of the pilgrim galley, and he was much blamed for this. Many of the pilgrims, especially the Ultramontanes, murmured, saying that this was an invention made on purpose to extort many ducats from the pilgrims, as had been asserted already. In consequence, the captain, reassurred by his officers and *galeotti*, having sent the letter, determined to continue the voyage.

Thus, at the hour of Vespers, the trumpet was sounded among those ruins to give notice to the pilgrims and to the *galeotti* who were outside with their goods to sell, that all must be on board the galley that evening. And his magnificence, together with Don Frate Francesco, and those belonging to his mess, having had supper, entered the galley, and so did the others.

On Monday, the 14th of July, after sunrise, when the anchor was heaved, we set out and went to anchor at a place called La Canute, six miles, so the sailors said, from

DEPARTURE FROM CYPRUS—PIRATES

Limasol, where there are many common woods, from what I could understand. Many *galeotti*, skilled in that work, were sent to cut down wood enough to supply the galley all the time it had to stay at Jaffa, because wood is not to be found there for love or money, and also to get a supply of water, because there were the springs freshly made, as I said above. Close by, there was a place called the *Cape of the Cats*,[1] where, as the persons said who knew it well, there used to be a hospital which kept many cats. Because that place was uninhabitable on account of the multitude of serpents, and many cats were brought there who destroyed the said serpents which infested those places.

While we were there, the secretary of the galley or the scribe, as they call him, arrived at the twenty-third hour. He had remained at Limasol to await the reply to the letters written to the Captain or Vice-Governor of the island of Cyprus to secure our way, for the reasons above stated. He brought letters, in reply to those written, which said, in short, that our captain might confidently continue his voyage, and that those two galleys he had asked for, for his protection, had gone to recover the ship of the Commander of Cyprus (of which I spoke above when I described the events at Rhodes), which had been seized by Arigi, the Turkish Corsair, and that, finding it had been recovered, they would return towards Syria. When he had read this letter the captain ordered a mortar to be fired, and gave orders that every man must return aboard because he wanted to set sail, and this he did without losing any time in the world.

On Tuesday, the 15th of July, we sailed through the great Gulf of Satalia with all the three sails spread to

---

1. The ancient Cape Curias of Herodotus. There was a monastery there of Greek Monks of St. Basil who had charge of the immense swarms of cats (Porro).

catch the wind, which was *garbino* and not a stern wind. There was no land to be seen here save on board the galley; sky and sea were to be seen, nothing else, though the sailors comforted us continually with the assurance that on the morrow we should reach Jaffa.

On Wednesday, the 16th of July, there was a calm at sea for a while, which did not at all please the company, beginning with the captain, because no land was to be seen in any direction, as had been hoped. After midday there arose a considerable war of words between the *comito*, the councillor and the pilot (or guide, as he may be called), who was taken by order at Modone. One said we were near our destination, another said no; at length a *galeotti* was sent up to the masthead of the galley to look carefully if he could make out land on any side. And remaining thus, at the twentieth hour, two towers at Jaffa were sighted, which greatly cheered the company.

While the captain was preparing letters to send to the Governor of Rama [1] and to the Governor of Jerusalem, we arrived at Jaffa, with the aid of a little good wind, which sprang up a little before the twenty-third hour. The scribe, bearing the letters, was at once put into a small boat and sent to Rama for permission to land, as is the custom, and all the rest of us remained on board the galley in the greatest heat I ever experienced in all my life. The Te Deum Laudamus was sung by the pilgrims, especially by the priests and friars, and many prayers said at the good pleasure of each one.

---

1. The modern Ramleh, not far from Jaffa and close to Lydda.

CHAPTER X.

The Galley Anchored near Jaffa.—Sermon by Fra. F. Trivulzio.—Letters Received from Jerusalem.—Death of a Young Pilgrim.—Another Sermon from Fra. Francesco.—Amusements Provided by the Captain for the Pilgrims.—Some Moors Visit the Galley.—Guinella.—Pilgrims Discontented.—Arrival of the Prior of Mount Sion.—Conference with the Deputy-Governor of Jerusalem.—The Moors again Visit the Galley.—Irritating Delays in Landing.—Some Pilgrims go Ashore followed at Intervals by the Rest.—3rd Sermon by Fra. Francesco.—The Governor of Nabule Extorts 100 ducats from the Captain.—Arrival of the Governor of Gaza.—The Pilgrims Ransom Ten Slaves.—Death of a French Pilgrim.—Casola Lands.—His Description of Jaffa.

ON Thursday, the 17th of July, the anchors were cast, and the galley anchored near to Jaffa, because there is no port there. While we were waiting for the Scribe or for the permission to land, the Venerable Fra Francesco Trivulzio, in order that every man—the *galeotti* as well as the pilgrims—should carry some good spiritual provision to the Holy Land, gathered all the company (both pilgrims and *galeotti*) together before dinner, by means of the *comito* of the galley, with his whistle, in his usual place, that is, the poop of the galley. And when there was silence he preached a beautiful sermon exhorting the company to prepare their consciences well, if they wished to gain the indulgences and the merit of that pilgrimage.

He took for his text, certain words of the Gospel for the previous Sunday, according to the use of the Court of Rome; that is, "Omnis arbor qui non facit fructum bonum excidetur et in ignem mittetur."[1] And there, in the first place, he laid down what he wanted to say, namely, that belief is of the heart, confession of the mouth; and he concluded by saying that without the confession of the mouth faith has no merit. Then he proceeded to the sermon, comparing the tree to the Christian and repeating that he that bringeth not forth fruit is hewn down. And here, condemning sins in general and exhorting the company to amendment, he preached a very remarkable sermon, so that the indulgences might be obtained by every person.

On Friday, the 18th of July, while we were waiting thus in expectation of being able to escape from this exile—which indeed appeared to us as hard as exile and very cruel—written papers were brought from Jerusalem together with a letter written by the Reverend Father the Prior of the Monastery at Mount Sion *(Note 75)* to the Venerable Father the preacher. These writings were signed in Moorish by the hand of one Abrayno Grasso, who, by the will of the Usbech, as he is called—that is, the chief Minister near the person of the Sultan, who is really, after the Sultan, the chief Lord of Jerusalem—administers like a Commissioner the affairs of Jerusalem as to the revenues, and is more powerful than all the others, especially the Governor of Rama.

The said letters ran as follows, according to the translation made into Latin:—The one, that the said Abrayno would set out and come to Jaffa according to custom, and that he would do all he possibly could for the Christians.

---

1. "Every tree that bringeth not forth good fruit is hewn down and cast into the fire."—Matthew, vii. 19.

JAFFA—DEATH OF A PILGRIM

The other writing was addressed to the Custodian of Jaffa, called Marano, who knew Italian well, and ordered him to permit four friars of the Franciscan Order to go on shore. This was written because Fra Francesco had written to the Prior, asking him to provide animals for riding, and obtain permission for him to go on instead of remaining in this state of uncertainty.

The said animals, however, did not appear at the time the aforesaid Fra Francesco hoped. At that hour the Governor of Rama, hoping to get something better in return, sent a present to the magnificent captain of the galley consisting of a young ox (at home we say a *jucho*), black and very thin, and certain very over-ripe apples, plums and grapes. It must be understood that the Governors, who will be mentioned in speaking of places subject to the Sultan, are like our Commissioners. The said Governorships are bought from the Sultan, and are given to the highest bidder, except that of Jerusalem.

On Saturday, the 19th of July, we remained still in this exile, and there was nothing new, except that a young pilgrim, a Datian,[1] passed from this life. It was said that he had fallen ill at Candia through eating unripe grapes. The truth is that hardly enough money was found on him to bury him. With the permission of the Custodian of Jaffa, who represents there the Governor of Jerusalem, he was carried on land and buried in a cave on the seashore.

On Sunday, the 20th of July, in order to provide some food to cheer the souls so vexed by that exile, Don Fra Francesco, by means of the *comito* of the galley, as usual, summoned every man to the poop, the accustomed place, to hear the sermon, which was announced by a whistle.

---

1. Casola wrote "Natione Datianus," but Röhricht in his summary of the voyage of Bemmelberg and Parsberg, who travelled on the same galley, says, "Before they left the ship however on arriving at Jaffa, one of the Pilgrims, *Lorenz Heuglin* from *Denmark*, died and was buried on Shore." *Deutsche Pilgerreisen*, p. 184.

When the company was gathered together he preached a beautiful sermon, taking for his subject: "Facite vobis amicos de mammona iniquitatis, ut cum defeceritis recipiat vos in tabernacula sua."[1] And he took this from the Gospel appointed for the said day at Mass, according to the use of the Court of Rome. There he expounded the Gospel fully, and drew from it most remarkable moral lessons, beginning at the beginning: "Erat quidam homo qui habebat villicum, et cetera."[2] There was not a word which was not very well applied to the galley and those on board; and (he explained) who was that certain man. Although on account of the language all did not fully understand him, nevertheless he was understood by the majority, and after the sermon he was magnified by all.

That evening a Mameluke arrived, who said he was sent by the Governor of Gaza for the protection of the Christians. It seemed to me that his protection would not be of much account, for he was barefooted; true he was dressed in camlet, and full of every virtue—Spanish ones I mean. In my opinion he had come rather to extort something from the Christians than for any other purpose, and the majority agreed with me.

On Monday, the 21st of July, the Venerable Father Don Francesco, being eager to go ashore, left the galley with his companions. When he landed, a Mameluke of the Governor of Gaza[3] would not let him depart, and he returned to the galley. For, all those Governors, hearing that the pilgrims galley had arrived, had set out for Jaffa and pitched their tents opposite the galley, so that it appeared as if there was an army there, preparing to make war, as was the case—at least on the purses of the pilgrims.

---

1. "Make to yourselves friends of the Mammon of unrighteousness, &c."—Luke, xvi. 9.
2. "There was a certain rich man which had a steward."—Luke, xvi. 1.
3. Gaza or Guzzeh is on the southern frontier of Palestine, three or four miles from the sea, and on the road leading to Egypt.

Many Moors also began to come from the surrounding villages, who brought victuals to sell to the pilgrims; and preparations were made to begin the fair—usually held by the Moors and *galeotti*, while the pilgrims remain in the Holy Land—which is carried on by means of barter and also with ready money. Seen from the galley it seemed a great affair.

Nevertheless we remained, like they say Tantalus does in the Inferno. He has the water up to his lips and cannot drink. We saw the land we had come so far to enter, and those Moorish dogs would not let us go on our way. They made difficulties, now about one thing, now about another, as they had never done before, from what I could hear from those who had been there on previous occasions. However, it was necessary to tie everything up in the sack of patience, as we did not want to loosen the sack of money.

Each one who goes on the voyage to the Sepulchre of our Lord has need of three sacks—a sack of patience, a sack of money and a sack of faith. The first two sacks had been used several times up to that hour; the third was still untouched.

As no conclusion was arrived at, the captain sought to procure us a little amusement, and he permitted some fishing; he even allowed anyone who wished, to leave the galley and go to certain places where it was said Saint Peter used to fish. On this day, with certain contrivances of very strong cord and great hooks, an immense fish was caught. There was great difficulty in hauling it up out of the water, because it defended itself boldly and resisted with force all the efforts to draw it out of the water; so that it was necessary to hold it thus tied in the water until it was exhausted. The hook that caught it was so big that it took a large sheep's lung to bait it. The men wounded the fish with certain iron weapons suitable for the purpose. It made the sea so red that it seemed as if there had been great slaughter done, and the company enjoyed all this greatly, and the more so because they hoped to have something good to eat. Afterwards it was found to be a shark, and the mariners said it had such an evil nature that if anyone had courage enough to swim in the sea and met this fish he would be killed, because it is such an enemy to man. It was skinned. The hide was like iron. Some of the poor pilgrims, though only a few, ate some of it. It was a fearful thing to see both before and after being skinned.

We had another pleasure that day. A turtle, called in our language a *bissa scudelera*, appeared in the sea and swam round the galley. It was so large that its case would cover the body of a man. If I had not seen it I would not have believed anyone who told me about it; yet so it was, and almost every day it showed itself as long as the galley remained there. We also took pleasure in watching certain long slender fish which went in great numbers and seemed like a great sea-wave when they were pursued by some large fish.

At this juncture, while we were so occupied, the Venerable Father Don Fra Francesco Trivulzio returned to the galley and certain Moors came with him. We could not understand anything they said or did except certain actions; as, for example, when one of them, as soon as he arrived jumped on to the table where the captain was and those who ate with him—I also amongst them—and sat himself down on it as the tailors sit on their benches. He was barefooted, though he was dressed in camlet.

Another action could be understood. Many pilgrims having gathered to see the said Moors, and to hear them—

for all the company hoped to have news of the end of that exile—one of the Moors, wishing to spit, opened the breast of his garment and spat within, in order not to spit amongst the company. It seemed to all a much more honest action than that of Guinella,[1] which someone recounted. Guinella was in the chamber of the Marquis of Ferrara, which was much decorated even to the pavement, and wishing to spit, he spat in the face of the Marquis, saying that in that room he had not been able to find an uglier place for spitting than the face of the Marquis.

On Tuesday, the 22nd of July, the day of Saint Mary Magdalen, the pilgrims began to murmur still more against the captain, as did the children of Israel against Moses when he was leading them through the desert into the country where we also desired to go. For it seemed to them that our delay in landing, prolonged beyond the usual time, was now out of all reason; and certain of them said that the captain was not using his accustomed diligence with the Moors, so that we might leave the galley and go on our way. Certain of them, especially the French, said many biting things to the captain's face; and he very justly replied that he lost more than they did by the delay, because as long as they remained on the galley he was obliged to maintain them, and that it would be a good thing for him to end the journey quickly. As well as he could, he calmed the irritation of the discontented.

On Wednesday, the 23rd of July, the Prior of Mount Sion came on board the galley, and talked with the captain a long time about the iniquity of the Moors who kept the pilgrims in such embarrassment. Then they

---

1. A famous court fool at the Court of Ferrara in the 14th century. His real name was "*Gonnella.*" See "Memorie di Ferrara," by Antonio Rizzi, vol. ii. p. 798.

went ashore to speak to Abrayno, whom I mentioned above, and another *Sabbatino*,[1] sent by the Governor of Gaza, and other Mameluke lieutenants who were encamped there, as I said before, and would not allow any of the pilgrims to land.

When they returned to the galley, the only news they brought was, that the captain could put the pilgrims ashore if he liked, but they would not be allowed to depart before the arrival of the Governor of Gaza. When the captain came back late, without the Prior of Mount Sion, he gave notice to the Pilgrims, through the *comito* of the galley, that they must be ready to go on land in the morning. All were overjoyed at this, for the eighth day of this terrible exile was already ended, and happy he who was ready first.

On Thursday, the 24th of July, the vigil of the day of Saint James the Apostle, very early in the morning the pilgrims, amid a great noise, shouting and rejoicing, prepared to leave the galley, each with his baggage, flasks and his wooden stirrups—I had iron ones and no others—each one according to his needs and his choice. It seemed a camp in movement; one trod on the heels of the other in the anxiety to be first. When they approached the place where they were to get off the galley and enter the boats, it was found that the captain had changed his mind and did not wish any of the pilgrims to leave the galley. He said that they were better off where they were than they would be ashore, where they would have to suffer many hardships. Indeed he spoke the truth, and there were some who proved it, for they lost their lives because of their anxiety to be amongst the first and

---

1. "*Sabbatino*" seems to be used in the sense of Commissioner or Deputy-Governor. Casola applied the term to Abrayno Grasso, the deputy-Governor of Jerusalem, and to the representative of the Governor of Gaza.

because they would not listen to the orders or even to the persuasions of the captain.

As the pilgrims remained on board, the captain sent renewed entreaties to those dogs to see if they would change their minds and let us go on our way according to custom, without waiting further for the Governor of Gaza, but those dogs would not listen to us.

On this day the chief Moors came aboard the galley to amuse themselves, and a great festival was made. The ship was decorated with carpets and hangings, the trumpets were sounded, the cannon fired and the *galeotti* shouted, as is the custom of sailors. That *Sabbatino* presented to the captain some wax, sugar and a *scxula*—that is, one of the white cloths the Moors wear on their heads—and a large sack of snow. It was a great marvel to all the company to be in Syria in July and see a sack of snow. It was also a comfort to many, because some of the snow was put into the water—which was hot—and cooled it.

Nothing else could be got from these dogs, except that when lunch was over, which had been prepared very sumptuously for them, Abrayno restored to the galley, in the sight of every man, what he had eaten on board the galley and outside. Then, throwing himself on the carpets, which were spread all over the poop, where they had been received on the galley by the captain, he stayed there to rest, with his slaves, for the space of two hours. The *Sabbatino* and the other dogs who had come, departed immediately when they saw the festival of Abrayno, and went ashore.

On Friday, the 25th of July, Saint James's day, in response to the earnest prayers of Fra Francesco Suriano *(Note 76)*, Prior of Mount Sion, and of the scribe of the galley, who was on land representing the captain, those dogs consented to allow the pilgrims to go on shore—that is, to suffer for lack of everything. But when two boat-loads had been sent, the rest were stopped because the Scribe of Jerusalem said he could not stay any longer in the sun to count the pilgrims, and that the others must wait until the following day. There was great distress in consequence, on the part of those ashore and those who remained on the galley, because we saw that we were ill-treated and separated, and we could not understand why. One thing was evident, however, that no pilgrims in that place had ever been so badly used as we were. Nevertheless, as well as possible, we laid hands on one of those sacks we had brought on board the galley—I mean the sack of patience.

Many of the pilgrims, seeing how badly we were treated, told the captain that he should not hesitate to lay hands on the other sack if necessary—I mean that of the money—rather than suffer such torments. In truth he always treated the pilgrims courteously and with great consideration; and now he begged them to have patience, saying that he did not want to create bad precedents with those Moors, and that if we did not show them our teeth they would do worse.

On Saturday, the 26th of July, the magnificent captain made the rest of the pilgrims get up early, thinking to send them all on land; and two other boat-loads went. In obedience to the advice given me the first day I entered the galley—that is, never to be among the first to go off the galley—I always let the Ultramontanes—who trod on each other's heels in their haste to leave—rush in front. When the boats returned for the rest, that often-mentioned Abrayno wanted to come on board the galley to see the merchandise which had been brought; and when he had seen it, and also bought what he wanted, and, further, settled his accounts with his mouth as much as he could (I speak as covertly as I can not to disgust the readers of this chapter), he departed, saying that he did not want any more pilgrims to be sent on land that day, as the sea had upset him and he did not feel he could attend to the counting of them. And this—to torment further the poor pilgrims who were already eleven days in this exile.

On Sunday, the 27th of July, the rest of the pilgrims were put ashore save five, who, according to his wish, remained with the captain; amongst them were Fra Francesco Trivulzio and the priest Pietro Casola, both Milanese.

When the Dry Mass had been said, Fra Francesco caused the *galeotti* to be summoned to the usual place, and preached them a beautiful sermon, taking for his subject; " Et coepit ejicere vendentes et ementes in Templo." [1] He gave thereon a beautiful dissertation on trading—buying and selling—and what was lawful and unlawful in that connection, and he expounded everything very fully.

On his return to the galley the captain was accompanied by the Governor of Rama and the Diodar[2] of Gaza, who remained on board looking at a great many cloth goods; then they went away about their business.

On Monday, the 28th of July, the captain went ashore, and while he was there, an Arab chief (as they say) called the Governor of Nabule,[3] a place in Samaria, arrived, and, as the captain afterwards recounted, took from him by force a hundred ducats before he would let him return to the galley. The captain was in a very bad humour

---

1. "And he began to cast out the buyers and sellers in the Temple."—Matt. xxi. 12; Luke. xix. 45

2. This appears to be the same person as the "Sabbatino" or representative of the Governor of Gaza, mentioned before.

3. Shechem or Sichem, the original capital of Samaria, now called "Nablus," a corruption of Neapolis, the name given to it by Vespasian.

because of the money and also on account of the wretched life he saw the pilgrims leading in those caves, where they were badly off for everything and could neither go on their journey to Jerusalem nor return to the galley, as they would have done very gladly. About the twenty-first hour the said Governor of Nabule came to the galley and bought certain cloths and other things. Still we remained in exile, on the galley and outside the galley, and this was the twelfth day.

On Tuesday, the 29th of July, in the morning, the Governor of Gaza arrived at Jaffa with a large company, and established himself on the highest place there, which looks like a hill—really there are extensive ruins there which have formed a sort of small hill. At the sight of so many tents pitched, the *parono* and the scribe were sent from the galley; and having heard everything from the Prior of Mount Sion, they returned to the galley and told the captain that the Governor of Gaza wished him to go ashore to send off the pilgrims. As he delayed somewhat, the aforesaid Prior came to fetch the captain, and they went ashore together, and visited the said Governor of Gaza.

While they were arranging for the expedition, the Governor of Nabule, the Arab chief, departed, and went home with the hundred ducats he had taken from the captain. In the evening, the aforesaid captain returned to the galley, saying, that he had come to terms and arranged everything with the Governor of Gaza.

On Wednesday, the 30th of July, in order that we should not go on our journey too quickly, certain mushrooms [1] sprang up among those ruins of Jaffa which we had to eat before we could depart. For when the captain—who had gone with two boat-loads of different things to offer to

---

1. *i.e.*, Difficulties, annoyances.

JAFFA—THE PRISONERS RANSOMED

the Moors according to custom in order to have the license to depart—was in the tent of the Governor of Gaza, the said Governor caused ten Christians, natives of Cyprus, whom he had taken prisoners, to be brought into his presence in chains. According to what they said, they had left Acre, otherwise Ptolemaida, in a ship loaded with merchandise; but a storm arose and the ship broke up. As, in the opinion of the sailors, there was nothing else to be done, they begged to be put ashore to save themselves, and while they were in a wood they were found by the Moors, who seized them saying that they had gone there to steal.

The Governor of Gaza said to the captain and also to the Prior of Mount Sion, that the pilgrims must redeem the prisoners, or that he would flay them alive before their eyes. As an altercation followed, he caused one of the prisoners to be stripped and stretched out by the executioner, and made as if he would have him flayed. The Prior—as a monk, and belonging to the Order he does—moved with compassion, put an end to the scene; and thus, just as we ought to have arisen and gone on our way, it was necessary to stay there and bargain for those chained men, for whose ransom the Governor of Gaza demanded a thousand ducats. Finally he was brought down to a hundred and fifty, and the collection was made among the pilgrims, so that the prisoners were redeemed and taken naked and famished on board the galley. I was taxed a ducat, which I paid.

Seeing that the ground was soft, and that the Christians were compassionate, those dogs brought in a Jew and a Frenchman, and the Governor of Gaza threatened to flay them if we did not ransom them. The captain told him he could do as he pleased provided he let us go on our way. The Jew was well beaten, and that coward of a Frenchman denied Christ, and the *sexula* was placed on his head.

By this time, as the sun had almost set, they said we should depart in the morning; for the present we remained there. The pilgrims suffered much in those caves, for they were not even at liberty to go out and make a little water, so many were there of those Moorish dogs there.

On Thursday, the 31st of July, when we thought to set out, those dogs began to bark and to try and extort more from the captain—some one thing and some another. The trouble was two-fold—that of the captain who saw the outrages inflicted by the Moors, and the other of the pilgrims who suffered more than usual on land, and many were ill in consequence.

That morning, one of the pilgrims—a Frenchman—died, and was buried on the seashore. This was the third pilgrim who died before we could go to Jerusalem. As the pilgrims saw that we were in great danger, at least from sickness, they said to the captain that he must either take them back to the galley or conduct them from that place; if not, proceedings would be taken against him for damages and interest.

In the opinion of many, the said captain did his duty, and would gladly have departed or taken the company back on to the galley, but those dogs wanted nothing but money.

Many pilgrims fell ill on account of the great privations of every kind they had to endure; and when anyone fell ill he had need to recommend himself to God, for there was no other remedy or medecine to be had. The captain remained on land that night, but I stayed on board the galley by his order, and felt compassion for those outside.

On Friday, the 1st of August, in the morning, the captain received license to depart, having satisfied those dogs up to that point; and he sent for me to go ashore. Taking the baggage I had already prepared, I gave the rest of my possessions in charge to a *galeotto*, and landed at

JAFFA

Jaffa, anciently called Joppa, which was built by the descendants of Ham, the son of Noah, who was cursed by his father. This country, inhabited by Canaanites, fell to him by lot when he divided the world with his two brothers, one called Shem the other Japhet.

Saint Peter performed many miracles in Joppa; amongst others he raised Tabitha from the dead. To judge by the ruins and also by the numerous marbles found there by the great Sultan—and used by him for building a new mosque which they say is a very beautiful building—the said Joppa must have been a beautiful citadel. It has a fine circuit of ruins, but one cannot understand what they were. Towards the sea there are certain vaults, one behind the other, where the poor pilgrims were lodged on the bare ground very uncomfortably. On the other side, that is, towards Rama, there are certain vestiges of a wall, as if the place had been surrounded by a wall. As I said before, what looks like a hill is formed by ruins which have fallen one on top of the other and made a sort of hill. The two towers there, were built for protection on the side facing the sea, because the Moors are always on the alert. This place or city was always without a harbour; there are continual tempests there, and it is dangerous to go among those ruins.

I find that the Romans destroyed Joppa after the destruction of Jerusalem. When I inquired why it is called Jaffa and not Joppa, I learned that there is a large village near, with a population of perhaps a thousand souls, which is called Jaffa, and as Joppa has ceased to exist, the port has taken the name of Jaffa. Just as people speak of the port of Turbigo,[1] and yet Turbigo is some distance away, and sometimes that same port is called the port of Galliate.[2] There is nothing else to be said about this shore of Jaffa.

1. *Turbigo* is on the west bank of the Ticino to the north of Magenta, and north-west of Milan.
2. *Galliate* is on the east bank of the Ticino, almost opposite Turbigo.

CHAPTER XI.

Pilgrims leave Jaffa.—Casola's Bargain with his Mule Driver.—Ride from Jaffa to Rama.—Hostel at Rama.—Sermon Preached by the Prior of Mount Sion.—Visit to Lydda.—Christians of the Girdle.—Description of Rama.—Death of Cypriano de Porri.—Ride from Rama.—Casola's Adventure.—Arrival at Jerusalem.—The Pilgrims' Quarters there.—The Captain's Lodgings.—Father Fran. Trivulzio Attacked by Fever.—The Prior of Mount Sion and His Treatment of the Pilgrims.

At Vespers, with great shouting from the Moors and Christians, the pilgrims mounted—some on asses, some on mules, some on horses, and each beast had a pack saddle on its back and a cord or chain round its neck. These animals were all provided by that Abrayno Grasso named above, in accordance with the agreement he had made with the captain of the galley. The captain paid him so much a head for the pilgrims, and he furnished the animals for them. In addition, the pilgrims had to give something to the owners of the animals; otherwise they cause you many annoyances, and are very disagreeable. Sometimes they make a rider tumble off his animal and then extort several *marchetti*[1] before they will help him up.

Chance gave me a mule, and as I was advised to do so by the captain, I bargained with the owner of the mule to give him a ducat extra as a gratuity,[2] for the whole journey, with the understanding that I was not to pay him

---

1. The *Marchetto* was coined by Francesco Dandolo about 1330. It was worth twelve piccoli, and was also called a soldo. (Gallicciolli, i. p. 580.)
2. Casola uses the word "*Cortesia*."

PILGRIMS LEAVE JAFFA FOR RAMA

until he had brought me back to Jaffa. He was satisfied with this, and asked my name, and I asked his; he was called Balzi. In this way I had no further annoyance from those gratuities, though, truth to tell, the said driver was of little service, even to me, on the way.

When all the Christians were mounted, and also the Moors—that is, that grand escort given us by Abrayno Grasso, of barefooted Mamelukes, armed with bows and quivers full of arrows—we set out, in the name of the Most High God, for the city of Rama through a beautiful plain. The heat was great and there was a great deal of dust. There was little shade by the way, and very few green boughs were to be found with which to drive away the flies. All the country round is cleared—that is, of trees, but very full of cotton, which at that time was beginning to ripen. Half way between Jaffa and Rama there is a place called Malcasale, because sometimes there are great robberies there. The said Mamelukes had a hunt through that country with horses only, and they caught a hare without dogs.

In the evening, all sunburnt and dusty, we reached Rama, and those Moorish dogs made us dismount a good way from Rama because we had to pass by a place where they bury their dead; and when we had dismounted, every man carried his baggage to the place where we went to lodge near the gate of Rama.

The said place [1] belongs to the friars of Mount Sion, although there are not always friars there. It is taken care of by a Christian of the Girdle *(Note 77)* called Moyses. There is not a stool to be found in the place; it is like a disordered hospital. The entrance is like a square window large enough to admit one person. I felt

---

1. The monastery at Rama was given to the friars by Philip the Good, Duke of Burgundy, so that they might give shelter there to pilgrims.—Porro.

as if I were going into the Stinche *(Note 78)* at Florence. There was no order in the lodgings; he was wisest who seized a place first. There was nothing but the ground. Whoever was willing, however, to spend a few *marcelli* [1] could get matting from the Moors; there was no straw.

I followed the captain, to whom a certain wretched room was assigned, where he placed his mattress which he had caused to be brought from the galley. I accompanied him as his secretary; he had no one else with him save me and his steward. I do not think he paid a tax for us two, by order, from what I could understand. My place in that poor room was a certain wooden plank, between a third and a fourth [of a *braccio*] thick, raised from the ground on two stones. As long as we were at Rama, both going and returning, my folded mantle was my bed, and under my head I kept my purse containing all I possessed. Poor Don Fra Francesco could not find a comfortable spot. A certain place apart from the others was assigned to all the friars, but neither here nor there pleased him. A mattress brought from the galley was given also to him; no other person had one.

As soon as we entered the said place, as it was evening, many of the inhabitants of Rama came there, both Moors and Christians of the Girdle, as they are called. I could not find out with certainty the reason for this name; some say one thing some another, so I leave the matter. These men brought bread, cooked eggs, much fruit and rice cooked in milk to sell to the pilgrims. Wine is not sold by the Moors; those Christians sell a little, but it is dear. Many barrels of it were brought from the galley and sold at a high price. In the said lodging there was a good cistern which greatly alleviated the thirst of the pilgrims.

---

1. The Marcello was a piece of silver money coined first in 1472 or 1473. It was worth ten soldi, and seems to have taken its name from the Doge Nicolo Marcello, at whose election "Marcelli" were thrown to the populace.

As to eating and drinking, I did not lack good things because I ate with the captain; so did Frate Francesco, who was always summoned at meal times; and at table there was no lack of the best things that could be found.

On the morning of Saturday, the 2nd of August, after Mass and a sermon preached in Latin by the Prior of Mount Sion, the said Prior ordered certain of his friars to direct the pilgrims, some on foot, some on horseback, to a certain little village *(Note 79)*, where there was formerly a beautiful church built of square blocks, which contains an altar on which they say Saint George was beheaded. It is much venerated also by the Moors, according to what those Christians of the Girdle said. I am sure I do not know in what way, because when I saw the place it was very neglected. It is true that those Moors took a *marchetto* from each Christian who wished to enter.

After gaining the indulgence, whoever wanted to mount there mounted; whoever wanted to go could do as he liked. I was not in a hurry because we were near Rama, and I stayed a while to watch the cotton making *(Note 80)* because many of the Moors in the little village were busy at that work; nevertheless I was back at Rama as soon as the others. And after such a dinner as could be got, for there were no other provisions for the pilgrims save the hard-boiled eggs sold by the Moors, some went to rest, others went to see the place.

I went to see what I could with certain of those Christians of the Girdle who knew a little Italian, only a little, but on that occasion I made good use of them. In the past the city of Rama must have been a beautiful city. It covers a large area, is situated in a plain, and has walls and gates, though they are not strong enough to resist the attack of an armed force. The gates are carefully closed, nevertheless they can be opened easily. There are many vestiges of what seem to have been fine houses there in former times, but now they are all tumbled down. There was a palace where Abrayno lodged which was very beautiful to look at, but it was partly in ruins. I pass over the dwelling of the Lord of Rama, which is beautiful and which has its mosque and a very beautiful bell-tower, on which during the night a man stood who, to my hearing, did nothing but yelp.

In the said city I saw two beautiful streets called bazaars. In one street, on one side, nothing is sold except things to eat, both cooked and raw; in the other there was their merchandise. This city has a more abundant supply of fruit than Jerusalem. From what I could understand, the supply of fruit came at that time from the city of Gaza; and this I understood because the sellers frequently invited the buyers by saying that their wares came from Gaza. Indeed the Prior of Mount Sion said to me several times that they were the best fruits in those bazaars. He had been many years in those parts, both as a layman and as a friar, so that he knew the Moorish tongue well; and he told me further that he had seen bunches of grapes at Gaza which weighed thirty-six pounds of twelve ounces. As he belongs to the Order he does I took his word for this, although it seemed to me an extraordinary thing. I saw very large grapes, larger than I ever saw in our country, and much better than ours. Besides other fruit, Rama has a greater abundance of dates than any place I saw in the Levant. The pilgrims bought also a great quantity of *melanzane*,[1] cooked and well prepared.

The houses have flat roofs which collect all the rain-water. Besides the tower I mentioned, which is called the

---

[1] The Melanzana is a herbaceous plant which bears white or blue flowers. The fruit, which contains a white pulp, is long in shape and violet in colour. It is generally fried.

Governor's Tower, there are other very beautiful bell-towers. At night the priests or *cathibissa*, as they call them, go up and yelp like dogs. When I asked our interpreter what they said, he told me that after midnight they called to those who had wives to increase and multiply on the earth; whether that be true or not I cannot say. They have indeed many women for wives, so that they can increase in the world.

The provision market is not bad. The bread is unleavened, but otherwise good; there are fine cooked fowls for three *marchetti* each, and four cooked eggs cost a *marchetto*. I stood to watch all these things, though I bought nothing for myself. When the captain went to table I went also; the rest of the pilgrims, however, fared badly.

On Sunday, the 3rd of August, after Mass, the Moors began to swarm into the hostel where we were, because of a great controversy which had sprung up since our arrival at Rama, between our captain and Abrayno on account of certain unusual extortions Abrayno wanted to make—and not a few either. For that reason a sermon which Father Fra Francesco wished to preach was prohibited, and thus we were delayed in port longer than usual.

At Vespers one called Cipriano de' Porri passed from this life. He said he was a Milanese, and paymaster for Count Filippo Rosso, captain of some men-at-arms of the Signoria of Venice. He was buried in a certain place outside Rama, said to have been bought for that purpose by the pilgrims. The funeral service was held in the hostel, and then after a certain sum had been paid to those Christians of the Girdle, he was carried outside in the evening on a piece of matting as secretly as possible.

In consequence of the disputes between the captain and the Moors the pilgrims suffered great hardships, sleeping on the ground, and many fell ill. As well as I could I kept myself on that plank mentioned above.

On Monday, the 4th of August, after a great altercation with that Abrayno often mentioned—who provoked new ones every hour to extort money—which was calmed by the intervention of the Prior of Mount Sion, and after the pilgrims had been counted like sheep, at the hour of Vespers, we all—both those who were well and those who were sick—left Rama in immense heat. And those dogs compelled us to go a good way on foot in great disparagement of the Christian faith, because we had to pass by a place where they buried their dead. When we had passed that place, with loud shouts and contemptuous acts they made us mount the animals prepared for us by the said Abrayno according to the agreement made at Jaffa. As the sun continually beat down upon us, and as we rode through a plain where there was not a plant as long as a finger, we were consumed with the heat; nevertheless this malady was doctored, though badly, by laying hands on the second sack I mentioned above.

At sunset, when it was rather dark, the Mamelukes, who preceded us as an escort to defend us from the attacks of the Arabs, rode back towards the pilgrims in great haste, saying that they had been assailed by Arabs. They stopped the pilgrims, and it appeared as if they were doing great things for our protection; and that commotion was arranged with ten ducats.

As night fell we began to leave the plain and to ascend, following the Moors who had large lanterns on the tops of long poles, so that we could see for more than half a mile. As we rode thus some trees could be seen, but we could not distinguish what they were. The way was very stony, so that the beaten track could not be recognised. One person went behind the other, and perhaps the animals we were riding knew the way.

CASOLA FALLS OFF HIS MULE

An adventure befel me. The Moor to whom my mule belonged had heaped so many sacks on its back, both for feeding the mule and also of the merchandise he was taking to Jerusalem to sell, that I was very uncomfortable, and could hardly move. As the mule had no bridle, but only a cord round his neck, I could not control him; he went where he pleased. Besides this, in the evening the owner put a boy up behind me on the croup, who, he said, was his son. Thus riding, the boy fell asleep and tumbled off the mule, dragging me, the sacks and the pack-saddle to the ground, or rather on to a stone, and I hurt my arm and foot so badly that when I got back to Milan my wounds were not yet healed.

As best I could I put my wallet and the stirrups on my back and went lamenting and limping behind the caravan in order not to lose myself, leaving the mule and all he had without any other guard. It was a piece of good luck for me that we were near the place where the Moors wanted the pilgrims to stop and rest in a large olive grove. With some difficulty I sought out the captain, who had kindly sent to look for me. When he heard my woes he could do nothing for me but console me by saying that I should not lack a mount. While we were waiting thus on the stones my arm swelled so that it was necessary to unsew the whole of the sleeve of my doublet. As well as I could I made use of the first sack—that is, of patience.

On Tuesday, the 5th of August, at sunrise, the order was given to get on horseback, and in a moment all were mounted on their animals. By order of the captain I had already taken a horse, when suddenly the Moor appeared who owned the mule I had left behind and had a great dispute with the owner of the horse. Finally I was obliged to get off the horse and mount again on the mule, but I gave the owner to understand through the interpreter that I would not have a single thing on the mule.

Thus we set out towards Jerusalem by a very stony, mountainous and disagreeable road. By the way a few ancient but ruined houses were to be seen—habitations for goats. The country seemed to me very bare and wild; there was no fruit to be seen, nor did we come across any beautiful fountains. These are not like the countries of Italy.

God willing, at an early hour we reached the Holy City of Jerusalem, almost dead of heat and thirst, and those dogs made us dismount outside the city near a castle called the Castle of the Pisans. It is said that the Pisans were formerly Lords of Jerusalem, and built the said castle. I have not found any authentic record of the fact, nor did I open the third sack on this account.

When we were all gathered together and counted again we were conducted into the city by certain friars of Mount Sion who had come to meet us, and quartered in the Hospital of St. John, as it is called. When we entered, after asking for a little fresh water, we began to lie down on the ground; then certain persons appointed by the friars gave each pilgrim a carpet to spread on the ground. The magnificent captain was in the habit of lodging with two persons in Mount Sion, which is a good way outside the city; but this Prior, however, in order to appear wiser than his predecessors, had taken him a house within the city [1] near to the Sepulchre. He went there to rest, and then in his goodness he sent to fetch me from the hospital, and made me lodge with him.

The Venerable Don Fra Antonio Regna, a true and excellent friar, with whom I made good friends because he was a Milanese, seeing that my arm, foot and almost

---

1. See Introduction, pp. 96-98.

all my body were badly hurt, provided me with two carpets and a mattress as large as my person, and two leather cushions. A good room was assigned to me, which I shared with Don Simone Fornaro of Pavia and Giovanni Luchino of Montecastello, companions of the Venerable Father Don Fra Francesco, who, although he lodged with the friars in Mount Sion, could not obtain permission for these two companions to join him. In general they took their meals in Mount Sion, but at night they came to sleep in the room with me.

I took rest for that day because I had need of it, but I did not lose courage. Father Fra Francesco at once fell ill of a fever; however, he lacked nothing in the world; he had a good doctor and excellent medicine. We lived like lords in the house and at the table of the captain, but the poor pilgrims fared badly, and it was all the fault of that Prior who had little charity for the pilgrims; not a single person was satisfied with him, beginning with the captain. All the friars shrugged their shoulders and excused themselves because they could not treat the pilgrims as they used to do in the time of the former Priors. And worse befell us when he gave the order that we were not to go out of the house without his permission.

CHAPTER XII.

The Pilgrims visit the Mount of Olives, the Valley of Jehoshaphat, and other Holy places.—Casola's description of Jerusalem.—The Great Mosque and the Temple of Solomon.—The Palace Miraculously Ruined.—Mount Sion and the Friar's Church and Monastery.—Castle of the Pisans.—The Inhabitants of Jerusalem.—First Visit to the Holy Sepulchre.—Death of a French Pilgrim.—Expedition to Bethlehem.—Second Visit to the Holy Sepulchre.—Ten Knights Created there for whom Casola wrote Letters of Testimony.

On Wednesday, the 6th of August, Mass having been said in the midst of the hospital, all the pilgrims set out early, guided by certain friars of Mount Sion, who were familiar with all the places to be visited by the pilgrims.

Leaving Jerusalem and passing that torrent called in the Holy Scriptures the torrent Cedron, we came to a monument built in the ancient fashion which was said to be that of Absalom, the son of David, who was killed by Joab, David's captain, when he was hung up by his hair while he was pursuing his father. On seeing it, I thought it was more probably the monument of Helena, Queen of the Adiabene, because so I had read in Josephus' wars of the Jews.

Then, going further, we visited all those sacred places on the Mount of Olives where the mysteries which preceded the passion of Our Lord Jesus Christ were shown to us: where he remained to pray, where the three disciples were when he prayed "Pater si possible est transeat a me calix

JERUSALEM—THE HOLY PLACES

iste," [1] and where he was apprehended. Then we mounted higher to where there was a small church, or part of one, and over the altar there was a stone still bearing the mark of the foot of Our Lord Jesus Christ when he ascended into heaven, and this was touched with the rosaries and other objects of devotion. In these places—because they are so despised by those Moorish dogs and are not otherwise venerated—it is necessary to open the third sack, called the sack of faith, otherwise the voyage would be made in vain. I do not mention that any antiphons or prayers were said there, because those Fathers did not say any; they only explained in Latin and in the vulgar tongue what those places were and nothing else. Many itineraries, however, both Italian and Ultramontane, written in the vulgar tongue and in Latin, mention that formerly antiphons and prayers appropriate to the places visited used to be said. I can only say that in fact this was not done. I can well believe that as the friars were in such a hurry to show us those places, they omitted some of the usual ceremonies.

Afterwards we descended the Mount of Olives and, turning to the right hand, we went into the valley of Jehoshaphat, who was King of Jerusalem. It is a small valley, nevertheless it is said that it will be the place of the Last Judgment of Our Lord Jesus Christ. In this valley there is a beautiful church containing the Sepulchre in which the body of Our Lady was placed by the eleven Apostles. The place of the Sepulchre proper is governed by the Latin friars—that is, by those of Mount Sion. In the same church there are several other altars served by Greek priests. The said church, from what I could hear, is held in great veneration also by the Moorish women. At the entrance to that church the Moors made

---

1. "O my Father, if it be possible, let this cup pass from me."—Matthew, xxvi. 39.

a charge for each person. I do not know how much it was because the captain paid.

After the prescribed prayers had been offered in the said church, which descends many steps, we returned to Jerusalem by the gate called the gate of St. Stephen, where he was stoned. Above the torrent Cedron, outside the gate on the left-hand side of the entrance, there is what looks like a little church. When I asked a Christian of the Girdle what it was, he said that the Lord of Damascus had built it in memory of one of his sons who was buried there, and that he had placed there a reservoir of water for wayfarers, which is never empty; and this is the will of the said Lord, even though the water should have to be brought from Damascus. And all this he has done for the repose of the soul of his said son.

Within the said gate, a house was pointed out which they said was the house of Pilate, and another which they said was Herod's. We went to a certain place said to be the pool of Siloam, where the blind man was sent to bathe his eyes. There is no water now, and the place is full of ruins.

We went to see the Probatic pool.[1] This has running water, and there are even a few vestiges of the five porches which the Holy Scripture says were there at the time of Christ. This was a pool which had the virtue that an angel descended from heaven into the said pool and moved the water, and the first sick person who entered the pool after the moving of the water was cured of all his infirmities. Therefore, under those porches, there used to lie a great multitude of sick persons in order to be ready to enter the water quickly; and Christ with a word only healed one who had been there eighteen years. Now, as could be seen, the Moors washed there the hides which had

1. The Pool of Bethesda.—John, v. 1-9.

been in lime. Many of the pilgrims drank the water. When I saw that filth I left it alone, it was enough for me to wash my hands there.

As it was on our way, we afterwards saw the Mosque which they say stands on the site of the temple of Solomon. It is a beautiful building to look at from the outside, and strong compared with the greater part of the habitations in Jerusalem. It is wonderful to see the courts—so well paved with the whitest marble—which are built around at the base of the Mosque.

When we had seen what the friars wanted us to see— opening the first and third sacks where it was necessary and where I judged it advisable to do so—we arrived at the hospital all hot and covered with dust, and took a little repose and also some refreshment, and whoever had a lodging went there. The Prior of Mount Sion now sent to tell the pilgrims that every man must be ready to enter the Holy Sepulchre that evening. But when he wanted to arrange for the entrance with Abrayno, who was the person in authority, he demanded first a thousand ducats. An altercation followed, and in consequence the project of entering the Sepulchre was given up.

As the captain's house was frequented by a very agreeable Moor who had formerly been forced into slavery at Rhodes, and who knew a little Latin, to while away the time, I got him for a few *marchetti* to take me and certain other pilgrims to see as much as possible of the city; and I studied it as carefully as I could.

The city of Jerusalem is very ancient. Its first founder was Canaan,[1] the grandson of Ham, son of Noah—that son as I said who was cursed by his father Noah because seeing him uncovered he mocked him. When the three sons of Noah—that is, Shem, Ham and Japhet—divided

---

1. Canaan was the *son* of Ham.

the world amongst them after the deluge, that part called Judea fell to the progeny of Ham, and in Judea Jerusalem has always been the chief city.

At first it was called Solyma,[1] and was an insignificant place, but afterwards from time to time it was enlarged, as Rome was. Although it lies between various mountains or rather hills, it seems that there are many flat parts, nevertheless it is in the mountains. As is generally known, Titus Cæsar in the second year of the reign of Vespasian destroyed it so completely that no one who looked on the ruins could have imagined that it had ever been inhabited. He did not leave there one stone upon another except in three towers preserved as a record that the Romans had subdued such a great city. I saw the foundations of the said towers; they are very wonderful. They are on the way down from Mount Sion before crossing the torrent Cedron.

After a long time Hadrian caused the city to be re-built and wished it to be called Helias.[2] To judge by the ruins it was not re-built as it had been at first, and he gave it for a habitation to the Christians. Since that time it has been attacked very often—now by the Saracens, now by the Christians. As all the histories relate, Saint Helena, mother of the Emperor Constantine, caused all the mysteries of the humanity of Our Lord Jesus Christ to be adorned, but afterwards many of them were destroyed and few remain to us because those Moorish dogs will not permit any restorations to be made.

As I went about the city I did not see beautiful dwelling-houses. There are a great number, and they are close together, but they are ugly. All the houses appear to be vaulted and have vaults above vaults. The roofs are

---

1. That is "Salem," the City of Peace.—Psalms. lxxvi. 2; Genesis, xiv 18.
2. Ælia Capitolina was the Roman name of Jerusalem.

flat, and there is little woodwork inside. The more a man wishes to say about this city the less he has to say, except that such a famous city, called by Christians the Holy Place, is a great *cavagniaza*.[1] There are some very honourable dwellings, though not many. Among the number is the house of the Governor, who, as I said, is like a Commissioner. There is also the habitation of the *Grand Cathibissa*, or as they call him the Old Man of the Faith,[2] to whom honour and reverence is paid as if he were a saint.

What pleased me most was the sight of the bazaars—long, vaulted streets extending as far as the eye can reach. In one of them all the provisions are sold—I mean also the cooked provisions, as they sell the chestnuts at home. When I marvelled at this I was told that not a single person in Jerusalem does the cooking in the house; and whoever wishes to eat goes to buy in the bazaar. However, they make bread at home—that is, flat cakes made without leaven; they are good when there is no other bread to be got. Leavened bread can only be had in the Monastery at Mount Sion. Cooked fowls, cooked meat, eggs and all other eatables are very cheap. I saw another long bazaar like the other, with both sides full of merchandise, and of the things the people know how to make, and this was a beautiful sight.

The city has one beautiful building; that is its Mosque *(Note 81)*. Neither Christian nor Jew can enter there. Outside one can see what a beautiful place it is with those courts round it as I mentioned above. I heard from the Moors that there are neither paintings nor images inside. They say that there are a thousand lamps within, which on certain occasions are all lighted at the same moment.

1. "Cavagniaza"=a market basket made of rushes. Casola's idea in applying the term to Jerusalem is not clear to me.
2. The Turkish title "Sheik-el-Islam"=the Old Man of the Faith.

Many people say that this Mosque is the Temple built by Solomon. But I cannot believe it, because I have not found any writing which would give me a reason for believing this, or that it is on the site of the Temple of Solomon; because the Holy Scripture relates that Nebuchadnezzar, King of Babylon, caused the Temple of Solomon to be thrown to the ground. We know also that Ezra, with the permission of Cyrus, King of the Medes and Persians, caused it to be re-built from the foundations. Then in true histories we find that Herod the Great—the one who was King of Judea at the time of the birth of Christ—caused it to be rebuilt. And besides all that, the Temple of Solomon was built on a mountain, and on that mountain called Mount Moriah, which was pointed out by God to Abraham when he told him he must sacrifice his son Isaac. This was also the place where the sleeping Jacob saw in a dream the ladder which reached from earth to heaven, and the angels ascending and descending, and said: "This is the house of God and the gate of Heaven"; and it was also the place where David saw the angel, sword in hand, striking the people with the plague, and prayed God to pardon the people and strike him instead. And God commanded him to build an altar there and offer sacrifices, and David did at once as God commanded him. He bought the site from Hornan, who was a Jebusite—that is, a Gentile; and he commanded Solomon, his son, to build a temple there after his death, and this was done. Therefore this Mosque cannot be on the site of the Temple of Solomon because it is in the valley, and that was on a mountain. Further, there is authentic record that, after Titus caused the Temple to be levelled to the ground because it was the greatest fortress the Jews then possessed, —it has never been re-built.

It appears to me that there are no vestiges remaining

JERUSALEM—THE MOSQUES

of the said Temple, and that this Mosque was built according to the will of the Moors after the Christians had lost Jerusalem, which was in the reign of Saladin, Lord of Babylon, and they have never been able to recover it since. However that may be, like the other smaller one which the Usbech—the present Governor of Jerusalem—caused to be built ten years ago, it is a stupendous thing; and it appears to me that the Moors do not lack good master workmen for their buildings. I heard from certain of the friars at Mount Sion that he used many of the marbles which were found at Joppa—that is, Jaffa—buried under the ruins; and some were also raised out of the water. Our magnificent captain assured me that this was true, because a few years ago he was obliged with his boats to help to raise certain columns which were in the water there at Jaffa, and which were afterwards dried and taken to Jerusalem to be used in the building of the new Mosque about which we have been talking. So that, in my judgment, there is not a vestige left of the said Temple of Solomon.

At the side of this Mosque there is a beautiful dwelling, almost the most beautiful in Jerusalem, where lives one who is called the Old Man of his Faith. He is a handsome man, and besides the Faith he is worth looking at. He has the care of these mosques, and especially of this new one. It is not an article of belief or unbelief—what was said while our magnificent captain was with the said old man—that is, that in the said new Mosque there were a thousand lamps constantly burning. I wanted to find out for certain, but it was impossible. I saw nothing else beautiful in the said city.

I saw indeed a thing worth recording; that is, a miracle. There is a palace ruined on one side. It is built in the modern style, rooms above rooms; in short, there is not its equal in Jerusalem. It belonged to a rich Moor. When the friars of Mount Sion were building at the side of their monastery a certain chapel of Our Lady, which was greatly venerated, the said Moor stirred up all the people on account of the said building to such an extent that all the Moors in a state of fury rushed there and destroyed the said chapel. And immediately the said palace was ruined, and no one has been able to re-build it since. I recount this because I saw both places, and heard the story from the Fathers of Mount Sion.

The Mount of Sion is the highest in Jerusalem, and in ancient times it was called the rock or city of David. The said rock was so strong that the children of Israel—that is, the Jews or Hebrews—even when they had entered the Promised Land and divided it by lot could never conquer it until David became King, and even he was King several years before he could take it. At last he took it and made it his dwelling. Now the observant friars of St. Francis live there, and they have a very well kept convent, and as the friars say, if it were not for the prohibition of the Moors who will not let them build, they would make it much more beautiful.

The friars' church is very beautiful, but it is not very large. They say that at the time of Our Lord Jesus Christ this church was the large room in which he ate the last supper with his disciples before his passion. Where the high altar stands was the place where, after supper, he first ordained the Sacrament of his Body and Blood and gave it to his disciples. At the right of the said altar there is another altar said to be the place where Our Lord Jesus Christ washed the feet of his disciples. In these two places, in spite of my unworthiness, I said Mass and prayed to God for all my friends.

Outside the said church, on the right-hand side going

THE FRANCISCAN FRIARY

in towards the habitation of the friars, there is the place where the Apostles were gathered together when the Holy Spirit descended upon them. Under the said church there is a certain little chapel, where it is said that Saint Thomas put his hand into the side of Our Lord Jesus Christ, when he said to him: "Be not faithless but believing."

The convent is in good order considering that there are so few friars; they say there are always twenty friars who administer their part of the Sepulchre and also the place at Bethlehem. As I said above, if it were not for the prohibition of the Moors, the friars would do great things. As to building, they can do nothing, and if they do any repairs in the house they do them very secretly.

At the side of the church there is a chapel of Our Lady which was destroyed by the fury of the Moors, as I mentioned before, and immediately the house of him who caused the evil fell down.

The said friars have certain gardens round the monastery, but when we were there everything was dried up. When I went into the said gardens I saw many ruins all round, which showed that the city of Sion had been an important place in the time of the Kings. Near the said monastery there is what looks like a grand palace, and within the gate there is a little church belonging to certain Christians of the Girdle. They say that Saint James, who was said to be the brother of our Lord, was beheaded in that place by order of Herod, the son of that Herod who killed the Innocents.

A little further on, going towards the gate of Jerusalem —because the Mount called Sion is a good way outside Jerusalem—there is the castle of the Pisans. Seen from outside it appears to be strong. In my opinion no care is taken of it. I never saw a guard there, although I often passed that way, going from the lodging of the captain where I also lodged, to the monastery of the friars at Mount Sion.

The said city, as I said above, has not strong walls nor any moat. I have not said anything yet about the place of the Holy Sepulchre because up to this day I had not seen it.

Among the inhabitants of Jerusalem there are many of good condition and handsome men. They all go about dressed in the same way, with those clothes that look like quilts.[1] Many are white, others are made of camlet, and of other silks of the Moorish kind. According to their means they display great care and magnificence in the white cloths they wear on their heads. This cloth is called a *sexula* if it is all white, and *moro naturale* if there are some black stripes woven in the said *sexula*.

Whether they are renegade Christians or true Christians of the Girdle, they all live in the same way, and eat on the ground on carpets; they have a few white cloths, but they are rare. They do not drink wine—I mean in public—but if they get the chance they take a good long drink of it. They like cheese very much. They would not eat a fowl which had had its neck drawn, as is the custom with us. They always cut the fowls' throats; otherwise they are clean in their cooking. For sleeping they have no place but the ground. They lie upon carpets, of which they have a great many. In their manner of eating they are very dirty; even persons of importance thrust their hands into the dishes. They do not use knives or forks or spoons, but they thrust their hands into everything.

With regard to their prayers, I observed—from a window which overlooked certain Moors who slept in the open air because of the extreme heat—that in the morning

---

1. Casola writes: "Vano tuti vestiti a uno modo, con quilli panni pareno preponte: assaj ghe ne sono de bianche, ghe ne sono de zembeloti, e de altre siede a la morescha.'

JERUSALEM—THE INHABITANTS

when they rose they went through so many genuflexions—throwing themselves all their length stretched out on the ground—that it was a marvel to see them. When I inquired further I learned that when they go to pray in the Mosqué they go barefooted, and first they wash themselves in certain places set apart for that purpose, but only from the waist downwards, and then they uncover their heads, which they never uncover even in the presence of the greatest lord in the world. It is great madness to talk to them about our faith, because they have no rational sentiment in them. They are very impetuous and easily excited to anger, and they have no gracious or courteous impulses or actions. And I declare that they may be as great and as learned as you like, but in their ways they are like dogs.

In Jerusalem I was never able to see a beautiful woman; it is true that they go about with their faces covered by a black veil. They wear on their heads a thing which resembles a box, a *braccio* long, and from that, on both sides, a long cloth, like the white towels in Italy, hangs down.

I know nothing more about these Moorish people, except that they are very disagreeable to us Italians and to other kinds of Christians in asking for money, which is an extreme annoyance. On this account I was obliged to use a great deal of two of the three sacks.

On Thursday, the 7th of August, all the pilgrims went to Mount Sion, and there many confessed and also communicated in that most holy place where this most Holy Sacrament was instituted; and many said Mass there. We had amongst us sixty-three priests of different Orders. I said Mass and communicated one of our Milanese—Bernardino Scotto by name—and two Ragusans. Then the friars chanted very solemnly a Mass of the Holy Spirit,

R

and a beautiful sermon was preached in Latin by one of the friars of Mount Sion, in which he expounded all the mysteries contained in the said church of Mount Sion. When Mass was ended a procession was formed to the places of the said mysteries; and when the said procession was finished the said friars of Mount Sion refreshed all the pilgrims with a good dinner.

After dinner all the pilgrims were advised to go and take a rest in order to be ready that evening either to enter the Holy Sepulchre or to go to Bethlehem. At a very late hour the order was given to enter the Sepulchre. And this was because of a new extortion which was invented out of the ordinary way. Thus in the evening, at the twenty-third hour, all the pilgrims congregated before the door of the church of the Holy Sepulchre in a little court very beautifully paved with slabs of marble. In the middle of the court there is a stone which is honoured because it is said that Christ rested there on the way to the place of his passion.

The deputies who had been appointed to count the pilgrims were now ready. They were ten Moors—men of imposing appearance and not priests—who wore dresses as white as snow and had those large *sexule* on their heads. It made me feel very hot only to look at them. These men were seated on a certain small platform raised about two *braccia* from the ground and arranged with mats over the boards, because the said platform was made of wood; and there they were all seated on their legs, like the tailors sit at home. They made, however, a fine picture.

We waited until sunset expecting the Moor who keeps the keys and who could not be found. You must know that although the Sepulchre is governed by the friars of Mount Sion and by other sects of Christians, as you will

FIRST VISIT TO HOLY SEPULCHRE

hear, nevertheless they cannot go in or out at pleasure, but must do so at the pleasure of that dog who always keeps the keys. He is the Moor who auctions the tolls on the pilgrims and on those who wish to visit the Sepulchre even at other times. It is indeed true that in the door of the church there are certain cracks through which victuals and other things can be passed to those within.

The pilgrims were finally dismissed, as it was said that for that evening they could not enter, and the company therefore began to depart. The captain had already gone some distance when he encountered the man who had the keys. After much altercation and many words which I did not understand because they were in Moorish—although the Prior of Mount Sion understood them—we returned to the church of the Sepulchre and the door was opened to the praise of God. The deputies mentioned above began to count the pilgrims like sheep in Moorish, and the interpreter in Italian; and by the grace of God we entered that Holy Church *(Note 82)*.

Because it was already night every pilgrim immediately lighted his candle, and the friars of Mount Sion who had come for that purpose began to form the procession, beginning at a Chapel of Our Lady where the offices are said continually by the friars who are shut up there all the year. In that place Christ appeared to his blessed Mother after the Resurrection. When an anthem had been chanted there and the appointed prayer said, one of the friars declared in Latin all the mysteries and relics contained in the said chapel; in which, besides the apparition I mentioned, a large piece of the Cross of Christ is honoured. It is placed in a window in the said chapel on the gospel side of the altar, and can be seen but not touched. On the other side of the said altar a large piece of the column at which Our Lord Jesus Christ was scourged is honoured. It is a wonderful relic, because the marks of the blows can be seen sculptured upon it; but they cannot be touched too much or they would disappear. This column may be touched with one hand, and also with a few rosaries. In all the places there are large indulgences.

On leaving the said chapel the procession entered the body of the church and visited all the other places usually visited, and first the place where Christ appeared to Mary Magdalen in the form of a gardener. All the time the appointed anthems were being sung, and the Litanies chanted by the way. We then visited the place where Christ remained in prison whilst the hole was being made in which the Cross was erected. Then we visited the place where the garments of Christ were divided, and where the lots were cast for them. Then we went into the Chapel of Saint Helena, which goes down several steps, and after descending several other steps we saw the place where the Cross of Christ was found, which is below the place of the Calvary. Then returning above, we visited a chapel where there is the column to which Christ was bound when the crown of thorns was placed on his head. Then we mounted to the place of the Calvary, by a wooden staircase, with the greatest reverence.

There a beautiful sermon was preached on the passion of Christ by one of the friars of Mount Sion, in such a way that I believe that if those Moorish dogs had been present, together with all the pilgrims, they would have wept. We stayed there for over an hour, and when the sermon was finished and the usual prayer had been chanted we descended to the Holy Sepulchre and entered one by one.

When the offices commenced by the said friars were

finished, the company set about refreshing themselves as well as they could—that is, those of the pilgrims who had laid in a store of provisions. I went with the magnificent captain to a small place belonging to the friars of Mount Sion, and had supper, although it was late, because he had made good provision. The other pilgrims stayed in the church on the floor, some in one place, some in another. When the refection was over some lay down on the ground to sleep, others did not.

As soon as I saw that the crowd of Ultramontanes had diminished, I went again with my lighted candle to make all the visitations, and I touched the places and relics with my rosaries without any impediment. Then after the scrutiny had been made, and the number of the pilgrims taken by the friars—I mean of those who wanted to say Mass—they made out the clear lists, and we were divided between three places—that is, the Sepulchre, the place of the Calvary and the Chapel of Our Lady. Mass could also be said in the place where the body of Christ was laid when he was taken down from the Cross, while he was being anointed with the mixture brought by Nicodemus and by Joseph of Rama,[1] before he was laid in the Sepulchre. In that place anyone who wished could say Mass without any other order. According to this first arrangement I said Mass above the Sepulchre.

On Friday, the 8th of August, at the third hour of the day, we were let out of the church of the Sepulchre, and each of the pilgrims went to his lodging to rest as well as he could.

On Saturday, the 9th of August, early in the morning, all the pilgrims were gathered together in Mount Sion, and we were led by two friars of the monastery on a

---

1. According to some authorities Rama is the ancient Arimathea, the country of Joseph, who buried the body of Jesus.

pilgrimage—that is, to seek certain places usually visited by pilgrims, and which we had not yet visited. Meanwhile the Venerable Father Don Fra Francesco was ill with the fever and suffering pain; he was doubtful, but full of courage.

After the said visitation we all returned to Mount Sion, and that day a Frenchman, also a pilgrim, who had been ill from the time we went on board the galley, was buried.

Immediately after Mass had been heard, every man went to prepare to go to Bethlehem according to the order given by the friars, and thus at the nineteenth hour we set out in extreme heat, riding the usual animals; and we went along a very gay and beautiful road with beautiful gardens on both sides. In my opinion, the road from Jerusalem to Bethlehem is the most beautiful we saw in those parts, there are so many beautiful things there—grapes, figs and olives. By the way, we came to three springs. The Prior said that those springs began to flow when the star appeared to the wise men as they went from Jerusalem to Bethlehem to seek Our Lord Jesus Christ to adore him. Further on, near to Bethlehem, I saw the sepulchre of Rachel, the wife of the Patriarch Jacob, who died in childbed. It is beautiful and much honoured by the Moors.

At the twenty-third hour we reached Bethlehem. It was the vigil of Saint Lawrence, and we went to the convent of the friars, which is a very comfortable place. Immediately the procession was set in order by the friars and we went into the grotto where Christ was born, and there a sermon was preached. Then we sought out the other places usually visited.

After the devotions were performed, the pilgrims were lodged as well as possible. As I have said several times, thanks to the captain, I fared extremely well compared with the others.

BETHLEHEM

At midnight the pilgrims began to say Masses in the place where Christ was born, and where he was laid in the manger. The places are near together. In the same grotto, down several steps, there was the place where Saint Jerome made his dwelling for many years. Mass was also said there. I said my Mass where Christ was laid in the manger.

On Sunday, the 10th of August, the Prior, having made instance, whoever wished to visit those holy places again could do so—that is, where Saint Jerome translated the Bible from Hebrew into Latin, where his body was laid, and where the Innocents were killed by order of King Herod, who sought thus to slay Christ, when he was deceived by the three wise men.

The church at Bethlehem *(Note 83)* seems to me the most beautiful between Venice and Bethlehem. It is not only fine but extremely beautiful. Besides the body of the church in the centre, it has two shoulders, or as we say, two naves, each supported by eleven columns, so thick that one man alone cannot put his arms round them. They are very tall and all of one piece. The church is all adorned with most beautiful mosaics that look quite new. I was never tired of looking at the many beautiful pillars. I counted up to forty-four of them.

The said church is inhabited by a sect called Armenian Christians, although it is administered by the friars of Mount Sion. The Armenians, both big and little, male and female, live there on the ground, like pigs. They did nothing but cry out all night without intermission. At the entrance to the church it is necessary to pay money to the Moors.

From the ruins which are to be seen, the city of Bethlehem must have been a beautiful place. The country is fine and fruitful. There are few inhabitants now. A few families live there in certain ruins arranged for keeping cattle, which they keep even up to the door of the said church, to our great shame.

When day broke and the pilgrims had finished saying their Masses, the order was given that every man must mount the animal assigned to him, and we went to the hills of Judea. There we visited a ruined church said to be the place where Saint Elizabeth greeted Our Lady, and where she made that canticle: " Magnificat Anima mea Dominum ";[1] and then another church. Although this last was not in ruins and was a fine body of a church, yet those Moorish dogs keep their animals inside, and make all kinds of filth.

We visited the place where Saint John the Baptist was born, and the place where Saint Zachariah, his father, made the canticle: " Benedictus Dominus Deus Israel quia visitavit, etc."[2] Then we departed from there and returning to Jerusalem by another way, we visited the Church of the Holy Cross, which is in very good order and served by certain Greek monks. They say that the wood was cut down there of which the Cross of Our Lord Jesus Christ was made.

After this visitation we returned to Jerusalem to rest a little, because in truth the heat exhausted us greatly. The Venerable Don Fra Francesco Trivulzio, who, as I said, was more ill than well, and who yet wanted to visit every place, remained behind in Bethlehem, saying that he did not want to ride in so much dust, and that he wanted to make that visitation with certain friars of Mount Sion.

The rest of us went again that evening into the church of the Holy Sepulchre, but without the captain, because

---

[1]. My Soul doth magnify the Lord, &c.
[2]. Blessed be the Lord God of Israel for he hath visited, &c.

SECOND VISIT TO HOLY SEPULCHRE

between age—for he is old—the great heat and the great trouble given him by those Moorish dogs, he was very sick. We made the visitations as we did the first time we entered, but without either procession or friars, and each one performed his devotions as his feeling dictated. A new list was made, arranging how Masses were to be said by the pilgrims, in order that there should be no confusion. I said Mass in the place of the Calvary because this was the order.

That night ten knights were created in the Sepulchre *(Note 84)*, and they belonged to every nation of Italy. One was Don Giovanni Simone Fornaro of Pavia, who, as I said, had come with Fra Francesco from Ferrara; another was Don Giovanni de Burgho of Antwerp, in Burgundy; others were Germans and also Spaniards. As there was a dearth of scribes, I wrote several letters testifying that they had been created knights at the Sepulchre, according to the form given me by the Superior, and he sealed the letters.

CHAPTER XIII.

Visit to the River Jordan.—Jericho.—Fountain of Elisha.—Illness of Fra. Francesco Trivulzio.—Mountain of the Quarantina.—Return to Jerusalem. — Some Pilgrims Arrested. — Accusations brought against them.—Casola remains at Mount Sion, and Visits the Sepulchre of Our Lady.—Mass celebrated there by Georgian Christians.—Difficulties arranged and the Pilgrims released.—Third Visit to the Holy Sepulchre.—Tombs of Godfrey and Baldwin.—Description of the Church of the Holy Sepulchre.—Casola Visits Bethany.—History of the Sultan and the Usbech.

On Monday, the 11th of August, at the usual hour, we were let out of the church of the Sepulchre, and all the pilgrims were told that those who wanted to go to the River Jordan must be ready at the nineteenth hour. For my part, I was not anxious to go, because of the extreme heat, and also because it appeared to me that the expedition was prompted rather by curiosity to see the country than by any sentiment of devotion. Nevertheless the aforesaid Don Fra Francesco, ill as he was, said he wanted to go at all costs, and I who was well and strong felt ashamed of myself and mounted the accustomed mule. At the twenty-first hour all those who wished to go were gathered together in Mount Sion ready mounted, and there we remained in the blazing sun until the twenty-third hour waiting for the escort, which the Governor of Jerusalem was to send to protect us against the Arabs. At last a Mameluke arrived with certain barefooted soldiers; it is true that they had a bow apiece. And with this escort we set out, though many even at the last moment remained behind because of the intensity of the heat.

We rode fast because night was overtaking us, and we passed by Bethany without being able to see it. In response to the entreaties of one of the Venetian gentlemen deputies, whom I mentioned in the beginning, called Don Giovanni Bernardo Valessi,[1] who came with us instead of the captain, who had remained in the house with the fever, we stopped for a short time, as the pilgrims were already very tired, at a fountain called the fountain of the Apostles, and there we refreshed ourselves a little. Why the said fountain was called the fountain of the Apostles I could not find out. At the command of the Mameluke every man mounted immediately, and riding through the night, it appeared to me that all the way we went was very wild and stony.

At last we came to Jericho, that famous city which God miraculously destroyed in order to give it to the children of Israel. It was the first city taken by them in the Promised Land. As many of the pilgrims were much afflicted in consequence of the night riding—amongst whom was the Venerable Father Fra Francesco, who was completely exhausted—those Moorish dogs were persuaded to let us stop there. And having stopped and dismounted we located the aforesaid Father as well as we could beside a tower there (there was no other dwelling), on the bare ground; there was nothing else to be got save some chaff— that is, the part left when the wheat is purged. The aforesaid Father had already begun to repose when all at once those Moorish dogs began to bark that every man must mount, and it was necessary to obey, although with

---

1. Don Giovanni Bernardo Vallaresso.

great suffering on the part of the Father. We rode so fast that we came by many thorny and arid ways to the River Jordan, and there the order was given that whoever wanted to enter the river must do so quickly. The sun had not yet risen.

Before sunrise on Tuesday, the 12th of August, we reached the River Jordan. I and many others who could swim entered the water naked; many, however, only washed their feet and hands there. Within the space of an hour the order was given to mount at once, and this was done.

The River Jordan in that part is not wider than our Naviglio,[1] which comes to Porta Ticinese. It is deep and the mud is high and sticky, almost like bath mud;[2] and the water is muddy, like that of the Po. When it is purified it is beautiful to look at. Many drank it from devotion, and I let them drink.

We returned by the same way by which we had come. It was very clear, and we could see well and examine the country, which is flat as far as Jericho. There is not a fruit tree to be seen, nor any other plant save abominable thorns, both large and small. I made acquaintance with them, for the mule I was riding carried me off the road among those thorns, and they tore my mantle and doublet. I showed the torn garments when I got home; my flesh was already healed when I arrived.

As we passed by I looked well at that city of Jericho. There was nothing left but ruins and the tower I mentioned above, and a hut or two propped up against the ruins. Neither bread nor wine is to be found there for money or as a gift. The men and women of that country are not black, but they are burnt and dried

---

1. The Naviglio is the great canal which goes through Milan and connects the city with the Ticino, Lago Maggiore, and the Po.

2. Casola was probably thinking of the mud-baths at Abano and elsewhere in Italy.

up by the sun. This is all that can be said about Jericho. True, we read in the Holy Scriptures that when God had caused Jericho to be destroyed he laid a curse on anyone who should ever re-build it again.

When we had passed by Jericho we were led to a spring of water called the spring of Elisha. It is a large spring, and the water gushed out through two large stones. It is cool and good to drink, and if it were in our country there would be good mills built there and many meadows around, but in that country it is not used. That fount is called the fount of Elisha because when the Prophet Elisha lived in those parts the water was bitter, and especially the water of that spring. As he was prayed to do so by those who visited him—that is by the sons of the other prophets—he blessed all the waters, especially the water of that spring, and threw salt therein, and those waters became good to drink, as they are at present; therefore this fount is called the fount of Elisha.

When we got there both Moors and Christians wanted to rest and eat. We lodged the Father and his company under a certain plant that was covered with brambles and formed by itself a sort of pavilion. We laid him there as comfortably as possible. He was suffering greatly, and I doubted very much whether we should be able to take him back to Jerusalem, because he did not want to eat, but only to drink. With gentle words and also a little scolding we got him to take some refreshment, and then we covered him in order that he might sleep.

After a good meal I left the company, and seeing some other pilgrims about to ascend a mountain near there, which is called the Mount of the *Quarantina*, and hearing that they were going to the place where Christ fasted forty days and forty nights, I also went there. Whoever wanted to go up had to pay certain *marchetti* to the Moors.

When I saw those places they were very arid and desert. I saw many cells among the stones; it was said they were places where in ancient times many hermits dwelt to do penance. One thing may be recorded, namely, that the day we were there it was so hot that the stones burnt my feet, although the boots I had on my feet had double soles. When I had visited the said *Quarantina* I returned to the company; then I refreshed myself in the said fount while waiting for those Moorish dogs to cry, "Get up."

Thus, after midday, in the hour when the sun was hottest, we set out towards Jerusalem, where we arrived suffering greatly from heat and thirst at the third hour of the night, and dismounted in Mount Sion. We had difficulty in entering Jerusalem because the guards at the gates wanted money. Having calculated and collected the tax amongst us and paid, we were allowed to go in.

Whoever had seen many pilgrims by the way and because of the extreme heat, drink water in which at home they would have disdained to wash their feet, would have been moved to great compassion. Some among them fell ill, and even died in consequence.

On Wednesday, the 13th of August, the Prior of Mount Sion gave the order to enter the Sepulchre for the third time. The pilgrims were already in order for entering, when the Governor of Jerusalem sent to the hospital where the majority of the pilgrims, as I said, were lodged, and caused six of them to be seized and chained and cast into prison. Then he sent to the house where our magnificent captain lodged to seize him and conduct him chained to the prison, together with all the pilgrims found with him in the house, but because he was ill it was impossible for him to go. They chained all the pilgrims who were with him, however, and took them to the prison where the others were. At that hour I was at Mount Sion, where I had gone for certain affairs of mine. If I had been in the house I should have been led in chains like the others. Owing to this unexpected occurrence the project of entering the Sepulchre was given up for this day.

Meanwhile the Prior of Mount Sion and Don Frate Antonio Regna, a true Milanese, succeeded in inducing the aforesaid Governor of Jerusalem to release all the prisoners from the prison, which was in truth a wretched place, and send them all to the house of the captain, where they were guarded by certain Moors. The reason why those dogs had treated the Christians in this unexpected way was the following:—

A Jew who lives in Jerusalem—a doctor, brought up in Italy, who had made great acquaintance with me, and with whom I had talked much because he speaks our tongue as if he were a Milanese—had accused the Christians to the said Governor, saying that certain of the pilgrims had refrained from going to the River Jordan in order to spy out and explore Jerusalem, and that he had heard certain of the pilgrims say that within two years the Christians would be masters of Jerusalem. Upon this accusation he caused those poor men to be chained.

I remained in Mount Sion—though I was very uncomfortable, especially for the sleeping—because the said Don Frate Antonio Regna advised me to do so in order to escape from the fury of those dogs, who appeared to be dogs indeed.

On Thursday, the 14th of August, the vigil of the Assumption of Our Lady—as the said Lord of Jerusalem persisted in the wickedness of trying to rob more money than usual from the pilgrims for the reason above mentioned—we all remained dismayed and alarmed, and we had not courage to go and seek any indulgence in all the world. We were all prisoners, some here, some there;

some at the hospital, some in Mount Sion and some at the house of the captain, which was guarded by Moors; so that we began to weary of this pilgrimage, although it procured us great merit in the sight of God—for all the time we drew on that sack of patience.

On Friday, the 15th of August, the festival of the Assumption of Our Lady, as I had remained at Mount Sion and slept with some pilgrim friars, I got up before daybreak, together with certain friars of the place—that is, of the Friary of Mount Sion—appointed to say the offices, and went into the valley of Jehoshaphat to visit the Sepulchre of Our Lady. It is situated, as I said above, in a very well-kept church which goes down many steps below the level of the ground. I paid certain *marchetti* before entering, and then visited the aforesaid sepulchre and heard the Mass which was said over the sepulchre.

Afterwards I stayed there a good while to hear another Mass chanted by a certain sect of religious called Georgians. They chanted it at an altar apart from the altar of the sepulchre. After watching their gestures and hearing the cries they made, I got tired of staying there, perhaps because I did not understand them as they were Greeks; and as certain friars of Mount Sion were returning to the house I joined them, for it was not yet quite light.

When we got back, having said my offices, I said Mass in the place where Our Saviour instituted the Sacrament of his body and blood.

All this time the Prior, together with Frate Antonio Regna—who appeared to me to have much more experience in dealing with the Moors than the Prior, but who did not speak their language; he had been nine years there without being able to learn it—and the magnificent captain, used every effort to put an end to this exile, for so it might be called. The pilgrims were all inclined to go or send word to the Sultan rather than pay a single *marchetto*; so for that day also nothing could be done.

As it came into my mind that the captain had appointed me his scribe, I went into the city and returned to his lodging, and there I found the pilgrims guarded by the Moors like prisoners and the magnificent captain sick of a fever. He made me write several letters to Beyrout, in Damascus, and also to Cairo (where the Sultan lives), addressed to certain Venetians who live there, telling them of the ill-treatment and grievous injury he was victim of on the part of the Moors, and asking them to report those things to the Sultan, and to the Usbech Governor of Jerusalem; and then he sent a messenger who promised to go and return very quickly. After that, as my lodging was occupied by the prisoners, I wanted to return to Mount Sion, but I was obliged to remain—I also—as if I were in prison. Finally, by means of another Moor who frequented the house of the captain, I paid a tribute of certain *marchetti* to the guard and thus obtained permission to return to Mount Sion, for my lodging was occupied by those other pilgrims guarded as if they were in prison. And that Moor guided me by certain roads where I was somewhat afraid.

Very early on Saturday, the 16th of August, the Prior and the captain, ill as he was, went to the Great Cathibissa, who is, as I said, the oldest [priest] of their faith. A word from him has more weight than that of any other Moor. They told him about the malice and iniquity of that Jew, and begged him to use his influence with the Governor of Jerusalem, so that he might let the pilgrims go on their voyage; and they assured him that those who had refrained from going to the River Jordan had remained behind because they were afraid of falling ill, and not to spy out the city. They used their best efforts with the said Governor, doing their duty before the Old Man of his Faith; but that dog of a Governor, who wanted to make extortions at all costs, would not give them any other reply for that time. All the pilgrims in consequence remained in great confusion and depression of mind, the more so because the said Governor had sent an order forbidding the captain to leave his lodging. Finally, at a late hour it was necessary to call in the help of the Venerable Don Fra Antonio Regna, our Milanese, who has greater courage in dealing with those mastiffs than any other person who was there. When he has to deal with those Moors he seems indeed another Judas Maccabeus in word and sometimes also in act; and this I say from what I saw.

They remained—that is, he and the Prior—to contend with that Old Man of his Faith and that Governor about the accusations made against the pilgrims. At last that business also was settled for money, the sum being reduced from a thousand ducats to twenty-five. Thus at the third hour of the night they arrived in Mount Sion and gave the good news to the pilgrims that everything was well arranged.

On Sunday, the 17th of August, the pilgrims gathered together in the morning at Mount Sion and comforted each other again on account of the good news brought by the Venerable Fathers aforesaid. We had been afraid of being kept there until we were dead or at least half dead, because it had been decided to appeal to the Sultan rather than pay a *quattrino*.[1]

When the magnificent captain arrived he gave notice to the company that they were to enter the Holy Sepulchre for the third time according to custom, and so we went

---

1. The quattrino was a copper coin worth four bagattini; that is to say, it was the third part of a soldo.

THIRD VISIT TO HOLY SEPULCHRE

there in the evening, and he also insisted on going, although he felt ill. The father preacher, too, was very sick. He had never been well since he returned from the River Jordan, and everyone advised him to remain in Jerusalem and doctor and nurse himself, and then come back with the trading galleys at Christmas.

Before daybreak on Monday, the 18th of August, at the accustomed hour, I said Mass at the altar of Our Lady, where Christ appeared to her after the Resurrection. Then when I had visited and re-visited the sacred places, and it had become quite light, as the Masses which were being said by the pilgrim priests were not yet finished, I set myself to examine carefully that sacred Temple *(Note 85)* which contains so many beautiful mysteries of our redemption.

The Temple is large. It has two doors, which seem to me to be in the middle of the body of the said Temple towards the west. One of the two doors is walled up, and only one is open; nor is there any other entrance. On the left hand of the said door outside there is a beautiful bell-tower, but at present there are no bells.

Immediately on entering the church there is the place where the body of Christ was anointed when it was taken down from the Cross. At the side there is the ascent to the place of the Calvary, which is governed by a sect of Christians called Georgians. Underneath there is a dark chapel, said to be the centre of the world.[1] In this same place there are two very humble monuments *(Note 86)*. One is said to be that of Godfrey, who was the first King after the Christians had rescued Jerusalem from the hands of the Saracens. On the other there are certain Latin

---

1. It was a general belief in the middle ages that Jerusalem was the centre of the earth. The belief was based on a literal interpretation of the words in Ezekiel, v. 5, "This is Jerusalem: I have set it in the midst of the nations and countries that are round about her."

letters in the ancient style, beautiful still and legible, which set forth that there lies one Baldwin, who descended from the said Godfrey, and was King also. The inscription reads thus:—"Balduinus qui fuit alter Machabeus."[1] At the side there is the chapel, which goes down by many steps under Mount Calvary, and is administered by another sect of Christians called Armenians. Then there is another chapel, where Our Lord Jesus Christ was bound, when the crown of thorns was placed on his head; it is in the hands of another sect of Christians called Abyssinians. There are other places also around the body of the said Temple which are governed by various sects of Christians called, some Syrians, some Maronites, some Golbites, and all have different services *(Note 87)*.

The cupola above the Holy Sepulchre of Our Lord Jesus Christ is very remarkable, and was built with great magnificence. It is indeed a miracle that those Moorish dogs have left it standing, but if God does not provide, I think it will tumble down. A piece has already fallen from the vault near the Latin friars, and those dogs will not allow it to be repaired, notwithstanding that the true Governor of Jerusalem—that is to say, the Usbech—obtained from the Sultan permission for them to make repairs; so those friars told me who went for it.

At the first glance the said cupola, seen from below, resembles that of Santa Maria Rotonda at Rome, because it also is somewhat low and decorated, and has a large hole in the centre which gives all the light, not only to the said cupola, but to all the rest of the Temple. After a more careful examination, however, the said cupola is seen to be built on the same plan as that of San Lorenzo the Greater at Milan, for below one can walk all round by means of a gallery, and the same above.

1. Baldwin, who was a second Maccabeus.

DESCRIPTION OF HOLY SEPULCHRE 277

Below, towards the west, there are two square pillars, which show signs of having been formerly encrusted with slabs of marble. Beside the said pillars, on the right as well as the left, there are three columns on each side as thick as two tall men could embrace. Behind these columns on both sides, in the same order and of the same size, there are two other square pilasters, which were formerly encrusted with slabs of marble. Then, in the order aforesaid, on each side, follow two columns of the same thickness as the aforesaid. Then, behind these, on each side, there are three columns a *braccio* thick, and almost all three together; and over these six columns there springs a large arch: and the cupola remains round in this order. The gallery above is as large as that below, but its columns are a *braccio* thick, and arranged in this order—a column and a square encrusted pilaster alternately all round the circle.

The Holy Sepulchre is in the middle. It is like a little round chapel, carved in stone, which has the diameter of the Sepulchre on which Mass is said; and when four persons are in the said little chapel there is no room for more. It is entered by a hole, as there is no door, and a man has to stoop greatly in order to enter there. In front there is a sort of square cell annexed to the said chapel, and there is a stone, somewhat raised, before the hole at the entrance to the Sepulchre. It is said to be the stone on which the angel was seated when he told the Maries that Christ had risen.

Behind the said little chapel, there is a sort of chapel served by a sect of Christians called Jacobites. They have a very strange way of chanting the offices. At night I stood a while to watch their ceremonies and chants, which rather provoked the company to laughter than anything else. The *calogeri*, as their priests are called, had little hammers in their hands, and as they chanted they beat with the said hammers on a piece of iron. I could not understand why they did so.

In the galleries which go round above and also below, the sects of Christians I have mentioned are lodged with their wives and families. They arrange their lodgings with matting and canvas, but everything they do can be seen.

After passing that arch which springs from those three columns on each side, as I said above, forming the cupola, there are two vaults higher than the cupola, which form the body of the church; and this is, as it were, the beginning of the Temple with its altar, which appears to be the principal altar. This body is surrounded by a wall, except the part towards the Sepulchre, which indeed has a wall, but it is low. I think it has been left so in order to receive light from the hole which is in the cupola, because it cannot obtain light in any other way. This place is administered by the Greeks who chant their offices there.

Outside one can walk all round this place, and there are certain chapels where various mysteries of the passion of Christ are honoured, as I said above. The habitation of the minor friars, who are called the Latins, may be said to be outside the circuit of this Holy Temple, although they have no other entrance or exit except that of the Temple. These friars have the care of the Sepulchre and of the little chapel in front. It is very commonly said that Saint Helena, the mother of Constantine, caused this wonderful Temple to be built, nor do we read anywhere that it was built by anyone else.

On Monday, the 18th of August, when God willed—it was after the second hour of the day—notice was given to all the pilgrims to be ready at Vespers to escape out of

DEPARTURE FROM JERUSALEM

the hands of those Moorish dogs who were never tired of tormenting the Christians, now about one thing, now about another.

After dinner I went with certain others as far as Bethany to see the tomb out of which Christ raised Lazarus, the brother of Martha and of Mary Magdalen, when he had been dead four days. I had passed twice by Bethany, but I had never seen the said monuments. It is very well worth seeing. I had to pay a few *marchetti* to the Moors in order to see the said monument.

After this I returned to my lodging to get my baggage, and then went to Mount Sion, where the pilgrims were gathered together anxiously waiting for the animals for riding, and for the moment when those dogs would say, " Get out of this," so that one hour seemed a year to us.

Finally, at the nineteenth hour, without entreaties from anyone, we all mounted the usual animals, and praising God, we left the Holy City of Jerusalem—about which so much has been written by saints and others—which is extolled in the sacred Scriptures, which has been the dwelling-place of so many holy men, and, finally, the habitation of Our Lord Jesus Christ, Our Saviour, in which he willed to endure so much opprobrium and so many blows, and, finally, a cruel death to redeem the human race. Now, owing to the great strife and discord among Christians, it is ruled by those renegade dogs, because no one can reign over the Moors who is not a renegade Christian. And if one of the renegades should take a wife and have sons, these sons cannot succeed the father in any dignity. Such sons as these are called sons of the people, even though they be the sons of the Sultan *(Note 88)*.

In the said office, when the holder dies, the man who has most influence with the soldiers, who are all renegade Christians, succeeds him, and the oftener he has abjured the more he is esteemed. The present Sultan was seized in the field together with the Usbech, on whom he bestowed the Governorship of Jerusalem. They are Circassians, belonging to a country near the possessions of the Sultan. They both abjured the Christian faith and were sold as slaves several times in their youth. As they grew up they became sworn brothers, and so valiant in arms that the late Sultan set them over all his army.

When he died these two sworn brothers were masters of the situation, because they had the army under their control. And when they were talking together—that is, the present Sultan and the Usbech—about this dominion, the Sultan said that if the Usbech would help to procure him this honour he should be Sultan as much as himself. These words were no sooner said than the Usbech went out and made all the Mamelukes proclaim the other, Sultan, while he himself remained at the head of the army and received the Governorship of Jerusalem. In course of time the Usbech, Governor of Jerusalem, sold this Governorship to another for many ducats, nevertheless he is still the Governor.

The Usbech has a great friendship for the minor friars, and gives them large alms. Whenever they go to Cairo and whenever they appeal to him on account of any trouble given them by the Moors he inflicts heavy punishments on the Moors and fleeces those malefactors right well *(Note 89)*.

CHAPTER XIV.

Pilgrims leave Jerusalem and reach Rama, where they are delayed.—The Governor of Gaza and the Ten Slaves.—Sermon from the Prior of Mount Sion and Warning to Intending Pilgrims. — Rumoured Night Attack on the Hostel.—Messengers sent to Jaffa.—Giovanni Simone Fornaro and his Parrot.—The Slaves Given up.—The Pilgrims leave Rama for Jaffa.—Death and Burial of a German Pilgrim.—The Galley sets Sail for the West.

We left Jerusalem, as I said, and set out towards Rama, following the road to Emmaus, the castle where Christ appeared after his Resurrection to those disciples who said to him: "Tu solus peregrinus es in Jerusalem?"[1] And he replied to them: "O stulti et tardi ad credendum."[2]

When we reached the said castle, as there was a fountain there, the owners of the animals wanted to give them to drink. I looked at the place meanwhile. There are still a few dwellings there, but not many.

Then when it was already evening Abrayno Grasso and his companions wanted to stop in the open country to sup; and thus all the pilgrims dismounted to refresh themselves and wait for the moon to rise before starting again. Our lodging was on many stones, because in the open country there, there was nothing but stones.

As soon as the moon had risen, we all mounted, by order of the Moors, and rode all night until we came near Rama. Here those dogs, making a great noise, thrust us

---

[1]. "Art thou only a stranger in Jerusalem?"—Luke, xxiv. 18.
[2]. "O fools and slow of heart to believe."—Luke, xxiv. 25.

off the animals' backs because they did not want us to ride past the places where their dead are buried. Thus on foot, dead with sleep, we carried our baggage on our shoulders as far as our lodging, and there the ground on which we could throw ourselves down and sleep a little seemed a great luxury to us because we were half dead and already the day was at hand.

The Venerable Father Don Fra Francesco had insisted on coming with us, though he was ill. Certain sick persons, however, of various countries had remained behind in Jerusalem.

On Tuesday, the 19th of August, when the company arose, the Venerable Prior and the magnificent captain began to make arrangements for going to Jaffa before any other obstacle arose, because some new mushrooms [1] sprang up each day. But our solicitude could not outrun the fury of those dogs who were not yet satisfied with what they had extorted from the Christians, so the arrangements came to nothing.

On Wednesday, the 20th of August, the Governor of Gaza, who had come to Rama on hearing that the pilgrims had arrived there, invented another bewildering fraud. He said he wanted back the ten slaves who had been redeemed after we left the galley to go to Jerusalem, or that he wanted five hundred ducats. This was a more than diabolial invention, because there was no court of justice there, and the Sultan was ten days' march away, according to what people said. There was no remedy. However, on the intervention of the Prior the robbery was compounded for a hundred and twenty-eight ducats, and this was a great consolation to the pilgrims, who hoped to depart at least the following day.

In the evening the captain went to take him the money,

---

1. Difficulties, obstacles.

but because the coins were his ducats called seraphs, that mastiff, the Governor of Gaza, would not take them, saying that he wanted ducats from the Venetian Mint. The captain and all the pilgrims were in despair, because our departure was retarded; and the pilgrims were suffering great hardships of all kinds, especially lack of water, for the cistern in the hospital where we were lodged was exhausted and we had many sick among us.

On Thursday, the 21st of August, as the pilgrims were cheated out of the departure, the Prior of Mount Sion said Mass very early in the morning. Then, wanting as well as he knew how, poor man, to comfort the company, he preached a sermon in Latin, racking his brains *a prisiano* [sic] as dexterously as he could, and exhorting the pilgrims to have patience under the tribulations inflicted on us every day by those Moors, and this with most excellent authority of the Holy Scriptures and also the examples of the saints, " quia oportet per multas tribulationes intrare in regnum Dei." [1]

In the second part of his sermon he asked pardon of all the pilgrims if he and his friars had not shown them all the attention that perhaps they hoped would have been shown them both in Jerusalem and elsewhere.

In the third part of his aforesaid sermon he admonished all the pilgrims when they returned to their countries and native places, to exhort all those who might have the intention of visiting the Holy Sepulchre, either because of a vow made, or out of devotion, not to go there for the next two years; and he gave as a reason for this warning the great vexations inflicted on the pilgrims by the Moors, and said that they will do worse in the future until the Sultan hears about it and takes steps.

After this sermon the door of the hospital was opened

---

1. Since it is necessary through many tribulations to enter into the Kingdom of God.

in order to admit all those who carried victuals to sell to the pilgrims. When dinner was over, the Venerable Prior had an interview with the aforesaid Governor of Gaza, and worked so hard that he finally persuaded him to accept the plunder already agreed upon, and instead of insisting on being paid in ducats from the Venetian Mint to take what could be found, in order that we might at length depart.

When the captain went to pay the sum agreed upon, however, the said Governor of Gaza began to do as Pharaoh, King of Egypt, did to Moses when God wanted him to lead the people of Irael into the Promised Land where we were. He began a new tyranny, saying he did not want money for the slaves who had been redeemed and were on board the galley, but he wanted them back again. And now he said one thing, and now another, till both the aforesaid Prior and the captain were thoroughly perplexed, and we did not know what to do in order to satisfy that raging dog of a Governor of Gaza.

Finally, it was agreed to send a messenger to Jerusalem to the Old Man of his Faith and await until his opinion on the matter was known. The messenger was sent, and for that day there was nothing else to be done.

There was never a day of greater murmuring among the pilgrims, because the wine and the water had come to an end, and the heat was very great. A great company of Ultramontanes arose and went to the captain's lodgings, crying out as did the children of Israel against Moses when they lacked water in the desert. It was more painful than I can say to hear the words spoken by the pilgrims and to see the affliction of the captain who had so many men, as it were, in prison. As well as they could, the Venerable Father Don Fra Francesco, who had a great reputation among the pilgrims, and the Prior, comforted the company and told them that provision would be made as to the drinking, in the morning. The pilgrims calmed down, because the sun had already set and they had had supper.

At this juncture, I think it was a Christian of the Girdle who warned the captain that certain Moors intended to attack the hospital that night in order to rob the pilgrims. The captain summoned those who appeared of most importance as representing the different nations, and told them what that Christian had said, adding that he thought guards ought to be posted for the night, and this was done.

About midnight one of the guards thought he saw armed men near the door of the hospital, and began to call out, and the cries so increased right up to the room of the captain, that at the first moment we thought we were all cut to pieces.

I slept, as I said before, in the captain's room with certain others, and I was lying on a plank raised perhaps half a *braccio* from the ground. On hearing the noise, half asleep as I was, I fell from the plank to the ground in such a way, that there was not a single pilgrim who came to grief on account of those cries except Casola who fell off from his perch. There was no real cause for all the alarm, nevertheless everyone was very much frightened.

When the company had breathed again somewhat, I began to laugh, saying: "And if there had really been an attack what resistance could we have made?" In all the hospital there was not a stick a *braccio* long to be found, nor a sword, nor a knife half a *braccio* long; in short, not a weapon of any kind. There were not even stones without pulling down the hospital. Every man said I was right, and we went back to rest on the beds several times mentioned, until the morning.

On Friday, the 22nd of August, in order to give a little satisfaction to the company until the messenger came back from Jerusalem, certain barrels of wine were brought in and distributed among the persons there. While we were waiting thus in expectation, some messengers came from the Moors and urged the pilgrims to mount the asses, etc., at once to go to Jaffa. As we thought that Abrayno had given this order we rejoiced greatly, but immediately after we heard that it was not true, and that the Moors were only mocking the Christians.

At that hour the messenger arrived from Jerusalem from that old Man of his Faith, who wrote to the Governor of Gaza and told him, that he was on no account to give up the redeemed slaves sent on to the galley, unless he had as many Moorish slaves in exchange, and that if he had received money for the slaves he should restore it. This was a great affliction for us and a great misfortune for the men who had been ransomed.

The captain was now obliged to write with his own hand to the *comito* of the galley and to the scribe, ordering them to bind those poor men and give them up to the Mamelukes who carried the letters.

While the Mamelukes went to the galley, in order that we should not find the delay tedious, Don Giovanni Simone Fornaro, a pilgrim belonging to Pavia, who had been created knight in the Sepulchre, was accused before the Governor of Gaza of having brought a fine parrot from Jerusalem, and the said lord sent a Mameluke to take it away by force. It was defended a good while by Frate Antonio Regna, both with words and acts, but at last he was obliged to give it up to the Mameluke, who took it away with peril of a scandal and injury to the pilgrims, because those Moors sought nothing but some excuse for spoiling us.

The captain immediately followed the man who carried the parrot, in order to make excuses for the disturbance made, and the said Giovanni Simone insisted on following the captain against the advice of his friends, who were all of the opinion that he ought not to go. When they were all in the presence of the said Governor, the Moors accused the said Giovanni Simone of having stolen the parrot in Jerusalem. The said Giovanni Simone sought to exculpate himself by saying that he had bought it, but he was told that he must either name the seller or lose his hand or pay fifty ducats; and with these words they put him in "cima,"[1] as the prisons are called. However, the matter was arranged for ten ducats of the Venetian Mint, which he paid. He also gave certain *maydini*[2] to those who guarded him, and he left the parrot behind with that Governor for that time. But the game of the dogs was not yet finished.

This was one of the festivals we enjoyed while waiting at Rama for the ten slaves to be brought from the galley. And worse befell us after the affair of the parrot, for at the third hour of the night, a Frenchman, who said he was of royal blood, passed from this life. He was buried in the place set apart by the friars.

On Saturday, the 23rd of August, the Mamelukes who had gone to the galley to fetch the slaves returned with empty hands, because the officers of the galley, believing that the captain's letters had been extorted by force, refused to give the prisoners up. Before the said Mamelukes left the sea, they had put thirteen *galeotti* who happened to be on shore, in chains and placed them in custody in one of the two towers at Jaffa.

---

1. Cima in Ital = the top, summit.
2. The Maidino was a small piece of silver money whose value varied according to the place and the time. The Maidino of Cairo was worth twice as much as that of Damascus. (Porro).

When they arrived at Rama without the slaves, there was a great outcry amongst the pilgrims, who all thought that they would never escape out of the hands of the Moors, and from such hard exile, where everything was lacking except extreme heat. The Prior, Fra Antonio Regna and the captain went at once to the said Governor of Gaza, who was very angry on account of these things; and, seizing the excuse that the officers of the galley had refused to give up the slaves on account of the *galeotti* who had been put in chains, they finally, with much difficulty, persuaded him to send once more.

The Mamelukes were therefore sent back, accompanied by a certain Don Giovanni Bernardo—belonging to the Valessi [1] family, who was one of the gentlemen appointed to the galley by the Signoria—with the stipulation that if the slaves were not brought back by midday on the following day, the Governor of Gaza would exact two thousand ducats. They departed at the twenty-first hour, and the said Don Giovanni Bernardo said afterwards that they arrived at the sea at the second hour of the night. The said Don Giovanni Bernardo did all he had been commissioned to do by the captain in my presence, and vehemently abused and threatened the officers of the galley. He was in truth very much disturbed.

On Sunday, the 24th of August, the day of Saint Bartholomew, when all the pilgrims had arisen and heard the Masses, and we had recommended ourselves to God, we waited in great anxiety of mind to know the result of the work of the messenger who had gone to the sea; and we remained on the roof of the hospital in the sun with that great desire to escape.

By the will of God the messenger and the Mamelukes arrived before the hour fixed and brought those poor

---

1. *i.e.*, the Vallaresso family—one of the Venetian patrician families

wretches of slaves chained. The poor men were weeping, and they had good reason, because they had been ransomed and now they found themselves again in the hands of the Moors. The hardest heart would have been moved to compassion at the sight of them; even the Moors were sorry when they saw them behave in the way they did.

The men of the galley sent word to the captain that he need not hesitate to add to the first sum paid because everything would be refunded, and they informed him that three of the slaves belonged to Candia and were well off at home.

I spoke to them, and found that they knew Italian well, though whether they were from Candia or elsewhere I did not otherwise inquire. I was very sorry for one thing, and so were the other pilgrims, and that is, that when the slaves were ransomed I paid a Venetian ducat for my share, but when the money was returned, the captain would not give it back to me.

As soon as those poor chained men had been handed over to those dogs, we had licence to go on our journey, and every man prepared himself until the animals were brought which we were to ride. Meanwhile the Governor of Gaza, who had kept the parrot and had received ten ducats from Don Giovanni Simone Fornaro, sent to say that he was to take that parrot away and that he wanted five *braccia* of scarlet cloth. When they heard this, the Prior and the captain went to the Governor of Gaza. I did not hear what they did, but the parrot was taken on board the galley by order of the captain.

At this time the pilgrims were mounting in great haste, some on mules, some on asses. It appeared to us as if we should never escape from that cruel prison where we had been kept so many days contrary to custom.

We departed without further delay, and arrived at

T

Jaffa very early, so that if those dogs had been weary of eating our flesh the pilgrims could have gone on board; but they wanted also to gnaw the bones. We were weary, afflicted and a great many of us were sick; but that mastiff, Abrayno Grasso, compelled us to pass that night also on the seashore, on the bare hot ground. I really think that was our worst night, although we had many bad ones before which we had forgotten. The Venerable Father preacher alone, in consequence of the entreaties of the Prior and the captain, was allowed to go on board the galley with his servant, because he was ill.

On Monday, the 25th of August, as those dogs were satiated, they consented to let the pilgrims be put on board the galley; and thus by the grace of God we were all carried by the boats with great speed to the galley. Nevertheless, as long as the captain, who remained behind us a good while, was not also on the galley, it seemed to us as if we must be summoned on shore again.

The officers of the galley and the *galeotti* gave us such a cordial and affectionate greeting that if we had been their brothers and sons they could not have done more.

After the pilgrims were on board the galley the captain and the scribe were detained until the following night, and Abrayno did not let the captain leave his tent until he had got all he wanted from him.

On Tuesday, the 26th of August, when the captain had been dismissed by those dogs and had entered the galley, he found that one of the German pilgrims [1]—one of those who had been created knights in the Sepulchre—was dead. It was necessary to come to terms with those dogs, who insisted on having ten ducats before they would let us bury him on land. He was buried on the seashore. This

---

1. The name of this pilgrim was *Albrecht Maetsch aus Preussen*, as we learn from Ludwig Freiherr von Greiffenstein, and two other German pilgrims, Reinhard von Bemmelberg, and Konrad von Parsberg. See *Deutsche Pilgerreisen*, by Reinhold Röhricht.

pilgrim was rich and of noble family; he was buried as you have heard.

When the boat which had carried the body on land returned, the captain, to the great consolation of the living, decided to set sail before eating. The poor gentleman had been so maltreated by the Moors that he was in a great hurry to depart. Thus at the fourth hour of the day he ordered the anchors to be heaved, and to the praise of God and of our glorious Lady we set sail towards the West.

CHAPTER XV.

Galley Carried out of its Course.—Arrival at the Salines of Cyprus.—Galley Touches at Limasol.—Contrary Winds.—Sermon from Fra Francesco Trivulzio.—Death of Andrea Alemano.—Last Sermon Preached by Fra Francesco.—Contrary Winds and Calms.—Fra Francesco complains of a Swelling on his Neck.—Fears of the Plague.—Precautions taken.—Beyrout Fleet Encountered.—News of the West.—Contrary winds and Storms.—Death of a Native of Zara and of Fra Francesco.—Arrival at Rhodes.—Burial of Fra Francesco Trivulzio.—The Galley leaves Rhodes.

ALTHOUGH there was not a favourable wind, nevertheless, by tacking, we navigated so far that the towers of Jaffa were lost to sight. Then the sea began to rise so much against us that, between the hard times we had endured on land and the contrary sea, we almost all fell sick, and we felt better lying down than eating and drinking.

Thus navigating against the wind from the aforesaid hour, the galley was carried so far out to sea that no land was seen again until the last day of August, which was a Sunday. On that day, at midday, a cape on the island of Cyprus was sighted, called Cape Greco. This greatly comforted the pilgrims because we believed that we should never again see land. Already the firewood began to run short, as the galley had remained at Jaffa beyond the usual time, and wood cannot be procured there because there are no woods. And we who sat at the captain's

THE SALINES OF CYPRUS

table had begun to use salt water for washing our hands—a thing which had never happened before—and the drinking water was so bad that it turned my stomach.

The desire for many things made us cheer up a little; but we were disappointed in our expectations, because we arrived very late at a place called the Salines of Cyprus *(Note 90)*, where there was not a single thing to be had. Four other Venetian ships were there on their way to Beyrout, and they had taken everything.

As the captain heard that at Nicosia, one of the principal cities of Cyprus, people were dying [of the plague] he made a general exhortation to the pilgrims, and advised them not to go to that city. There were, however, certain impatient Germans, who, when they heard that the captain had to stop there some time, went to see the island at their pleasure. I was obedient, being afraid of risking my life. Certain of the pilgrims also, who had suffered greatly from the sea, landed and went by land to await the galley at Limasol, where the captain intended to call, in order that whoever wished to buy and sell might do so, and also to get a supply of biscuits.

We stayed so long at the Salines that whoever on the galley wished to do so got a supply of salt. The salt costs nothing there, and all the world could be furnished without exhausting the supply. There is a lake there like certain of our lakes of the Seprio *(Note 91)*, which can be seen all at once. It is called the lake of San Lazzaro, and is said to have taken the name because of the favour he asked from God that salt might never be lacking there; and thus the said lake appears always as if frozen, and it is the salt. The *galeotti* enter with hatchets or other tools and take out as much as they want and carry it away; when morning comes the lake is the same as ever.

The whole island of Cyprus is supplied from there and all the ships that pass by, and the salt is never lacking. It appears to me to be a miracle, though certain persons think it may be the nature of the place. The said salt is white as snow, and salts excellently. It cannot be taken to Venice, except in secret, under a penalty. In the galley they used the salt very liberally, and salted everything, even the skins of the animals which were killed.

When the galley was supplied with the said salt, at the second hour of the night, a slight wind arose, and all the night we navigated as well as possible in the circumstances, making as much progress as a snail would have done.

On Monday, the first day of September, we advanced very slowly on our voyage, because there was a calm at sea, and the galley could not be driven with the oars, as I have said several times, because it was too large a ship, so that I felt vexed that I also had not gone by land with many others as far as Limasol. Suffice it to say that we took eight days to go the two hundred and sixty miles from Jaffa to Cyprus. It is true, as the sailors said, that we really made more than eight hundred miles, because the course followed was in the shape of a great curve which carried us far into the high sea. There was no help for this on account of the wind, which was contrary to our path.

On the above-mentioned day we came to a place called "A la Canuta," and there stopped, for there was such a calm at sea that the galley did not move.

On Tuesday, the 2nd of September, as the galley could not proceed, the captain ordered the anchor to be cast, and many of the pilgrims went ashore to go to Limasol, thinking to procure some good refreshment; but all were deceived. I took the advice of the captain, who said to me, "Don't go," and I bore the hardships patiently.

Two hours before daybreak on Wednesday, the 3rd of September, they began to work the oars, because, as I said, there was a great calm at sea; and the poor men worked so hard that we arrived at Limasol.

The captain stopped there and fastened the galley with the anchors, because there is no port there to which the cables could be attached, but only the seashore.

Every man went on land, where, however, provisions were not found to refresh the company as we had hoped. There was nothing but bread and a few grapes. The dearth was due to the fact that a few days before, a Venetian galley, one of those of the guard, had put in there because the greater number of those on board were ill, and the *galeotti* had so harried the peasants—taking away their goods and refusing to pay for them—that they were afraid to show themselves.

Nevertheless, on our arrival they were somewhat reassured, and began to come with some things to sell, and bought some of the merchandise carried on land by the *galeotti*, though not as much as we had thought. There was an abundance of melons good for the teeth of old folks, not after the Lombard fashion where they like them hard; there you could eat them with a spoon.

The quantity of *carobs* or ultramarine beans was almost incalculable. A great trade was done in them, and the quantity brought on board the galley was stupendous. Whoever could find a place for them in the galley was lucky; a sack of a *moggio* was sold for three *marcelli*. I did not buy any, because I do not care for that fruit. It seemed to me that the carobs brought on the galley were sufficient to supply all the world; but after seeing the quantity held by the agents of certain Venetian merchants who live there, and which was all to be sent to Venice, I changed my opinion. I can assure you that the trade in this fruit is of immense importance and value, and I can say the same of the sugar I saw there.

Although the captain had decided to depart that same day, he was unable to do so, because the supply of biscuits and the cattle he had ordered were not ready in time, so he was obliged to wait until the following day.

On Thursday, the 4th of September, the pilgrims and the *galeotti* who had gone on land, some for one thing, some for another, were recalled by the firing of mortars and the blowing of trumpets. At the third hour of the night we set sail, and by the morning we had gone about forty miles.

On Friday, the 5th of September, in the morning, the *provenza*,[1] a wind directly contrary to our path, was blowing, and so hard that although all the sails were furled it drove us back. As well as possible the galley was brought under control by means of the oars. All the sailors sweated copiously and shouted, because in truth they were exerting themselves beyond their strength. The sight of them roused one's compassion. At a place near what is called Cape Bianco[2] there is a certain stretch of quite white coast which forms part of the island of Cyprus.

On Saturday, the 6th of September, the captain, seeing that he could not go ahead, ordered the anchors to be cast. We were then so near land that the *galeotti* were sent out in a certain little boat called a *copano*, and went to get wood and water, and also a few sheep. To obtain these, it was necessary to go some miles distance from the shore.

As this weather continued all Saturday and also all the following night, the captain and the pilgrims were very

---

1. West wind.
2. Cape on the south coast of Cyprus not far from Paphos or Baff.

depressed, beause, as I said above, it had not been possible to supply the galley with what was necessary at Limasol on account of the other galley which had touched there and remained there so many days before us.

On Sunday, the 7th of September, as the *provenza* had dropped and the sea was calm, the captain ordered all the sails to be spread as quickly as possible in order to leave the place where we were. We made so little progress, however, that it appeared to the company as if we were going back; nevertheless we really went ahead, at least obliquely.

In order to assuage in some degree the great sadness on board among the pilgrims and also the *galeotti*, due to the lack of what the company wanted—that is, some good victuals—the Venerable Don Fra Francesco de Trivulzio caused all the company to be gathered together in the usual way, by means of the whistle sounded by the *comito* of the galley, and they came to the usual place in the poop at the second hour of the day.

There he preached a beautiful sermon—the last but one preached by that holy man—and encouraged the company not to have so much anxiety about the things of the world as they appeared to have. It was all very well for him to talk, because he did not lack anything, but for many of his hearers, to whom they were lacking, talking was not enough.

He took for his subject: " Primo quaerite regnum Dei et justitiam ejus."[1] And in the first place, following the text, he expounded the Gospel which occurred in the Mass according to the use of the Court of Rome. Then he proceeded to his sermon by way of a question—namely:— Whether a person can be solicitous about temporal things without sin; and this because Christ said: " Respicite

---

1. " Seek first the Kingdom of God and his righteousness."—Matt., vi. 33.

volatilia coeli quomodo non serunt neque nent"—that is, "Regard the fowls of the air, who toil not, neither do they spin."[1] There he quoted Alexander of Hales: and distinguished between four kinds of solicitude, and said some very beautiful things. Finally, he concluded his sermon by saying that there could be solicitude about temporal things without sin, provided that it be not of such a nature as to cause the neglect of spiritual things. The sermon was very acceptable to the company. At the end he playfully told the company to go to breakfast, and named certain officers of the galley—very agreeable men—who took their meals very frequently.

Before we left this place news was brought to the captain that one, Andrea Alemano, a knight,[2] from Cambray, in Brabant, son of the Governor of Antwerp, and the only son of his father, had passed from this life. As the galley was quite motionless and near land, the *parono*[3] with certain strong *galeotti* undertook to carry the body ashore and walk until they should find a church of some kind in which to bury him; and this was done. When he returned the *parono* said that he had gone more than four miles, and that he had found a poor little church. His compatriots could tell the father, who was very rich, so they said, that his son was buried in Cyprus.

Two hours before daybreak on Monday, the 8th of September, which was the nativity of Our Lady, as it appeared to the *comito* of the galley that a little wind had arisen favourable for our journey, he at once ordered the anchors to be heaved and the sails spread; but in spreading the *artimone*—that is, the main sail—a great rent was made, and it was necessary to let it down again. It was said that Our Lady wanted something from us.

1. Casola confused here two texts. Matt. vi. 26 and 28.
2. The phrase in the text is "Andrea Alemano Cavalero, fiolo del governatore de Anversa, Cameracense in Barbantia.
3. See p. 160.

While it was being mended—for it was a long job—the wind dropped, and the sea settled into a calm, and this made us very sad.

Then the aforesaid Venerable Don Fra Francesco caused the company to be summoned to the last sermon he ever preached in this world in the midst of the sea. When the company was gathered together he preached a beautiful sermon on the nativity of Our Lady, taking for his subject: "Exiet Virga de radice Jesse." Thereupon he said most beautiful things in praise of Our Lady, which greatly pleased the company. It was the last time he preached.

During the whole of that day we did not go more than six miles towards Paphos, and it was necessary to cast the anchor, because the *provenza*, which was a contrary wind for us, began to blow so terribly. Nevertheless in the evening, as the sea had called down, the *comito* decided to trust to fortune, and ordered the anchor to be heaved and all the sails to be spread, saying that he wanted to navigate at all costs even if he had to go backwards.

At sunrise on Tuesday, the 9th of September, we were found to be more than sixty miles out of our course, and when we had well boxed the compass and almost returned to land it was said that we had only gone eighteen miles on our way. Nevertheless in the evening the sails were turned to another side, and it was decided to navigate all the night, because, in that gulf of Natalia, there is no danger from rocks; by the grace of God it is wide and ampler than the gulf of Sclavonia.

On the morning of Wednesday, the 10th of September, we were so far out at sea that the island of Cyprus could not be seen any more. Nevertheless, according to what the pilot, who was a Greek and an old sailor, said, we were right opposite Paphos. This was bad news, not only for the captain, but also for the mariners and the pilgrims, because the stores were running short. So many mouths as there were on that galley took some feeding. At that moment the captain had to provide for not less than four hundred persons, because every man looked to him. The company was the more alarmed, because the captain said, that such a thing had never happened to him before, in that sea. It really appeared as if God had determined to consume us in that gulf.

After dinner the Father preacher, Don Fra Francesco complained, when only the captain and I were with him, of a swelling [1] which had come on his neck. The captain and I examined it and told him not to touch it nor have it medicated. He said he would take our advice, but afterwards it was found that he had had it medicated, and that caused his death.

As soon as the swelling on the neck was mentioned, the captain said he wanted to use every remedy in order not to perish together with the pilgrims,[2] and he sent criers to order all those who had brought water from the River Jordan to throw it into the sea.[3] The order was not much obeyed by certain persons, principally Italians. Then he had a search made to see if there was anything aboard which had been stolen from a church; and proceeding further, together with the Father preacher, he proposed that a vow should be made to Our Lady in order to escape from this anxiety; but no ear was given to this. It appeared to me that that galley was full of all iniquity,

---

1. Casola uses the word "Brusarola" (Ital: Brufolo), which may mean, according to circumstances, boil, carbuncle, tumour, &c. I have preferred, therefore, to adopt in translating the general term, "swelling."

2. The captain evidently feared an outbreak of the plague on board.

3. It was a superstitious medieval belief that Jordan water brought bad luck on board. For example Santo Brasca was told "that as long as there is any Jordan water on the Galley the sea always remains calm," that is, the ship is becalmed. The priest who wrote the voyage to the "Saincte Cyté" heard that as long as there was a drop of Jordan water aboard, it was useless to hope for a favourable wind, but he stigmatizes this as "foolishness."

considering the places we were coming from, and that we deserved much worse than we got, because, although the wind was contrary, nevertheless we had not a storm. Although I was discontented like the others, I did not marvel in the least at what befell us, for the reason given above.

Very late in the day three galleys were sighted belonging to the Levant Trading Fleet, which were on their way from Venice. The captain-in-chief was Don Juliano Gradenigo, and they were called the Beyrout galleys.[1] They had a stern wind, which was unfavourable for us. They recognised us immediately, and when they came near, the two largest lowered their sails in order not to pass us by. At the second hour of the night we were so very near one another, that there was general rejoicing on the one side and the other; the cannon were fired, and there was much shouting, as is the custom of sailors.

A small boat, or rather, as they say, a *copano*, was lowered into the water from one of the Beyrout galleys, and many persons came to visit our captain, and many letters were brought to him from Venice. They told us the news of the West, especially about the movements of the King of France; and, amongst other things, a Franciscan friar, belonging to the Zorzi family *(Note 92)*, said, that in Venice, on the Vigil of Saint Lawrence, it was said publicly, that the King of France was expected at Milan on the 16th of August *(Note 93)*, and much other news.

They remained on board, and there was a great illumination for nearly an hour, and then, having taken leave of the friends, they returned to their galleys, which looked like the daughters of ours. We still remained with

---

1. In the month of August or September every year, from three to five trading galleys went together to this Syrian port and returned about Christmas to Venice. The Patroni or Captain-owners were always Patricians.

the wind contrary, and they went flying away with the wind in the stern.

On Thursday, the 11th of September, the sails were not moved. We went on drifting until the evening with a violent wind, desiring indeed to come to some good place if God willed; but we were not on our proper course. One person said we were in one place, another said we were in another. The mariners did not understand where we were at all.

On Friday, the 12th of September, Saturday the 13th, Sunday the 14th, and Monday the 15th, I did not note down anything, because, although we were navigating day and night in that gulf with all the sails spread, and with a high though contrary wind, nevertheless the mariners had gone so far out into the high sea that no one knew where we were, and the many navigating charts on board were no help. The captain said one thing and the *comito* and the *parono* another, and the pilot another. There was great confusion in the said galley, and the pilgrims who saw this confusion felt very depressed. Then a storm arose so violently, especially at night, that it appeared as if the galley would split open and break up, and, as has been said, all the stores were running short.

When the captain lost courage, as he showed by calling us all together and saying that if we thought it best he would return to Cyprus, I began to lose courage also to such an extent that I thought it was all over with me. Although, seeing so many Observant friars and other good people on the galley, it appeared to me too much to suppose that God would destroy so many souls all at once. It made me very low-spirited to see the Father Preacher, who, amid this general depression and because of his own special suffering from the swelling I spoke of above, had quite lost heart. I was accustomed to amuse myself alone, but this day I was quite unable to do so; rather I said: "Casola, we are lost! I shall never again see Rhodes, which I have so desired to see." Vows were made by every man. I never thought to see land again after so many days without seeing any.

Two hours before daybreak on Tuesday, the 16th of September, the Most High God, wishing to show us that all things are in his hands, and that he wills to be prayed to without any other expectation, sent a stern wind so favourable for our journey that it appeared a miracle.

Immediately afterwards a headland was sighted which belongs to the Turk, and is called Phenice.[1] The galley approached it, which greatly cheered everybody. Thus navigating with a good wind, we passed a castle in the mountains of Phenice called Castle Rugi. Judging from the outside, it must be strong. It belongs to the King of Naples, though I think it is little use to him; enough, however, that it is not possessed by the Turk. In those mountains there are two cities, one called Patera[2] and the other Saurinia.[3] In the one Saint Nicholas was born, and in the other he was afterwards bishop. They are far from the coast, however, and could not be seen from the sea.

On this day there passed from this life a man, who said he belonged to Zara, that he had escaped from the hands of the Turks, and afterwards reached Cyprus. He had come on board the galley to go to his own country, but when he was on the galley he fell ill, and, as I have said, not being able to get remedies any more than the others, he died. The sea was given to him for his monument.

On Wednesday, the 17th of September, it was said that we were making good progress, and although the company

---

1. Casola seems to have confused Phenicia with Lycia. From the position of the Galley it was evidently the mountains of Lycia which had been sighted at this point.
2. Patera, Patara or Panthera, a city of the province of Lycia, where St. Nicholas was born.
3. St. Nicholas was bishop of Myra in Lycia.

had not all they desired, yet all took some comfort except Don Fra Francesco, who had entirely let himself go.

At the dinner hour, as he did not come as usual to the poop, the captain's servant was sent to tell him to come, but he sent word that he could not come, and that he felt very ill. The captain was much disturbed about his illness, and sent to ask him if there was anything he wished for, and ordered all his subordinates to take care that the Father did not want for anything there was on the galley. After dinner I went to see him, and stayed a long time with him. I discovered that he had had the swelling medicated and with medicines that were not suitable. I did my best to cheer him. He asked constantly if we were yet at Rhodes, and I replied that we should be there immediately.

On Thursday, the 18th of September, we came near Rhodes very very slowly. In the evening, when we hoped to enter the port, such a terrible *provenza* arose, that, whereas we had been only eighteen miles from Rhodes, we were driven more than a hundred miles out to sea. A turn, however, was made which at last brought us into port.

When I saw the violence of the wind I took leave of the Father Preacher, whom I had been visiting, and who was in a high fever and suffering greatly from thirst, and went to my own quarters, which were far away from his. He was at the prow and I was near the poop beside the canteen. About midnight I was summoned to go to the Father Preacher by one of his companions named Frate Michele da Como. I jumped up immediately, wrapped myself in my cloak, and went to see his Reverence, who was in the last agony. I could not get him to say even one word, nor to open his eyes. He raised himself unaided to render a service to nature, and then fell back again in a heap on his pallet. I got a Florentine hermit—who had also come out of sympathy to visit him at that hour—to take him in his arms. Then, as the other friars of every Order began to come to say the appointed offices, and as the place was small, I took leave of them and went in a very high wind to my quarters, carrying to my neighbours very bad and distressing news of the preacher, because he was loved and revered by all.

When I had been resting a couple of hours or less, a *galeotto* came to tell us that he had passed from this life, and everyone felt very pained and sad.

On Friday, the 19th day of September, at the second hour of the day, we reached the port of Rhodes; but as the other ships which had arrived before us had spread the news that in Cyprus, especially at Limasol, the people were dying of the plague, when the galley entered the port, the sanitary officers came at once and ordered that not a single person was to be allowed to leave the galley. While the matter was under discussion it came to their ears that the Preacher had died of a suspicious malady, which had manifested itself on the throat. On this account it was necessary to desist from going ashore.

The news spread throughout Rhodes that the galley had come, and immediately the quay was crowded with friends, especially Ultramontanes, of whom indeed there are many there, come to visit their friends whom they were expecting eagerly. Finally, through the efforts of the friends, and especially of the Lord of Longo, a Genovese, about whom I said a great deal before, the Grand Master was persuaded to accept testimony to the effect that the galley was not infected, and that the Preacher had left Jerusalem with the fever. In consequence of these impediments the pilgrims left the galley very late.

It must be confessed, that, in the matter of dinner,

the aforesaid Lord of Longo made such provision at the captain's table as almost made me forget many wretched meals I had had during the preceding days; for sometimes the only dish they had given me was red beans and vinegar.

As to the body of Fra Francesco, whom the magnificent captain and all the galley desired to honour, permission could not be obtained to carry it off the galley until the evening, when the pilgrims were already scattered here and there about Rhodes with a great desire to eat a good meal. In the evening the body was taken off the galley and accompanied to a gate leading to his monastery, called Santa Maria della Vittoria, which is being restored. I think we were four Italian pilgrims who did him honour as well as we could. We did not go through the city because of the prohibition of the Grand Master. That great preacher was buried before the high altar with few words.

On Saturday, the 20th of the month of September, we— that is, the magnificent lord our captain and many pilgrims of every nation—gathered together at the said church of Santa Maria della Vittoria, where the once great preacher was buried, and we remained there until the obsequies were over, and many Masses had been said; then all went freely about the city occupied in restoring afflicted bodies and minds with good things and also in buying some carpets.

As I had not much business to attend to, and also in order to fare better as regards living, I never left the captain, who received many attentions from many people, and especially from the Governor of Longo, who kept him to meals with him as long as he was on land, and Casola as well, because Casola is a Milanese and he a Genoese. He did not entertain us after the Rhodian fashion, but

MONUMENT TO FRA. F. TRIVULZIO

like a great noble and true Italian; there were banquets and very sumptuous ones every day.

On Sunday, the 21st of September, in the morning after Mass was heard, as the captain had been invited, we went to do honour to a certain bride who was accompanied to the church for the benediction and afterwards to her husband.

When dinner was over at the house of the Lord of Longo, the captain ordered the trumpet to be sounded to give notice, that, at the hour of Vespers, every man must be on the galley, because he intended to set sail. But he changed his mind, because a great flaw was discovered in the helm of the galley, and on Sunday no master could be found who would repair it. The pilgrims were glad to have the chance of resting a little longer.

On Monday, the 22nd of September, every man being supplied with carpets, which were numberless—I was told that between the *galeotti* and the pilgrims more than four thousand were carried aboard, though according to my reckoning there were seven thousand of them—and the helm of the galley having been repaired, the captain ordered the trumpet to be sounded and certain cannon to be fired to give notice to the company to come on board the galley, and he ordered all the cables to be loosened in order to set sail. But in spite of all his haste and the many signals given, he could not depart until it was already the first hour of the night.

We Italians wanted to leave orders for a stone to be prepared with a few affectionate words and placed over the tomb of Fra Francesco, in order that some record should remain of him. The captain was of the same opinion, and I offered to leave the money it would cost, but the Governor of Longo, with whom these matters were discussed, would not agree to this. He said that the Grand Master himself wanted to erect the monument at his own expense, and that he did not wish for anything from us except the name of the Father's family and of his country.

With the help of his companions, I put together a few words which were left with the Prior of the Monastery of Santa Maria della Vittoria, where he lies, with the request that he would hasten the matter.

When this was arranged we entered the galley, and at the first hour of the night we set sail, heading towards Turkey, because the wind was not favourable for going in the direction of Candia; though we hoped that as soon as we were out at sea some good wind would spring up for us.

CHAPTER XVI.

The Island of Cos or Longo Sighted.—The Watch Dogs there.—Galley in the Archipelago.—Contrary Winds.—The Island of Santorin.—The Galley Anchors at Enios or Ios.—Discontent of the Ultramontane Pilgrims.—Bad Weather.—Arrival in Candia.—Productions of the City and Island.—The Quails.—The Ex-Duke and Ex-Captain of Candia go on Board the Galley to return to Venice. — Departure from Candia.— Favourable Winds.—Modone.

AT sunrise on Tuesday, the 23rd of the month of September, we found that we had made forty miles towards Candia, leaving Turkey always on the right hand and on the left hand the island of Rhodes. After this, very little way was made until the evening on account of a great calm which came on at sea.

When we lost sight of Turkey, the island of Longo, formerly called Choo [1] by writers, was sighted. As I said, it is subject to the knights of Saint John, and is a single commendam which is held by Don Eduardo de Camardino of Genoa, who, because I am a Milanese, did me such honour and made me such generous offers as I cannot describe. I think he was very demonstrative to me because the captain of the galley, Don Agostino Contarini, gave him to understand that I was a person of importance at Milan. However that may be, I fared well under this shadow.

To return to our subject. The said island of Longo has

1. Cos.

amongst other things a beautiful castle, called the Castle of Saint Peter, which, as it is near the Turkish borders, has forty large dogs to guard it who are trained carefully and very intelligent. They go out of the castle without any guide in large bands by night and by day. They go a long way—two, three and four miles away—and if by chance they encounter one or more Turks in the woods they recognise them immediately, and if they cannot escape they worry them to death. If, however, they meet one or more Christians they recognise them at once and show great joy, and in their way lead them to the castle.

Those dogs eat in a very orderly fashion. A bell is rung three times which can be heard a long way off. At the third sound all the dogs assemble there as if they were friars. If one should be missing, some of the oldest dogs immediately go outside and search until they find the missing one, and when he is found, after giving him a few bites, they conduct him to the others. They are worth their keep. I heard about them while I was in Rhodes at the house of the Lord of Longo, from one of his servants who had just come from Longo. Afterwards I heard about them also from the captain, who said that in his voyages he had been to that castle and seen this thing.

On Wednesday, the 24th of September, with calms and some contrary winds, we went thus navigating amongst the islands belonging to the Rhodians, and we greatly desired to enter the Archipelago, which, as the experienced sailors said, is otherwise called the Sea of Greece.

On Thursday, the 25th of September, we finally entered the desired sea, which has so many rocks and islets that they cannot be numbered; and there the sea, almost as if by a miracle, calmed down so completely that we remained where we were all Thursday, the Friday following, which was the 26th, and also a part of Saturday. The mariners did not know what to say, because usually the passage from Rhodes to Candia takes at the most two days and two nights, and we had already taken four. Further, we were in a difficult position, for, trusting to arrive quickly in Candia, very few provisions had been taken at Rhodes, where everything was dear, and so everything began to run short.

Very late on Saturday, the 27th of September, a wind arose called *garbino*,[1] which drove the galley so much out of our course that the captain would gladly have approached an island called Santurin.[2] And there was a great dispute in consequence between the captain and the *comito* and the pilot, who said to the captain that it was not a suitable place to stop at—that is, to cast the anchor. The captain maintained that on other occasions he had anchored there; and he related that one time when he was in the Canal of Santurin with several galleys, a storm arose in the West which continued for the space of three days, and was not only violent but very terrible—great thunder, great flashes of lightning, and noises as if there had been battle chargers there; and all on board the galleys were so terrified that they did not know what world they were in. On the morning of the third day an island as black as coal made its appearance; and the aforesaid captain said that they made every effort to approach it, but could never discover the bottom, and that he had never been able to anchor there since. The *comito* and the pilot would have their own way, and we did not anchor near the said Santurin.

On Sunday, the 28th of September, owing to the contrary

1. South-west wind.
2. *Santorin* or Thera is the most southern island of the group of the Cyclades. It was formerly united to the neighbouring islands of Therasia and Aspronisi, and the three together formed the crater of an immense volcano. The volcanic eruptions in the island of Thera have been numerous and violent.

winds, which had increased so much that the company began to be upset, it was necessary to take refuge beside an island called Nio,[1] in a place where there was an excellent port. Although it was not walled, nevertheless it was a safe port and capable of holding very large ships. It was almost surrounded by mountains, and had an excellent bottom right up to the shore.

When the anchor was cast, those who desired to do so went on land, and the company climbed to a castle called Nio, high up on the summit of a mountain, and bought many necessary things except bread, because there was only badly made barley bread there; some was taken, but very little. There were excellent wines of our kind, meat and fowls, good grapes, pomegranates and other things for whoever wanted to buy. For a short time it was very agreeable to stay at this place, especially in order to obtain a supply of water, because the water was excellent, both the spring water and that of a river which came down from the island.

With many others I climbed up to the said castle in order to see several things. It is situated on a great rock, very difficult to get at. If it were in Italy, especially in Lombardy, it would be made into a very important fortress; here it appears to me to be a pigstye. I should not have courage to stay a night there, for fear it would tumble down, because the walls of the houses are built without mortar: one stone is simply placed over another, and nothing more. Nevertheless there are a great many houses, and also many inhabitants. There are a great many females, both great and small; one cannot imagine how so many persons can live in the said castle. Although the women are Greeks and live in such a remote place,

---

1. Enios, the ancient Ios, said to be the burial place of Homer.

DISCONTENT AMONG THE PILGRIMS

they are beautiful; also the men we saw were handsome; there are only a few.

The said castle is subject to a Lord called the Lord of Nissa,[1] an island near there and fertile. The said Lord had died a few days before we arrived there. He was the brother-in-law of our captain's brother. He left one young son, and the Signoria of Venice to whom he is recommended, has appointed his uncle as his guardian, according to what the aforesaid captain said *(Note 94)*.

On Monday, the 29th of September, Saint Michael's day, we were kept in the said port, to our great vexation, waiting for favourable weather in order to depart.

On Tuesday, the 30th of September, the leaders of the Ultramontane pilgrims gathered together and came to the poop to see the captain, who at that time had finished dinner; and when all the company were arranged according to their order and dignities the captain asked what they wanted. The first of them in order said that they had come on behalf of all the pilgrims to beg him to lead them out of that place, because they were not satisfied with a single thing, and especially with what was given them to eat. The captain replied very amiably, saying, in the first place, that he was not keeping them there for his pleasure, and that the greatest loss was his. He then explained that, because of the contrary winds and in order not to jeopardise both himself and them, he had made a port he never touched at, that he had done his best to leave there, but the weather had been unfavourable, and that the voyage as far as Candia could not safely be made at night on account of the innumerable rocks, because, as there was no moon and the winds were adverse, the ship might easily run into danger. Before the interview was over very injurious words had been said on both sides,

1. Naxos, the largest of the Cyclades.

because the pilgrims went on to speak of their discontent with the food given them to eat. I calmed the discussion as well as I could. There was right on both sides, and therefore a satisfactory sentence could not be pronounced. The matter remained undecided.

When the aforesaid Ultramontanes had departed, the captain ordered two cannon to be fired to call back the company, both of pilgrims and of *galeotti* who were on land idling and amusing themselves, for there was no trade to be done there. The greater number were ashore, some in one place, some in another, but, owing to the dearth of boats, they could not return as quickly as they did in the frequented ports, where there are many other boats beside those of the galley. By the time the company was at last on board the sun was not less than twenty-two hours old. As the weather was very clear the captain set sail immediately, but many were afterwards very sick, for before the third hour of the night very bad weather came on, and then the captain chanted the Litanies, while the French stayed below deck and said never a word.

On Wednesday, the 1st of October, we navigated against the wind, and went so far, that, according to what some said—but secretly so that the captain should not hear—we had passed by Candia, and were nearing Modone. But the captain, who wished at all costs to go to Candia, turned back because of the promises he had made to the Duke and Captain of Candia, and also in order to fulfil the agreements he had made with the *galeotti*.

On the way we met some ships going from Candia to Venice loaded with wines. This made the pilgrims discontented, for they desired to go to their own countries and not to Candia to buy wine or malmsey.

On Thursday, the 2nd of October, at sunrise, we reached Candia, to the great joy of the Candiots, who were

CANDIA

expecting us eagerly, and especially also of Don Lorenzo Venier and Don Luca Zeno. Don Lorenzo Venier had been Duke of Candia, and now, because his term of office was ended, he wanted to go home; and so, too, Don Luca Zeno, who had been captain of the island of Crete, and lived in Candia, wanted also to return to the mother country; but in order to be safer they wished to return on board our galley. The Candiots were rejoiced at the opportunity of selling a quantity of malmsey and muscatel, many cheeses, and many articles made of cypress wood.

As soon as we arrived in port it was marvellous to see the crowd that assembled. The pilgrims, who had suffered greatly from the sea, and had complained because they had not been taken to Venice without touching at Candia, immediately began to enjoy themselves a little with the good malmseys and muscatels and also with some rough wine.

On Friday, the 3rd of October, the feast of Saint Titus was celebrated all through Candia. The principal church bears his name, and he is the patron saint of the Candiots. For that day no other business was done. We visited the churches, our friends and also the taverns.

On Saturday, the 4th of October, there was an even greater festival, that of Saint Francis, and neither the shops nor the warehouses were opened for trade. I remained the greater part of the day at the Convent of Saint Francis. In the morning all the magistrates, both new and old, came there and all the pomp of Candia.

On Sunday, the 5th of October, the merchants began to examine the malmseys and muscatels in the warehouses. I, who did not want to trade, went to see what was being done, and I often went on the sea,[1] which was so agitated

---

1. Casola writes:—" E spesso andava *sopra* el mare el quale era tanto turbato chel pariva non se dovesse maj piu quietare." He may have meant that he went to some point *above* the sea from which he could look down on the harbour and the shipping, and not that he went *on* the sea.

that it seemed as if it would never again calm down. A wind called the *bora* [1] was blowing so hard that the ships could not leave the port. There were many in the harbour, loaded and ready to go to Venice, and the wind made them all tremble and dashed them one against another.

On Monday, the 6th of October, all the shops of Candia were opened. They are filled with every kind of work they do there, especially cypress work, of which there is a great variety, and they do good business. The warehouses of the malmseys and muscatels were also open, and many agents invited people to buy. The great warehouses full of cheeses floating in the brine made me marvel greatly that the skin of those who stand in it with their legs bare did not crack on account of the salt. I spent the whole of this day in looking at these things in order to be able to tell about them, not with the idea of trading.

In the morning I went also to a gate on the land side, where there is a market for all kinds of victuals. It was a pleasant sight to see so much beautiful bread. I seemed to be in Italy. The bread is cheap. One thing displeased me greatly. I saw many barrels of quails, skinned and salted like the mullet or *muzeri*.[2] It was a pity to see them, with their white feet; they looked like *zati* [3] or toads. I and certain other Italians bought some to try if they could be made good to eat, but it was impossible; whether roasted or boiled they always tasted like a piece of leather prepared for eating. Seeing such a quantity of them I asked Don Nicolò de Domo, doctor-in-law, our good Milanese, who does excellent business in Candia, why there was such a quantity of quails, and all thus salted. He

---

1. *The Bora*, Acquilone or Tramontano. A north-east wind, very dangerous at sea.
2. *i.e.*, the Muggine, another term for the "Mugil cephalus" or mullet.
3. This word "zati" is probably a softened form of the Milanese "sciatt"—a rospo, or toad.

said that that was not because a great many were not eaten fresh, but that a few days before we arrived, for eight days continually at a certain place in the island of which he told me the name, such a number appeared that two persons with a light caught four thousand of them in one night. Afterwards on the voyage our magnificent captain showed me the said place. This day I saw a great abundance of cheap fruit of every kind, especially pomegranates. They are sweet, though not as fine and good as those at Rhodes, where they are larger and finer than any I saw in any place during this voyage.

On Thursday, the 7th of October, accompanied by the aforesaid Don Nicolò, I went to see all the different kinds of work done in cypress wood, and also the articles of devotion painted in the ancient style. Everything was shown to us out of regard for the aforesaid Don Nicolò, who is much esteemed by the people on account of his profession which he exercises publicly before those Lords, the Duke and Captain and Councillors very boldly. Following the example of the other pilgrims, I also spent a few ducats on the articles of devotion and the things made of cypress.

On Wednesday, the 8th of October, the pilgrims began to behave to the captain as did the children of Israel to Moses when they were in the desert, and, weary of the manna they had every day, they asked for meat and began to murmur. So did the pilgrims, satiated with so much malmsey and muscatel. They began to say to the captain that he must take them away from there, and that if he wanted to trade in malmsey or anything else he could do so at his good pleasure, provided he sent the company to Venice.

He excused himself on the ground that the weather was very unfavourable; but the company received the excuse with very high and injurious words. I was the judge of the controversies which arose between the pilgrims and the captain, and they said some hard things to me also, declaring that I supported the captain, because, even when we remained on land, he paid my expenses and not theirs. This was the truth, but I paid more than they did.

On the morning of Thursday, the 9th of October, the weather changed, and immediately the captain gave notice to his friends, and sent word to certain Venetians who wanted to come to Italy, and by means of the trumpet warned the pilgrims who were on land, that every man must be on board the galley by the twenty-third hour, because if this weather continued he intended to set sail without fail.

At the appointed hour no time was lost. First came the old Duchess—that is, the wife of Don Lorenzo Venier,[1] who, as I said, was the retiring Duke of Candia, and the wife of Don Luca Zeno,[2] the retiring Captain. They were accompanied by the wife of Don Domenico Bollani, the new Duke, and the wife of Don Francesco Foscarini, the new Captain, and attended by many ladies, so adorned and so magnificent that I seemed to be in Venice on a great festival; and they went first on board the galley.

After them came the aforesaid retiring Duke and Captain preceded by the new Duke and the new Captain. All the magistrates of the island and an infinite number of gentlemen of Candia (if those can be called gentlemen who neither do nor want a single thing), and the trumpeters and the pipers escorted them to the galley very honourably and also with great dust.

---

[1]. Ser Lorenzo Venier, son of Ser Marco, had been Duke of Candia since July, 1492. His successor, Ser Domenico Bollani, son of Ser Francesco, was elected on the 14th Sept., 1494.

[2]. Ser Lucas Zeno, son of Ser Marco, knight, was apointed in September, 1492. His successor, Ser Nicolo Foscarini (and not Ser Francesco as Casola says), was elected in September, 1494. Both Duke and Captain held office for two years. Segretario alle Voci, Reg. vi. p. 80, Venice Archives.

When the company heard that the aforesaid Duke and Captain with their families had gone on board the galley, all flew with their baggage on their shoulders, and no one looked behind. I was accompanied by the aforesaid Don Nicolò de Domo, doctor, and greatly recommended by him, more than I wished or needed, living as I did at the captain's table. In addition, he insisted on my accepting a barrel of excellent malmsey and some fowls, pomegranates and grapes. I kept the fruit for myself as I am very fond of it, the rest I gave to the *galeotti*.

In spite of the firing of so many cannon and the many signals of departure given, it was past the second hour of the night before leave had been taken of all the friends. Then to the praise of God and of Our Lady, at the third hour of the night (it was moonlight), the cables and other fastenings of the galley were loosened, and at the fourth hour we left the port with great cries from the mariners and blasts from the trumpets, and set sail towards the West, although the wind was not favourable for our voyage, but rather contrary.

On Friday, the 10th of October, God willed to give some little consolation to the pilgrims, so often troubled now by one thing, now by another, and he suddenly sent a wind so favourable for our journey and so strong, that without a single stroke of the oars it drove us between the said Friday and the Saturday following, right opposite Modone. The *artimone* (that is, the main sail) only was spread, and there was no need to move even a rope, so that every man was in good spirits.

On Saturday, the 11th of October, at the eighth hour, it was found that we had passed beyond Modone, and if a calm had not come on towards Sunday, the captain had decided with that wind to go on without putting in at the port; but as the sea calmed down he ordered the anchors to be cast.

On Sunday, the 12th of October, as the galley was already anchored, but some distance from the port of Modone, the captain gave license, to anyone who wished, to go ashore, especially to hear Mass; and he ordered the anchors to be raised because he wanted to approach the port and go and hear Mass also. But the moment the anchors were heaved such a favourable wind sprang up that nothing better could be desired. He was thereupon entreated by Don Lorenzo Venier not to trouble about landing there, but rather to go to Venice; and being also urged to do this by the *comito*, he changed his decision, and at once ordered three cannon to be fired and sent a trumpeter on land to recall to the galley all those who had gone on land. In the shortest possible time every man was back on board, and without delay he set sail with an excellent stern wind, amid general rejoicing. We made more than ten miles an hour.

CHAPTER XVII.

Pilot left behind at Modone.—Don Bernardino Contarini goes on Board the Galley.—Zante Sighted.—Great Storm.—Curzola.—Lesina.—Description of this Island. — Franciscan Friary. — Sermon in the Cathedral.—Galley Anchored at La Murata near Sebenico.—Several Pilgrims leave the Ship.—Death of a French Pilgrim.—Zara.—Storm in the Quarnero.—Brioni.—Istrian Stone.—Church of the Four Crowned Heads.—Majority of the Pilgrims take small boats to go direct to Venice.—Parenzo.—Pilot taken Aboard and the Galley sets Sail for Venice.

At Modone the captain left the pilot whom he had taken there on the way out, and he took on board the galley one of his relatives named Don Bernardino Contarini, who wanted to go to Corfu; but he and all the others who desired to go there were disappointed, because it was not possible to touch there on account of the weather.

When the galley was well started in the name of God, and after dinner was over, the said Don Bernardino, who had dined with the captain and those other Venetian gentlemen, in reply to questions addressed to him, because he had just come aboard, began to speak of the affairs of the West—of the Pope, of the King of France and of our Lord Lodovico. I think he spoke of what he knew and what he did not know, and far from the truth; nevertheless some of the things he said, which we did not believe, were afterwards found to be true. I appeared to believe them like the others, and the more so, when they redounded to

V

the praise of the aforesaid Lord Lodovico, although he said them with another object. I supported what he said with good arguments, and they themselves—I mean the Venetians—remained silent.

Thus we spent the time until late; then the sky became very dark, and the company thought there would soon be heavy rain. The said weather began in the sea towards the North, and for the space of over an hour a tail of cloud was seen, like a great beam, which came from the heavens and entered the sea; it seemed to raise a great mass of water from the sea. All on board the galley, the mariners as well as the pilgrims, stood in great wonder to watch this thing. The captain said that it was a very evil beast called *Scio*, and that if it encountered a ship, no matter how large, unless that ship could get out of the way, it would be thrown upside down. However, at the third hour of the night the weather cleared, and good weather continued and also a good wind.

On Monday, the 13th of October, in the morning, the island of Zante as it is called was sighted. It is a very fertile island, and subject to the Signoria of Venice. During the preceding night it was found that we had made over a hundred miles, although the weather was so good that we pilgrims, who had been crowded together below deck for fear of a storm, thought that the galley had never moved. We all declared, that on the whole voyage, we had never had such a good night before. But in truth we behaved as did the children of Israel when they waxed fat with the favour of God, and instead of praising Him they gave themselves up to idolatry, and did everything in direct opposition to his Commandments, until they provoked Him to do them some harm. Because of the good weather we had and the excellent passage God had granted us, we ought to have been occupied continually in good works and in praising God; but all the contrary prevailed throughout the galley, and the good works were limited to a very few persons, so that within myself I marvelled greatly, that having experienced so many perils at sea, those on board had not become better and did not recognise the Divine Power in a very different manner.

God, however, chastises whom He will at the right time, and like our excellent Father as He is, when He sees that of our ownselves we do not walk in the good way of His Commandments, at once He sends the punishments. Thus at the hour of Vespers, when we thought to reach Corfu that night, the weather was so good, and when we were already opposite the island of Jacinthos, commonly called Zante, a hundred miles from Corfu, such a terrible storm arose and of all the winds together—now *scirocco*,[1] now *garbino*,[2] now *ostro*[3]—that the officers of the galley did not know what to do, and having furled the sails they waited to see what would happen.

The following night the sea was so agitated that every hope of life was abandoned by all; I repeat by all. We were driven out of our course, and the galley was launched out into the open sea on chance, and a certain sail called the *cochina* was hoisted which had never been used all the voyage. The storm became so violent that every man fled below deck, and it was no use to say: "This is my place," because in that hour all things were common in our despite. Death was chasing us.

During the night such heavy waves struck the ship that they covered the castle in the poop and the *pizolo* and the whole galley in general with water; not a single person was exempt, from the least to the greatest. The water came from the sky and from the sea; on every side

---
1. South-west wind.
2. South-east wind.
3. South wind.

there was water. Every man had "Jesus" and the "Miserere" constantly in his mouth, especially when those great waves washed over the galley with such force, that, for the moment, every man expected to go to the bottom.

Thus the night wore away amidst such cries that it seemed as if all the souls tormented in hell were there, so to speak. From time to time, the *galeotti*, who remained on deck exposed to the weather in order to navigate the galley, came below drenched to the skin, and in such a state as to merit all compassion even if they had been more wicked than they were.[1] I gave up my place to them very willingly, in order that they might put on dry clothes. How many bargains were made with the Judge who will not accept frivolous things nor chatter! I made very many, if they were only accepted! That time there was no lack of vows, both general and particular. Amongst the general, it fell to me to draw out of a hat a written one, containing a promise to say certain Masses at Venice. I have not forgotten the private ones I made, and I will carry them into execution as soon as I can.

As that terrible tempest continued, on Tuesday, the 14th of October, by order of the captain and also of Don Lorenzo Venier, three pilgrimages were arranged—one to Our Lady of Loreto, another to Saint Anthony of Padua, and the third to Venice.[2] Much money was collected for the purpose, and many pilgrims volunteered to undertake these pilgrimages.

During this storm we drifted at the mercy of the sea, with nothing but the sail I mentioned above. Three very

---

[1]. The original runs: "De hora in hora venevano li galeoti sotto coperta, bagnati in tuto, chi staveno di sopra a la sparata a governare la galea, degni de ogni compassione vedendoli, se ben fosseno stati anche *più scelerati* che non erano." Though free men, the sailors were drawn from a low class, and their habits and language were no doubt calculated to shock a priest like Casola.

[2]. See Introduction, pp. 80—81.

STORM CONTINUED

strong men remained always at the helm of the galley, and it was as much as they could do to manage it. I remained on deck because the sea did not upset my stomach as it did many of the others.

I stood to contemplate the fury of the sea, which was greater than I can describe to anyone who has not seen it. When it was angry, those mountains, as they seem of water, appeared as if they would engulf the galley. I reflected that these were among the things I had not believed when I heard about them. When those mountains reached the galley they gave her such blows that it seemed as if she would break up, as indeed she would have done if she had not been so excellently built. The old and experienced mariners said that no other galley could have resisted so many and such terrible blows, and I shall always be able to testify to this from what I saw.

The storm lasted until the following midnight. It was impossible in such weather to make a port, so we left Corfu behind, though it was desired by so many, beginning with myself.

On Wednesday, the 15th of October, a little before daybreak, the sea began to mitigate its terrible fury somewhat. At sunrise, the *cochina* was taken down and the *artimone*—that is, the main sail—was spread, and we began to make good way towards Albania, leaving the Morea behind us. At the twenty-third hour the weather began to change again, and in great haste the *artimone* was let down and furled and the *cochina* was hoisted again. Heavy rain came on with thunder and lightning, which lasted until the morning, when we found ourselves at the point of an island called El Sasino, in Albania.

As I went about everywhere on the galley quite freely, I came to the conclusion that the past evils, and those we still feared to encounter, proceeded from the fact that there were too many commanders aboard. First, the captain ordered one thing; next Don Lorenzo Venier ordered another, and insisted on having his own way; then the *comito*, because of the altercations, flew into a passion; and finally, in the midst of these disputes, the bad weather overtook us.

At dawn on Thursday, the 16th of October, the *cochina* was taken down and all the other sails were spread, as the sea was somewhat calmer and a wind favourable for our journey had sprung up. More than twelve miles an hour were made, so the experienced sailors said, and with this weather we hoped to be able to touch at Ragusa, having passed by Corfu so much desired by the company; but Don Lorenzo Venier, according to whose pleasure the ship was navigated, wanted to touch at a castle in Albania called Antivari, where one of his nephews was Governor.

We passed Dulcigno, and a river called the Boyana,[1] which comes from a lake and winds for two hundred miles. It generates terrible fish, especially eels of enormous size and other fish, and it is subject to the Turk.

After all, as the weather was so steady and so much in our favour, it was impossible to stop and make the port of Antivari.

In the evening, in order to avoid running on a rock, for there are many in those parts, all the sails were taken down and the *cochina* alone was spread. With this, however, the galley made such progress that it was a marvel and in the morning we found that we had left Ragusa at least sixty miles behind, to the great disappointment of many who wanted to leave the galley and go on board other ships, in order to cross to the kingdom of Naples.

On Friday, the 17th of October, late in the day, we

1, The Boyana issues from the south-east of the Lake of Scutari, and after a long sinuous course enters the sea between Dulcigno and San Giovanni de Medua.

reached Curzola,[1] a citadel in Dalmatia, and as bright and clean as a beautiful jewel. It has no drawbridges, but it has strong walls, and it will be stronger still when a wall is finished which has been begun towards the sea. At first sight the said citadel appears to be flat, but one perceives on entering it that all the streets ascend a little. The streets are narrow and dark, but they are paved with stones. The city is built on a rock. Many of the houses are built in the modern style and are handsome enough for a great city. They are built of white stone like marble and sculptured. It was a marvel to me to see so many beautiful houses in that place. The Cathedral Church, considering its importance and also that of the city, is beautiful. It is entirely built of beautiful squared stones. The choir is beautiful and the church is well served.

The said citadel is full of people. The men dress in public like the Venetians, and almost all of them know the Italian tongue. When I asked the reason, I was told it was because they often go to Venice. Their women cannot fear the cold. They go about with their chests and shoulders entirely uncovered from the breasts upwards, and they arrange so that their breasts hold up their clothes and prevent them from falling down on to their feet.

The place seems to me poor in everything save wine, which is abundant and good. The island is not much cultivated because the greater part of the men are *galeotti* and continually at sea.

Most of the pilgrims landed, thinking to find a good supper. But there is no fish to be had there, although the place is in the midst of the sea, no eggs, no cheese. There was hot bread, for, as soon as the people heard of the

---

1. In 1494 the Venetian Count or Governor of Curzola was Ser Simon Capello, who remained there three years, until January, 1496. Segretario alle Voci, Reg. vi. p. 68. Archives of Venice.

arrival of the galley, every man ran to make bread in order to earn a little money; it was good, and so was the wine. There were dried figs and also some raisins, but everything was dear.

We stayed there until the following morning, every man being warned, however, that if he wanted to come further, he must sleep on board the galley. Certain Ragusans remained behind and some friars who wished to return to Ragusa, which we had passed by owing to the force of the wind.

On Saturday, the 18th of October, which was the festival of Saint Luke the Evangelist, we left Curzola. Only one sail, the *terzarola*, was spread, because there was a very high though favourable wind—that is, the *scirocco*, and with the said sail alone we made, according to the estimate of the mariners, fifteen miles an hour.

It was a lordly sight, for anyone who did not fear the sea, to see such a great ship fly along. In four hours we went from Curzola to Lesina, and there made the port, in obedience to the wish of Don Lorenzo Venier, who was afraid of being carried further by the violence of the wind—although it was favourable for us—because the rocks were so numerous in Dalmatia.

The anchors were thrown out on all sides of the galley because of the force of the wind, and as that was not enough they also threw on land certain cables called *provexe*. It seemed indeed as if all the world would be engulfed, such was the fury of the wind.

When the galley was brought to and secured, the greater part of the pilgrims went ashore, hoping to find some refreshment besides the wind, but they did not find anything save wind and water—no eggs, no fish, hardly even a little bread and wine; and all returned to the galley expressing great marvel that the captain had touched at such a place. As to provisions, they had fared better at Jaffa. Everybody was very astonished also that Lesina should be reckoned a city, when there is not to be found there lodging for a single person.

This city of Lesina [1] is called in Latin, Fara. It looks a more important place seen from the sea than it is found to be when one is on land. It stands on two hills, one higher than the other. In my opinion, it must have taken its name because the higher part is built as a fortress and walled, and goes up to a point like a *lesina*.[2] I think the lower part is more ancient, and it is called Fara because the Episcopal Church is there and the Bishop is called the Bishop of Fara and not the Bishop of Lesina. I inquired about this both on the galley and ashore, but I did not get any explanation.

Suffice it to say that on entering this city it seems flat, nevertheless on two sides it ascends, and more on the left side than on the right, and the part on the left is walled. It must be said that the place is strong, for it has a large port on the right hand, and on two other sides—because it can be described as triangular—it is dominated by the hills. On the top of the left-hand side there is a castle which appears to overlook the whole sea.

As to the buildings, I saw nothing beautiful there, except the palace of the Government. The other houses are very humble, and there are very few of them. There are some which have been begun above the seashore. They will be beautiful when they are finished. I heard that they belonged to certain Ragusans who went away because of the heavy taxes. The people are poor and of a bad condition. They are proud, even to the women, so that the officials do not know how to carry out their duty there.

1. In May, 1494, Ser Alvise Barbo was elected Count or Governor of Lesina, and remained there until 1497. Segretario alle Voce, Reg. vi. p. 67.
2. Lesina (Italian)=an awl.

The longer a stranger remains there the more he lacks. There is wine there and not much else. The town has to live on the bread of Apulia. The Cathedral is in the lower part, and is dedicated to Saint Stephen.

On Sunday, the 19th of October, we all went to hear Mass at the Church of Santa Maria delle Grazie, where the Observant friars of Saint Francis live. The Friary *(Note 95)* is being built with the offerings of sailors. It stands on a white rock, and when any building is added it is necessary to excavate the rock.

The Church and Monastery were founded by a certain Don Giovanni Soranzo, because of a great miracle worked for him by Our Lady; and the sign is to be seen as you enter the church door. One night he was at sea in a great storm; the ship's rudder broke; he recommended himself to Our Lady, and found himself again safe at this rock. This was the origin of the building. It was afterwards enlarged, and in it there live as many as twelve friars. Don Lorenzo Venier had a Mass chanted there because of the vow he had made at sea.

After hearing Mass we went to the Cathedral to hear the sermon. It was not like those preached by the departed Don Fra Francesco Trivulzio, which stimulated a man to listen; this instead incited one to talk and even to sleep. The day ended very sadly for the pilgrims, for the reason I gave above.

On Monday, the 20th of October, we remained in port, with great loss to the pilgrims, who murmured, although the captain excused himself on account of the weather. It must be said that the sea had so calmed down during the night that the galley could not be moved. In order to remain on good terms with the captain, I went to see the sights and did not take part in any assembly that might displease him. Certainly, I also would have been glad to depart, nevertheless, by standing aside, I was always among those chosen to accompany the captain and the other gentlemen and go with them everywhere.

Before daybreak on Tuesday, the 21st of October, we left the port of Lesina with a little favourable wind, and up to the second hour of the day we sailed along gaily enough. Then the sea calmed down so much, that, with much fatigue—for the oars had to be used—we were taken for safety to stop at a place called Cape Cesto, because it was feared that an unfavourable wind was about to rise, and there we remained. No one went on land, and there was nothing to be done save contemplate the sea, which was so quiet that it appeared a glass of water.

On Wednesday, the 22nd of October, we departed from the said place, thinking to be able to navigate as a little wind had sprung up; but immediately there was a calm again, and afterwards a *provenza* arose which was unfavourable for us, and it was necessary to take refuge in a place called La Murata, where there was nothing except high and very bare mountains. It is called La Murata, because of a wall which the Signoria of Venice has caused to be made in the manner of a fortress with a drawbridge. It is said to have been made in order to fortify a certain islet, and that formerly, when the Turks harried those parts, the peasants used to take refuge in that islet and save themselves from the raids. Although it is such a desert place, vestiges of dwellings are to be seen there; they are also built of stone. La Murata is twelve miles from Sebenico.

While we were in this place the fishermen came from Sebenico and from certain hamlets three or four miles distant, and brought on to the galley an abundance of good and cheap fish; there was nothing else to be had. With certain other persons I want wandering a long time on those mountains, because I wanted a salad. As I have said, they are so dry and bare that there was not a herb to be found the length of one's finger.

On Thursday, the 23rd of October, we still remained in this straitness with great murmuring on the part of the pilgrims, who said that if we had not stopped at Lesina we should have already arrived at Venice with the weather we had. And murmuring thus, sixteen pilgrims of various nations left in several barques to go to Zara. Although I was invited to accompany them, I determined not to abandon the captain, even if it took up to Christmas to go to Venice; and he strengthened me in this resolution, taking care, that, as far as the living was concerned, I should lack nothing.

While we were at La Murata, this day, at the twenty-second hour, a French pilgrim passed from this life, and was buried beside the wall.

On Friday, the 24th of October, when the moon arose, as there was a little *Greco-Levante*, we set sail; but it left us very quickly, and it was necessary to anchor near a rock, suitable for the purpose, twenty miles from Zara.

On Saturday, the 25th of October, at daybreak, the said wind having sprung up again, we set out with the intention of passing by Zara without stopping, in order to make up the time lost at the preceding rocks, but the opinion of Don Lorenzo Venier's wife, who wanted to visit certain relatives at Zara, won the day, and the port was made. The pilgrims who remained and those gentlemen with their wives went ashore, on the understanding, however, that every man must be aboard again by the evening, because it was decided to set sail before dawn. There we did nothing save stand and watch the partridges sold for six *marchetti* the pair.

On Sunday, the 26th of October, at daybreak, we left

Zara with such a strong stern wind that we made fifteen miles an hour quite smoothly. But at midday, when we were in a certain gulf called the Quarnero,[1] such a storm arose that it seemed as if we must founder. The captain was of the opinion that we had not yet had the worst, and already I began to envy the pilgrims who had left the galley and gone by other ships. The blows given by the sea were so heavy, and such a quantity of water was thrown on the galley, and came down through the hatches, that I thought we should be drowned below deck.

For my part I considered that we well deserved it all, because, as at the pleasure of a woman we had entered port, so, in the judgment of God, we ought to have remained on land long enough to hear Mass on Sunday. Nevertheless, when it pleased God, we approached a rock called the rock of Saint Jerome, twenty-eight miles from Parenzo, in terrible rain, which put an end to the violence of the *bora* which had sprung up so furiously. The anchors were cast there, and we waited the favour of God until the morning, for the wind was contrary.

On Monday, the 27th of October, we took refuge, as well as possible, in a port very well protected from the violence of the winds, according to what I heard. On one side there was a village called La Fasana, on the other side another village called Briona.[2] I think the name has been altered, and that it should be "Priona,"[3] because there are mountains of rocks and very beautiful stones of different kinds, although there are no marbles. They are like the stones of Angera,[4] and it seems really as if the veins of stones had been first squared before being put into those mountains, for they are all cut as if to measure.

1. The Quarnero or Gulf of Fiume.
2. The Istrian stone used for important buildings in Venice came principally from Brioni and Rovigno in Istria.
3. In the dialect of Como "Pròna" means a steep rock without vegetation.
4. Angera or Anglera is on the south-east of Lake Maggiore opposite Arona.

It is a very extraordinary thing to see those stones. The greater part of the stones used in Venice are obtained from there.

At Briona whoever wished to do so went on land. I found there a man from Cremona, and another from Como, employed in stone cutting, and from them I learned about the nature of the place.

The land is cultivated by the women, because the men are entirely occupied in cutting out the stones. I saw one thing in that place which I must not omit to mention, namely, that the greater number of their houses are built without mortar, and nevertheless there are some beautiful ones. The stones are so well put together one upon the other that the buildings are strong, though these are without cement. The cracks are filled up outside with tow.

The men are honest, and have had enterprise enough among them to build a beautiful church, called the Church of Saint Germanus and the four Crowned Heads, and they have had enterprise enough also to cause an altar piece to be made of the value of three hundred ducats, as they themselves say. There are five large figures made by the hand of an excellent master. They only lack the voice, otherwise they would be alive, and the gold has not been spared on them. At the foot, there is carved the history of the four crowned heads who were carvers in stone *(Note 96)*. I have not seen an altar piece like it at Milan.

On Tuesday, the 28th of October, as the contrary wind persevered, the captain and the other Venetian gentlemen left the galley, and I did not abandon them. It was very cold, and we were not ashamed to go to the good fires.

As many pilot boats had come there, the majority of the pilgrims who suffered much from the inconvenience of the place, entered those boats and departed to go to Venice. For my part, not being too bold-spirited, I determined not to leave the galley, although I was anxious to depart.

On Wednesday, the 29th of October, at the second hour of the day, as there was a little favourable wind, we departed, and sailed towards Parenzo, leaving on the right a city which looks large and beautiful seen from a distance. It is called Rovigno, and appears to have a beautiful church dedicated to Saint Euphemia, whose body is said to lie there.

With this weather we arrived at Parenzo at the first hour of the night, and when the anchor was cast, the captain, urged by Don Lorenzo Venier, went ashore alone and took a pilot according to the regulations. When he returned to the galley bringing the pilot with him, as the air was clear, he set sail out of the usual order, for we thought to leave the galley here and go by a small boat as far as Venice. The galley set out towards Venice to the praise of God and of the glorious Virgin Mary, and to the great joy of those who remained board; they were only a few.

CHAPTER XVIII.

Arrival in Venice.—The Custom House.—Festival on All Saints' Day.—Casola says Mass at the Frari.—Visits the Milanese Ambassador and meets Philippe de Comines.—Palazzo Delfini.—Dominican Convent.—Casola takes leave of Friends in Venice and goes to Padua.—Vicenza.—Abbey at Villanova.—Verona.—Peschiera.—The Muster.—Brescia and its Bishop.—Encounter with Friends from Milan.—Calci.—Caravaggio.—Casola Arrives in Milan.

On Thursday, the 30th of October, about the first hour of the day, we reached a place called Sopra Porto,[1] said to be ten miles distant from Venice. There was a very heavy sea, and the captain ordered the anchors to be cast there.

As the arrival of the galley had been announced by an English pilgrim who had left Zara in a barque, many pilot boats came to meet us, and other boats also came to take off the pilgrims, because, as I said, there was a heavy swell on, and the pilot thought it better not to proceed further for the present.

The captain, who did not feel very well, took one of the boats, and permitted me to accompany him. I left all my possessions except my breviary on board the galley. That swell was a great comfort to me, so great was my desire to reach Venice.

To the praise of God, at the nineteenth hour, I arrived in Venice, and found that the pilgrims who had left the

---

1. This may have been what is now called "Pelorosso" on the sea side of Malamocco, where there is good anchorage.

galley in various places before us, had not yet arrived because they had taken another route, nor did they arrive until the evening. When I had taken an affectionate leave of the captain and thanked him, I was received by the Italians, especially by my fellow countrymen, with great rejoicing, because I was the first Italian pilgrim who arrived. Everyone was glad to see me. Nicolò Delfinono, at whose house I had left the emblem of my pilgrimage, brought me and a certain native of Friuli back from death to life, so to speak, for we were both dying of hunger and thirst. We had an excellent meal, after which I set about paying the visits due, beginning with the Magnificent Don Tadiolo Vicomercato, the ducal Ambassador, who kept me with him until the evening, and even then he would hardly let me depart.

On Friday, the 31st of October, the galley came into the Grand Canal of Venice to the Custom House *(Note 97)*. Although it was raining heavily, as I found I could do so, I had all my things taken off the galley and put into a gondola. For this I paid certain *marcelli* to someone. I do not know who he was. Immediately after, by order of the Lord Advocates, the door of the Custom House— that is, the place where the merchandise was stored and where the pilgrims had slept—was sealed. This was very inconvenient for many pilgrims, especially for the Ultramontanes, who wanted to go to their own countries.

In consequence of this sealing—as complaining produced no effect in Venice—they had to stay there against their will more than six days. It excited one's sympathy to see those pilgrims go with so many complaints to the Signoria; nevertheless the said door was not opened until it pleased the authorities. My experience proved that it helped matters greatly to shake one of the three sacks I had carried with me—I mean that of the money.

Saturday, the 1st day of November, being the festival of All Saints, I went to Saint Mark's Church, and there found the Most Illustrious Don Agostino Barbarigo and the royal and ducal Ambassadors at the Mass for All Saints' day, which was chanted very solemnly with the usual ceremonies as I described above.

When Mass was finished the aforesaid Doge ascended to the palace, accompanied by the aforesaid Ambassadors, and followed by so many gentlemen in couples that it was a marvel to see them. I counted up to a hundred of them, then I remembered the lesson read at Mass which spoke of the multitude which no man can number, and I gave up counting and contemplated their superb and sumptuous dresses—so many togas down to the ground of crimson or of scarlet as you please; and they all walked two and two, as I said, after the Doge in perfect order. This is very different from the practices I have witnessed at many Courts, both ecclesiastical and secular, where the moment the Prince has passed all go pell-mell (as we say in our tongue *a rubo*) and without any order. In Venice, both before and behind the Doge, everyone goes in the best order imaginable.

After dinner, with the aforesaid ducal Ambassador, we went to hear very solemn Vespers at a Monastery for women, called All Saints *(Note 98).*

On Sunday, the 2nd of November, as I was not yet ready to return to the mother country, although I greatly desired to do so, I went with certain Milanese to the Church of Saint Francis, or as it is called the Church of the Minor Friars, where the Milanese, as I said before, have a beautiful chapel dedicated to Saint Ambrose, and having borrowed an Ambrosian missal, I said Mass there in the Ambrosian fashion, not without exciting the admiration of certain Venetians who remained to hear it.

VENICE—VISIT TO PALAZZO DELFINI

Then I went to see the magnificent ducal Ambassador, who with great courtesy had sent to seek me, and for the rest of that day he would not let me leave his magnificence. After dinner he very kindly took me in his boat, together with the Ambassador of the French King *(Note 99)* and Don Girolamo Zorzi *(Note 100)*—a very good man and facetious, though somewhat deformed in his person, that is to say, slightly hump-backed—who had just been appointed Ambassador for the Signoria to the Pope. We went first to hear Mass at San Giorgio Maggiore, which was so disagreeable to listen to, because of the manner in which it was celebrated by the friars, that we were obliged to leave.

We then entered the boat and went together to visit the wife of a gentleman of the Delfini family who was in childbed. I think this visit had been arranged by the aforesaid Don Girolamo to show the magnificent Ambassadors, and especially the Ambassador of the King of France, the splendour and great magnificence of the Venetian gentlemen. The aforesaid royal Ambassador said truly, that neither the Queen of France nor any French noble would have displayed so much pomp in similar circumstances. The ducal Ambassador said the same, and declared that our most illustrious Duchess would not have such ornamentation on a similar occasion.

As the room was not capable of holding many persons, the aforesaid ducal Ambassador chose me specially to enter with him so that I might see and also report what I had seen elsewhere. While we were standing in the room he asked my opinion several times, now about one thing, now about another. I could only reply with a shrug of the shoulders, for it was estimated that the ornamentation of the room where we were and where the invalid was—I mean the permanent structure—had cost two thousand ducats and more, although the length of the chamber did not exceed twelve *braccia*. The fireplace was all of Carrara marble, shining like gold, and carved so subtly with figures and foliage that Praxitiles and Phidias could do no better. The ceiling was so richly decorated with gold and ultramarine and the walls so well adorned, that my pen is not equal to describing them. The bedstead alone was valued at five hundred ducats, and it was fixed in the room in the Venetian fashion.

There were so many beautiful and natural figures and so much gold everywhere that I do not know whether in the time of Solomon, who was King of the Jews, in which silver was reputed more common than stones, there was such abundance as was displayed there. I had better not try and describe the ornaments of the bed and of the lady—that is, the coverings and the cushions, which were six in number, and the curtains—as I fear I should not be believed. They were in truth most wonderful.

I must tell about one other thing, however, which is true, and yet perhaps I shall not be believed, though it is certain that the ducal Ambassador would not let me lie. In the said chamber there were twenty-five Venetian damsels, one more beautiful than the other, who had come to visit the invalid. Their dress was most decent, as I said above, in the Venetian style. They did not show, however, less than four or six fingers' width of bare skin below their shoulders before and behind. Those damsels had so many jewels on the head, neck and hands—that is, gold, precious stones and pearls, that, in the opinion of those who were present, these must have been worth a hundred thousand ducats. Their faces were very well painted, and so was the rest of the bare skin that could be seen.

After staying a good while and contemplating the room

and the persons in it, every man departed fasting; the custom in this respect differing from that observed at Milan, where at similar visitations a magnificent refection is provided. I think the Venetians consider that the refreshment of the eyes is enough; and I like the idea, because the refections offered at Milan on such occasions are a great expense, and those at Venice cost nothing.

On Monday, the 3rd of November, being the day of the commemoration of the dead, there was a festival, as on Sunday. I went to the Observant Monastery of Saint Dominic. The friars are good men. Having borrowed vestments from them I said a Mass for the souls of the departed.

On Tuesday, the 4th of November, I went again in the morning to the Monastery named, and there I said a Mass in fulfilment of a vow which fell to me by lot during the storm at sea. After this, as the weather had turned very cold, I set about making a provision of warm clothes to protect me, and attended to certain other affairs because I wanted to leave for Milan.

These things occupied me all Wednesday and the following Thursday, on which day I took leave of those to whom I was debtor, beginning with the Magnificent Don Tadiolo de Vicomercato, the ducal Ambassador, and then all the others, especially the Milanese.

On Friday, the 7th of November, I heard Mass in the Church of San Salvatore, and then, after taking a meal in the house of Don Giovanni Toretino, a citizen of Lucca, who, by reason of the great courtesy he had shown me during my sojourn in Venice, both going and returning from this voyage, had been a most delightful host, I went on board a boat near the Rialto in company with two Milanese merchants; and at the seventh hour, with the favour of God, we left Venice and set out towards Padua, where we arrived at the third hour of the night. We had a great deal of difficulty in entering the city. Finally, after mingling entreaties and gratuities, we were admitted by a certain postern gate and went to lodge at the Sun Inn, where, because the inn was full and we were late, we fared as the proverb says: "He who comes late has a poor supper and a worse bed."

On Saturday, the 8th of November, I took a horse on hire from the host, and having first dined, we set out towards Vicenza, which we reached at the twenty-second hour. There I found Raphaele da Palazzolo, a Milanese, who was on his way from the fair at Treviso, where he had bought three horses. He gave me one to ride as far as Milan, and I gave back the horse I had hired.

We left Vicenza without further delay and went to lodge at a place called Le Tavernelle, for no other reason except that we wanted to ride before daybreak.

On Sunday, the 9th of November, we left Le Tavernelle very early, and arrived in very good time at a place called Villanova, where there is an excellent abbey.

After finding lodgings, we went to the abbey to hear Mass in order to do our duty. Although the abbey is rich there was only one friar to be found in the monastery. He had already said Mass, and if we wanted to hear Mass it was necessary for me to say it in very dirty vestments, to the shame of the person who holds the abbey in commendam. Enough! I do not want to say any more; but I marvelled greatly that the Signoria permits such a state of things.

Having said Mass as well as possible, and commended ourselves to God, according to the Commandment of the Holy Mother Church, we went to restore our bodies which had need of refection. Then we mounted on horseback and went as far as Verona, where we lodged early. As it was a festival, and we were warned that if we went further there was no good lodging to be found for a very long way, we decided to put up at the house of a good innkeeper who had been recommended to us. Then we went about the city to see the things we had not yet seen until supper-time.

On Monday, the 10th of November, we started out and made our first halt at Peschiera, where, because it was the Vigil of Saint Martin's day, and also because we saw a fine quantity of fish, we had a Lent dinner. Then riding on, we put up at a certain little inn called Saint Mark's Bridge, where we fared very badly. But we were constrained to stop there as it were by necessity. We had planned to pass the night at Lonato, but we heard that the place was everywhere full of soldiers gathered there for the muster, and we thought it wise to keep away from such company *(Note 101)*.

On Tuesday, the 11th of November, Saint Martin's day, we rose early and rode to Brescia, where we dismounted and went to hear Mass at a little church situated in the Bishop's Court. A great festival was being held there in honour of Saint Martin, and a very solemn Mass chanted in the presence of the aforesaid Lord Bishop *(Note 102)*. In my opinion he must have been very little at the Court of Rome to learn ceremonies and episcopal dignity, or if indeed he had learnt these things he practised them very little; and let that suffice.

When we returned to the inn we found certain Milanese who told us that some of my friends, hearing at Milan that I had arrived in Venice several days ago, had waited there two days to meet me, and that they had departed to return to Milan that very morning.

After dinner we mounted on horseback and set out towards Milan. When we reached Cuchai, we found those who had come to Brescia to meet us. They had stopped there because they had heard from certain merchants that we had left Brescia. They received us very affectionately. Amongst them there was the Secretary of the Magnificent Don Fermo Secchi, sent by his Magnificence to conduct me to a property of his called Calci. So we left Cuchai, notwithstanding that it was evening, and went to Calci, where we were excellently lodged.

On Wednesday, the 12th of November, after dinner at Calci, we went very early to Caravaggio, and how cordially we were received by the aforesaid Don Fermo I will not say, because it would have been oppressive for me to have accepted all he offered to me and to all my companions, for we were seven. If I had been a great prelate he could not have done more for me. And there I stayed until the following day.

Very early on Thursday, the 13th of November, I went to fulfil a vow I had made at sea—that is, to say a Mass at Our Lady of the Fountain at Caravaggio. After Mass I returned to the house because I wanted to mount with the company, but the aforesaid Don Fermo insisted on our having dinner before we departed, although it was early.

When dinner was over we took leave of the aforesaid Don Fermo and set out towards Milan, the city I had so greatly longed for both by sea and by land. When I heard, however, that his Excellency the Lord Lodovico Sforza, the new Duke of Milan, had made his entry at the eighteenth hour with the usual solemnities, I left my companions for several reasons, and especially because I did not want to enter Milan with so large a company—we were twenty horsemen—and remained alone at the Cassina di Rotuli in the house of Don Jacobo Rotulo, a Milanese Patrician. Although it was night and there was no one there save an old woman, nevertheless great honour was done me, and I rested there until the following morning.

On Friday, the 14th of November, by the grace of the Most High and Excellent God, I reached Milan and entered the city by the Porta Orientale, in pilgrim's dress and alone, although many of my friends had come to meet me at an early hour.

I first visited the principal church and thanked Our Lady for the notable help vouchsafed to me in the many perils I had passed through on this voyage, both by sea and by land. Then I went to see our Most Reverend Lord the Archbishop, who, as I said before, had given me the cross and bestowed his blessing upon me. He received me in his chapel most graciously, and did and said over me all that is laid down in the Pontifical to be done to a pilgrim when he returns to the fatherland. Thus with his blessing I went home, and was very joyfully welcomed by my friends.

If I have described this voyage at too great length I beg my readers to excuse me, because those who asked me to tell them about it wished me to write thus.

I have not said anything about the voyage to Saint Catherine in Mount Sinai because I could only do so from hearsay. When we were in Jerusalem, I, and certain other pilgrims, had already made provision for the journey as to the expense, but the friars of Mount Sion told us that it was impossible to go there. They said that the Arabs had plundered the monastery which has charge of the body of Saint Catherine, and killed the abbot and certain of the monks, and that until the Sultan takes measures no one will be able to go there in safety. On this account we gave up the idea of undertaking this journey.

Praise be to Thee, O Christ!

Notes.

NOTES.

NOTE 1.

The Ambrosian Liturgy. The local Milanese Liturgy attained its greatest splendour towards the end of the fourth century. The Oriental elements it contains may have been due to some one of the first bishops who had come from the East, or have been introduced by St. Ambrose, Bishop of Milan, 374—397. It was afterwards called the Ambrosian Liturgy, either because it was arranged and enriched by St. Ambrose, or because it had been used by a man of such great merits and authority. It was used in the Milanese Church all through the Middle Ages, and its continuity was never seriously threatened until the time of the Council of Trent, when it was decided to compile a universal liturgy. In consequence, the Roman Breviary was published in 1568, and the Roman Missal in 1570. The Curia was determined to impose the new liturgies on all the Latin Churches, and they prevailed by degrees everywhere save at Milan. In 1578 the then governor of the city obtained a papal letter authorising him to have mass celebrated daily according to the Roman rite, in any church he pleased. The Archbishop, St. Charles Borromeo, however, procured the immediate revocation of the brief, and since that time no attempt has been made to suppress the Ambrosian liturgy.

NOTE 2.

The Cathedral of Milan, in which Casola received the benediction of Archbishop Arcimboldi, was not the Duomo, but the Basilica of Santa Tecla, then called the Basilica Metropolitana Estiva or Summer Basilica, because the Archbishop and the Canons ordinary officiated there from Easter until the first Sunday in October. According to Count Giulio Porro, "there can be no doubt on this point, because Casola says that he was blessed on the third day of the Rogations after the services. Now we know from ancient documents and from Puricelli, who in his "Nazariana" gives us the description, that the procession on the third day started from the Summer Basilica of Santa Tecla, and after visiting the churches of Santa Eufemia, S. Celso, and others, returned to S. Tecla. In fact, in 1494, there were two cathedral churches in Milan, Santa Maria Maggiore and Santa Tecla.[1]" The Summer Basilica

---

1. Note 3 to Porro's printed edition of Casola's voyage, Milan, 1855.

of S. Tecla, also called S.S. Tecla and Pelagia seems to have been the older of the two. It was demolished in the fifteenth century, because it was threatening to fall from old age, and immediately rebuilt. It was finally destroyed in 1548.

NOTE 3.

St. Ambrose (Bishop of Milan 340—397) was born at Treves in 340, and in 387 he founded a new church at Milan on the ruins of a Temple of Bacchus. It was first dedicated to the Saints Gervasius and Protasius, whose bones were transferred there from the place miraculously revealed to St. Ambrose. After the death of Ambrose, who was laid between them under the high altar, the church took his name. St. Ambrose became the great patron Saint of Milan, and the Milanese have always been proud to call themselves 'Ambrosiani,' or Sons of St. Ambrose.

NOTE 4.

Saints Gervasius and Protasius were twin brothers, who suffered martyrdom at Milan under the Emperor Nero, A.D. 69. A good man buried their bodies honourably in his own garden, where they remained undiscovered until 387 A.D. In this year St. Ambrose had built his new church at Milan, and the people desired him to procure for it some holy relics. The Bishop thereupon went to pray in a neighbouring church, and fell into a trance in which the burial place of Saint Gervasius and his brother was miraculously revealed to him. The relics were borne in solemn procession to the new basilica, which was dedicated to them, and wonderful miracles were worked by them as they passed along the street. After the death of St. Ambrose, who was laid to rest between them, the church was called by his name. The bodies of the three saints (St. Ambrose in the centre), all dressed in gorgeous vestments and lying in a magnificent sarcophagus, may still be seen in the crypt, under the high altar of the remarkable old church, which preserves in the beautiful atrium and the façade, the form of the original building.

NOTE 5.

Erasmus of Narni (not *Narma* as Casola wrote), surnamed Gattamelata, perhaps on account of the quiet catlike astuteness he displayed in his military strategy and tactics, was one of the most celebrated Condottieri chiefs in the service of the Venetian Republic during the fifteenth century. His most famous achievements were (*a*) the victory won at Rovato (July, 1438) over Niccolo Piccinino, who commanded the troops of the Visconti; (*b*) his skilful retreat with his troops, the same year, from Brescia towards Verona; for which he received generous gifts from the Republic, and his family was admitted to the Venetian Patriciate;

(*c*) the battle he won near Arco (9 Nov., 1439) over the Marquis of Mantua and Piccinino. Gattemelata retired from active service 1440 to Padua, where he died 1443. An equestrian statue in bronze, the work of Donatello, was erected to his memory in the Piazza in front of the Church of St. Anthony. In the same church, his wife caused the chapel of the sacrament to be built, to contain the ashes of her husband, and of her son who died 1456. The bas reliefs in bronze which adorn the chapel were designed and executed by Donatello between 1446 and 1449.

NOTE 6.
Antenor. In 1274, while excavations were being made near the Hospital of the Casa di Dio at Padua, a cypress coffin was discovered, with a lead coffin inside it which contained the body of a man with a sword lying by his side. Near the coffins two vases were also found full of gold coins of considerable value. The results of later research made it probable that the body was that of a Hunnish soldier. A certain Lovato or Lupato, however, promptly declared the corpse to be that of Antenor the famous Trojan, to whom legend attributed the foundation of Padua. He thereupon persuaded his fellow-citizens to celebrate the discovery with sumptuous festivals, and to build a tomb, magnificent for its day, to contain the remains. This tomb is still to be seen near the University and the Ponte di San Lorenzo.

NOTE 7.
The pilgrims, whether Italian or Ultramontane, who chose Venice as their port of embarcation, came on foot or on horseback as far as Pavia, or Padua, or Treviso, or Mestre, according to the route selected, and then performed the rest of the voyage to the Lagoon-City by river or canal. Those who had come on horseback generally either sold their horses, or left them with an innkeeper, or a friend, to be kept for them till they came back, others however sent them back home. Casola tells us that before entering the boat at Padua to go to Venice, he recommended the horse he had ridden from Milan, to the innkeeper, " as is the custom." Something must have happened to the animal, however, because on his return to Padua he was obliged to hire a horse from the host, which he gave up at Vicenza, having obtained another from a Milanese whom he met there.

NOTE 8.
Don Taddeo Vicomercato. A large number of despatches sent by Don Taddeo (or Tadiolo, as Casola calls him) Vicomercato to Milan, while he was Milanese Ambassador to Venice in the years 1491—1496, are preserved in the Archives of his native city. There are few, how-

ever, for the month of May, 1494, and Casola is not mentioned in them. On the 16th of June, 1494, Don Taddeo wrote to his master amongst other items of news :—"The mercantile galleys which leave Venice every year are twenty-two in number, including the pilgrim galley, which has gone on its way."[1] On the 31st of October, 1494, the Milanese Ambassador informed the Duke that "This morning the pilgrim galley arrived. Frate Francesco Trivulzio died on board of it, and was buried at Rhodes on the way back from Jerusalem. I have not heard anything else of sufficient importance to be worthy of being brought under the notice of your Highness."[2] Later on Don Taddeo was ambassador for Milan to Lucca, Imola, Bologna, Siena and Florence. He died in 1509.

NOTE 9.

The chapter in Sansovino,[3] which is devoted to a description of the private palaces in Venice, concludes thus :—"So many and such splendid edifices, with others near them of greater or less importance, form a most great and spacious city; which to subtle observers reveals itself to be not one city alone, but many separate cities all joined together. Because, whoever looks at a plan in which the bridges are not marked will see that the city is divided into many large, fortified places and cities, each surrounded by its own canals; and people pass from one to the other by means of bridges—whether of stone, as they are for the most part, or of wood—which bind the whole city together. The shops also, which are scattered over the whole body and circumference of the said city, also make it appear to be made up of many cities joined into one. Because every *Contrada*[4] has not one church alone, but several churches. There is also a piazza with wells; and it has bakehouses, wineshops, the arts of the tailors, the fruitsellers, the grocers, the chemists, the schoolmasters, the carpenters, the shoemakers, and everything else necessary for the use of human beings in great abundance. The result is that on going out of one *Contrada* and entering another, you will say without doubt that you have gone out of one city, and entered another."

NOTE 10.

The Ducal Palace, begun by Angelo Partecipazio in 809 or 810, was in great part destroyed by fire during the revolution which led to the death of the Doge Pietro Candiano, and rebuilt between 991 and 1009 by the Doges Pietro I. and II. Orseoli. It afterwards suffered from four other great fires which did inestimable damage. The first of these great

---

1. Archives of Milan, *Potenze Esteri, Venezia*.
2. Idem.
3. *Venezia descritta*, da M. Francesco Sansovino, Venetia, 1604.
4. *i.e.*, District or quarter.

fires took place in 1106, but the damage was soon repaired, and the Palace enriched with the marble and other treasures brought from the East after the fall of Constantinople. In the second half of the fourteenth century the Hall of the Great Council was built. In 1422, on the proposal of the Doge Tommaso Mocenigo, it was decided to reconstruct the rest of the old fabric facing the Piazzetta, in harmony with the work already carried out.[1] Thus under the Doges Foscari and Moro, the outside of the Palace was completed as it stands at present, but the eastern side of the Courtyard remained as in ancient times until the second great fire broke out on the night of the 14th of Sept., 1483, according to Malipiero.[2] (Sanuto gives the date of the fire as 1479.) This fire did great harm, especially to the Ducal apartments, which were completely gutted. When the question was raised, the majority of the Venetian Patricians "did not feel like spending more than 6,000 ducats in repairing the Palace, because of the hardness of the times."[3] Nicolo Trevisano, on the other hand, proposed to buy all the houses opposite the Palace on the other side of the Canal as far as the Calle delle Rasse, and build there a new residence for the Doge, with a large garden, and join it by a stone bridge to the Sala del Collegio in the old building, which was to be restored and used for purely business purposes. It was, however, finally decided to rebuild the original Palace with the addition of another story; and it is this decision, which Casola, who was fascinated by Trevisano's scheme, so much regrets. Antonio Rizzo, the architect, was appointed at a salary of 100 ducats a year to direct the work. In 1494 Casola saw the so-called Giant's staircase in process of construction, and the new façade of the Ducal apartments, which internally also impressed him with the splendour of the new furniture and decorations. It was only in March, 1492, that the Doge Agostino Barbarigo, after giving a dinner to a hundred poor people to celebrate the event, left his temporary residence in the Palazzo Diedo, and went to sleep for the first time in the "New Palace." In 1498 Rizzo had already spent 80,000 ducats and only about half of the necessary work was yet done. As it was discovered at this time that he had embezzled 12,000 ducats, he fled, and died shortly after at Foligno. The work of restoration went on and may be said to have been completed in the middle of the sixteenth century.

NOTE 11.

Prisons. The *chief prisons* in Venice in the Middle Ages were in the Ducal Palace itself, though every "*Sestiere*" or sixth part of the city had its own separate prisons for debtors and persons guilty of slight

---

1. See F. Zanotto in *Venezia e le sue lagune*, vol. ii. part ii.
2. Malipiero, see Annals of, in the *Archivio Storico Italiano*, vol. vii.
3. Malipiero, p. 673.

offences. In 1321[1] and 1326[2] two decrees of the Maggior Consiglio ordered—the first the construction, and the second the enlargement of certain prisons "Desubtus Palatium" (underneath the Palace)—two houses which existed there, and the apartments of certain subordinate officials being devoted to this purpose. These details, together with the fact that the Ducal apartments and all the chief Government offices—in fact the Palace proper—were above the ground floor, remove all suspicion that by the words "Desubtus Palatium," subterranean prisons are to be understood. No such prisons ever existed in the Palace, and it was the long, dark, narrow staircase, down which they were conducted, which gave prisoners the idea that they were going into the bowels of the earth. The "upper prisons" referred to in decrees relating to the prisons, were evidently those in the *Torresella*, which was probably the eastern tower of the original ducal palace, while the "lower prisons" were on the ground floor, and occupied part of the space now devoted to the lower of the two open arcades surrounding the courtyard. These latter prisons included the so-called *Pozzi* or wells, which still remain. On the upper floor of the Palace, on the side facing the canal, were the prisons popularly known as the *Piombi* or leads, though under the lead roof there was a wooden ceiling formed of heavy beams; these *Piombi*, however, only began to be used as prisons in 1591. Casola refers to the "lower prisons," that is to the *Pozzi* on the eastern or canal side and to others on the south side known by quaint names such as the *Liona* (the lion), *Forte* (the strong), *Orba* (the blind prison, because it had no windows), *Frescagioia* (fresh joy), etc., and he must have been quite right in thinking that they spoiled the general effect of the Palace. Between 1589 and 1602 the present prison building, connected with the ducal palace by the Bridge of Sighs, was constructed, and the prisoners were removed there. The outer walls of some of the old prisons were then thrown down and replaced by the pillars which form the lower arcade. See Romanin, *Storia documentata di Venezia*, vol. iii., pp. 74—78; iv., pp. 51, 52; vi., p. 75. Sansovino, *Venetia descritta*, p. 251*b*; Edizione, 1604. Mutinelli, *Lessico Veneto*, p. 310. Tassini, *Curiosità Veneziane*, p. 157. *Venezia e Le sue Lagune*, vol. ii., part ii., p. 347e, 348. *Codice Italiana alla Biblioteca Marciana*, class vii., No. ccxcv.

NOTE 12.

Broletto was the popular name at Milan for the *Palazzo di Corte*, the early residence of the Visconti and the seat of the government offices, especially of the Courts of Justice. It stood on the site now occupied by the S. W. part of the enlarged Duomo (which it was destroyed

---

1. *Maggior Consiglio*, vol. vii, 5th July, 1321, p. 19*b*.
2. *Maggior Consiglio*, vol. vii. 2nd March, 1326, p. 127.

NOTES

piecemeal to make way for), and by the modern Palazzo Reale. *Brolo* in the Milanese dialect (*Broglio* or *Brogio* in the dialect of Venice), means a garden. The Palazzo di Corte took its name from the *Broletto*, or small garden, which lay on its eastern side, as distinguished from the *Brolo Grande* or large park which is believed to have extended behind the Palace from San Nazaro to Santo Stefano, and perhaps included the present Piazza Fontana.

NOTE 13.

The date of the institution of the College or Tribunal known as the *Signori di Notte*, i.e., The Lords of the Night, cannot be given precisely. According to Marino Sanuto the elder, it existed before 1250, and this chronicler asserts that it consisted at first of one, and then of two persons, who divided the inspection of the city between them, until, in 1262, their number was increased to six, one being elected for each Sestiere of Venice. In any case from that time there were always six of them, and their duty was to watch over the safety of the city, especially at night, protect it from fire, and punish murderers, thieves, fornicators, bigamists, swindlers, tenants who did not pay their rents, etc. They were empowered to pronounce sentence of death, but there was an appeal, first to the magistrates known as *Del Proprio*, and second to the highest criminal and civil court, called the *Quarantia*. In 1544 the Maggior Consiglio created a second College of six Lords of the Night. Henceforth the older body was known as the *Signori di Notte al Criminale*, and dealt with criminal matters. The new body called the *Signori di Notte al Civile*, had jurisdiction in Civil cases. see *Venezia e le Sue Lagune*, vol. i., p. 72, and p. 155. Mutinelli, *Glossario*, p. 370. Ferro, *Diritto Comune e Veneto*, vol. ii., p. 693.

NOTE 14.

The Church of S. Maria della Carità was one of the oldest in Venice, and built at first of wood. In 1120 the Patrician Marco Zulian offered all his substance to the Papal Legate to erect it in stone together with the Convent, which in 1134 received a certain number of Regular Canons of St. Augustine. Pope Alexander III. consecrated the church and enriched it with indulgences; whence arose the custom that every year the Doge and the Signoria went there in state on the 5th of April, to take advantage of the same. The church was rebuilt in 1446 and beautified in the following century. The famous congregation or Scuola della Carità, instituted 1260 in the Church of St. Leonard, erected its meeting hall in 1344, beside the Church and Convent of the Carità. Tradition relates that Pope Alexander III., fleeing before the Emperor Barbarossa, came to Venice in disguise 1177, and passed the first night, either on the bare ground near the Calle del Perdon at S. Appollinare, or as others recount, under the porch of the Church of S. Salvatore; that he went the next morning to the Monastery of the Carità, and was received as a simple priest, or according to another version, as a scullion, and that he remained there six months. V. Tassini, *Curiosità Veneziane*, pp. 148, 150 and 550.

NOTE 15.

The Pregadi [from Pregare Ital=to pray, to beg]. The Venetian Senate was also known as the "Pregadi," because in early times the Doges, on occasions of special importance were in the habit of summoning, and begging for the counsel of certain of the leading citizens. The number and the choice of the individuals depended entirely on the Doge's good pleasure. The citizens thus gathered together formed a purely consulting body; all real power being reserved to the Great Council. As, however, the latter generally accepted the advice of the Pregadi which was open to the suspicion of unduly favouring the policy of the Doges, it was decided, early in the thirteenth century, to replace the irregular and arbitrary body by a permanent one elected from the Great Council itself. The new Council was called the Senate; at the same time it kept the old name of "*Pregadi*," though the members were no longer invited but elected.

NOTE 16.

As the palace in Venice belonging to the Duke of Milan had been confiscated and sold during the wars which preceded the Peace of Lodi (1454), the Venetian Government bought a house at San Polo from the heirs of the famous Condottiere Gattamelata, and presented it to Francesco Sforza in 1458. A few years later (1461) the latter sold the house at San Polo to Marco Cornaro, father of Catherine of Cyprus for 12,000 ducats, and at the same time bought from Marco Cornaro for 20,000 ducats the foundations of a magnificent palace begun by Marco's brother Andrea in 1453 on the Grand Canal. The difference in the price (8,000 ducats) was to be paid by Duke Francesco in five annual rates of 1,600 ducats each, beginning with the 1st of January, 1463. But Cornaro had to wait for his money. Finally Sforza decided to pawn the ducal jewels for 5,500 golden ducats to pay his debts in Venice, and through the intervention of the Doge, Marco Cornaro, received in February, 1465, two instalments. Not long after, Francesco Sforza died, and his son Galeazzo turned a deaf ear to Cornaro's requests for payment. In 1478, however, the Duchess Bona authorised Marco Cornaro to collect a ducat above the usual price (fixed in 1460 at ten ducats) on every moggio of salt brought into Milan from Venice—and this up to the extinction of the debt. The Palace begun by Andrea Cornaro, and designed by Master Bartolomeo Bono, the mason and architect, was described in the Act of

Sale as "The house begun on the Grand Canal in the Contrada of Saint Samuel," etc. And with more precision by Marco Cornaro, in the description he sent to Francesco Sforza as follows :—" The façade on the Grand Canal has two towers on that side, which are of marble cut diamond fashion, and the riva between the two towers has very large columns of marble." By these descriptions, the foundations, which never seem to have been carried any further, may still be recognised. For, after passing under the Academy bridge on the way to the station, there is to be seen on the right-hand side, at the corner of the *Rio del Duca*, and nearly opposite the *Rio Malpaga*, a group of very ordinary looking houses rising from a foundation evidently intended for a large and imposing palace. This is the *Ca' del Duca*, that is the *House of the Duke*, and according to the popular tradition the Venetian Government, alarmed at the size and strength of the building, stopped the construction. There does not seem, however, to be any authentic record of any such prohibition; and the money difficulties of Francesco and his successors, together with the complications produced by the French Invasions, sufficiently explain why the building was not continued. In 1494, when Casola saw the beginning of the handsome structure and wished "for the honour of the Milanese" that it had been completed, it still belonged to the Sforzas; and it is not certain when it passed out of their hands. Probably it was confiscated in 1499, when the Venetians, in league with Louis of France against Lodovico il Moro, conquered Cremona. On that occasion the Venetian "Provveditori," who were with the army— Melchiore Trevisan and Marcantonio Morosini—brought home some famous marble trophies. Trevisan's grandson fixed two of these into the walls of the courtyard and garden of their house at the Giudecca; while Morosini built those that fell to his share into the wall of the courtyard in his house at Santa Giustina. Early in the 16th century the *Ca' del Duca*, that is the simple building set up on the Colossal foundations of Andrea Cornaro and Bartolomeo Bon, was occupied in part by Master Bartolomeo himself; and Titian kept models here for the pictures he was commissioned to paint for the hall of the Great Council. In the time of Francesco Sansovino it belonged to the Grimani family. (See *Cronaca Magna*, Marciana, Venice. Sansovino, *Venezia Descritta*, Edition of 1604, p. 266b. Tassini. *Curiosità Veneziane*, p. 241. Luca Beltrami, *La Ca' del Duca*, Milan, 1899. Cantu, *Scorsa di un Lombardo negli Archivi di Venezia*, Milan, 1856.)

NOTE 17.

The large number of warehouses and the immense accumulation of merchandise in mediæval Venice was due to the trading system pursued. The merchant galleys were not allowed to go directly, from a port where goods were bought, to the port of exchange; but every voyage was required to begin and end at Venice. Venice became, therefore, the place of deposit until at least the following year, when the new voyages were made; and foreign merchants crowded there to make their purchases. Two great events, however, which immediately preceded and followed Casola's visit very soon changed the current of trade and began to empty the Venetian warehouses. If the discovery of America in 1492 had not made its due impression on the Venetians, things were very different when a few years later tidings came that Portuguese ships had circumnavigated Africa, arrived in India, and returned laden with spices and other Eastern products, which were sold cheaply at Lisbon. "All the city of Venice was greatly impressed and alarmed, and the wisest men held that this was the worst news that could ever come to the city . . . . Because the spices which came to Venice, passed through the whole of Syria and the countries subject to the Sultan, paying exorbitant duties in every place, so that when they arrived in Venice the value of an article which, in the beginning, was worth a ducat, was raised as high as sixty and even a hundred ducats. As the voyage by sea was exempt from these oppressive taxes, it came to pass that the Portuguese could sell the goods they brought at a much lower price." (*Girolamo Priuli Diarii*, p. 108, in Romanin, *Storia Documentata di Venezia*, vol. iv., p. 461.)

NOTE 18.

Fondaco dei Tedeschi. From very early times various nations such as the Germans, Greeks, Tuscans, etc., having extensive trading relations with Venice, had houses assigned to them for their representatives and their merchandise, by the Government of the Republic. From at least the thirteenth century, the Fondaco which stands to-day on the same site, was allotted to the Germans or *Tedeschi;* and in 1268 three Patricians called "Visdomini" were appointed to direct the affairs of the *Fondaco dei Tedeschi.* In 1505 a violent fire reduced the building to ashes; and during the reconstruction, completed in 1508, the senate lodged the Germans provisionally in the house of the Lippomano at Santa Fosca. The outer walls of the New Fondaco, were decorated with frescoes by Giorgione and Titian. The pilgrims to Venice were met as they entered the city by a crowd of agents who with noisy importunity extolled the merits of the hostels they represented. Some went directly to quarters bespoken in advance, at the houses of friends or agents. Priests and monks were received at certain of the monasteries. Knights and merchants established themselves at one of the inns which existed in Venice from very ancient times; and amongst these there were several German houses. The chief of the German hostels was the Fondaco dei Tedeschi on the Grand Canal, just below the Rialto Bridge. Ordinary pilgrims might go where they liked; but all German merchants were obliged to live here, and deliver up to the House Steward on their arrival, their weapons, their money, and their merchandise. Here the whole German trade in Venice was concentrated and placed under the control of the State officials, who in spite of their close protective system and high duties, favoured the German merchants on the whole. The Fondaco contained not only dwelling rooms and bed rooms, but also a large restaurant, where good eating and drinking was to be had. If, however, the Germans had little to complain of with regard to their treatment in general, the time limit imposed on the visits to the eating room formed a standing grievance; they wanted it open night and day after the well-known German necessity—long ago noted by Tacitus— To take just one more drink. (See Röhricht, preface to *Deutsche Pilgerreisen*, Innsbruck, 1900.)

NOTE 19.

"Round the roofs" (of the palaces and houses) "run the gutters of hard stone, by which the rain water descends through hidden pipes into the wells" (which are provided with an ingenious system of filtration), "where it is purged of the grosser material and turns again to the benefit of man. Because as there are no rivers there (*i.e.*, in Venice), nor foundations of solid earth where springs of sweet waters could be found, the cisterns are used, and their water is healthier and more easily digested than spring water, which is very crude. There are a great number of these wells or cisterns—both public and private— throughout the city, so that every piazza, or campo, or corte, has its well, made at the public expense, and for the greater part on special occasions." (Sansovino-Venetia Descritta, p. 261.) The modern system of reservoir, aqueduct, and pipes in the separate houses has supplemented but not superseded the old system in Venice, especially for the poorer classes. The water carriers and water sellers formed themselves into a guild in the 14th century, and elected as its protector St. Constantius, because this saint "caused the lamps to burn with water without any liquor or oil as Messer St. Gregory relates." [1]

NOTE 20.

Fra Francesco Trivulzio belonged to one of the noblest of the aristocratic families of Milan. He was one of the five sons of Pietro Trivulzio, Lord of Codogno in the district of Lodi, by his wife Laura Bossi.[2] In the Trivulzian Library I saw an engraving of a portrait which bore the legend "B. Fran. Trivultius. Ord. Min. obyt 1482." The portrait is that of a gentlefaced, beardless friar, holding a lily in his hand, and

---

1. Tassini, *Curiosità Veneziane*, p. 6.
2. See notes on the life of Fra. Fr. Trivulzio by Carlo Trivulzio, inserted on loose leaves, in the MSS. copy of Casola's voyage, in the Trivulzian Library, Milan.

bears a strong resemblance to the traditional portraits of Saint Anthony of Padua. The date is clearly a mistake. In the same library a book of the quattrocento is preserved, which contains a written inscription on the 1st page, stating that it was "For the use of Brother Francis de Trivulzio," and begging the reader to pray for the Soul of the Magnificent Lord Peter de Trivulzio—through whose bounty the book was bought,—who died on the 1st of December, 1473, when "I, brother Francis his first born was present, and I believe that through the mediation of the order of the Minor Friars he is saved because he closed his life well."[1] Francesco married Veronica dei Secchi,[2] but persuaded his wife to embrace the religious life. Francesco assumed the habit of the minor friars in the Convent of Sant' Angelo, then a mile outside Porta Comasina (Milan); and in time was appointed Provincial Vicar of his order for the province of Milan. Fra Francesco "was very frugal in his food, and very assiduous in his prayers, most vigilant in conserving his virginity perfectly pure, and of no ordinary perfection—skilled in both laws and endowed with a most profound and tenacious memory; and he preached so unweariedly throughout Italy, that he became famous everywhere not only as an excellent, but also as a most saintly preacher. The people themselves rendered public testimony to his fervent preaching, his doctrine, his holiness, and his exemplary life when he drew sinners to repentance, reconciled enemies and excited those who were most inveterate in their vicious habits to amend their ways."[3] Fra Francesco's reputation for sanctity and eloquence is enthusiastically confirmed by Casola, who sought out "The venerable religious and most remarkable evangelist of the word of God, Don Frate Francesco Trivulzio" as soon as he heard that he was in Venice, and kept much in his company during the voyage "as long as he was well," "because in truth he was treated with great respect and everything was shown to him without much difficulty." On the voyage, although there were 63 priests among the Pilgrims. Father Francesco's sermons are the only ones Casola records, and presumably the only ones delivered. They were preached on land as at Zara and Ragusa; and in the midst of the sea, as when on the Vigil and the feast of Saint John, he expounded the famous nine meditations on the saint of the day; and so comforted the passengers and crew that he made them forget their sufferings from

---

[1]. See "Panteologia seu Summa Rainerij" in the Trivulzian Library. The inscription runs thus :—Ad usum fratris Francisci de Trivultio et pertinet loco Sci Johannis apud Lande. Recordare lector exorare pro anima Magnifici Domini Petri de Trivultio de cujus elemosyna emptus est liber iste, qui obiit anno Domini MCCCCLXXIII die prima Decembris in civitate Terdene (?) Ill͞mi D͞ni Nostri Galeaz Marie Ducis Mediolan : quinti ultra Padum tunc comissarius, ubi ego frater Franciscus primogenitus suus fui presens et credo quod mediante ordine Fratrum Minorum sit salvus quia vitam suam bene finivit."
[2]. It was don Fermo de' Secchi, a member of this family, who entertained Casola hospitably at Calzi on the outward and homeward journey.
[3]. History of the Minor Friars in Milan, by Brother Pier Nicola Buonavilla, Milan, 1733.

heat, bad weather, and bad and insufficient food, and preached for two hours at a stretch "to the great satisfaction of every nation, and especially of the learned persons, who came crowding round Casola afterwards to know who that Venerable Father was." "And I," writes Casola, with the pride of a fellow-countryman, "not only for the honour of the Fatherland, but also that the truth should not remain hidden, told all I could about him." At Lesina, on the way back, Casola regretfully remembered his lost friend when he went to hear a sermon in the cathedral there. "Not like those preached by the departed Don Fra Francisco Trivulzio which stimulated a man to listen; this instead, stimulated one to talk and even to sleep." Father Francesco was not destined to see Italy again. Just as the ship entered Rhodes he died and was buried in the Franciscan Church of Santa Maria della Vittorie.

NOTE 21.

Don John Simon Fornaro of Pavia. In Register 61, in the State Archives at Milan, which contains the "Immunità, Salvo Condotti, Grazie," etc., for the years 1493 and 1494, I found on page 206, the following:—"The eve of the 22nd April, 1494. On the aforenamed day, letters of safe conduct, valid for two years, were granted to John Simon Fornaro, citizen of Pavia and *Cubiculario*, who intends to go to Jerusalem and the Holy Sepulchre, with six companions." Perhaps Don John Simon was chamberlain to the young Duke Gian Galeazzo Sforza, who died in the Castle at Pavia on October 20th, 1494. The unpleasant adventures which befel Don John Simon, through his desire to bring home a parrot as a memento of his voyage, are very graphically described by Casola (chapter xiv. of the Translation).

NOTE 22.

The church and monastery of Sant' Elena or St. Helena. Casola was mistaken in attributing the foundation of this church to Alessandro Borromeo in 1420. Between 1170 and 1173 or 1175, Vitale Michael, bishop of Castello, founded a monastery on the island which lies beyond the present public gardens, and a hospice was attached for poor persons and pilgrims. In the beginning of the fifteenth century, however, Alessandro Borromeo contributed, together with a certain Tommaso Talenti, to the building of a new church, which he enriched. Borromeo also erected a chapel (in the Church), begun in Nov., 1418, where he and several relatives were afterwards buried. He came from San Miniato (Florence) and was brother of Giovanni who settled in Milan and became the ancestor of Saint Charles Borromeo. The first persons who occupied the monastery of St. Helena were regular canons living under the Augustine rule. In 1407, as the monastery, hospice, etc., had fallen into decay,

Pope Gregory granted it to certain monks belonging to the congregation of the blessed virgin of Monte Oliveto—or Olivetani—founded by Saint Bernard Tolomei of Siena (born 1272). Casola is therefore mistaken also when he says that the monks of St. Helena belonged to the Camaldolese Order. The church of St. Helena has been turned to secular purposes in modern times. See Porro—Note 9 to printed edition of Casola. Cicogna, *Inscrizioni Venete*, vol. iii., p. 337. Mrs. Jameson, *Legends of the Monastic Orders*, p. 149.)

NOTE 23.

The church and monastery of Sant' Antonio or St. Anthony the Abbot stood almost on the extreme point of Venice, looking towards the two Castles of Saint Andrew and Saint Nicholas (on the Lido). The church was founded in 1346, and the building was occupied, first by the regular Canons of Saint Anthony, and after 1471 by the regular Canons of St. Saviour: not, therefore, by the Olivetani, as Casola declares. In 1807 church and convent were destroyed to make way for the new public gardens. (Tassini, *Curiosità Veneziane*, p. 35.)

NOTE 24.

San Cristoforo della Pace or Saint Christopher of the Peace. A certain Frate Simone (born at Camerino 1404) who was versed in philosophy and theology, and a man of handsome, dignified presence, and also of rare eloquence, founded a hermitage for the hermits of Saint Augustine on one of the two small islands between Venice and Murano, granted to him by the Senate for this purpose. (v. Commemorali, xii., 1436.) Saddened by the wars which desolated Italy, he made several journeys to Milan, and finally his efforts and those of Paolo Barbo, succeeded in bringing about the Peace of Lodi, 1454. Aided by the grateful Senate and by other devout persons, he built soon after, a church on the island which had been granted to him; and church and island were known henceforth as St. Christopher of the Peace. The church and monastery were demolished in 1810. Later on, the canal which separated them having been filled in, the island of St. Christopher was joined to that of St. Michael, and the two together form the present cemetery of Venice. (See Sansovino, Edition of 1604, p. 175. Romanin, *Storia Documentata di Venezia*, vol. iv., p. 225. Mutinelli, *Glossario*, p. 120.

NOTE 25.

S. Giorgio Maggiore or St. George the Greater. Casola did not see the existing church of San Giorgio. The rebuilding was begun in 1556 by Palladio, and finished in 1610. The monastery has always been occupied by Benedictine monks.

NOTES

NOTE 26.

Sant' Andrea or S. Andrew. The church and monastery of Saint Andrew, belonging to the Carthusians, lay on an island beyond the island of St. Helena. The island of St. Andrew, otherwise called Sant' Andrea del Lido, was connected at low water with another island occupied by the fortress or castle of Saint Andrew, which as Casola writes, was about a bow shot from the other fortress or Castle of St. Nicholas, on the N. W. extremity of the Lido.

NOTE 27.

San Francesco delle Vigne or Saint Francis in the Vineyard. Among the many vineyards in Venice in early times the largest was that belonging to the Ziani family. This contained a tiny chapel dedicated to Saint Mark, because according to tradition this was the place where the evangelist passed the night to escape from a terrible storm, and where the angel appeared to him and prophesied the future foundation of Venice. The vineyard and chapel were bequeathed 1253 by Marco Ziani, son of the Doge Pietro to the minor observant friars who erected a new church dedicated to St. Francis. This was the building Casola saw. As it was in danger of falling, however, at the beginning of the sixteenth century, it was decided to build a new church. The first stone was laid in 1534; and it was consecrated 1582.

NOTE 28.

San Francesco dei Conventuali, as Casola calls it, is *Santa Maria Gloriosa dei Frari,* which belonged to the Conventual Friars of Saint Francis, some of whom came to Venice as early as 1227. The convent which was called the "Ca' Grande," or the big house, because of its size, was founded in 1236, and rebuilt after a fire in 1369. The church began to rise in 1250. It seems to have been rebuilt as it is at present in the fifteenth century, and it is certain that it was consecrated in 1492 by Bishop Pietro da Trani. With other foreign merchants the Milanese had their Guild in Venice. Its hall was in the Campo dei Frari, and in the Friars Church they had a side chapel and altar on the left, dedicated to Saint Ambrose. The magnificent altar piece was begun by Bartolomeo Vivarini, and completed after his death by Basaite, 1498. It represents the Archbishop, Saint Ambrose, seated on his throne in his episcopal robes, with attendant saints. It is uncertain when the Milanese first took possession of the Chapel of St. Ambrose, but it was probably not long before 1421.

NOTE 29.

The church and monastery of the Servants of Mary or Santa Maria dei Servi, were begun in 1318 by certain friars who had lately come to

Venice from Florence, the cradle of their order. The church was only finished in 1474. Church and monastery were almost totally destroyed in 1813, and the few remains were incorporated in a modern building It was in this monastery that Fra Paolo Sarpi passed his life; and he died here in 1631. Early in the fourteenth century a number of merchants and workmen driven from Lucca by faction, settled in Venice, where they perfected, if they did not found the silk industry. A certain part of the city was assigned to them for their residence. It lay between the well-known tortuous Calle della Bissa (or Snake) and the church of all the Holy Apostles. With the permission of the Venetian Government, they formed in 1360 a guild, under the protection of the "Volto Santo," the name given to a marvellous crucifix venerated at Lucca. In 1370 they obtained a piece of ground near the Church of the Servi, where they built an oratory with a cemetery attached. Finally in 1398 they secured from the Servite fathers a piece of empty ground opposite the Church of the Servi, where they erected their Guild Hall.

NOTE 30.

San Nicolo o San Niccoletto del Lido or Saint Nicholas of the Lido. Saint Nicholas the patron Saint of Sailors was naturally one of the patron Saints of Venice. The church dedicated to him at the entrance to the Lido port was built by order of the Doge Dominico Contarini, whose body was buried there. The monastery was filled with Benedictines from San Giorgio Maggiore.

NOTE 31.

The Monastery of San Giorgio in Alga or *de Alga*—that is Saint George among the Seaweed—stood on a small island between Venice and Lizza Fusina on the mainland. The first monks were Benedictines. They were replaced by Regular Canons of St. Augustine, with whom San Lorenzo Giustiniani, afterwards the first Patriarch of Venice, embraced the religious life. In 1690 the Augustine Canons were succeeded by Carmelite friars of the reform of St. Theresa.

NOTE 32.

Santa Maria dell' Orto or Saint Mary in the Orchard, commonly known as the Madonna dell' Orto, was first dedicated to St. Christopher. In 1377, however, an image of the Virgin was discovered in a neighbouring garden, and placed in the church which took the name of the Madonna dell' Orto, or Santa Maria Odorifera. The monastery was first inhabited by the monks called the "Umiliati"—a congregation instituted at Milan by San Giovanni di Meda. They were expelled in 1462 and replaced by some of the exemplary canons from San Giorgio in

NOTES

Alga. In 1668 the regular canons were suppressed and succeeded by Cistercians from Torcello. The church was erected towards the middle of the fourteenth century by Fra Tiberio of Parma. Though church and convent were restored, the façade of the church probably remains as it was built.

NOTE 33.

According to the legend, the church of *San Zaccaria* or St. Zaccharia was one of the eight churches founded in consequence of a revelation made to St. Magnus bishop of Ereclea. The annexed convent was filled with Benedictine nuns. In 1105 church and convent were burnt down; but they were soon rebuilt. About 1456 the modern renaissance church was begun, in which, part of the previous church, including the nuns' choir was incorporated. From a certain analogy in the style, it has been attributed to Martin Lombardi the architect of the School of St. Mark. The church was not completely finished until 1515.

NOTE 34.

Opposite the church of *San Pietro or Saint Peter* in Castello rose the Convent of the Nuns, called the Virgins, who professed the Augustine rule. On the 15th of November, 1487, Malipiero wrote in his diary— "The Convent of the Nuns, called the 'Verzene,' was burnt for the second time," and he added : " It has been rebuilt by public and private offerings, and by means of indulgences obtained at Rome." In the nineteenth century church and convent were destroyed, and the site included in the enlarged arsenal.

NOTE 35.

The Church and Convent of *Santa Maria de Caelestibus*, commonly called *della Celestia*, or the *Zelestre*, was begun in 1237 in Castello for the use of Cistercian nuns who came from Piacenza to Venice. In 1810 the Church and Convent were absorbed into the Arsenal.

NOTE 36.

For the laxity of monastic discipline in Venice, see the Registers called the *Raspe;* various chronicles such as that attributed to Savina; and also Gallicciolli *Memorie Venete II.*, and Tassini *Curiosità Veneziane*, pp. 174, 175, 179, etc.

NOTE 37.

It is curious at first sight that Comines, the French Ambassador to Venice from October 1494, to May 1495, made the same observation in almost the same words :—" C'est la plus triumphante cité que j'aye jamais veue," he says, " et qui plus faict d'honneur à ambassadeurs et estrangiers, et qui plus saigement se gouverne, et où le service de Dieu est le plus sollempnellement faict : et encores qu'il y peust bien avoir d'aultres faultes, si croy je que Dieu les a en aide pour le reverence qu'ilz portent au service de l'Eglise." Memoires de P. de Comines. Liv : vii. Ch : xviii. It will be noted, however, that on his return to Venice from the Holy Land, Casola met the French Ambassador at the house of Don Taddeo Vicomercato the Milanese Ambassador, and passed a good deal of time in his company. On that occasion as Casola gives us to understand, they exchanged their impressions about many things in the city which was new and fascinating to both of them, and very probably discussed amongst other topics the attitude of the Republic towards religion and the Church. This probably explains why they expressed themselves in such similar words on the subject in writing their Memoirs.

NOTE 38.

San Giovanni e Paolo. In 1234 the Doge Giacomo Tiepolo gave to the Dominican friars a tract of land on which to build their church and convent. The latter was entirely finished in 1293, and its two centuries of life qualified Casola's admiration when he saw it in 1494. The church, begun in 1246, was only completed in 1430. It is dedicated to the Roman brothers and martyrs Saint John and Saint Paul, who were put to death by Julian the Apostate. The Dominicans who settled in Venice were emigrants from the convent of these saints at Rome. The friars of SS. Giovanni e Paolo (Saints John and Paul) granted in 1438 a piece of land beside their church to the brothers of the School of St. Mark, who built their hall there and went to it in solemn procession on St. Mark's day. In 1485 the Assembly Hall was accidently burnt. Malipiero the Chronicler writes : " In 1485, on the 1st of April, the evening of Holy Thursday, the brethren of the School of St. Mark, met in their Hall to go to the Church of St. Anthony, and departed, leaving the candles alight on the altar. The wind opened a window on the west, and blew the curtain on to the candles; the curtain then set fire to the altar and the roof, so that in four hours everything was burnt. And it was fortunate that the Church of San Zuan Polo [SS. John and Paul] was not burnt as well. Afterwards, with the help of the Signoria and the brethren, the Hall has been rebuilt finer and larger than it was before." The architect was Martin Lombardi; and the work was finished not long before Casola visited Venice.

NOTE 39.

The Church of San Domenico belonged to the Dominican friars. Church and convent were built early in the fourteenth century with a legacy left by the Doge Marino Zorzi. In the beginning of the nineteenth century church and convent, like those of St. Anthony, were destroyed to make way for the public gardens.

NOTE 40.

The Church of the Madonna dei Miracoli, or Our Lady of the Miracles. In 1480 Malipiero wrote in his diary :—"This year, has begun the adoration of the Madonna dei Miracoli, which was at the door of the Corte Nuova, opposite some houses belonging to the Amadi in Calle Stretta. Owing to the concourse of the people, it was necessary to take away the image and carry it into the Courtyard of the Palazzo Amadi. And great offerings of wax, statues, money, and silver were made, amounting to about 400 ducats a month. And the inhabitants of the Contrada created six Procurators, among the others, Leonardo Loredano, procurator. And in process of time 3,000 ducats were collected, and with them the Corte Nuova was bought from the Bembo, Querini and Barozzi families. And there, a most beautiful temple has been built with a monastery attached, and in the convent nuns have been placed from St. Clara at Murano." The miraculous Madonna referred to was a picture of the Virgin which had been painted by order of Francesco Amadi, and put upon the wall near his house. The beautiful renaissance Church begun in 1480 was completed in 1487, and the image was placed there.

NOTE 41.

The Arsenal. In the Diary of Malipiero [part I., p. 662] there is the following notice :—" 1472 in the month of June, the 'Arsenale Nuovissimo" was begun—between the Arsenal and the Convent of the Virgins—in remembrance of Giacomo Morosini the uncle, patron of the Arsenal. It is capable of holding a hundred galleys; and this place is called Babylon." Casola refers to this, the third extension of the Arsenal, which was transferred to its present site at the beginning of the twelfth century. The first extension was begun in 1303 or 1304, and continued up to 1390; the second, called the New Arsenal, was begun in 1325; the third in 1473; the fourth in 1538 or 1539; and the fifth in 1564. Two centuries later, the Austrians twice enlarged the Arsenal, in 1810 and in 1820—28. The place outside the Arsenal, where the cords were made, was called the "Casa del Canevo" [from "Canapa," hemp; and "Canapo," a cable made of hemp] or the "Tana." It was not only a department of the Arsenal (though separate from the latter); but also the emporium, where all the hemp belonging to the State or to private individuals was warehoused. The best was chosen for the heavy ropes and cables of the ships of war and commerce; and no one was permitted to manufacture ropes, having more than a certain thickness, elsewhere.

Three Patricians who held office for 16 months, presided over the Tana. In the fourteenth century they were called "Ufficiali alla Camera del Canevo"; in the sixteenth century "Visdomini alla Tana." The Government of the Arsenal was entrusted to two distinct bodies of magistrates. The superior officials, called the "Sopra Provveditori," were chosen from among the Senators and united ripeness of judgment with the theory and practice of maritime affairs. They had civil and criminal authority over the employés; observed and regulated the conduct of the Provveditori, over whom they formed a sort of inspectorship; decided on the general line of policy to be pursued, and referred all matters to the Senate. In the beginning, that is in 1490, there were only *two* Sopra Provveditori (as Casola observed also in 1494); their number was raised to three in 1498. The second body, formed of what were called the "Provveditori," or "Patroni," that is the Directors of the Arsenal, was a very ancient magistracy. It consisted of three Patricians, not necessarily Senators, who had experience of naval affairs. By a law of 1442, the Provveditori were obliged to reside, during their term of office of 32 months, in three separate palaces near the Arsenal, called, one Paradise, another Purgatory, the third the Inferno. The reason for these quaint names is not precisely known, though it is probably to be sought in the more or less advantageous positions of the palaces, and the more or less comfortable arrangements of the rooms inside. Each Provveditore had also to take turn in sleeping for fifteen nights inside the Arsenal and keep the keys by him. Besides the material custody of the Arsenal, the business of the Provveditori was to arrange and distribute the work and direct its execution, manage the accounts, punish offences on the part of their subordinates and so forth.

NOTE 42.
Saint Augustine and the Trinity. "*The famous subject called in general, the Vision of St. Augustine*, represents a dream or vision related by himself. He tells us that while busied in writing his discourse on the Trinity, he wandered along the seashore lost in meditation. Suddenly he beheld a child who, having dug a hole in the sand, appeared to be bringing water from the sea to fill it. Augustine inquired what was the object of his task. He replied that he intended to empty into this cavity all the waters of the great deep. "Impossible!" exclaimed Augustine. "Not more impossible," replied the child Christ, "than for thee, O Augustine, to explain the mystery on which thou art meditating." (Mrs. Jameson. *Sacred and Legendary Art*, vol. I., p. 313.)

NOTE 43.
The Galeotti. From early times, and certainly until nearly the middle of the sixteenth century, the oarsmen on board the "Biremi" and the

"Triremi"—that is the Venetian Galleys which had had two or three men to each oar, were free men of Venice and of the subject territories. Every commune was obliged to furnish for the State ships a certain number of "Galeotti" between twenty-five and forty years of age; and when they had completed this term on board, their places were taken by others. Amongst the peasants of the country districts, the obligation to serve at sea was very unpopular, because it took them far away from their homes, into unhealthy, unfamiliar climates, and to a life contrary to their habits—making them exchange the liberty of the open fields for the narrow limits of a mediæval ship. It was quite different with men who belonged to Venice itself, or the Eastern shores of the Adriatic. And the Signoria, in course of time, came to draw its recruits more and more exclusively from the poorer districts in Greece, Dalmatia, etc., where as Cristoforo da Canale, one of the Vice-admirals, wrote in 1539: "Either because of some special property which heaven has bestowed on those provinces, or because of the general poverty, or because the inhabitants are familiar with the sea from their childhood upwards, the largest number of suitable men is obtained." These men also formed the crews of the galleys and sailing ships equipped and sent out by private enterprise. When a ship was ready the Captains—with the permission of the Senate—set up a table or "banco" in the Piazza, and enrolled the Volunteer Crew. These *Galeotti* must be carefully distinguished from the *Galley slaves*, or condemned criminals who were kept chained on board hulks in the "Bacino di S. Marco," opposite the Ducal palace and the piazzetta. In the pamphlet referred to of 1539, Messer da Canale asks the question :—"Whether it is better for a prince or a republic to equip the Galleys with Volunteers and free men *as we do*, or with chained Galley slaves"?[1] The reply given by Messer Alessandro Contarini, the Procurator, who advocated the Galley slave system, is a confirmation of the fact, that up to that time (1539) Venice had not used condemned prisoners on board the National Galleys as she began to do soon after.

NOTE 44.

The Chief Secretaryship. Casola refers to the chief of the ducal secretaries called the "Cancelier Grando," and does not mean to imply that he was a foreigner in the sense of not being a Venetian, but that he was not a Venetian Patrician. This was the highest position open to a man of the citizen class which came between that of the nobles and the people. The "Cancelier Grando" was appointed for life by the Senate, and he was created Cavalier. In public documents he was addressed as "Magnifico," in private he was usually called "Eccellenza." He accom-

[1]. Quoted in *I Triremi*, by Admiral L. Fincati.

panied the Doge on all state occasions, and had the right of keeping his hat on in the ducal presence, while the senators were obliged to uncover their heads. The election of the "Cancelier" was marked by great festivities which lasted three days; and after his death a very magnificent funeral service was held in the Basilica of St. Mark.

NOTE 45.

The Corpus Domini. It was a very ancient custom in Venice for the Doge to go publicly in procession on certain days and visit certain churches. The oldest was the procession on St. Mark's day; and one of the most important was the festival of the Corpus Domini instituted 1295. On the 22nd May, 1407,[1] it was decreed by the Maggior Consiglio, in order to make the festival more solemnly imposing, that :—"On the morning of the said day every year, a solemn procession should be made, and the body of Christ borne along under a handsome canopy supported by four poles, to be carried by four noble knights, and if there were no knights there, by four other nobles chosen by the Lord Duke and Councillors. At which procession should be present the serene Lord the Duke who approves, and the Councillors and other nobles who desire out of reverence for the glorious Jesus Christ our Lord, and to do honour to their country to take part in the said procession. At which procession should be present the Canons and other priests attached to the Church of St. Mark." The procession was to go out of the church, round the Piazza, and back to the church again. In 1454 it was further decreed that :—"Every year on the day of the Corpus Domini, a regular and solemn procession should be made in St. Mark's—in which should take part, the Great Schools, the regular orders of friars and monks, the congregations of secular priests, and the Bishops and mitred abbots according to custom, all well in order and wearing their vestments and ornaments. And that the Piazza of St. Mark should be covered all round with cloths which should be furnished by those engaged in the woollen industry, and that the necessary poles should be contributed by those who worked in wood. And lest the Piazza should be broken, the Procurators are to cause hard stones to be prepared, which are to stand on the ground, and in which the Poles are to be fixed."[2] This is a summary of the scene Casola describes so graphically. As every year about this time, the pilgrims who were going to Jerusalem assembled in Venice, each Venetian gentleman appeared in the procession with a pilgrim on his right hand. After the throng of pilgrims ceased, towards the end of the sixteenth century, the nobles walked, each with a poor man on his right hand, and so kept alive the

1. Maggior Consiglio deliberazioni. Leona. Carta 162 *b*.
2. This decree is given by Gallicciolli. *Memorie Venete*, Book ii. p. 272.

memory of the old custom to the downfall of the Republic. In later times, on the evening of the Corpus Domini, after the services in the church in the Sestiere of Cannareggio, dedicated under this name, there was a "Fresco"—that is a Gondola procession in the neighbouring canal.

NOTE 46.

Agostino Barbarigo was one of the five sons of Francesco Barbarigo, (surnamed the wealthy), Procurator of St. Mark's, by his wife, a daughter of Nicolo Morosini.[1] Three of Francesco's sons became in their turn Procurators of S. Mark's, and two of them, Marco and Agostino, doges. Agostino was born either in 1419 or 1420. In 1482 he was Captain for the Venetian Republic at Padua; from there he was sent to assume the government of Rovigo and the Polesine just conquered from Ferrara. Shortly after he distinguished himself as *Provveditore* of the Venetian army in the war against the Duke of Ferrara and his allies, until, falling ill, he asked and obtained permission to return home. In 1485 he became Procurator, when his brother Marco was created Doge. The Barbarigo family was so rich, so influential, and so popular in the city that there was a time when even three of the brothers were regarded as possible candidates for the dukedom.[2] Girolamo, who was also a procurator, died, however, in 1468; but at the death of Marco, in 1486, Agostino was chosen to succeed his brother—an event so extraordinary, that it made a great impression on the writer Capellari, who qualifies it as an "unheard of occurrence." The Senator, Domenico Malipiero, described the new doge at the time of his election as "a man who in a short time has gained much experience in the government of this country; but he is very obstinate in holding to his own opinion." Other chroniclers declare that the death of the doge Marco Barbarigo, was due to violent anger caused by his brother Agostino.[3] The events which marked the reign of Agostino Barbarigo, belong to the general history of Venice between 1486 and 1501. During the last months of his life, "As he had become decrepit from old age, he wanted to resign, but the Fathers of the City would not let him."[4] He died in 1501, "In worse repute," says Sanuto, "than any other doge since the time of Missier Christofal Moro. It was amazing to hear the maledictions everyone bestowed upon him for his arrogance, greed, obstinacy, and avarice, and for the way in which he used to accept presents."[5] After his death,

1. Capellari. *Campidoglio Veneto*, Class vii. No. 8304.
2. The Annals of Venice from 1457—1500, by the Senator Domenico Malipiero, published with preface and notes in vol. vii. of the *Archivio Storico Italiano*, by Agostino Sagredo.
3. See note, p. 680, Annals of Malipiero, by Agostino Sagredo.
4. Capellari, Campidoglio Veneto.
5. *Diario* of Marino Sanuto, vol. iv. p. 113.

the Government, not content with the revision of the *Promissione Ducale*, instituted an inquisition into the acts of the dead Doge. The result seems to have fully explained and justified his unpopularity. In his will Agostino Barbarigo left ten thousand ducats to complete the Church of Santa Maria degli Angeli at Murano, and twenty ducats a year each to his daughters who were nuns in the convent there; while to each of his married daughters he left two hundred ducats a year.

NOTE 47.

The Doge's seat. "The ducal throne was usually placed within the choir, on the right-hand side and almost facing the high altar. It was made of carved, inlaid and gilded walnut wood. In the middle of the back there was a very fine piece of inlaid work representing Justice with the Sword in the right hand, and the scales in the left. The throne used to be draped with crimson satin; but now instead of that it is all upholstered in cloth of gold." (Sansovino, *Venezia descritta* edition of 1604, p. 33.)

NOTE 48.

Don Nicolo Donato was a son of Ser Bernardo Donato. In 1491 he was elected patriarch of Aquileia, in opposition to Almoro Barbaro, nominated by the Pope. However, in 1494, after the death of Barbaro, Nicolo Donato was confirmed Patriarch of Aquileia by Pope Alexander VI. According to Ughelli he died in Cividale, 1497; others say in 1505. (Capellari, *Campidoglio Veneto.*)

NOTE 49.

Don Tomaso Donato was a son of Ser Almorò Donato, and belonged to another branch of the Donato family. He was a friar of the order of St. Dominic, and one of the most learned prelates of his time. He died 1504, and was buried in the Church of St. Dominic in Venice. (Capellari, *Campidoglio Veneto.*)

NOTE 50.

The Gesuati. The religious movement which led to the institution of the order of the Gesuati was begun at Siena by Giovanni Colombini (a contemporary of St. Catherine), who was born at Siena 1304, and died at Monte Amiata 1367. He was a merchant, married to the noble Biagia Cerretani, and already father of a son and daughter at the time of his conversion 1353. When his son was dead, he gave his substance to the Convent of Santa Bonda (corruption of the names of two saints Abbondio and Abbondanzio) outside Porta Romana—where he placed his daughter Angela—on condition that his wife should be suitably maintained by the convent as long as she lived. The letters of Colombini addressed for the most part to the Abbess and Nuns of Santa Bonda bear some resemblance to the flowers of St. Francis. Either in 1366 or 1367 the order of the Gesuati was approved by Pope Urban V. It was suppressed in 1668. In the second half of the fourteenth century the Gesuati established themselves in Venice. S. Bonda is now a private villa. When at Siena, I heard the following legend :—Once upon a time, one of the nuns was in much distress about her soul. She was oppressed by the fear that her sins were so great that it was impossible for her to obtain salvation, and she wept constantly. Her companions tried in vain to comfort her. In vain they reminded her that Christ is merciful, and the Blessed Virgin full of pity for human weakness. One day she was on the Loggia of the Convent, and in reply to the consolation offered by a friend, she said : " If this branch of olive can grow where I place it in this crack between the stones, then I will believe that my sins can be forgiven." The unexpected happened ! The olive branch took root and grew into a goodly tree. As it grew the nun dried her tears and lived happily in the conviction that she had found pardon.

NOTE 51.

"*The Messa Secca*" or dry mass "was used for the services on board the ships." (Galliccioli, *Memorie Ven*, Lib ii., p. 437.) There were prayers, chants, etc., and the benediction, but the Host was neither consecrated nor consumed. A Catholic friend of mine suggests that probably the Dry Mass was ordered at sea, because of the danger of sea sickness. When the patient is in danger of vomiting, the consecrated wafer is not given even to the dying.

NOTE 52.

The cases referred to by Casola, which were arranged down the centre of the deck in the " Corsia," and round the main mast, contained goods belonging to the officers of all ranks aboard the galley. The common sailors and galeotti kept their boxes and chests under the benches where they worked, slept, and probably ate also. According to the earliest known maritime statutes, issued in 1229 by the Doge Jacopo Tiepolo,[1] it was provided that each merchant, sailor, knight or priest on board a Venetian ship should be allowed to have a chest and carry in it what he pleased; no servant, however, was to have such a chest. This was confirmed in the statutes of 1255.[2] In course of time the chests which were carried by the officers and crew so increased in size, number and weight, that they constituted a source of danger, especially to the galleys. In

1. *Gli Statuti Marittimi Veneziani fino al 1255*, edited by R. Predelli and A. Sacerdoti, Venice, 1903.
2. Idem.

1418[1] the Senate ordered that the chief and petty officers alone were to store their chests on deck, that they were to have there only one each, and that these were not to exceed the ancient measures. In 1446[2] the Senate took up the matter again as the result of abuses on the Merchant Galleys and it was decreed that the chief officers were not to carry more than 2,000 lbs. weight each in their chests on deck; the carpenters and calkers, not more than 1,500 lbs. each, and other officers having chests in the Corsia not more than 1,200 lbs. each. The cooks and stewards were not to carry more than 800 lbs. each in their chests on deck. "*The rowers, however, who keep their chests under their benches*, may not carry more than 150 lbs. each." All the chests were to be of the legal measure. The scribes on the large galleys were allowed to carry 2,000 lbs. weight, and on the small galleys 1,500 lbs.[3] In February 1418,[4] the pilgrim galleys were forbidden to carry merchants or cargo. The officers, etc., who were doubtful as to whether the prohibition applied to the goods they were in the habit of carrying in their chests, and in the appointed places, declared to the Senate,[5] through their representatives, that unless they could carry such goods they "could not with their present pay maintain their families." It was therefore decreed that the comitos, sworn patrons, councillors, scribes, carpenters, calkers, and helmsmen of the said pilgrim galleys, in the matter of their chests, and the places allotted to them, were to be treated in the same way as similar officers on board the merchant galleys, except that they were not to carry goods which could only be carried by the ships of the regular trading fleets. The statutes of Jan., 1418, and of May and August, 1446, applied therefore to the Pilgrim Galleys equally with the others.

NOTE 53.

The two gentlemen appointed to the galley by the Signoria, and whose names as we learn later were Don Alvise Morosini and Don Giovanni Bernardo Vallaresso, were what in modern times would be called midshipmen, if on a man of war; or apprentices to the sea if on a merchantman. In the Venetian Navy they were known as "Nobili di poppa," or Nobles assigned to the poop, where the Captain's quarters were. It was a very ancient custom to send a certain number of patrician youths to sea in this way to learn their business; and was instituted and encouraged by "our most wise ancestors," as a decree of 1493 states, "not only to obviate the many inconveniences and disorders which occur

1. *Senato Miste.*, Reg. 52 p. 72 b, 27th January, 1417 (*i.e.*, 1418, modern style).
2. *Senato Mar.*, Reg. ii. p. 143, 17th May, 1446.
3. *Senato Mar,*, Reg. ii. p. 172 b, 26th August, 1446.
4. According to Venetian reckoning February, 1417, because the new year began on March 1st.
5. *Senato Miste.*, Reg. 52. p. 86 b, 7th April, 1418.

when our noble youths remain in this city; but also to provide an opening for those who have no other means of supporting themselves, or of increasing the fortunes of their families." The number of young nobles each galley was to carry varied from one to eight, according to the epoch and the size of the ships. In course of time the practice was being abandoned; and in 1493 the Senate declared that "The greater number of ships which ought to carry nobles of the poop, perform their voyages without them, against our orders." It was therefore decreed[1] that eight days after a captain-owner had decided to undertake a given voyage, he was to notify the fact to the Magistrates over the Armament, who would assign a certain number of young patrician apprentices to his ships, whom he was obliged to carry with him under a penalty, after giving in their names and surnames at the office before departure. The law had been so recently passed that whatever may have been his usual procedure, Don Agostino Contarini was pretty sure to have his right quota of apprentices on this occasion.

NOTE 54.
Before and for long after the invention of gunpowder and firearms, the *Balestrieri* or Crossbowmen, furnished a powerful arm to the Venetian fleet. All young men without distinction of caste were required to keep themselves in practice, and were eligible for appointment to a particular ship after attaining the age of eighteen. Targets were established on the Lido, and at various other places in Venice, and young men were expected to go there once a week if they belonged to the better classes, and on all great holidays if they were of poorer condition. Each armed galley or other ship carried a certain proportion of patricians among the Crossbowmen, and the importance of their position may be judged from the fact that in 1396, when permission was given to Ser Benedetto Delfino, one of the Captain-owners of the Beyrout fleet, to visit the Holy Sepulchre, he was ordered to leave one or two of his brothers in command during his absence; or "in case his brothers were not with him, one of the Noble Crossbowmen who were on board the Galley."[2] For the protection of the Pilgrim Galleys the Senate decreed 1414, that for the future, each of the galleys carrying pilgrims should be equipped with two rowers to each bench and with 20 Crossbowmen, of whom two were to be Noble.[3] The Crossbowmen were selected after having demonstrated their skill at the arsenal itself, as we learn from a decree of the Senate 1446. Ser Fantin Zorzi had been Balestriere on board a galley which had come to grief, and he had lost nearly all his goods. The Senate, therefore decreed that "the

1. *Senato Mar.*, Reg. 14, p. 6, 1493, 30th March.
2. *Senato Miste.*, Reg. 43, p. 135, 8th June, 1396.
3. 1st March, 1414, *Senato Miste.*, Reg. 50 p. 80 *b*.

said Ser Fantin Zorzi shall, according to custom, be taken as Crossbowman, *without shooting in the Arsenal*, on the first ship that sets sail for the place where he wants to go."[1] As he had succeeded in one test, it was not considered necessary to subject him to another. Laws were repeatedly passed in the fifteenth century to compel young nobles to go as *Balestrieri* on the ships, as for example that of 1458 which supports the measure, "Because in this way, these gentlemen of ours, become expert in the sea which is the chief foundation and sustenance of our State."[2] The *Balestrarie* or posts as Crossbowmen were granted to young patricians by the highest Criminal Court, the Quarantia Criminale. "So that each of our poor gentlemen may have his share of such appointments as is just and honest." It was found, however, in 1493, when as the decree states "there is a greater number of poor gentlemen than ever before," that these posts were begged from the Signoria for certain persons to the injury and exclusion of the poor nobles; and that some of the Captain-owners bought the appointments and then sailed without filling them up—effecting thus, no doubt, a considerable economy. It was therefore decreed[3] that the appointments were only to be made by the Quarantia Criminale; that each Noble Crossbowman elected was to go in person or send another noble in his place; and that Captain-owners were not to buy such posts, or set sail without duly filling them up.

NOTE 55.

Bernardino Scotto. Porro says: "I could not find anything else referring to this Bernardino Scotto son of Beltrame, save the inscription placed by his children over his tomb, which stood in the Church of the Peace. From this it appears that Bernardino Scotto was forty-seven years of age when he undertook the pilgrimage to Palestine. Scotto is mentioned once again by Casola, who on the 7th of August administered the Holy Sacrament to him and to two natives of Ragusa in the Church at Mount Sion.

NOTE 56.

Parenza and Istria generally. Istria and Venice had always an affinity of interests and customs, and from Roman times they were united in a single province. In 732 they were also united under the Jurisdiction of the Patriarch of Grado. Two centuries later the Istrian Cities asked for the friendship and alliance of the Republic of Venice, which were granted. But they did not observe their promises, and soon became nests of Pirates as of old. In 1150 a Venetian fleet reduced Parenzo, Pola, Rovigno and other cities to submission; but

---

1. *Senato Mar.*, p. 174, 12th September, 1446.
2. Register Regina M.C. 9th July, 1458, given by Romanin, vol. iv. p. 478.
3. *Senato Mar.*, Reg. 14, p. 6, 30th March, 1493.

for a century their fidelity was not to be relied on. However, in the middle of the thirteenth century, the growing power of Venice induced the Istrian and Dalmatian Cities to place themselves under its protection and even accept its dominion. Parenzo yielded first 1267, and the other cities followed the example and received Venetian Governors. Parenzo became the great station for the certificated pilots, who took home-going ships through the intricate channels to Venice, and outward bound ships as far as Modone in Greece. There was much legislation regulating the admission of the Pilots and their duties. Their supervision was entrusted to the magistrates known as the *Cattaveri*.

NOTE 57.
Zara and the Province of Dalmatia. Dalmatia was attached to the Greek Empire, though as the latter was unable to protect it, it drew always closer to Venice. In 998 Zara, Spalato and other cities placed themselves under the protection of Venice, entering at most into a condition of Vassalship, and the Doge Pietro Orseolo on his return to Venice was proclaimed Duke of Dalmatia, and the title was added to that of Doge of Venice. By degrees Venetian power increased, and Dalmatia became subject to the Republic; though the cities from time to time tried to throw off the yoke and called in the King of Hungary to help them. After numberless revolts, Dalmatia, with the cities of Zara, Trau, Spalato, Sebenico, Lesina, Curzola, etc., was finally taken by the Venetians from the King of Hungary between 1409 and 1420. Each city had its Count or Governor sent from Venice, and a Provveditore-Generale aided by a Council of Nobles was placed over the whole.

NOTE 58.
Curzola. The battle referred to by Casola took place in August, 1483. During the war between Venice and Ferrara (1482—1484), King Ferdinand of Naples, in support of his son-in-law the Duke of Ferrara, sent a fleet against Curzola. It was defeated by the inhabitants under Giorgio Viario, the then Count or Governor.

NOTE 59.
Ragusa. This city came under the Venetian domination with the rest of Dalmatia in the time of the Doge Orseolo 998. In early times the Venetian power weakened in Dalmatia until it became a simple protectorate, and the proof lies in the frequent renewal of the pacts between Venice and the Dalmatian cities, which on every propitious occasion freed themselves from foreign domination, and either governed themselves independently, or placed themselves under the protection of some powerful neighbour. Between 1122 and 1152, and again between 1204

and 1358 the Venetian Government was established solidly in Ragusa, and the series of Counts or Governors sent by the Senate is continuous for the latter period. In 1358, however, having made a secret treaty with the King of Hungary, the Ragusans, with his aid, established their independence of Venice and maintained it. In 1365 they placed themselves under Turkish protection, paying tribute, but preserving, as under the Venetians, their own proper laws. At the same time they frequently paid a small tribute to their nearer protector the King of Hungary. (Romanin, *Storia documentata di Venezia*, vol. viii., p. 96—97 and 455—465.)

NOTE 60.

Moorish fasting. Roberto di San Severino, in describing his journey to Mount Sinai, says:—" On Friday, the eleventh of August, as their 'Ramatana," that is their Lent, was finished, and it was their Easter day, the Interpreters, Moors, Arabs, etc., wanted to remain where they were from the morning until Vespers. Their 'Ramatana' lasts a month, and every day they fast. They neither eat nor drink until the evening, that is until the hour of the stars; and this custom is followed by the Moors as well as the Arabs. Then all night they eat and drink as much and as often as they like until sunrise on the following day."

NOTE 61.

The Island of Corfu, with the rest of the Ionian Islands, was acquired by the Venetians 1205, as part of their share of the spoils of the Greek Empire destroyed by the Fourth Crusade. It was immediately let out as fiefs to certain Venetian nobles, each of whom undertook to maintain at his own expense twenty horsemen, forty foot soldiers, and pay a tribute in addition. Within ten years the Island was lost, however, and Venetian power was not established again there permanently until 1386, when Corfu was induced to withdraw itself from the dominion of the King of Naples, and surrender to Venice. With the rest of the Ionian Islands it remained subject to the Republic until the end of the eighteenth century.

NOTE 62.

"*Brugh.*" I succeeded in obtaining a specimen of the plant known in Milan and the neighbourhood as "*brugh*," through the courtesy of Monsignor Marco Magistretti, Canon of Milan to whom I am greatly indebted for much kind help, especially in the interpretation of words and phrases in the Milanese dialect, in Casola's voyage. I sent it to Miss Clotilde von Wyss of the London Day Training College. She kindly replied as follows:—" I knew the plant at once as '*Erica Carnea*,' belonging to the natural order Ericaceae; it is one of the heaths or heathers. It grows on the Alps and Fore-Alps up to a height of 2,600 metres. I do not think it has been found at a greater height. In some localities, it is used as fuel, and I know that bees feeding on it are considered to produce very delicate honey. I am nearly certain I have found Erica Carnea in England; but not absolutely so; what I came across may have been only an allied species. I may mention that the plant chiefly grows in limestone regions; but only this summer I saw a healthy patch of it on a conglomerate The 'brugh' certainly belongs to the class called 'bruyère' in France."

NOTE 63.

"*Eduardus de Camardino* was as Casola states, one of the most distinguished members of his order. In the great chapter of 1478, he was appointed 'Baglivo' (Commendator) of Longo, more correctly called Langò. In 1481, after the famous siege of Rhodes, when the Council of Knights determined to conquer Mitylene, he was elected Captain-general of the troops; but the enterprise was abandoned on account of the damage caused by various earthquakes which devastated Rhodes during that year, and of the peace made a little later with the Turks. Camardino was one of the knights sent to escort the Sultan Zem, or Gem (son of Mahomet II.), who, hard pressed by the army of his brother Bajazet, had asked permission to take refuge in Rhodes; and on several occasions he bravely defended his *commendam* against Turkish attacks. He died on the 13th of October, 1495, and bequeathed the third part of his large fortune to the order to which he belonged. At his death, the island of Langò (the country of Hippocrates, the Cos of the ancient Greeks, now called Stanko by the modern Greeks, and Istankoi by the Turks), which had been conquered by the Knights of Rhodes in 1315, ceased to be granted *in commendam*, and was henceforth governed directly by the Grand Master. When the Knights lost Rhodes, Langò also fell into the power of the Mussulmans." (Note to the printed edition of Casola's Voyage, 1855, by Count Giulio Porro.)

NOTE 64.

Capo del Ducato. After the fall of Constantinople in 1204 the Ionian Islands, Corfu, Zante, Cephalonia, and Leucadia or Sänta Maura, etc., fell to the share of Venice. The *Capo del Ducato*, or Cape of the Duchy, was in Leucadia or S. Maura. The latter island was seized by the Turks in 1472 and recovered by the Venetians in 1502. It was restored to the Turks in 1573, and finally regained by Francesco Morosini in 1684. It was of great importance to the Venetians from its position between

Corfu and Cephalonia, and close to the coast of Acarnania. Originally a peninsula of the mainland, it became an island when the Corinthians, in 665 B.C., dug a canal across the isthmus.

NOTE 65.

Modone and Corone. In 1204 the Morea fell to Venice on the division of the Byzantine Empire. The chief strongholds of the Republic there were Modone and Corone. In 1500 they were seized by the Turks. *Modone or Methone*, 7 kilometres south of Navarino, was the Pedasus of Homer. *Corone* on the Gulf of Messina occupied the site of the ancient Asine. Both cities were in the ancient Messenia on the S.W. of the Peloponnesus.

NOTE 66.

Wines of Modone and Cyprus. The pilgrim who wrote the voyage to the "Saincte Cyté" in 1480, confirms Casola's opinion. He says: "Il y a bon marché de pain et de chair" at Modone, "Mais les vins sont si fors et ardans, et sentent le poix si fort qu'on n'en peut boire."[1] Later on at Cyprus, Casola observed "everything in that island pleased me except that they make the wine with resin and I could not drink it." While the author of the "Saincte Cyté" remarked, p. 56 :—"In Cyprus sont les plus maulvais vins qu'on puisse trouver, et sent si fort la poix qu'on n'en peult boyre." Modern travellers are equally displeased with the resinated wines of Greece.

NOTE 67.

Candia was assigned to Venice on the division of the Byzantine Empire, 1204. The island was invaluable to the Republic for its products and commerce, but the inhabitants did not easily tolerate the new dominion. The Venetians were obliged to repress many revolts, and to do so more easily sent several Colonies of Nobles and others, to whom land was granted on condition of defending it for the Republic. The chief authority was the Duke or Governor-in-Chief (elected by the Maggior Consiglio) who was also Commander-in-Chief of the forces. He was aided by two Councillors, and by a Council formed of all the Venetian and Cretan Nobles in the island. A Captain-general was sent from Venice to manage military affairs, and there were separate governors in the principal cities. The Cretan citizens had a share in the management of subordinate offices. The two religions, the Greek and the Roman Catholic, were equally protected. St. Mark and St. Titus were the two patron saints

---

1. *Le Voyage de la Saincte Cyté de Hierusalem . . . fait l'an mil quatre cens vingtz*, published by Ch. Schefer and Henri Cordier.

of the island. In August 1645, Canea was taken by the Turks, who in June 1647 advanced on the capital, Candia, which was besieged and held out for twenty-two years. In 1669 the heroic siege came to an end, Candia surrendered, and the whole island passed into the hands of the Turks.

NOTE 68.

The Turkish pirates Arigi (also called Erichi) and Camalio were very famous in their day, and they and their exploits are frequently mentioned in the early volumes of Marino Sanuto, which refer to the years 1496— 1506. In 1492 the Venetian Senate ordered the Admiral of the Gulf if possible "to seize the said Camali and others who have inflicted damage on our subjects, and drown them or hang them by the throat without any remission or regard; for besides that they merit this treatment, the terms of the peace we have with the Signor Turk, provide that the Corsairs shall be taken and punished."[1] Similar orders were also issued in 1493.[2] In 1496 Camali was seized by Turkish officials at Negropont, and taken to Constantinople where it seems Arigi had preceded him.[3] He was well received by the Sultan, to whom he made acceptable presents, and after reproofs pro forma, and a solemn order "not to exercise the *art* of a Pirate any more" he was taken into the Turkish naval service and placed in command of one of the two largest ships. At the same time Arigi was given the command of a large galley. Sanuto remarks sarcastically, "In this way the Signor Turk has collected all his Corsairs in Constantinople, and he will make great men of them." Arigi and Camali did not seriously think of changing their occupation; they only did their "Pirating" now in the interests of the Porte. In 1497 Arigi commanded one of a numerous Turkish squadron, which—in spite of the peace then existing between Venice and the Sultan—attacked the pilgrim galley of that year, commanded by Alvise Zorzi, near the Morea, on its way to Jaffa. The attack failed by a miracle, and Arigi presented his excuses and explained that he had made a mistake; a mistake which cost the pilgrim ship much material damage in addition to numerous dead and wounded.[4] Camali was sent several times as Turkish Admiral against the Knights of Rhodes.

NOTE 69.

The Siege of Rhodes, 1480. Santo Brasca who arrived at Rhodes, on his return from Jerusalem, on the 9th September, 1480, wrote:—"I went to see the damage done by those cursed Turkish dogs to that poor city," and then went on to describe the famous siege which had just

1. *Senato Secreta*, Reg. 34, p. 132, and p. 144.
2. *Senato Secreta*, Reg. 34, pp. 169, 171, 172.
3. Marino Sanuto, *Diarii*, vol. i. pp. 10, 83, 625, 977.
4. See Introduction, pp. 102, 103.

been raised. The author of the "Saincte Cyté," who was a fellow pilgrim with Santo Brasca gives interesting details of the siege. In July, 1522, Rhodes was again attacked by the Sultan with a formidable army. After several months resistance the Knights were obliged to capitulate, and the Grand-master embarked for Candia. The headquarters of the order of St. John of Jerusalem were afterwards fixed at Malta, granted to the Knights by the Emperor Charles V. in 1525. Together with Rhodes, eight other islands which had belonded to the Knights of St. John, including Cos or Lango, Leros and Telos fell into the hands of the Turks.

NOTE 70.

In the wars between the Knights of Rhodes and the Turks no quarter was given on either side. Robert of San Severino recounts under date Sunday, the 11th of June, 1458, that on the preceding day news had come that a galley belonging to the Knights of Rhodes had taken three Turkish ships which were to be brought to Rhodes that day or the next, "And as soon as they arrived, the captured Turks, two hundred and fifty in number, were to be cut to pieces or impaled, as is the custom to do to them when they are taken by the Knights of Rhodes. Because they do the same and worse to the Knights, when they happen to get hold of them."

NOTE 71.

Robert of San Severino relates that he and his companions went in 1458, "to see the said thorn which is in the said Castle" at Rhodes, "in a chapel, and kept in a silver tabernacle. And every Good Friday—according to what the said Knights said, and also all the people of Rhodes, who have seen this miracle,—at the sixth hour, it begins to flower and remains in flower until the ninth hour." *Santo Brasca* saw the thorn in 1480, and relates:—"Amongst the relics, there is a miraculous thorn taken from the crown which was placed on Christ's head during his passion, and it lies in a crystal which is kept in a silver tabernacle. At the sixth hour on Good Friday, this most holy thorn begins to blossom and remains in blossom until the ninth hour. Then the flowers retire within the said thorn. This miracle has been seen by many witnesses, and it is certified by those gentlemen, the Knights, and by all the people of Rhodes. This miracle happens, they say, because it was one of the thorns, which pierced the most precious head of our Lord."

NOTE 72.

Cyprus. The first treaty between Venice and Cyprus was arranged in 1306. The island was most important to Venetian commerce, because of its products (especially wine) and its proximity to Syria. There was a long fight to establish Venetian supremacy over that of the Genoese, her great rivals in the Mediterranean, until finally in 1472 King James of Cyprus married Catherine Cornaro, daughter of Marco and of Fiorenza Crispo (daughter of Nicolo Crispo, Duke of the Archipelago). After the death of King James, 1473, the Genoese renewed their efforts to oust the Venetians, by supporting the rival candidate to the throne. The island was also threatened by the Sultan of Cairo and the Ottoman Turks, and the Government of Catherine was too weak to cope with the situation. In 1488, therefore, her brother George Cornaro was sent to persuade her to resign and come to Venice, where she died 1510. In 1489 the government of Cyprus was directly assumed by the Venetian Republic, which was confirmed in the possession of the island by the Sultan of Egypt. It was governed by a Lieutenant elected by the Senate for two years, who resided at Nicosia. He was aided by two Councillors. There was also a Captain, who resided at Famagosta. On the 3rd July, 1570, the Turks landed at the Salines, and in August of the same year they took Nicosia. Famagosta defended by Captain Marcantonio Bragadino was obliged to surrender August, 1571, after a resistance of two months. Bragadino and the other defenders were cruelly killed by the Turks, who violated the terms of surrender. Bragadino after the terrible tortures, was flayed alive in the Piazza of Famagosta.

NOTE 73.

Porro says: "The King of England who, according to Agostino Contarini, destroyed Limasol, must have been Richard Coeur de Lion, because he was the only English King who went on a Crusade to Palestine. However this may be, in 1248, when Louis IX. of France landed there, the city was still flourishing. We find the real causes of its ruin in the History of Cyprus by Loredano. Speaking of the terrible hurricane which burst over the island on the 10th of November, 1330, he says that Limasol was entirely destroyed and 2,000 persons perished. The decadence of Limasol then probably dates from that period, and the wars, and invasions of the Moors, no doubt afterwards contributed to its total ruin."

NOTE 74.

Episcopia. "After the downfall of the Latin States in Syria, amongst other branches of industry transferred to the island of Cyprus, one of the most important was the cultivation and manufacture of Sugar. The plantations were scattered over the island, but the cultivation was principally concentrated in the districts of Baffo and Limasol. The Kings of Cyprus occupied themselves personally with this industry.

The sugar was generally sold to Venetian merchants, though it was not refused to those of other nations. The great Venetian family of the Cornaro, possessed vast plantations at Episcopia (or Piskopi) near Limasol. Gistèle calls them 'the chief factories for the manufacture of sugar in the whole island.' The Cornaro property touched that of the Casal de Colossi, belonging to the knights of Rhodes, who had extensive fields of sugar canes there."[1] When Roberto da San Severino reached Cyprus June 16th, 1458, he noted "A small castle called Episcopia, which produces large quantities of sugar. It belongs to a Venetian gentleman called Don Andrea Cornaro, who was banished to Cyprus by the Signoria of Venice." Don Andrea was a brother of Marco, and therefore uncle of Catherine, Queen of Cyprus.

NOTE 75.

The Prior or Guardian of Mount Sion was the Prior of the Franciscan friary there, as well as Superior-general of all the houses belonging to that order in the Holy Land, and Papal Vicar and Legate for all the countries of the East. When a pilgrim ship reached Jaffa it was always obliged to lie at anchor, until in answer to the captain's letters, the acting governor of Jerusalem, the Prior of Mount Sion or his deputy, and the Emirs of Rama and Gaza arrived. The Prior's duty was to accompany the pilgrims to Jerusalem and back to Jaffa, and to aid the Captain in making arrangements for their comfort, and for facilitating the expedition as much as possible; though he was generally helpless to prevent a great many annoyances or worse, as Casola and other writers of pilgrim voyages plainly demonstrate. On shipboard, before they landed, or if not then, either at Jaffa or Rama, the Prior was in the habit of giving the pilgrims in Italian and in Latin, a series of rules for their guidance, which other pilgrims, or the interpreters attached to the party, translated for the benefit of those who did not understand these two languages. Although Casola does not distinctly say that he did so on this occasion, it is hardly likely that Fra Francesco Suriano—departing from the custom of his predecessors,—omitted to give the usual general instructions.

NOTE 76.

Fra Francesco Suriano was a Venetian patrician, a Franciscan friar, and the historian of the Franciscan Missions in the Holy Land. His *Treatise on the Holy Land* has been sympathetically edited in 1900 by Father Girolamo Golubovich. Suriano was born in Venice in 1450, and went on his first voyage to the Eastern Mediterranean at the age of twelve. Between 1462 and 1475 he accomplished at least sixteen

---

1. Heyd, *Hist. du Commerce du Levant*, vol. ii. p. 687.

voyages, always trading in the merchandise of his own father, as he himself says. In 1475, at the age of twenty-five, he became a friar, and shortly after he went to settle in Umbria. In 1480 or 1481 Fra Francesco was elected Prior of the Franciscan convent at Beyrout. He remained at this post until 1483, when he went to join the brethren at Mount Sion, probably as secretary of the Prior. He returned to Venice in 1484 on board the pilgrim galley commanded by Agostino Contarini. The voyage took nearly five months and was full of peril. In a great storm which arose after leaving Candia, Suriano tells us that "as there were not many men on board the galley who thoroughly understood their business," he was obliged "to show his skill as a sailor somewhat" to the great astonishment of the company. In another storm he recounts that he tucked up his friar's gown and took the command of the ship which he brought safely to Corfu. Afterwards he went to live in Umbria. There, at the request of the sisters of the convent of Foligno, where his sister was a nun, he wrote, in 1485, his treatise thus entitled :—"*Incomenza lo tractatello de le indulgentie de Terra Sancta cum le sue dechiaratione. Compillato per frate Francesco Surian de l'ordine de li frati del Observantia de Sancto Francesco: ne l'anni del Signor: mile quatrocento otanta cinque: nel loco de Sancto Anthonio de Piscignano de la provintia de Sancto Francesco, ad requisitione de una soa sorela carnale, monaca de Sancta Chiara nel Monasterio de Sancta Lucia de Foligno: chiamata Sora Sixta. In modo de Dialogo: Introducendo lei addimandare et lui ad respondere.*" The Treatise was revised by its author in 1514 and again in 1524. In the latter year it was printed and published in Venice by Francesco Bindoni. It appears probable that Suriano remained in Umbria until 1493. In May of that year, by the General Chapter of the Observants held in Florence, he was elected Prior of Mount Sion, and a few months later he embarked again for Palestine. Very likely Suriano himself obtained from the Venetian Senate, and carried with him on this occasion, the severe decree of the 12th of July, 1493, which forbade the Captains of the Pilgrim ships to take up their residence in the Monastery at Mount Sion, under a fine of 200 ducats. The new Prior passed the winter of 1493 and 1494 in Egypt, where he went to appeal to the protection of Myr Isbech; and he preached the Lent sermons in Cairo. It must have been on this occasion that Suriano undertook the journey to Sinai, of which he has left an interesting description, without however giving the date of his visit. On his arrival he found the twenty-six monks of the Monastery of St. Catherine on Mount Sinai in a state of consternation. They were beseiged by a crowd of armed Arabs, who had just killed their Abbot. It will be noticed that in the last paragraph of his voyage Casola explains why he did not visit Mount Sinai. The friars of Mount Sion told the pilgrims that it was impossible to go there, "because the Arabs had plundered the monastery which has charge of the body of Saint Catherine, and had killed the Abbot and certain of the Monks." No doubt the news of these events had been brought by Suriano himself when he returned to Jerusalem in time for the arrival of the Pilgrims of 1494. In 1495 Fra Francesco preached the Lent Sermons at Damascus, and shortly after ended his first guardianship of Mount Sion. Little is known of his later life. In the years 1510—1512, he endured, with the rest of the friars of Mount Sion, a two years' imprisonment, and on his release he was immediately elected again Prior of Mount Sion. In this second period of office, the friars were victims of all the old abuses on the part of the Governors and the hostile population; and Suriano had good reason to deplore the deaths of the former protectors of his house, Myr Isbech and the Sultan Kaiet-Bey. Towards the end of 1514, Suriano was sent as Papal Legate to the Maronites in Syria. It is not known when he returned to Italy, nor even the date of his death. Father Agostino di Stroncone, however, who wrote towards the end of the seventeenth century, mentions in his chronicle that Fra Francesco Suriano was twice Prior of the convent of Santa Maria degli Angeli, or Saint Mary of the Angels, at Assisi—on one occasion in 1528 and 1529. It is evident that Casola was not, on the whole, unfavourably impressed by the Prior of Mount Sion. The disparaging remarks he makes in the beginning are clearly a reflection of Captain Contarini's irritation at changes unfavourable to himself. Casola was a Milanese, and probably knew nothing about the decree of the 12th July, 1493, or of the "grave abuses" which had provoked it. In any case it was his policy to keep on good terms with Agostino Contarini.

NOTE 77.

"*The Christians of the Girdle* are so-called because their ancestors were converted by the miracles performed by Saint Thomas the Apostle with the girdle of the glorious Virgin Mary, which he received from her when she ascended into heaven. In remembrance of this, and in sign of devotion, when they enter the churches for worship, they put on a girdle made like those sold for the measure of the Holy Sepulchre. According to what people say the girdle they wear is exactly like that of the glorious Virgin."[1] Santo Brasca and other pilgrims give similar accounts of the Christians of the Girdle. In enumerating the religious sects found in his time in the Church of the Holy Sepulchre, Fra Francesco Suriano says[2]:—"The eighth are the Syrians, that is the Christians of the Girdle."

1. *Voyage to Jerusalem*, undertaken by Roberto da Sanseverino in 1458.
2. *Il Trattato di Terra Santa*, by Fra. Fr. Suriano, edited by Father G. Golubovich, 1900 chap. xxiii. p. 64.

NOTES

NOTE 78.

The prisons called the *Ancient Stinche* were built by the Commune of Florence in 1303. They received this name because the first persons who were imprisoned there, were prisoners taken in an attack on a Castle of Val di Grieve, called *Stinché*. Later on the New Stinche were built. In these prisons were confined prisoners for debt and also those condemned to imprisonment for life.

NOTE 79.

The "*little village*" in question was *Lydda*, "which is nigh to Joppa" It was called in Roman times Diospolis, and believed to be the place of the martyrdom of St. George of Cappadocia, the dragon slayer, the patron saint of England, and one of the patron saints of Venice. He was beheaded in the great persecution of Diocletian after suffering cruel tortures. The church built over his tomb was destroyed by Saladin 1191. According to many mediæval pilgrims it was rebuilt by a King of England. The Christians occupied the Eastern part of the church, while the Western part was converted by the Mussulmans into a mosque, with a very tall minaret. Felix Faber (1480 and 1483) remarks that this mosque, for its beauty and good order, seemed a paradise compared with the ruined Christian Church adjoining it.

NOTE 80.

Cotton Picking at Rama. "It is well known that after the fall of Acre, the hate of Mahometanism awoke with a new energy and that under the influence of this passionate sentiment Sanuto the elder, proposed to the Christian universe, to break off all communication with the Mussulman world. He pointed out that people bought certain articles (some very important) from the Infidels, whilst they could procure them in Christian countries. He gave as examples sugar and cotton—especially cotton, which, according to him was produced in Apulia, Sicily, Crete, Greece, Cyprus, and Armenia. But in spite of Sanuto's appeal to Christendom, the traffic retook its course between Syria and the West, and the merchant ships of Europe went as regularly as in former times to load native cotton in Laodicea, Beyrout, Tripoli (in Syria), Acre, and Jaffa." (*Heyd, Hist. du Commerce*, vol. ii., p. 611.)

NOTE 81.

Porro says:—"*The mosque of Omar* rises in the midst of a vast quadrilateral, which occupies the Eastern part of the city, towards the valley of Jehoshaphat. This was the site of the Temple of Solomon, or to be more exact, the site of the Temple, which in place of the first destroyed by Nebuchadnezzar, was erected by Zerubbabel on the return from the captivity in Babylon—and entirely rebuilt by Herod of Ascalon. When Jerusalem was taken by Titus, the temple was also destroyed, and the few remains disappeared when, under Julian the

Questa e la forma del s̄c̄ō sepulcro de mi
ser yhu x̄

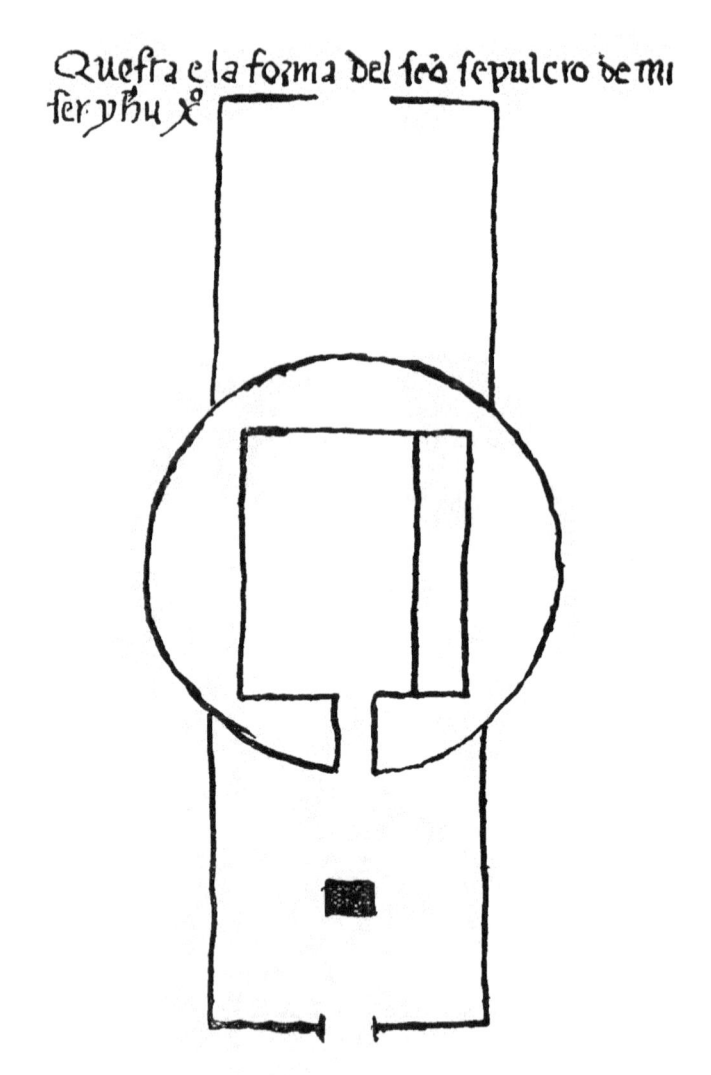

This drawing of the Holy Sepulchre is taken from the last page of the "Voyage of Santo Brasca" in the Trivulzian Library.

Apostate, an attempt was made to build another temple. From that time the area was abandoned until the year 635 when Omar seized Jerusalem. The Caliph began to inquire from the citizens of the conquered city, and especially from the patriarch Sophronius, where the temple of God destroyed by Titus used to stand. And the place being shown him he assigned a sufficient sum of money for the purpose and sent workmen there to build a mosque .... which was beautified by other Egyptian Caliphs who added vast structures round it. William of Tyre has left a description of this magnificent monument, well known to him because it was used for Christian worship during the dominion of the Latin Kings. The description is the more precious because Christians in later times were jealously excluded. He tells us amongst other details that the mosque was octagon shaped, the walls covered with marbles of different colours, and the cupola of gilded copper."[1]

NOTE 82.

The Holy Sepulchre. "This is the plan of the Holy Sepulchre of Miser Jesu Christo. The circle is the sepulchre proper. Those two cells you see, one in front of the circle and one behind the circle, have been added since the time of the passion of Our Lord. The little cell in front of the sepulchre was made in order not to leave neglected and without reverence, that square stone which you see in the middle; because it was the stone on which the angel was sitting when the Maries came and said : "Who shall roll us away the stone from the door of the sepulchre?" The other small cell behind the sepulchre was built by the Ethiopian friars or Abyssinians, in order to sacrifice there, and recite their offices and prayers." (Santo Brasca, *Viaggio al Santo Sepulchro* editions of 1481 and 1497.)

NOTE 83.

The church at Bethlehem. Porro says :—"The magnificent church at Bethlehem was built in the fourth century by Saint Helena, mother of Constantine the Great. . . . In 1480, as it threatened ruin, it was restored at the expense of the Minor Friars. In 1672 it was newly restored under the direction of the Patriarch of Constantinople. The beautiful mosaics which adorned it . . . were finished in 1169 A.D., as a Greek inscription which was there declared. In this church Baldwin the first was crowned 1101." From Fra Francesco Suriano we learn that the roof was made of cypress, cedar, and other very notable wood from Mount Libanon, and covered with the finest lead. It had, however, been allowed to fall into decay in the fifteenth century. "But the Virgin Mary, who watches that church continually, did not permit it to be ruined completely. She granted grace to the Venerable father Fra Giovanni Tomacello, who was Prior of Mount Sion about the year of our

---

[1]. Note to the printed edition of Casola, edited by Count Giulio Porro, 1855.

Lord, 1479, to rebuild the said roof for his perpetual memory. Having sought licence from the Sultan, he sent for two shiploads of prepared wood from Venice, and new lead that the King of England had sent, and with the divine aid, in a few days, the old roof was taken down and the new one built. But it was a marvellous thing that the poor friars were able to bring so much wood to Jerusalem over the rough mountain paths." Suriano, *Trattato di Terra Santa*.

NOTE 84.

The Knights of the Holy Sepulchre. From the account of his voyage left by Ludwig Freiherr von Greiffenstein, who was a fellow traveller of Casola's, we learn that eleven of the company were dubbed Knights of the Holy Sepulchre by John of Prussia. And this is confirmed by Bemmelberg and Parsberg, who were also Pilgrims in 1494.[1] In 1458, two friends of Roberto da Sanseverino were created Knights in the Holy Sepulchre by the English Pilgrim John, earl of Exeter. Bernardo Giustinian[2] devotes a long chapter to the Knights of the Holy Sepulchre, and described minutely the ceremony of initiation.

NOTE 85.

The Church of the Holy Sepulchre. Descriptions of this church, such as that given by Casola are valuable, because in modern times great changes have been made. The church took fire in 1808. When it was restored by the Greeks, the architecture was changed. The columns were replaced by massive pillars, the form of the cupola was altered, and the mosaics which adorned the upper part of the church were not replaced. (Note by Porro to the printed edition of Casola's Voyage, edited by him in 1855.)

NOTE 86.

The tombs of the Latin Kings are described by Denis Possot who saw them in 1532 as follows :—" En ladicte chappelle dessoubz le dict mont de Calvaire, à senestre est le sepulchre de Bauldoin, et sur iceluy sont escriptz ces motz :—

> 'Rex Balduinus, Judas alter Machabeus,
> Spes patrie, vigor ecclesie, virtus utriusque,
> Quem formidabant, cui dona tributa ferebant
> Cedar et Egyptus, Dan ac homicida Damascus,
> Proh dolor! in modico clauditur hoc tumulo.'

---

1. Röhricht, *Deutsche Pilgerreisen*, pp. 183-4.
2. Bernardo Giustinian, *History of the Origin of the Military and Religious Knightly Orders*, Venice, 1692.

Il est d'une pierre en façon de couverture de maison, troussé sur quatre pilliers. A dextre, est le sepulchre de Godefroy de Billon semblable à l'aultre et tout l'un devant l'aultre, sur lequel est escript tel epitaphe :— 'Hic jacet inclitus dux Godefridus de Billon que totam istam terram adquisivit cultui christiano. Cujus anima regnet in Christo. Amen !' C'est a dire : Cy gist le tres noble duc Godefroy de Billon, lequel acquesta toute ceste terre aux chrestiens. De qui l'âme puisse regner avec Jesu Christ." [1] The tombs were destroyed at the time of the fire in the beginning of the nineteenth century.

NOTE 87.

The Christian Sects, whom Casola found in the church of the Holy Sepulchre, were nine in number :—The Latins, Georgians, Armenians, Abyssinians, Syrians, Maronites, Golbites, Jacobites, and Copts. Francesco Suriano gives a good deal of interesting information on the subject in the various texts of his *Trattato di Terra Santa*. In the first text written in 1485 Suriano mentions eight christian sects living at that time in the Holy Sepulchre :—The Latin Friars or Franks, Greeks, Georgians, Armenians, Abyssinians or Indians, Jacobites, Syrians and Maronites. He mention the Copts, but says that they were not then there permanently. In chapter xxiii., p. 64, of the text revised in 1514, Fra Francesco wrote :—" In the afore-named Church of the Holy Sepulchre, ten kinds of religious, christians of different nations live. All celebrate divine service according to their own rite, and all have their habitations—separate one from the other—within the body of the church. They are the following :—The first are our friars, who are called Franks; the second are the Maronites, who are orthodox Catholics; the third are the Greeks; the fourth are the Georgians; the fifth are the Abyssinians, that is Indians; the sixth are the Copts; the seventh are the Jacobites; the eighth are the Syrians, that is the Christians of the girdle; the ninth are the Armenians; the tenth are the Nestorians." In the printed edition of the *Trattato* (Venice, 1524) Suriano adds that the Nestorians were not continually in Jerusalem. Commenting on these various bodies, Suriano observes that the Maronites "Are very placable, polite and pleasant to deal with. They are descended from the Italians." That the *Greeks* "are cursed," and "our worst and most atrocious enemies." The *Georgians* "are abominable heretics, like to the Greeks and equal to them in malice." The *Armenians* "are handsome people, rich and generous." The *Abyssinians* "are vassals of Prete Jane who reigns in Ethiopia, which is eleven months of day's journeys from Jerusalem. This Signor Prete Jane is a christian and has seventy-two

---

1. See p. 179 of *Le Voyage de la Terre Saincte*, composé par Maître Denis Possot, et achevé per Messire Charles Philippe seigneur de Champarmoy et de Grandchamp, 1532. Published, with notes, by Charles Schefer.

crowned Kings under his dominion. . . . The men and women [of this sect] dress badly; they are very slippery, lascivious, and carnal people. . . . They are extremely fond of the Franks and especially of us friars. . . . They are abominable heretics, adherents of the Jacobites." The *Jacobites* "love the Franks greatly, and especially us minor friars. They hate the Greeks, and every other sect except the Abyssinians who have adhered to their heresies. . . . These Jacobites use singing and music in their services in this way. They hold in the hand a piece of thin polished iron, and strike on it with a little hammer, harmonising the blows and the words." With regard to the *Copts* he remarked :— "As the Copts had left Jerusalem when I was there and gone to Cairo, I had no opportunity of talking to them, and so I cannot describe their abominable customs and rites as I have done in the case of the others. But to conclude, I can liken them to the other heretics and putrid members cut off from the most Holy Roman Church. The Copts are fewest in number of all the sects in Jerusalem, and as they are few, when the sons of their priests are born, they make them deacons and sub-deacons, and when it is necessary to chant the Epistle and Gospel, the fathers chant them in the name of their sons, holding the aforesaid infants in their arms the while."

NOTE 88.

The phrase "Sons of the people" ("fioli de la gente") used by Casola, is repeated many times by Marino Sanuto in the notices he gives of Egyptian affairs. It evidently means "sons of free men"—as distinguished from the sons of those who were slaves. In August, 1496, Sanuto mentions a letter (dated May 26th)—which had been received from the Venetian Consul in Alexandria—giving the news that as the Sultan "Caithbei" (*i.e.*, Kaiet or Qait Bey) was old and ill, he had sent for his son Mameth and named him Sultan "against their law," and consigned the Treasure to him. The Pachas and the Mamelukes were opposed to this "Because they did not want their rules to be broken, and that this dominion should pass to a person who was the *"fiol di la zente,"* but only to slaves who had been bought and sold as it had always been."[1] Another letter (dated July 22) from Damascus, announced the death of the Sultan Caithbei, in whose place his son had been declared Sultan with the aid of powerful supporters, "but they say, he will not reign many days because he is a *"fiol di la zente."*[2] After describing the origin of the Mameluke Dynasty in Egypt and Palestine, Suriano goes on to say :—"The first Sultan they elected had been bought and sold five times, and therefore, up to the present they

1. Sanuto, *Diarii*, vol. i. p. 262.
2. Idem, p. 288.

observe this custom, that a person who has not been bought and sold five times cannot be raised to the dignity of Sultan. And if it should happen that a person whom they wished to exalt to this place, had not this qualification, they buy and sell him in one day all the times that are lacking. No one but a renegade christian can be Lord of this country."[1] The Mamelukes were deprived of their Asiatic dominion by the Turks early in the sixteenth century.

NOTE 89.

The Usbech, the Sultan and the Minor Friars. In reply to the question addressed him by his sister :—"Are the friars at Mount Sion molested by the Moors?" Fra Francesco Suriano wrote[2] :—"At the time when, as a Layman, I frequented those parts, the friars were very badly treated by the Moors, so much so, that very often they dared not go out of their convent, and they were forced to give food to all who came to the door, otherwise the Moors threw stones at the place. And they were in great subjection to certain Moors in particular, who had the audacity to enter and search the whole house; and when in any cell they saw a good 'Schiavina'"—a bedcover that is of coarse wool,— "they demanded it, and the friars dared not refuse for fear of offending them. Similarly they went and poked their noses into the cooking-pots in the kitchen, and if there was a piece of meat that pleased them they took it—and so on everywhere else in the building. Many times there were riots and the people spilled all the friars' wine, and did many other contumelious acts which it would take too long to narrate in detail. But at present "—that is in the year 1485—" all this has ceased, the friars live in blessed peace; and happy the Moor, either small or great as he may be, who is considered their friend." In chapter sixty of his Treatise, Suriano explains how the miraculous change alluded to in the last paragraph had been brought about through the influence of the Usbech and the Sultan. After their deaths Suriano was elected a second time Prior of Mount Sion, and he says :—"This second term of office appeared to me very hard and wearisome when I remembered the immunities we enjoyed during my first guardianship. Because we had returned to the former anxieties, oppressions, extortions and intolerable burdens."

NOTE 90.

The Salines of Cyprus. In the middle ages the chief products of Cyprus were sugar and salt, and perhaps the revenue yielded by the salt was larger than that derived from the sugar. The salt was ex-

1. Suriano, *Trattato di Terra Santa.*
2. Suriano, *Il Trattato di Terra Santa.* Edited. 1900, by Father Girolamo Golubovich.

tracted with little trouble from the salt pits near Limasol and Larnaca.[1] In 1490 (July 11) the Maggior Consiglio of Venice passed the following decree by a large majority :—"The Salines of Cyprus are of the greatest importance (as everyone knows very well) for many reasons, and especially for the salt which is a great source of gain to our ships. It is therefore necessary to appoint a suitable governor for the place, whose duty it will be to see that the Salines are well kept, and to take care that the inconveniences which occurred last year, and have occurred also during the present year, are not repeated. For many of our ships, for lack of salt, returned empty from that Island with very great loss." It was decreed in consequence that "one of our Gentlemen" should be elected as Captain of the Salines of Cyprus; that he was to stay at his post for two years, and receive a salary of five hundred ducats a year.[2] In 1494 the Governor or Captain was "Ser Franciscus Mauroceno."[3] From Denis Possot we learn that these salt lakes were due to a "*miracle du Lazare*, lequel, une foys passant par là, et pour le chaleur qu'el faisoit, desirant appaiser la grand soif qu'il avoit, demanda à une femme qui là estoit, qu'elle luy donnast une grappe de raisin ou quelque liquer pour estancher sa soif; laquelle femme luy donna de la terre salée, et pour ce, le lieu et pais est fertile et abondant de sel, et moins de vignes."[4]

NOTE 91.

The Lakes of the Seprio. In the early middle ages the Milanese territory was divided into "Contadi," so-called because the administrators, at first called "Giudici," afterwards obtained the title of Count. One of these divisions was called the Contado of Seprio. It lay to the East of the Ticino, between Lakes Maggiore and Lugano, and extended also considerably to the South of both. The group of small lakes to the South-east of Maggiore, of which Lake Varese is the largest, are the so-called Lakes of the Seprio. ("Descrizione della città e della campagna di Milano nei secoli bassi," by Conte Giorgio Giulini, p. 87.)

NOTE 92.

Friar of the Zorzi family. Although it is not certain, the Franciscan friar in question may very well have been the celebrated *Francesco Zorzi*, a man of profound intelligence, versed in Hebrew and Chaldean, and a great student of Plato, who also wrote "De Armonia Mundi," and other works. He was born in 1460 and died at Asolo at the age of eighty. (Cappellari, Campedoglio Veneto, and Agostini's biographies of the *Scrittori Veneziani*." Tome ii., p. 332—362.)

1. Heyd, *Italian Commercial Colonies in the East in the Middle Ages*, pp. 312-3.
2. Maggior Consiglio, Register *Stella*, p. 103 *b*.
3. *Segretario alle Voce*, Reg. vi. 1.
4. *Le Voyage de la Terre Sainte*, par Maitre Denis Possot, 1532, p. 139.

NOTES

NOTE 93.

Arrival of Charles VIII. in Italy, 1494. This is one of the notices given by Casola which enables the year of his pilgrimage to be fixed with absolute certainty. He carefully abstains from commenting on this important political event; probably because he was much too wary and prudent to write anything which might cause him embarrassment in the future. As Lodovico of Milan had brought Charles into Italy, the topic was a dangerous one for the Milanese Canon. In the Spring of 1494, Venice was kept well informed of the projects on foot. In May, 1494, the new French Ambassador, Monseigneur de Citin presented his credentials to the Venetian Senate, and announced that his master had decided to come to Italy, and from there attack the Turks. He offered various ports and cities in the Kingdom of Naples to the Republic, if the latter—for payment—would furnish the French army with provisions. The Senate replied evasively and promised nothing. In July, 1494, in reply to the Neapolitan Ambassador who had come to find out the intentions of the Republic, the Senate assured him of Venetian friendship for Naples, and said that the French King lacked money, and that his preparations were not such as to excite alarm. Nevertheless, after passing the Summer at Lyons, Charles crossed the Alps, and on the 9th of September entered Asti, where he met Lodovico il Moro. From there Philippe de Comines, Seigneur d'Argenton was sent as the new Ambassador to Venice, to ask for a loan of 50,000 ducats, which he did not obtain. A month before Comines left Venice, that is in March, 1495, he was informed of the league between Venice, the Pope, Spain, and Milan, etc., against his master, which gained the so-called victory over the French army at Fornovo on the Taro in July, 1495. From Asti Charles VIII. went to Pavia, where he saw the Duke Gian Galeazzo, who had been ill for some time, and his young wife Isabella of Aragon, who implored his protection for her husband and herself, and sought in vain to dissuade him from advancing further. Without delay, the French King—without visiting Milan—left for Piacenza, and soon after he reached there news came that the young Duke Gian Galeazzo had died. From Piacenza Charles went on to Florence, and then to Rome, which he entered on the 30th December, 1494.

NOTE 94.

The Duchy of Naxos, or the Duchy of the Archipelago of the Cyclades. On the division of the Byzantine Empire after 1204, the part which fell to the Venetian Republic formed a continuous line of ports on the mainland and in the islands from Constantinople to Venice. But in many cases the possession was purely nominal, and in order to relieve the State of the burden of conquering and maintaining the new acquisitions, it was decided to grant a large number, especially of the

Islands, on feudal conditions, to those Venetian Nobles who were willing to conquer them at their own risk and expense. These feudatories were pledged to recognise the supremacy of the mother country, pay a tribute, defend the land they had won, supply a contingent of troops in the Wars of Venice, and grant liberty of trade to the Republic. In return they received a promise of protection. In this way Marco Sanudo obtained the lordship of Naxos, Paros, Melos, Delos, and other islands, and by the successor of Baldwin on the Byzantine throne he was created Prince of the Empire and *Duke of the Archipelago*. After six generations the duchy passed out of the Sanudo family, by the marriage of a daughter of Giovanni Sanudo with a prince of Negropont, and later it came into possession of the Crispo family, a powerful Greek family which had aided the Republic in the war against the Emperor Michael Paleologos, and was included amongst the patrician families of Venice in consequence. The members of the Crispo family intermarried frequently with those of the most conspicuous Venetian families. Agostino Contarini's more famous brother Ambrogio, who was ambassador to the King of Persia, 1474—1478, and wrote a very interesting account of his mission, married Violante, sister of Giovanni Crispo, Duke of Naxos and the Archipelago. Giovanni had died, as Casola reports, a few days before the pilgrim galley arrived there on the 27th of September, 1494. The tutor appointed by the Republic to govern the Duchy during the minority of the young Duke Francesco, was not his uncle Ambrogio Contarini, but Ser Pietro Contarini, son of the late Ser Adorni, a more distant relative of the same family, as I found on consulting the Register of the elections, and also the Register of the general proceedings of the Senate. The latter contains the following decree addressed on the 29th of May, 1495, to the Admiral of the Venetian fleet in the Archipelago:—"As the noble man Piero Contarini has lately died, who was our Governor of Nixia" [that is Naxos] "where he had taken his wife and children; it is convenient to grant a safe passage to his wife, so that she and all her possessions may be conducted to some safe place of ours"—the Admiral was therefore ordered to place a galley at the disposition of the wife of the defunct Ser Piero Contarini, so that she and her family and all her goods might be taken to Modone or Corfu.[1] In October, 1495, Ser Andrea Memo was elected Governor of Naxos, and he was succeeded in March, 1498, by Ser Ambrogio Contarini, son of the late Ser Georgio.[2] It is to be assumed that, after the latter's term of office expired, the young Duke took the government into his own hands. The Duchy of Naxos was taken by the Turks in 1566 and bestowed by the Sultan on a Jew. The Crispos took refuge in Venice. In 1579 the Duchy was incorporated in the Ottoman Empire.

1. *Senato Mar.*, Reg. 14, p. 64.
2. *Segretario alle Voci*, Reg. vi.

NOTE 95.

The town of Lesina or Fara [*Lat. Pharia*] is in Dalmatia, on the western side of the island of the same name. Santo Brasca visited it on the homeward voyage in 1480. He writes : " On the 14th of October we entered the port of Lesina, a city in Dalmatia, and there we stayed two days waiting for the wind to drop and the sea to calm down a little. As there was no other lodging to be found, the very reverend Misser frate Pietro da Canedo and I went to lodge at the monastery of the observant friars of the order of St. Francis, who received us with such affection, such joy, and such humility as I have no words to describe, and in spite of their poverty they did us great honour. I must tell you that in the Levant there is no comfortable lodging to be found, whatever you would be willing to pay for it, except in the monasteries of the observant friars of St. Francis." At one time Lesina was the permanent station for about thirty light galleys of the Venetian fleet, and there was an Arsenal there.

NOTE 96.

San Germano ed i quattro Coronati or St. Germanus and the four crowned heads. Legend relates that in the reign of Diocletian there lived at Rome four christian brothers, who were cunning artificers in wood and stone, and excelled in sculpture and architecture. "In those days," says Gibbon, "every art and every trade that was the least concerned in the framing or adorning of idols was, in the opinion of Christians, polluted by the stain of idolatry "—a severe sentence since it devoted to eternal misery the far greater part of the community employed in the liberal or mechanical professions; while those who refused to profane their art were as certainly condemned to poverty and starvation if not to martyrdom. This was the fate of the four crowned brothers. They refused to exercise their known skill in obedience to the command of the emperor and were put to death. Some time in the fourth century the bodies of four men who had been decapitated were found buried on the road leading from the Colosseum to the Lateran. Their names were unknown and they were merely distinguished as the " Coronati "—crowned that is with the crown of martyrdom. Afterwards their names and history were revealed to a holy man, and the church of the " Quattro Coronati " was built to their memory on the spot. They are the special patron saints of builders and stone cutters. (Mrs. Jameson, *Sacred and Legendary Art*, vol. ii., p. 624.)

NOTE 97.

The Custom House. In Venice, up to the year 1414, all goods were unloaded and weighed near San Biagio, in Castello. But as commerce increased the place became too small, and two Customs Houses were erected, one at the Rialto for goods which came from the mainland, the other on the site of the present Dogana for goods brought by sea. The old *Dogana da Mar* had a tower which is to be seen in the plan of Venice, in the year 1500, attributed to Albert Dürer. It was restored in 1525 and rebuilt in 1675. From the thirteenth century the Custom House business was regulated by a body of Patrician magistrates called *Visdomini da Mare*, or *Ufficiali della Tavola del Mare*.

NOTE 98.
The Festival of All Saints. Sansovino[1] notes in chronological order twenty-two occasions during the year on which the Doge, accompanied by the Signoria, went in state to High Mass at St. Mark's. "The first time is on Christmas Eve . . . and the twenty-second and last is on the solemn day of All Saints which is celebrated on the first of November." In 1472, on the site of the present Church of "Ognissanti" (All Saints), behind the Zattere, the Cistercian nuns of Santa Margherita in Torcello—who had abandoned that island, where the air was becoming every day more unhealthy,—settled in a poor convent, to which was added a wooden church, dedicated to the Virgin and all Saints. In the year 1505, certain miracles were worked by an image of the Virgin placed in an obscure part of the convent. It was brought into the church, and so generous were the gifts of the faithful that a new church and convent were commenced. The church was consecrated in 1586.

NOTE 99.
The Ambassador of the King of France in Venice between October 1494, and May 1495, was Philippe de Comines, Seigneur d'Argenton. His account of his entry into Venice is in his *Memoires*, Liv. vii., ch. xviii. Elsewhere I have called attention to the probable consequences of his meeting with Casola at the house of Don Taddeo Vicomercato.

NOTE 100.
Girolamo or Hieronimo Zorzi, surnamed the "Gobbo" or the hunchback, was the son of Francesco Zorzi. He became Senator and Knight, and enjoyed a great reputation because of the various legations successfully sustained by him, amongst others to the Sultan, the King of France and the Pope.

NOTE 101.
The Muster. This may have been a review of the mercenary troops in the service of the Republic, but it was more probably a gathering of

---

1. Sansovino, *Venezia descritta*, 1604.

the "cernide" or country militia raised for home defence in proportion to the population, and amounting to twenty-five or thirty thousand men. These were under obligation to appear for practice once a week in the separate communes; and once a month there was a general muster in each district. The men were only paid when called out for active service, otherwise they remained at home and pursued their ordinary occupations.

NOTE 102.

The Bishop of Brescia. Porro says : " In 1494 the Bishop of Brescia was Paolo Zane, a noble Venetian who was appointed bishop in 1481, at the age of 22, on condition that he was not to exercise his functions until he reached the age of twenty-seven. . . . In spite of the accusations made against him by Casola, he was a pious man, and very devoted to the Blessed Virgin, in whose honour he erected, at his own expense, the Church of S. Maria delle Grazie in Brescia. He died on March 12, 1531, and was buried in the Cathedral at Brescia."

Appendix.

APPENDIX.

Documents relating to Pietro Casola which exist in the State Archives of Milan.

DOCUMENT A.—Ducal rescript confirming Pietro Casola in the possession of the Benefice of Saint Victor at Corbetta, Milan, 13th August, 1467.

"Ducissa Mediolani, etc. Annuere volentes requisitioni nobis facte per presbyterum Petrum de Casolis, qui sicut nobis exposuit, obtinuit a sedde appostolica benefitium prepositure Sancti Victoris de Corbeta Mediolanensis diocesis prout vidimus, per bullas Sanctissimi domini nostri Pape, concedimus quantum in nobis est eidem tenore presentium plenam et liberam licentiam et facultatem quod in assecutione huusmodi (sic) prepositure juribus suis uti possit iniungentes quibuslibet offitialibus et subditis nostris ad quos spectat quatenus prenominato presbytero Petro seu procuratori suo in premissis patientiam prestent omnimodam et favoribus quibuscumque assistant opportunis licitis tamen et honestis, iniungentes et mandantes etiam Filippino Burro, yconemo ut dicitur dicte prepositure, quatenus dictam preposituram liberam et expeditam sine ulla exceptione dicto presbytero Petro vel eius procuratori relaxet et dimittat, ac de administratis eidem rationem reddat et amplius se de dicta prepositura neque de bonis dicte prepositure se intromittat. In quorum, etc. Datum Mediolani, die xiij Augusti, 1467."

Taken from the "Volume of Privileges and Exceptions of the Duchess Bianca for the years 1466, 1467 and 1468. Registro Ducale, CC, f. 199a. Milano, Archivio di Stato.

DOCUMENT B.—A supplication addressed by Pietro Casola, priest and canon of Milan Cathedral, to the Illustrious Princes and Lords of Milan, asking for authority to exercise his rights as canon of Santo Stefano in Brolio, and of the church of Corbetta, both of which had been usurped by others. The form of the address shows that it was written after the death of Galeazzo Sforza (1476), during the regency of Bona of Savoy, and before Lodovico Sforza took all power into his own hands—that is between 1476 and 1480, and most probably soon after the death of Galeazzo. The writing seems to be identical with that of the Manuscript of Casola's Voyage in the Trivulzian Library.

" Illustrissimi Principes et Excellentissimi Domini: per parte del fidelissimo servitore et dele Excellentie Vostre et a Dio oratore per quelle prete Petro Caxola Canonico ordinario de la Chiesia Maiore de Milano, se expone: che essendo più mesi passati richesto in siema con molti altri preti, e chierici de questa cità, per parte de le Illustrissime Signorie Vostre ad prestare juramento de esser fideli alo Stato Vostro et a Vuy benche non bisognasse el procuratore che richedeva tal juramento: disse, che essendo como he debito fideli subditi e servitori de le Celsitudine Vostre, ne serebbe facto quello debito tractamento se sole fare dali principi ali soy subditi, per il che confidandossi el prefato oratore che le parole et promesse deli principi non hano esser vacue, maxime non domandando lui senon justitia, se ricorre humelmente alo P^{te} Vostre Excellentie e suplicale se dignano de darli licentia possa in questa vostra cita de Milano uxare le rasone sue in uno Canonicato de Sancto Stephano in Brolio, et unaltro nela chiesia de Corbetta, el qual già piu anni he unito ala prepositura de dicta chiesia de Corbeta; li quali Canonicati gli sono ocupati contra ogni rasone e justitia e prega le P^te Vostre Celsitudine non vogliano denegare la justitia achi la richede per scaricho de le sue conscientie e como he di costuma e debito dele Illustrissime Signorie Vostre, e como crede firmissimamente sia el volere e la mente sua, Benchè li occupatori de li dicti canonicati per dare ad intendere altro che la verità a quelle siano defensati in la occupatione de dicti canonicati dale sue littere. Attento che, se le P^te Vostre Excellentie farano ministrare equalmente la justitia ali soy subditi precipue in queste cosse ecclesiastice, non bisognarà siano may in timore de turbatione de stato, per che lo altissimo Dio, el qual lha in protectione el conservara in perpetuo; e cossi pregara esso oratore nele sue messe dice de continuo il faccia: Attento etiam che qualuncha de quisti duy occupatori he inhabile ad havere dicti canonicati; quello de Sancto Stephano perche la età gliel denega, essendo lui uno puto: e bisognando sia prete chi debbe obtegnire dicto Canonicato de Sancto Stephano; e quello occupa lo Canonicato de Corbeta sia apto ad ogni altra cossa che esser prete; unde anchora in questo le P^te Vostre Excellentie hano a provedere che ale chiesie sia proveduto de persone ydonee ali loro benefitij. Esso oratore non ricorda altramente chel sia xvi. anni chel sta in Corte de Roma ali servitij de questo stato; perchè domandando justitia dali soy Signori gli pare non gli debia esser denegata, essendo la prima cossa che debbe fare li principi ali soy subditi: et indistincte farla administrare achi la domanda humelmente." Milano. Archivio di Stato. Sezione Storica. Famiglie, Casola.

On the back of the parchment there is the following:—

"Suplicatio Presbyteri Petri Casole Canonici Ordinarij Ecclesie Maioris Mediolani."

The supplication bears no date.

DOCUMENT C.—Minutes of a letter from the Milanese Ambassador at Rome dated August 14th, 1477, in which he mentions Pietro Casola who was probably one of the Secretaries to the Milanese Legation there.

" Rome, xiiij° Augusti, 1477.

Illustrissime. Le Vostre Illustrissime Signorie me scripseno per sue littere como era vacata la prepositura de Marliano e imposono la facesse suspendere donec deliberasseno a chi la voleno fosse conferita, e cosa fu facta lambassata, sucedete che un prete Bernardino de Robiate persona ben costumata, ben che altramente io non lo cognoscesse et, ut dixit, nepote de domino Bartholomeo de Calcho, Secretario de le Excellentie Vostre, partito de Milano, vene qua batando con speranza dé questo benefizio o de qualche unaltro, et dete supplicatione de questa prepositura, como se fa per tentare la sua fortuna, e capitando in le mane al Reverendissimo Monsignore de Tirasone in caxa del quale sta un prete Johanne Maria de la Mayrola, quale mera (sic) io e con difficulta al tempo de la sua promotione [e non senza difficulta],* como subdito de la Excellentia Vostra; E costuy temerariamente, vista tal vacantia, fece duy inconvenienti, l'uno de ocultare la supplicatione de questo Bernardino, l'altra de impetrarlo senza licentia de le Celsitudine Vostre. So [or questo] non peccò per ignorantia, et havendo io notitia de questo, manday per luy et ammonillo a desistere de la impresa, ricordandoli il suo bisogno; deteme bone parole e pur a proceduto a la expeditione de le bolle secretamente guardandosi da mi; e quando ho inteso questo, de novo a la presentia de domino Augustino Roso ho remandato per luy, e pur persisti in sua temerita. De poy anchora li ho facto

* These words are written thus and then cancelled in the original.

redire per pre(te) Petro Casola, et infine pare chel se confida havere de la persone chi lo adiutarano, apresso a le Celsitudine Vostre e che vole mandare le sue bolle, e che scriva che anche luy scrivara. E questo è il merito che'l me rende per haverlo misso in quella caxa, che me arguisse sia una persona molto temeraria; e in questo modo el scrivere ha facto le Excellentie Vostre per quello de Serenio, per questa prepositura non so havere loco. Ho voluto che le Vostre Excellentie intendano el tuto, per che mandando luy de là le sue bolle a li sui parenti, esse li faciano quelle provisione li parira. Che la ingratitudine sua di qua per la mia particularità remediarò io, non per farli male, perchè de mia natura, et etiam como prelato non voglio fare male ad alcuno: ne etiam cociezare con li pari sui. Bono e chel vincha."

Archives of Milan. Potenze Estere. Roma.

DOCUMENTS D.—Copies of two letters from the Dukes of Milan to Don Andrea de Fagnano, Canon of Milan Cathedral, ordering him to hear and settle a dispute as to the possession of the Chapel of Santa Maria de Cepis, claimed by Pietro Casola on the one part and on the other by Ambrogio de Cepis and Girolamo Cazaniga. The first letter is dated August 1478. The second February 1479.

Letter I.—" Venerabilis doctor nobis dilecte, vertitur controversia super quadam capella Sancte Marie de Cepis inter Venerabilem presbyterum Petrum Casolam et Hyeronimum Cazanigam, quorum dispendio parci cupientes de ipsarum partium consensu vobis iniungimus ut dictam controversiam, visis videndis et auditis audiendis, que partes producere, dicere et alegare voluerint sumarie, etc., terminetis providendo ut super possessione dicte capelle neutri fiat iniuria. Ambo in doctrinis et sinceritatis vestra confidunt, et nos optimam opinionem habemus.—Mediolani, tertio Augustij, 1478. Cichus.[1] Venerabili doctori, domino Andree de Fagnano, ordinario, Mediolani, Nobis dilecto." Milano. Archivio di Stato. Sezione Storica. Famiglie. Casola.

Letter II.—" Venerabilis dilecte noster, cum non pauci agantur menses quod commissa vobis fuerit vertens controversia inter Hyeronimum Cazanigam, et Ambrosium de Cepis pro una, ac presbyterum Petrum Casolam ex altera, ob eam causam que in vestra est commissione expressa putabamus in hanc diem expedictam per vos fuisse, sed quantum nuper intelleximus controversia ipsa adhuc inexpedicta esse videtur; et quia quo magis in longum cause protrahantur eo gravioribus partes afficiuntur sumptibus et incomodis, quibus semper occurendum est, ideo vos et ortamur et oneramus, ut cuiusmodi expediende controversie absque ulteriori dilatione incumbatis juxta commissionem vestram, quo tandem debitum finem capiat nec indecissa diutius futura sit in maximum partis utriusque dispendium. Datum Mediolani, die xvij Februarij 1479. Cichus. Venerabili dilecto nostro, domino Andree de Fagnano, decretorum doctori et ex ordinarijs Ecclesie Majoris Mediolani."

Milano, Archivio di Stato. Sezione Storica—from a packet of papers relating to the Casola family.

DOCUMENTS E.—Extracts from documents relating to the Cathedral of Milan, in which the names of certain of the Canons are given for several years between 1481 and 1504. Those have been selected in which Casola's name

---

1. *i.e.*, Cichus or Francesco Simoneta, the famous Milanese Chancellor.

appears. The extracts are taken from Volume III. of the "Annali della Fabbrica del Duomo di Milano."

P. 1.—"1481. Ordinarij. Guido de' Castiglioni arciprete, Filippo de' Calvi, Pietro de' Casoli, Andrea de' Fagnano, Lantelmo de' Majno, Giovanni de' Menclozzi, Leonardo de' Plati, Zanotto Visconti prevosto."

P. 73.—"1492 Arcivescovo Guido Antonio Arcimboldo. Ordinarij, Filippo de' Calvi, Pietro de' Casoli, Modesto de' Cusano e Giovanni de' Menclozzi."

P. 85.—"1496. Ordinarij. Carlo Baldo, Pietro de' Casoli, Gabriele della Croce, Cristoforo del Pozzo, e Giovanni Ambrogio Visconti."

P. 119.—" Ordinarij 1502. Petro Casola, Modesto Cusano, Taddeo Morone, Cristoforo del Pozzo e Gian Pietro Visconti."

P. 124.—"1503. Ordinarij. Carlo Baldo, Pietro Casola, , Modesto Cusano, Taddeo Morone, e Gian Pietro Visconti."

P. 127.—"1504. Ordinarij. Pietro Casola, Modesto de Cusano, Taddeo Morone, Giovanni Stefano Olgiak, Francesco de' Parravicino, e Stefano de' Tosi."

DOCUMENTO F.—Register of the death of Casola, taken from the " Registri Mortuarij (m. 81)," in the State Archives of Milan.

1507. Die Sabbati Sesto mensis Novembris.

Porte Ticinensis, Parrochie Sancti Victoris.

Reverendus dominus presbyter Petrus Casolus annorum LXXX ex gattarro prefocante egritudine non suspecta judicio Magistri Ambrosij Varisij Roxati.[1]

1. Printed in the article "Morti in Milano dal 1452—1552," by Emilio Motta. See Introduction, p. 14.

Index.

INDEX.

A

Abbiategrasso, 163.
Abbondio, 372.
Absalom, 246.
Abyssinian Christians, 276, 389, 391.
Acre, 6, 25, 39, 43, 44, 45, 53, 54, 233, 387.
Adalia, 212.
Adiabene, Queen of the, 246.
Adige, 121.
Adrianople, Treaty of, 60.
Advocates of the Commune, 97, 98, 99, 100, 105, 337.
Africa, Circumnavigation of, 358.
Agents (Missetæ), 40, 42, 48, 49, 51, 52, 72, 111.
Agostini, Biographies of, 394.
Agram, Bishop of, 32, 33.
Albania, 161, 183, 325, 326.
Albanian Sailors, 161.
Alemano, Andrea, 298.
Alexander, 298.
Alexander III., Pope, 126, 136, 355.
Alexandria, 4, 30, 45, 59, 108, 193, 391.
Alexandria Trading Galleys, 32, 46, 59, 60.
Alfano, Bishop, 6.
All Saints, Festival of, 338, 398.
Amadi, Francesco, 367.
Amalfi, 4, 6.
Amat di S. Filippo, Pietro, 3, 6, 8.
Ambrosian Breviary, 17, 18.
—— Library, 18.
—— Liturgy, 117, 349.
—— Mass, 147.
—— Missal, 338.
Ambrosiani, 350.
America, new route to, 358.
Amorea (Amorgo), Island of, 83.
Ancona, 5, 52, 54, 86, 188.
Anfosio (Alphonso) of Portugal, 46, 47.
Angel, 158.
Angera, 333.
Anjou, King of, 78.

Antenor, 122, 351.
Antiphons, 247.
Antivari, 183, 326.
Antoninus, Martyr, 5, 6.
Antwerp, Governor of, 298.
Antwerp, Johanne de Burgho of, 265.
Apostles, fountain of the, 267.
Apulia, 176, 181, 183, 330, 387.
Aquileia, Patriarch of, 147, 152, 372.
Arab Chief, 231, 232.
Arabs, 242, 266, 345, 385.
Aragon, Isabella of, 395.
Arcadia, 188, 191.
Archbishop of Milan, 8, 9, 18, 117, 345.
Archipelago, 196, 310.
—— Duchy of, 383, 395, 396.
—— Duke of, 383, 396.
Arcimboldi, Giovanni, 8.
—— Guidantonio, 8, 9, 17, 91, 117, 345, 409.
—— Nicolo, 8.
Arco, 351.
Arduina (Galley), 33, 36.
Arena (Verona), 120.
Argelati, 8, 13.
Arigi, 102, 103, 204, 210, 219, 381.
Arimathea, Joseph of, 261.
Arimondo, Nicolo, 63, 64.
Armenia, 387.
Armenian Christians, 263, 276, 391.
Arsenal, 66, 68, 71, 75, 79, 86, 98, 105, 106, 139, 141, 365, 367, 368, 397.
—— Experts, 86.
—— Heads of the, 141, 368.
Artillery, 105, 106.
Artimone, 158, 298, 319, 325.
Ascalon, 388.
Ascensiontide, 29, 86, 99, 106, 111, 116.
Asine, 380.
Asolo, 394.
Assisi, Saint Francis of, 6.
—— Santa Maria degli Angeli at, 386.

Assumption, Festival of the, 271, 272.
Asti, 395.
Astrology, 8.
Auction of Licences for Pilgrim Ships, 69, 75, 106.
—— of State Galleys, 55.
Augsburg, 96.
August Voyage, 69, 71, 75.
Autumn Voyage, 25, 76, 78.

B

Babylon, 387.
Baccano, forest of, 16, 153.
Bachino, Francesco, 38.
Baffo (Paphos), 212, 299, 383.
Bag of Money, 10, 13, 230, 337.
—— Faith, 13.
—— Patience, 10, 13, 230.
Bailo of Acre, 25.
—— of Corfu, 186.
Bajazet, Sultan, 379.
Balass Rubies, 145.
Baldwin, King of Jerusalem, 276, 389, 396.
Balestrieri, 56, 63, 79, 84, 85, 158, 159, 160, 375, 376.
Balestrarie, 376.
Balla d'oro, 95.
Balzi, 237.
Banchum, ponere, 59, 65.
Barbarigo, Doge Agostino, 142, 146, 147, 152, 338, 353, 371.
—— Giovanni, 37.
—— Girolamo, 371.
—— Doge Marco, 371.
Barbaro, Giosafatte, 96.
Barbarossa, Emp. Fred., 126, 136, 355.
Barbary, 25, 59, 191.
Barbo, Alvise, 329.
—— Paolo, 362.
Basaite, Marco, 363.
Bavaria, Dukes of, 31.
Bazane Ultramarine, 216.
Belgioioso, Galeotto di, 9.
Bellini, Gentile, 20.
Beltrame, Luca, 357.
Bembo, 35.
—— Lorenzo, 48.
Bemmelberg, Reinhard von, 2, 390.
Berths, measurement of, 102.
Bethany, 267, 279.

Bethlehem, 258, 262—264, 389.
Beyrout, 4, 32, 33, 39, 43, 45, 46, 47, 54, 55, 56, 57, 58, 59, 65, 77, 273, 385, 387.
—— Beyrout Fleet, 32, 33, 39, 43, 44, 45, 46, 47, 48, 55, 56, 59, 60, 67, 74, 77, 78, 80, 82, 301, 375.
Bianca, Duchess, 14, 403.
Bianco, Cape (Cyprus), 296.
Bianco, Paolo, 110.
Bindoni, Francesco, 385.
Biremi, 56, 368.
Birsa, Nicolaus de, 47.
Bissa Scudelera, 266.
Black Sea, 5, 59.
Bohemia, John Sartor from, 60, 61.
Boldù, Bernardo, 104.
Boleyn, Queen Anne, 36.
Bolingbroke, Henry, 33, 34, 35.
—— See Derby.
Bollani, Domenico, 318.
Bologna, 3, 352.
Bona, Duchess, 15.
Bonanza, 164.
Bono, Bartolomeo, 357.
—— Guglielmo, 37, 39.
—— Nicoletto, 38.
Borromeo, Alessandro, 134, 361.
—— St. Charles, 18, 349, 361.
Bossi, Laura, 359.
Botta, Leonardo, 9.
Botte, 203.
Bouillon, Godfrey de, 275, 391.
Boyana (river), 326.
Boza, Bartolomeo, 109.
Brabant, 298.
Braccio (measure), 144, 155.
Bragadino, Antonio, 33.
—— Marcantonio, 383.
Brasca, Santo, 6, 8, 9, 10, 13, 93, 96, 381, 382, 388, 389, 397.
Brenta (river), 132.
Brescia, 118—121, 350.
—— Bishop of, 343, 399.
Breviary, Ambrosian, 17, 18.
Brindisi, 5.
Briona, 333, 334.
Broletto, 126, 354.
Brolio, San Stefano in, 404.
Brown, Rawdon, 34, 35.
Bruges, burgomaster of, 47.
Brugh (plant), 187, 378.
Buatello, Jacobello, 39.
Bucentauro or Bucentoro, 32.
Budua, 183.
Burgho, Johanne de, 265.

INDEX

Burgundy, 63, 265.
—— Philip the Bold, Duke of, 53.
—— Philip the Good, 74, 77, 78.
—— Nobles from, 63.
Butigella, Giov. Matteo, 7.
Byzantine Empire, 5.

C

Ca' del Duca, 357.
Ca' Grande, 363.
Cairo, 7, 273, 280, 383, 385.
Calcho, Bartolomeo de, 406.
Calci, 118, 344.
Calogeri, 202, 277.
Camalio, 204, 217, 381.
Camardino, Ed. de, 188, 205, 206, 309, 379.
Cambray, 298.
Camerino, Fra Simone da, 362.
Canaan, 249.
Canala (Galley), 63.
Canali, Cristoforo, 369.
—— Francesco, 36, 38.
—— Girolamo, 64.
—— Vito, 45.
Cancelier Grando, 369.
Candia (Crete), 18, 22, 37, 42, 71, 83, 110, 111, 197, 198—203, 289, 311, 314—319, 380, 381, 382, 385, 387.
—— Duke of, 314, 315, 318, 319.
—— Captain of, 314, 315, 318, 319.
Candiano, Doge Pietro, 352.
Canea, 381.
Canedo, Fra Pietro, 397.
Canevo, Casa del, 367.
Canteen, Captain's, 157.
Canthari, 129.
Cantù, 357.
Canuta, la (Cyprus), 218, 294.
Capella (Galley), 46.
Capellari, 371, 372, 394.
Capello, Andrea, 46, 47.
—— Simon, 327.
Capitulum peregrinorum, 25, 27.
Capodilista, Gabriele, 6, 7.
Cappadocia, St. George of, 387.
Caravaggio, 118, 344.
Cardaro (Caldaio), 184.
Cardinal Federico, 18.
Carducci, Giosuè, 3.
Carob-beans (Cyprus), 216, 295.
Carpaccio, Vittorio, 20.
Carpets (Rhodes), 307.

Casanigo, Girolamo, 17, 407, 408.
Cases on the Galley, 159, 373, 374.
Casola, Pietro, Life and MS. of, 13—22.
—— meeting with Fra F. Trevulzio, p. 132.
—— —— with Agostino Contarini, 124, 253.
—— —— with Andrea Lanza, 184.
—— with Ed. of Camardino, 188, 206.
—— Visit to the Cornaro Sugar Plantations, 212.
—— Accident on the journey from Rama to Jerusalem, 243.
—— Adventure at Rama, 285.
Cassine, 139, 140.
Castelli, Francesco, 19.
Castelnuovo, 132.
Castiglione, Girolamo, 7, 10.
Castles, above the two, 155.
Castle of the Galley, 156.
Castle Rugi, 303.
Cathibissa, 241, 251, 273.
Cats, Cape of the, 219.
Cattaveri, 40, 41, 43, 44, 48, 49, 50, 51, 52, 54, 60, 61, 62, 69, 72, 73, 75, 79, 87, 88, 89, 90, 100, 101, 102, 107, 108, 110, 111, 124, 377.
Cavagniaza, 251.
Cavallo, Francesco, 59.
Caxi, 130.
Cedron, 246, 248.
Cepis, Ambrogio de, 17, 407, 408.
—— Santa Maria de, 407, 408.
Cephalonia, 188, 379.
Cerigo, 196.
Cernide, 399.
Cerro, 119.
Cesto, Cape, 331.
Chalk, 202.
Charles V., 382.
Charles Philippe, Messire, 2, 109, 391.
Chioggia, 5.
Chitrow, Madame de, 2.
Choo (Cos), Island of, 309.
Cicerigo, 196.
Cicogna, Emmanuele, 362.
Circassians, 280.
Citin, Monseigneur de, 395.
Cividale, 372.
Civrano, Pietro, 49.
Cleves, Duke of, 77.
Cocha (Cocca), 38.

Cochina, 158, 325, 326.
Colla, Paulo, 37.
Colombini, Giovanni, 372.
Colosseum, 120.
Colossi, Casal de, 384.
Colossians, 205.
Comines, Philippe de, 20, 365, 366, 395, 398.
Comito, 12, 160.
Como, man from, 334.
—— Fra Michele of, 132, 304.
Conder, Lieut.-Col., 3.
Confectera, 149.
Constantine, Emperor, 250, 278, 389.
Constantinople, 1, 2, 5, 6, 60, 113, 353, 381, 389, 395.
Contarina (galley), 81, 82, 84, 85, 86, 87, 99, 155—161.
Contarini, Agostino, 3, 9, 23, 56, 94, 95, 96, 99, 100, 101, 124, 153, 160, 168, 169, 171, 179, 181, 182, 183, 184, 187, 195, 196, 197, 199, 205, 213, 215, 217, 218, 219, 220, 223, 225, 226, 227, 228, 229, 230, 232, 233, 234, 236, 238, 239, 241, 243, 244, 253, 259, 261, 262, 267, 270, 271, 272, 273, 274, 282, 284, 287, 288, 289, 290, 294, 300, 304, 306, 307, 309, 311, 313, 314, 317, 320, 321, 324, 326, 330, 331, 332, 335, 337, 375, 383, 385, 386, 396.
—— Ambrogio, 95, 96, 98, 396.
—— Alessandro, 369.
—— Alvise (Luigi), 96.
—— Andrea, 81, 83, 84, 85, 86, 87, 95.
—— Benedetto, 95.
—— Bernardo, 74.
—— Bernardino, 22, 321.
—— Doge Domenico, 364.
—— Girolamo, 95.
—— Hector, 71.
—— Lorenzo, 60.
—— Luca, 95.
—— Marino, 65.
—— Pietro, 396.
—— Zaccaria, 71, 72, 95.
Conventual, monks and nuns, 136.
Cook's Agency, 22.
Copano, 296, 301.
Copts, 391, 392.
Corbetta, 14, 15, 16, 163, 403, 404.
Corcyra, 184.

Cordier, Henri, 2.
Coressa (Nave), 109.
Corfu, 42, 109, 183, 185, 186, 188, 323, 325, 326, 378, 385, 396.
Cornara (Nave), 109.
Cornaro Andrea, 356, 384.
—— Catherine, 383.
—— Federico, 216.
—— Giorgio, 383.
—— Giovanni, 64.
—— Marco, 356. 383.
—— Sugar Plantations, 212, 216, 384.
Corner (Cornaro), Federico, 30.
—— Francischini, 31.
Corone, 42, 103, 195, 380.
Corpus Domini, 29, 78, 112, 113, 135, 146—153, 370.
Correr Museum, 21.
Corsia, 159, 374.
Corte, Fra de, 214.
—— Palazzo di, 354.
Cortese, Martino, 39.
Cortesia, 236.
Cos (Lango, Longo), Island of, 188, 204, 209, 309, 310, 379, 382.
Cotton growing (Cyprus), 216.
—— picking (Rama), 387.
Couriers, Milanese, 123.
Cremona, 357.
—— man from, 334.
Creta, Pietro de, 38.
Crete. See Candia.
Crispo family, 396.
—— Fiorenza, 383.
—— Francesco, 396.
—— Giovanni, 396.
—— Duke Nicolo, 383.
—— Violante, 396.
Cronaca Magna, 357.
Crossbowmen. See Balestrieri.
Crusaders, 5.
Cuchai, 343.
Curias, Cape, 219.
Curlo, 126.
Curzola, Island of, 171, 327, 328, 377.
Cyprus, 30, 31, 46, 54, 63, 64, 77, 82, 87, 90, 92, 96, 109, 110, 111, 204, 215—219, 233, 293, 295, 296, 298, 305, 316, 317, 356, 380, 382, 383, 384, 387, 393.
—— Captain of, 217, 218, 219.
—— Cypress Work at, 316, 317.
—— Galleys, 82.
—— King of, 30, 215, 383.

INDEX

Cyprus, Pilgrim died at, 298.
—— Plague at, 293, 305.
—— Queen of, 356.
—— Salines of, 293, 383, 393.
—— Sugar Plantations at, 212, 216, 383, 384.
—— Wines of, 380.

D

Dalmatia, 327, 328, 377, 397.
Damascus, 56, 248, 273, 386, 392.
—— Lord of, 248.
Damietta, 6.
Dandolo, Andrea, 32.
—— Marco, 109.
—— Marcantonio, 105.
Daubusson, Peter, 206.
David, King, 254.
Delfini, Palazzo, 339.
Delfino, Francesco, 37.
Delfinono, Nicolo, 337.
Delos, Island of, 396.
Derby, Henry, Earl of, 33, 34, 35.
Diedo, Baldesar, 81.
Discords, musical, 200.
Diocletian, 387.
Diosopolis, 387.
Dogs of Longo, 310.
Dolfina (Nave), 109.
Domo, Nicolo de, 200, 316, 317, 319.
Donatello, 351.
Donato, Nicolo, 147, 372.
—— Tommaso, 147, 372.
Dono, Lorenzo, 37, 39.
Doppiero, 148.
Dry Mass, 156, 190, 231, 373.
Duca, Ca' del, 357.
Ducato, Capo del, 189, 379.
Duracino, Nicoletto, 38, 39.
Dürer, Albert, 20, 398.
Duyni, Dominus, 31.

E

Easter Voyage, 25, 53, 69, 71, 75, 82.
Earthquake at Candia, 198—200.
Eckher, Friedrich, 112.
Egypt, 60, 385.
—— Sultan of, 30, 36, 60, 66, 73, 75, 76, 94, 222, 273, 274, 276, 279, 280, 282, 283, 345, 383, 386, 392, 393.
Elia, Antonio de, 39.
Elisha, Well of, 269.
Ellis, Sir Henry, 35.

Emmaus, 281.
England, 3.
—— Henry IV. of, 35.
—— King of, 7, 47, 387, 390.
—— Niece of King of, 215.
—— Pilgrims from, 47, 336.
—— Richard, King of, 35, 383.
Episcopia, 64, 209, 216, 383, 384.
Erasmus of Narni. See Gattamelata.
Ereclea, 365.
Erichi. See Arigi.
Erizza (Galley), 56, 57.
Erizzo, Donato, 56, 57.
Ethiopia, 391.
Ethiopian Friars, 389.
Exeter, John, Earl of, 7, 81, 390.
Extimaria, 160.
Ezra, 252.

F

Faber, Felix, 9, 92, 96, 98, 387.
Fagnano, Andrea de, 17, 407, 408, 409.
Faith, old man of the, 251, 253, 274, 284, 286.
Famagosta, 215, 217, 383.
Fanatico, Sino, 164.
Fara, 171, 329, 397.
Fasana, la, 333.
Ferrara, 132, 227, 265, 377.
—— Duke of, 377.
—— Marquis of, 227.
Ferro, 355.
Festivals of, All Saint's, 338, 398.
—— Assumption, 271, 272.
—— St. Bartholomew, 288.
—— Corpus Domini, 29, 78, 112, 113, 135, 146—153, 370.
—— S. Francis, 315.
—— St. Gervasius and Protasius, 182, 183.
—— St. James, 228, 229.
—— St. John, 189, 190.
—— St. Lawrence, 262, 301.
—— St. Luke, 328.
—— St. Martin, 313.
—— St. Mary Magdalen, 227.
—— St. Michael, 313.
—— The Nativity, 298.
—— St. Peter and St. Paul, 196.
—— S. Titus, 315.
Fino, Pietro, 37.
Flanders, 48, 49.
Flemish Pilgrims, 83.

A 2

Florence, 352, 361, 364, 385, 386, 395.
Florentine pilgrims, 6.
Fondaco dei Tedeschi, 40, 129, 358.
Foligno, 353, 385.
Foreigners, Judges of the, 41.
Fornaro, Giovanni Simone, 132, 245, 265, 286, 287, 289, 361.
Fornovo, battle of, 395.
Foscari, Doge Francesco, 135, 353.
Foscarini Francesco and wife, 318.
Fountain, Our Lady of the, 118, 344.
France, 2.
—— Charles VIII. of, 22, 395.
—— King of, 301, 321.
—— Louis of, 102, 357, 383.
—— Queen of, 339.
Francho, Nicolo, 146.
Franciscan Friars, at, Candia, 198, 201.
—— Lesina, 330, 397.
—— Modone, 191, 193.
—— Parenzo, 163.
—— Ragusa, 173, 174, 177, 180.
—— Rama, 237.
—— Rhodes, 306, 308.
—— Venice, 135, 338, 363.
—— Zara, 166. See also Mount Sion, Friars of.
Franco, Pietro, 86.
Franks, 391.
French Ambassador, 20, 339, 365, 395, 398.
—— Pilgrims, 36, 78, 104, 227.
—— Pilgrims, deaths of, 234, 262, 287, 332.
Frescobaldi, Leonardo, 6.
Friuli, Pilgrim from, 185, 337.
Furiano, Frate, 210, 213.
Fyo, Constantino de, 110.

G

Gaeta, 5.
Galeotti, 56, 58, 79, 143, 160, 189, 231, 234, 290, 368, 369.
Galliate, 235.
Gallicciolli (Mem. Ven.), 365, 373.
Garbino, 164.
Gattamelata, 122, 350, 356.

Gaza, Diodar of, 231.
—— Fruit from, 240.
—— Governor of, 224, 228, 229, 232, 233, 282, 283, 284, 286, 287, 288, 289, 384.
Genoa, 4, 5, 53, 54, 57, 63, 206, 309, 383.
Georgian Christians, 272, 275, 391.
German Pilgrims, 36, 83, 89, 103, 112.
—— Pilgrim, death of a, 290.
Gesuati, 151, 372, 373.
Ghiringhelo, Fra, 153.
Gibbon, Edward, 397.
Gilforth, Duke of. See Guildford, Thomas, Duke of.
Gionchio, Castle of, 191.
Giorgione, 358.
Girdle, Christians of the, 237, 238, 239, 241, 248, 255, 256, 285, 386, 391.
Giulini, Count Giulio, 13, 394.
Giustiniana e Malipiera (Nave), 104.
Giustiniani, Bernardo, 390.
—— Francesco, 87, 96.
—— Giustiniana, 98.
—— San Lorenzo, 364.
Godfrey of Bouillon, Tomb of, 275, 391.
Golbites, 276, 391.
Golubovich, Girolamo, 3, 384, 386.
Gomene, 140, 159.
Gondolas, 141.
Gonnella (Guinella), 227.
Gonzaga, Lords of, 120.
Gradenigo, Juliano, 301.
—— Doge Pietro, 29.
Gradisca, 103.
Grado, Patriarch of, 376.
Grana, 186, 187.
Grasso, Abrayno, 222, 228, 229, 230, 236, 240, 241, 242, 249, 281, 286, 290.
Greco, Cape, 292.
Greece, 25, 75, 387.
—— Sea of, 310.
Greek Christians, 278, 391.
—— Empire, 5.
—— Monks, 264.
—— Rites, 18.
Greiffenstein, Ludwig von, 1, 390.
Greppo (Grippo), 110, 188.
Grimani, Nicolo, 65.
Grimming, Karl von, 112.

INDEX

Gritta (galley), 67.
Gritti, Andrea, 67.
—— Marino, 67.
Guides, Piazza (Tholomarij), 39, 40, 41, 49, 50, 51, 60, 61, 62, 72, 73, 87, 88, 89, 111.
—— Gastaldo of the, 60, 61, 72, 73.
Guildford, Thomas, Duke of, 35.
Guinella (Gonnella), 227.

H

Hadrian, Emperor, 250.
Hakluyt's Voyages, 3.
Havere Capse (Havere Capselle), 58, 63.
Helias, 250.
Hermits, 362.
Hermit, Florentine, 305.
Herod, 248, 255, 387.
—— House of, 248.
Heughlin, Lorenz, 223.
Heyd, William, 387, 394.
Hierusalem, Voyage to, 2, 9, 92, 96, 380.
Hippocrates, 379.
Holy Land, History of, 7.
—— Voyage to the, 7.
Homer, burial place of, 312.
Hornan the Jebusite, 352.
Howard, Thos., Duke of Norfolk, 36.
Hungarian, Andrew the, 52, 60.
—— Pilgrims, 36, 60.
Hungary, King of, 177, 377, 378.

I

Imola, 352.
Incantus Galearum Peregrinorum, 69, 75.
India, new route to, 338.
Indians, 391.
Inferno (Arsenal), 368.
Innkeepers and Inns, 52, 89.
—— Sun Inn, 342.
Instructions to Pilgrims, 10.
Ionian Islands, 378, 379.
—— Sea, 188.
Ios, Island of, 310.
Istankoi, 379.
Istria, 163, 376, 377.
—— Stone Quarries of, 333, 334.
Italian Pilgrims, 5, 6.
—— Republics, 4.
—— Voyages, 3.

Itinera Latina, 2.
Itinéraires Français, 2.
Itinéraires Russes, 2.

J

Jacob the Patriarch, 252, 262.
Jacobite Christians, 277, 391.
Jacinthos, Island of, 323.
Jadra. See Zara.
Jaffa, 9, 12, 32, 33, 37, 38, 39, 43, 44, 45, 46, 47, 53, 54, 58, 60, 70, 75, 77, 78, 81, 84, 85, 86, 89, 93, 99, 101, 104, 110, 111, 112, 170, 220, 221—235, 253, 287, 290, 381, 384, 387.
—— Custodian at, 223.
—— Fair at, 225.
—— Galley, 8, 76, 96, 98, 101, 103, 104, 105, 124, 155, 162.
—— German Pilgrim died at, 290.
—— St. Peter at, 225, 235.
Jameson, Mrs., 362, 368, 397.
Jehoshaphat, Valley of, 247, 272, 387.
Jericho, 267, 268, 269.
Jerusalem, 2, 3, 4, 5, 6, 7, 8, 9, 92, 102, 103, 110, 112, 124, 224—279, 381.
—— Godfrey and Baldwin, Kings of, 275, 276, 391.
—— Governor of, 220, 222, 253, 266, 270, 271, 273, 274, 276, 280.
—— Hospital at, 6, 244, 272.
—— Miracle at, 254.
—— Pilgrims left at, 282.
Joab, 246.
Joppa (see Jaffa), 235, 253.
Jordan, river, 90, 153.
—— Visit to, 266—268, 271, 273.
—— Jordan Water, 300.
Jorga, Mons. N., 2.
Josephus' Wars of Jews, 246.
Jucho, 223.
Judas Maccabeus, 274, 276, 390.
Judea, Hills of, 264.
Julian the Apostate, 366, 388.

K

Knights of the Holy Sepulchre, 265, 290, 390.
Knights of Rhodes (St. John). See Rhodes.
Kaiet Bey, Sultan, 386, 392.

L

Lanza, Andrea, 184, 187.
—— Pietro, 184, 185, 186, 187.
Larnaca, 394.
Latin Friars. See Mount Sion.
—— Empire, 5.
—— Kings, tombs of the, 275, 390, 391.
Lausanne, Johanne de, 204.
Lazarus, tomb of, 279.
——Miracle of, 293, 394.
Leghorn, 1.
Lent dinner, 343.
Leros, Island of, 382.
Lesina, Island of, 171, 328, 329, 330, 331, 377, 397.
—— Bishop of, 329.
Leucadia, 379.
Levant, 4, 54.
—— Trading Fleet, 301.
Liber Plegiorum, 24.
Liburnians, 164.
Lido, 363, 375.
Limasol, 213—218, 295, 383, 394.
Lissa, Island of,
Lisso, 217.
Litanies, 18, 19, 117, 211, 314.
Lodi, Peace of, 77, 356, 362.
Lodovico il Moro, 15, 321, 322, 357, 395.
Lombardi, Martino, 365, 366.
Lombardy, 7.
—— Sailors from, 161.
Lonato, 120, 343.
Longo (Lango), Island of, 188, 204, 309, 310, 379, 382. See Cos.
—— Governor of, 205, 206, 305, 306, 307, 310, 379.
Loredana (Galley), 67, 81, 82.
Loredano, Antonio, 67, 72, 76, 77, 81.
—— Bartolomeo, 65, 66, 68.
—— Daniele, 67, 72.
—— Jacopo, 83.
—— Leonardo, 367.
—— Lorenzo, 65, 66, 67, 68.
—— Pietro, 68.
Loreto, Pilgrimage to, 52, 324.
Lovato (Lupato), 351.
Luchino, Johanne, 132, 245.
Lucca, 8, 153, 341, 352, 364.
—— National Library at, 8.
—— Merchants from, 135, 364.
Ludolph, Heinrich Wilhelm, 1.
Lumiarez, Antonio di, 21.
Lupato. See Lovato.
Lydda, 239, 387.

M

Maccabeus (Machabeus), 274, 276, 390.
Maetsch, Albrecht, 290.
Magagnis, Jacobinus, 30.
Magistretti, Monsignor Marco, 378.
Majestate (Majestà), 166, 173, 174.
Malcasale, 273.
Malea, Cape, 196.
Malipiera e Giustiniana (Nave), 104.
Malipiero, Domenico, 99, 108, 353, 365, 366, 367, 371.
—— Giacomo, 108.
—— Giorgio, 63.
—— Marino, 36.
—— Tommaso, 108.
Malta, 382.
Mamelukes, 109, 224, 237, 242, 266, 267, 280, 286, 287, 288, 392, 393.
Mameth, 392.
Mantella (Nave), 78.
Mantua, Francis Gonzaga, Lord of, 46.
—— John Francis Gonzaga, first Marquis of, 351.
—— Priest from, 214.
Marano, 233.
Marcelli (Coins), 238, 337.
Marcello, Marcello, 48.
Marchetti (Coins), 236, 239, 249, 279.
Marconi, Bernardo di, 105.
Maritime Statutes, 23, 24, 26, 55, 373.
Maronite Christians, 276, 291, 386.
Marseilles, 113.
Mauro, of Amalfi, 6.
—— Lorenzo and Antonio, 71.
Maydini (Coins), 287.
Mayrola, Johanne de la, 17, 406.
Meda, San Giovanni di, 364.
Medes, Cyrus, King of the, 252.
Meissner, Dr. H., 1.
Melanzane, 240.
Melech-el-Daher (Sultan), 76.
Melita, 171.
Meloria, 4.
Melos, 396.
Merchants, Consuls of the, 26, 40, 56.
—— Council of the, 56.
Mergenthal, Hans von, 91, 93, 102.

INDEX

Messa Secca, 156, 190, 231, 373.
Mestre, 351.
Mezzana (sail), 157.
Methone, 380.
Michiel, Fantin, 106.
—— Francesco, 37, 38.
—— Jacopo, 105.
Midshipmen, 374.
Migliaia, Migliaio, 24.
Milan, 7, 9, 15, 17, 21, 22.
—— Archbishop of, 8, 9, 18, 117, 345.
—— Archives of, 13.
—— St. Ambrose, Bishop of, 117, 135, 349, 350.
—— Churches of St. Ambrose, 117, 163.
—— S. Celso, 349.
—— St. Dionysius, 118.
—— Santa Eufemia, 13, 349.
—— San Lorenzo, 276.
—— S. Maria de Cepis, 407.
—— S. Maria Maggiore, 349.
—— Metropolitan Church at, 13, 349.
San Stefano in Brolio, 15, 404.
—— S. Tecla, 349.
—— San Vittore, 14, 117.
—— Diocese of, 14.
—— Duchess of, 339.
—— Duke of, 7, 8, 63, 175, 344, 394, 407, 408.
—— Duomo, 17, 117, 349.
—— Annals of, 408.
—— Canons of the, 117.
—— Gates, Porta Ticinese, 14, 268.
—— Porta Orientals, 345.
Milan, King of France expected at, 301.
—— Noble Families of, 13.
—— Patron Saints of, 117, 182, 183, 350.
—— Registri Mortuarij, 13.
Milanese, Ambassador to Venice, 9, 20, 125, 339, 340, 341, 351, 366.
—— Rome, 16, 406, 407.
—— Merchants in Venice, 18, 123, 135, 363.
—— Pilgrims, 7.
Misseta, 40, 42, 48, 49, 51, 52, 53.
Mitylene, 379.
Mocenigo, Andrea, 29.
—— Doge Tommaso, 353.
Modone, 22, 42, 53, 67, 87, 102, 103, 170, 191—194, 314, 319, 320, 321, 380, 396.

Modone, Fair at, 191.
—— Wines of, 380.
Moggio, 129.
Money, bag of, 10, 13, 230, 337.
Monte, Gabriele da, 109.
Morea, 104, 188.
Moorish Fasting, 182, 378.
Moors, 83, 92, 225, 226, 229, 230.
Moro, Doge Cristoforo, 353, 371.
Morosina (galley), 82.
Morosini, Andrea, 36, 38, 83.
—— Alvise, 211, 374.
—— Dardi, 37.
—— Francesco, 379, 394.
—— Giovanni, 108.
—— Marcantonio, 357.
—— Piero, 108.
Mosque, 249, 251, 252, 253, 257, 387.
Motta, Emilio, 14, 409.
Mount Lebanon, 389.
Mount Moriah, 252.
Mount of Olives, 246, 247.
Mount Sinai, 7, 32, 345, 385, 386.
Mount Sion, 254, 257, 266, 270, 271, 272, 273, 274, 279.
—— Church of, 254.
—— Friars of, 348, 391, 393.
—— Monastery of, 96, 97, 244, 251, 255, 256, 385, 386.
—— Prior of, 93, 97, 112, 222, 227, 229, 232, 233, 239, 240, 242, 244, 245, 249, 259, 261, 270, 271, 272, 273, 274, 282, 283, 284, 288, 289, 290, 384, 385, 386, 389, 393.
Mowbray, Thomas, Duke of Norfolk, 35.
Moyses, 237.
Mudacio, Andrea, 60.
Murano, 142, 372, 367.
—— Church of Sta Maria degli Angeli, 142, 372.
Murata, la, 331, 332.
Muratori, 18.
Museum, Correr, 21.
Mushrooms, 232, 282.
Muster, the, 343, 398.
Mutinelli, 41, 354, 355, 362.
Myra, Nicholas, Bishop of, 303.
Myr Isbech. See Usbech.

N

Nabule, Governor of, 231, 232.
Nadal, Bernardo, 37.
Nali Bernardino di, 7, 8.

Naples, 5, 77, 171, 188, 303, 377, 394.
—— George of, 110.
—— King of, 303.
—— King Alfonso, 77, 188.
—— King Ferdinand of, 171, 377.
Narma (Narni), Erasmus of. See Gattamelata.
Nassau, Count of, 75.
Natalia, 55, 212, 219, 299.
—— Gulf of, 299.
Navarino, 380.
Navi and Nave, 11, 75, 78, 104, 106, 108, 109, 110, 111, 112, 139, 141.
—— The Santa Maria, 110.
—— Pilgrim Navi, 109.
Naviglio, 268.
Navilio and Navilij, 111, 112.
Naxos, 313, 395, 396.
—— Duchy of, 395, 396.
Nebuchadnezzar, 252, 387.
Negropont, 84, 381, 396.
Nero, Emperor, 350.
Nestorians, 391.
Nicodemus, 261.
Nicolai, Zanino, 38.
Nicosia, 215, 293, 383.
Night, Lords of the, 126, 355.
Nio, Island of, 312.
Nissa, Lord of, 313.
Nissari, 209.
Noah, 249.
Nobili di poppa, 374.
Norfolk, Thomas Mowbray, Duke of, 35, 36.
Normans, 4.
Notte, Signori di, 126, 355.
Nuremberg, 96.

O

Observants, 136.
Odorico of Pordenone, 3.
Omar, Mosque of, 387.
Ongaro, Andrea, 52, 60.
Orient Latin, Société de l', 2.
Orseolo, Doges Pietro I. and II., 352, 377.

P

Padua, 122, 132, 341, 342, 351.
—— Pilgrimage to, 324.
Palazzolo, Raphaele de, 342.

Paleologos, Emperor Michael, 396.
Palestine Pilgrims' Text Society, 3.
Palladio, 362.
Pandolfo, Lord, 48.
Pantaleone of Amalfi, 6.
Papal Legate, 146.
Paphos (Baffo), 212, 299, 383.
Paradise (Arsenal), 368.
Parenzo, 162—164, 170, 333, 335, 368, 376, 377.
Parma, Fra Tiberio of, 365.
Parono, 160.
Paros, Island of, 196, 396.
Parrot, Affair of the, 286—289.
Parsberg, Konrad von, 2, 390.
Partecipazio, Doge, 352.
Pascha, Roxata, 120.
Pasqualigo, Lodovico, 83.
Patera, 303.
Patience, bag of, 10, 13, 230.
Patrono, Patroni, Patronus, 11, 23, 49, 54, 55, 57, 59, 62, 65, 66, 67, 68, 69, 70, 71, 72, 74, 75, 76, 77, 78, 79, 80, 81, 82, 83, 84, 85, 86, 87, 88, 89, 90, 91, 94, 95, 96, 97, 98, 99, 100, 101, 102, 103, 106, 107, 111, 153, 160.
Pavia, 132, 265, 286, 351, 361, 395.
Pelorosso, 336.
Pentecost, 120.
People, Sons of the, 279, 392.
Pera, 84.
Peregrinorum, Capitulum, 25, 27.
Peregrinorum, Incantus galearum, 69, 75.
Persia, Ouzoun Khassan, King of, 96, 396.
Pesaro, 38.
Peschiera, 120, 343.
Phenice, 303.
Phidias, 340.
Piacenza, Sant' Antonino of, 6.
—— Bishop of, 184.
—— Nuns from, 365.
—— Charles VIII. at, 395.
Pianelle, 144.
Piazza Guides. See Guides.
Piccinino, Nicolo, 350, 351.
Piis, Ugolino de, 48.
Pilate, house of, 248.
Pilgrimages to Loreto and Padua, 52, 324.
Pilgrimage, emblems of, 117, 337.

INDEX

Pilgrims Books, 43, 44, 52, 124.
—— Complaints of, 313, 317, 318.
—— on the Contarina, 161.
—— Contracts, 51, 89, 90, 124.
—— Datian, 223.
—— English, 47.
—— Expenses, 94.
—— Flemish, 83.
—— Florentine, 6.
—— French, 36, 78, 104, 227, 234, 262, 287, 332.
—— Galleys, 3, 11, 22, 146, 381, 384, 385.
—— German, 36, 83, 89, 103, 112, 290.
—— Hungarian, 36, 60.
—— Instructions to, 10.
—— Italian, 6, 7.
—— Navi, 109, 110.
arrested as Spies, 270.
Pilot and Pilots, 170, 220, 299, 321, 325, 377.
Pioltella, 118.
Piombi (Prisons), 354.
Pirates, 91, 93, 105, 204, 209, 210, 212, 217, 219, 376, 381.
Pisa, 4.
Pisan Castle, 4, 244, 255.
Pisani, Filippo, 37.
Piskopi, 384.
Pius II., Pope, 82.
Pizolo, 156, 328.
Plague at Cyprus, 293, 305.
Plebanie, 138.
Plegiorum, Liber, 24.
Plimsol, Mark, 24.
Po, river, 168, 268.
Pola, 376.
Ponere Banchum, 59, 65.
Ponte, Zaccaria da, 56, 57.
Pontifical, 345.
Pope, Alexander III., 126, 136.
—— Alexander VI., 321.
—— Ambassador to, 339, 398.
—— Pius II., 82.
—— Urban V., 30.
Poppa, Nobili di, 374.
Pordenone, Odorico of, 3.
Porri, Cipriano di, 241.
Porro, Count Giulio, 15, 21, 22, 349, 362, 379, 383, 387, 389, 390, 399.
Porta Ticinese, 14, 268.
—— Orientale, 345.
Portugal, King John of, 46, 47.
—— Alphonso of, 46, 47.

Possot, Maître Denis, 2, 109, 390, 391, 394.
Pozzi (Prisons), 354.
Præneste, Bernardo of, 6.
Praxitiles, 340.
Predelli, Riccardo, 23, 24, 26, 373.
Pregadi, Council of the, 127, 356.
Prester John (Prete Jane), 391.
Priola (galley), 59.
Priuli, Girolamo, 104, 109, 358.
—— Marino, 76.
Priona, 333.
Prisoners, Christian, 233, 282—289.
Probatic Pool, 248.
Prodano, rock of, 191.
Promissione ducale, 372.
Provenza, 164.
Proveri (galeotti), 12.
Prussia, John of, 390.
Ptolemaida, 233.
Purchas's Pilgrims, 3.
Purgatory (Arsenal), 368.
Puricelli, 349.

Q

Quails (Candia, 316.
Quarantia, Council of the, 43, 47, 355, 376.
Quarantina, Mountain of the, 269.
Quarnero, 164, 333.
Quattro Coronati, 334, 397.
Quirina (galley), 55.
Quirini, Andrea, 55.

R

Rachel, tomb of, 262.
Rages of the Medes, 116.
Ragusa, 172—179, 181, 183, 326, 328, 377, 378.
—— Ragusans, 257, 328, 329.
Rama, 220, 237—242, 281—289.
—— Cotton-growing at, 239, 387.
—— Governor of, 220, 222, 223, 231, 240, 384.
—— Hospital at, 285.
—— Joseph of, 261.
Ramatana, 378.
Ramleh, 220.
Ranghoni, 139.
Raspe, 365.
Rationale, 18.
Registri Mortuarij (Milan), 13.

Regna, Fra Antonio, 244, 271, 272, 274, 286, 288.
Renegade Christians, 279.
Resin in the Wine, 194, 216, 380.
Rethemo (Candia), 202.
Rhodes, 21, 30, 31, 54, 57, 64, 65, 73, 77, 82, 83, 109, 204, 205, 304, 305, 307, 311, 352, 379, 381, 382.
—— Grand Master of, 30, 206, 209, 213, 305, 308, 382.
—— Knights of, 73, 82, 83, 188, 205, 208, 209, 305, 309, 379, 381, 382, 384.
—— Sanitary Officers at, 305.
—— Siege of, 381.
—— Church and Monastery of, Santa Maria della Vittoria, 306, 308.
Rimini, 61.
Rizo, Virgilio, 37.
Rizzo, Antonio, 353.
Robiate, Bernardino di, 406.
Rogations or Litanies, 117.
Röhricht, Reinhold, 1, 2, 3, 8, 359, 390.
Roma, Francesco di, 153.
—— Mario di, 39.
Roman Breviary and Missal, 349.
Romanin, S., 354, 358, 362, 378.
Rome, 16, 17, 52, 61, 62, 120, 127, 137, 188, 297, 343, 365, 395.
—— Milanese Embassy at, 406, 407.
—— Church of Santa Maria Rotunda, 276.
Roso, Don Agostino, 406.
Rosso, Filippo, 241.
Rovato, 350.
Rovere, 152.
Rovigno, 335, 376.
Rotuli, Cassina di, 344.
—— Jacobo, 153.
Russian Palestine Society, 2.
—— Voyages, 2.

S

Sabbatino, 228, 229.
Sacerdoti, A, 23, 24, 26, 373.
Sack of Faith, 225, 227.
—— Money, 10, 225, 230, 237.
——Patience, 10, 225, 230.
Saint Adrian, Cardinal deacon of, 206.
—— Ambrose, 117, 135, 349, 350, 363.

—— Andrea, Island of, 170.
—— Arsenius, 186.
—— Augustine, Vision of, 141, 368.
—— Athanasius, 193.
—— Blaise, 173.
—— Charles Borromeo, 18, 349, 361.
—— Catherine (Mount Sinai), 345, 386.
—— Elizabeth, 264.
—— Euphemia, Church of, 335.
—— George, 239, 387.
—— Gervasius and Protasius, 117, 182, 183, 350.
—— Germanus, 334, 397.
—— Helena, 250, 260, 278, 361, 389.
—— James the Apostle, 255.
—— Jerome, 263, 333.
—— John Baptist, birthplace of, 264.
—— John, Knights of. See Knights of Rhodes.
—— Leo, 193.
—— Mark's Bridge, 343.
—— Nicholas, Bishop of Myra, 303.
—— Paul the Apostle, 205.
—— Peter, 225.
—— Stephen, gate of, 248.
—— Titus, 201, 315, 380.
—— Thomas, 255, 386.
—— Zachariah, 264.
San Lazzaro, Lake of, 293.
—— Nicolo di Carichi (Rhodes), 209.
Santa Maura, Island of, 379.
—— Maria (Nave), 110.
Saladin, 253, 275, 387.
Salem, 250.
Salerno, Alfano, Bishop of, 6.
Salines (Cyprus), 293, 383, 393.
Salmoria, 203.
Salonicco, 60.
Salt, 293, 393, 394.
Sanitary Officers (Rhodes), 305.
Sanseverino, Roberto da, 3, 6, 7, 81, 378, 382, 384, 386.
Sansovino Francesco, 352, 354, 357, 359, 362, 372, 398.
Santurin, Island of, 311.
Sanudo, Giovanni and Marco, 396.
Sanuto, Marino, 8, 36, 101, 103, 104, 105, 353, 355, 371, 381, 387, 392.

INDEX

Saracens, 4, 6, 12, 29, 30, 49, 250.
Sarpi, Fra Paolo, 364.
Sasino, El, Island of, 325.
Satalia (Sadalia). See Natalia.
Saurinia, 303.
Savij, 47.
Savina, Chronicle of, 365.
Savoy, Bona of, 404.
—— Duke of, 48, 82.
Savoyard Nobles, 63.
Saxony, Duke of, 91, 103.
Scanderbeg, 84.
Schefer, Mons. Charles, 2.
Scio, 322.
Scirocco, 164.
Sclavonia and Sclavonians, 32, 161, 169, 179.
Scotto Bernardino, 161, 257, 376.
Seat, Doge's, 372.
Sebenico, 169, 331, 377.
Secchi, Don F., 118, 344.
Secretary, Chief, 144, 369.
Seprio, lakes of the, 293, 394.
Sepulchre, Holy. First visit to the, 259—261.
—— Second Visit to the 264—265.
—— Third Visit to the, 274—278.
—— Christian Sects at the, 391.
—— Church of the, 275—278, 390.
—— Knights of the, 265, 290, 390.
—— Plan of the, 388, 389.
Sepulchre of Our Lady, 272.
Serio, 118.
Sermons by Fra. F. Trivulzio at Zara, 167.
—— at Ragusa, 179.
—— on St. John's Eve, 189.
—— on St. John's day, 190.
—— at Jaffa, 221, 222, 224, 231.
—— at Sea on the return voyage, 297, 298, 299.
—— at Bethlehem, 262.
—— by Friars and the Prior of Mount Sion, 239, 258, 260, 283.
—— at Lesina, 330.
Sexula, 229, 233, 256, 258.
Sforza, Francesco, 6, 356.
—— Galeazzo, 404.
—— Gian Galeazzo, 15, 361, 395.
—— Lodovico, 8, 15, 321, 322, 344, 357, 395, 404.
Sforza palace in Venice, 128, 356.
Sichi. See Secchi.

Sicily, 387.
Siena, 352, 372, 373.
Signoria of Venice, 121, 141, 160, 165, 171, 184, 186, 188, 191, 192, 194, 195, 217, 313, 322, 331, 337, 342, 366, 369, 384, 398.
—— of Ragusa, 177, 178.
Sigoli, Simone, 6.
Silk Industry, 121.
Siloam, pool of, 248.
Simiteculo, Galeazzo, 109.
Sinai. See Mount Sinai and Saint Catherine.
Sino Fanatico, 164.
Sion, Mount. See Mount Sion.
Smith, Lucy Toulmin, 33.
Snow, 227.
Sophronius (Patriarch), 389.
Solomon, Temple of, 249, 252, 253, 387.
Solyma, 250.
Sopra Porto, 336.
Soranzo, Giovanni, 330.
—— Nicolo, 33.
Spain, 8, 188.
—— Nephew of the King of, 188.
Spanish Litanies, 211.
Spalato, 171, 377.
Spies, pilgrims arrested as, 270.
Spring Voyage, 25, 76.
Stagno, 172.
Staia, 185.
Stella, Raphaeletto de, 38.
Stinche, 238, 387.
Stone Cutters, 397.
Stone quarries, 333, 334.
Stradioti, 151.
Strapontino, 11.
Stroncone, Father Agostino di, 386.
Sugar Plantations, 216, 383, 384.
Sun Inn, 342.
Suriano, Fra Francesco, 3, 7, 93, 95, 98, 229, 384, 386, 389, 390, 391, 392, 393.
Symie, Island of, 208.
Syria, 5, 25, 27, 37, 39, 43, 53, 54, 58, 60, 67, 80, 212, 219, 383, 386.
Syrian Christians, 276, 386, 391.

T

Tabitha, 235.
Tacitus, 359.

Talenti, Tommaso, 361.
Tana, The. 367.
Tantalus, 225.
Tarì, 4.
Tassini, 354, 356, 357, 359, 362, 365.
Tavernelle, le, 342.
Tedeschi, Fondaco dei, 40, 129, 358, 359.
Telos, Island of, 382.
Terra Santa, Trattato di, 3.
—— Viaggio in, 3.
Terza, Ora di, 123.
Thera, 311.
Tholomarius, Tholomarij. See Guides.
Thorn, Sacred, 210, 382.
Tiberio, Fra, 365.
Ticinese, Porta, 14, 268.
Tiepolo, Doge Jacopo, 24, 55, 373.
—— Lorenzo, 65, 76.
—— Statute, 27, 373.
Timotheus, 201.
Tirapello, Zanino, 36.
Titian, 357, 358.
Titus Cæsar, 250, 252, 388.
Tobias, 116.
Tobler, Titus, 1, 3, 6.
Toga, 143.
Tolomei, Bernardo, 362.
Tomacello, Fra Giovanni, 389.
Torcello, 398.
Toretino, Johanne or Giovanne, 153, 154, 341.
Torre, George da, 103.
Torresella, 354.
Trani, Bishop Pietro da. 363.
Transylvania, Voyvode of, 32.
Trau, 171, 377.
Trevisano, Domenico, 76.
—— Melchiore, 357.
—— Nicolo, 353.
—— Stefano, 65.
—— Zaccaria, 76.
Treviso, 46, 146, 342, 351.
—— Bishop of, 146.
—— Fair at, 342.
Triduan Litanies, 18, 19.
Trieste, Gulf of, 162.
Trinchetto, 159.
Trinity. St. Augustine's Vision of, 141, 368.
Tripoli (in Syria), 217, 387.
—— Consul of, 217.
Triremes, 56, 83, 101, 102, 103, 369.

Trivulzian Library, 7, 15, 21, 388, 404.
Trivulzio, Carlo, 21.
—— Donna Evelina, 21.
—— Fra Francesco, 21, 132, 135, 142, 154, 155, 162, 164, 167, 172, 174, 175, 179, 180, 182, 189, 190, 191, 193, 196, 198, 207, 214, 218, 221, 222, 223, 224, 226, 231, 238, 239, 241, 245, 262, 264, 266, 267, 269, 275, 282, 284, 290, 297, 299, 300, 302, 304, 305, 306, 307, 308, 330, 352, 359—361.
—— Gian Giacomo, 9, 91.
—— Pietro, 359, 360.
Trono, Luca, 65, 107.
Turbigo, 235.
Tucher, J., of Nuremberg, 96.
Turks, 30, 55, 60, 82, 83, 84, 91, 96, 102, 103, 104, 105, 108, 109, 113, 177, 188, 190, 204, 205, 210, 212, 303, 310, 326, 331, 379, 381, 382, 383, 393, 394, 396.
Tyre, William of, 389.
Tyrol, Sigismund, Count of, 7.

U

Umbria, 385.
Ughelli, 372.
Umiliati, 364.
Urban, v. (Pope), 30.
Urbino, 38.
Usbech (Myr Isbech), 222, 253, 273, 276, 280, 283, 293, 385, 386, 393.

V

Valania, 187.
Vallaressa (galley), 63.
Vallaresso (Valessi), Giov. B., 267, 288, 374.
Varese da Rosate, Ambrogio, 14, 409.
Vasallo, Francesco, 104.
Veglia, Count of, 31.
Vendramin, Doge Andrea, 108.
—— Luca, 108.
Venice. Castles, 155, 362, 363; Chief Secretary, 144, 369; Churches and Monasteries of: All Saints, 338; Sant' Ambrogio, 135, 338; Sant' Andrea, 135, 363; Sant' Antonio, 134, 362; San Cristoforo, 135, 362;

INDEX 427

Carmine, 136; San Domenico, 138, 341, 366; Sant' Elena, 134, 361; San Francesco delle Vigne, 135, 363; San Giorgio in Alga, 136, 364, San Giorgio, Maggiore, 135, 339, 362; San Giovanni e Paolo, 138, 366; Santa Maria degli Angeli, 142, 372; S. Maria de Caelestibus, 136, 368; S. Maria della Caritá, 126, 136, 355; S. Maria dei Frari, 135, 338, 363; S. Maria dei Miracoli, 139, 367; S. Maria dell' Orto, 136, 364; S. Maria dei Servi, 135, 363; San Marco, 137; S. Nicolo del Lido, 136, 364; San Pietro (Castello), 137, 365; San Salvatore, 136, 341; Virgins, 136, 365; San Zaccaria, 136, 365; Custom House, 337, 397, 398; Ducal Palace, 126—128, 152, 352; Ducats of, 4, 10, 153, 283, 284, 287, 289; Gentlemen of, 142, 143; Hostels, 358; Islands of Murano, 372; S. Michele, 362; Mint of, 13, 153, 283, 284, 287, 289; Maritime Legislation, 23, 24, 26; Monastic Orders of S. Augustine, 136, 355, 361, 362, 364, 365; Benedictines, 145, 364, 365; Camaldolese, 134, 362; Carmelites, 136, 364; Carthusians, 135, 363; Cistercians, 365, 398; St. Clara, 139; Dominicans, 138, 366; Eremitani, 135, 362; Franciscans, 135, 335, 363; Gesuati, 151, 372, 373; Santa Giustina, 135, 151; Olivetani, 134, 362; Servites, 364; Umiliati, 364; Palace of the Sforzas, 128, 356; Parochial Churches, 138; Patriarch of, 147, 152; Piazzas, 128; Prisons, 353, 354; Provisions and Markets, 129—132; Great Schools, 138, 148, 149, 150, 355, 363, 366; Trading Fleets, 59; Warehouses, 129, 357, 358; Wells, 359; Venetian Women, 142—144.
Venier, Doge, 35.
—— Francesco, 68.
—— Lorenzo, 315, 318, 320, 324, 326, 328, 330, 332, 335.
—— Santo, 68.
Verdure, 131.

Verme, Jacopo del, 33.
Verona, 120, 342, 343, 350.
Vespasian, 250.
Vespers, 123.
Viario, Giorgio, 377.
Vicenza, 121, 342, 351.
Vicomercato, Vadiolo de, 125, 155, 337, 341, 351, 352, 366, 398.
Villanova, Abbey of, 342.
Visconti, Filippo Maria, 63, 77.
Viterbo, 119.
Vivarini, Bartolomeo, 363.
Volto Santo, 364.
Von Wyss, Clotilde, 378.
Voyages, in August, 69, 71, 75.
—— Autumn, 25, 76, 78.
—— at Easter, 25, 53, 69, 71, 75, 82.
—— in March, 71.
—— in Spring, 25, 76.
—— in Winter, 25.

W
Wax, white, 80, 129, 135.
Wurtemburg, Eberhard of, 92.

Z
Zaffo, Agostino dal, 95.
Zangola, 11.
Zane, 35.
—— Paolo, 399.
Zante, 36, 190, 322, 323, 379.
Zara, 165—167, 168, 169, 332, 336, 377.
—— Relic of S. Simeon, 166.
—— Death of a pilgrim from, 303.
—— Zanino, de cha de, 36, 37.
Zecchino, 4.
Zelestre, 136, 365.
Zem, Sultan, 379.
Zeno, Carlo, 53.
—— Luca, 315, 318.
—— Doge Rainiero, 26, 55.
—— Statute, 27, 28.
Zerubbabel, 387.
Ziani, Doge Pietro, 23, 363.
—— Marco, 363.
Zorza (Galley), 102.
Zorzi, Alvise, 101, 103, 381.
—— Friar of the Zorzi family, 22, 301.
—— Fra Francesco, 394.
—— Girolamo (Jeronimo or Hieronimo), 339, 398.
—— Doge Marino, 367.
Zulian, Marco, 355.

SHERRATT AND HUGHES

MANCHESTER UNIVERSITY PUBLICATIONS.

MEDICAL SERIES. No. 1.

No. I. SKETCHES OF THE LIVES AND WORK OF THE HONORARY MEDICAL STAFF OF THE ROYAL INFIRMARY. From its foundation in 1752 to 1830, when it became the Royal Infirmary. By EDWARD MANSFIELD BROCKBANK, M.D., M.R.C.P. Crown 4to (illustrated). 15s. net.

"Dr. Brockbank's is a book of varied interest. It also deserves a welcome as one of the earliest of the 'Publications of the University of Manchester.'"—*Manchester Guardian.*

"We have a valuable contribution to local Medical Literature."—
Daily Dispatch.

MEDICAL SERIES. No. 2.

No. II. PRACTICAL PRESCRIBING AND DISPENSING. For Medical Students. By WILLIAM KIRKBY, sometime Lecturer in Pharmacognosy in the Owens College, Manchester. Crown 8vo, 220 pp. Second edition. 5s. net.

"The whole of the matter bears the impress of that technical skill and thoroughness with which Mr. Kirkby's name must invariably be associated, and the book must be welcomed as one of the most useful recent additions to the working library of prescribers and dispensers."—
Pharmaceutical Journal.

"Thoroughly practical text-books on the subject are so rare that we welcome with pleasure Mr. William Kirkby's 'Practical Prescribing and Dispensing.' The book is written by a pharmacist expressly for medical students, and the author has been most happy in conceiving its scope and arrangement."—*British Medical Journal.*

"The work appears to be peculiarly free from blemishes and particularly full in practical detail. It is manifestly the work of one who is a skilled chemist, and an expert pharmacist, and who knows not only the requirements of the modern student but the best way in which his needs may be met."—*Medical Press.*

"This is a very sensible and useful manual."—*The Hospital.*

"The book will be found very useful to any students during a course of practical dispensing."—*St. Bartholomew's Hospital Journal.*

"The book is a model, being tutorial from beginning to end."—
The Chemist and Druggist.

"A very useful little book."—*Practitioner.*

34 CROSS STREET, MANCHESTER

SHERRATT AND HUGHES

MANCHESTER UNIVERSITY PUBLICATIONS—*continued.*

HISTORICAL SERIES. No. 1.
No. III. MEDIÆVAL MANCHESTER AND THE BEGINNING OF LANCASHIRE. By JAMES TAIT, M.A., Professor of Ancient and Mediæval History. Demy 8vo, 240 pp. 7s. 6d. net.

"Patient and enlightened scholarship and a sense of style and proportion have enabled the writer to produce a work at once solid and readable."—*English Historical Review.*

"A welcome addition to the literature of English local history, not merely because it adds much to our knowledge of Manchester and Lancashire, but also because it displays a scientific method of treatment which is rare in this field of study in England."—Dr. Gross in *American Historical Review.*

"La collection ne pouvait débuter plus significativement et plus heureusement que par un ouvrage d'histoire du Moyen Age dû a M. Tait, car l'enseignement médiéviste est un de ceux qui font le plus d'honneur à la jeune Université de Manchester, et c'est a M. le Professeur Tait qu'il faut attribuer une bonne part de ce succès."—*Revue de Synthèse historique.*

"The two essays are models of their kind."—*Manchester Guardian.*

ECONOMIC SERIES. No. 1.
No. IV. THE LANCASHIRE COTTON INDUSTRY. By S. J. CHAPMAN, M.A., M. Com. Jevons Professor of Political Economy and Dean of the Faculty of Commerce. 7s. 6d. net. Demy 8vo.

"Such a book as this ought to be, and will be, read far beyond the bounds of the trade."—*Manchester Guardian.*

"There have been books dealing with various phases of the subject, but no other has so ably breathed it from the economic as well as from the historical point of view."—*Manchester Courier.*

"The story of the evolution of the industry from small and insignificant beginnings up to its present imposing proportions and lightly developed and specialised forms, is told in a way to rivet the attention of the reader . . . . . . the book is a valuable and instructive treatise on a fascinating yet important subject."—*Cotton Factory Times.*

"Highly valuable to all close students."—*Scotsman.*

HISTORICAL SERIES. No. 2.
No. V. INITIA OPERUM LATINORUM QUAE SAECULIS XIII., XIV., XV. ATTRIBUUNTUR. By A. G. LITTLE, M.A., Lecturer in Palæography. Demy 8vo, 300 pp. (interleaved). 15s. net.

MEDICAL SERIES. No. 3.
No. VI. HANDBOOK OF SURGICAL ANATOMY. By G. A. WRIGHT, B.A., M.B. (Oxon.), F.R.C.S., and C. H. PRESTON, M.D., F.R.C.S., L.D.S. Crown 8vo, 214 pp. Second edition. 5s. net.

"We can heartily recommend the volume to students, and especially to those preparing for a final examination in surgery."—*Hospital.*

"Dr. Wright and Dr. Preston have produced a concise and very readable little handbook of surgical applied anatomy. . . . The subject matter of the book is well arranged and the marginal notes in bold type facilitate reference to any desired point."—*Lancet.*

34 CROSS STREET, MANCHESTER

SHERRATT AND HUGHES

MANCHESTER UNIVERSITY PUBLICATIONS—*continued.*

HISTORICAL SERIES. NO. 3.

No. VII. THE OLD COLONIAL SYSTEM. By GERALD BERKELEY HERTZ, M.A., B.C.L. Demy 8vo, 232 pp. 5s. net.

"Mr. Hertz gives us an elaborate historical study of the old colonial system, which disappeared with the American Revolution . . . . He shows a remarkable knowledge of contemporary literature, and his book may claim to be a true history of popular opinion."—*Spectator.*

"Mr. Hertz's book is one which no student of imperial developments can neglect. It is lucid, fair, thorough, and convincing."—*Glasgow Herald.*

"Mr. Hertz's 'Old Colonial System' is based on a careful study of contemporary documents, with the result that several points of no small importance are put in a new light . . . . it is careful, honest work . . . The story which he tells has its lesson for us."—*The Times.*

"Both the ordinary reader and the academic mind will get benefit from this well-informed and well-written book."—*Scotsman.*

ECONOMIC SERIES. NO. 2. (GARTSIDE REPORT, NO. 1.)

No. VIII. AN EXAMINATION OF THE COTTON INDUSTRY IN THE UNITED STATES. By T. W. UTTLEY, B.A. Demy 8vo. 1s. net.

"Mr. Uttley is to be congratulated on the performance of a not altogether easy task, and his book, in conception and execution, appears to fulfil admirably the intentions of the Trust."—*Manchester Courier.*

"The writer gives ample details concerning wages and other features connected with typical mills . . . and the information thus gathered is of interest and value to the factory operative as well as the student and economist."—*Cotton Factory Times*

"Mr. Uttley describes how he visited the mills in various States in a very systematic and detailed manner. Altogether the report makes an admirable and welcome collection of information, and will be found on many occasions worthy of reference."—*Textile Mercury.*

THEOLOGICAL SERIES. NO. 1.

No. IX. INAUGURAL LECTURES delivered during the Session 1904-5, by the Professors and Lecturers of the Faculty of Theology, viz. :—

Prof. T. F. Tout, M.A.; Prof. A. S. Peake, B.D.; Prof. H. W. Hogg, M.A.; Prof. T. W. Rhys Davids, LL.D.; Rev. W. F. Adeney, D.D.; Rev. A. Gordon, M.A.; Rev. L. Hassé; Rev. Canon E. L. Hicks, M.A.; Rev. H. D. Lockett, M.A.; Rev. R. Mackintosh, D.D.; Rev. J. T. Marshall, D.D.; Rev. J. H. Moulton, D.Litt.

Edited by A. S. PEAKE, B.D., Dean of the Faculty.

Demy 8vo, 300 pages. 7s. 6d. net.

"The lectures, while scholarly, are at the same time popular, and will be found interesting and instructive by those who are not theologians.

60 CHANDOS STREET, LONDON W.C.

MANCHESTER UNIVERSITY PUBLICATIONS—*continued.*
PRESS NOTICES (Inaugural Lectures)—*Continued.*

". . . The entire series is excellent, and the volume deserves a wide circulation."—*Scotsman.*

"This is a very welcome volume . . . All these lectures were delivered to popular audiences, yet they are far from superficial, and will be found of great value to busy pastors and teachers."—*Christian World.*

"We welcome the volume as a most auspicious sign of the times."—
Spectator.

"The lectures themselves give a valuable conspectus of the present position of Theological research . . . They are, of course, not addressed to experts, but they are exceedingly valuable, even when allowance is made for their more or less popular form."—*Examiner.*

"The whole volume forms a very important and valuable contribution to the cause of Theological learning."—*Record.*

"This is a most interesting and valuable book, the appearance of which at the present moment is singularly significant. . . . But it is impossible in a brief review to indicate all the treasures of this rich volume, to read which carefully is to be introduced to the varied wealth of modern Biblical scholarship."—*Baptist.*

"This volume is of the most exceptional value and interest."—
Expository Times.

"This is a book of more than common interest."—
Review of Theology and Philosophy

"The writers of these lectures do not attempt to offer more than samples of their wares : but what is given is good, and it may be seen that theology without tests is destitute neither of scientific value nor of human interest."—*Athenæum.*

ANATOMICAL SERIES. No. 1.

No. X. STUDIES IN ANATOMY from the Anatomical Department of the University of Manchester. Vol. iii. Edited by ALFRED H. YOUNG, M.B. (Edin.), F.R.C.S., Professor of Anatomy. Demy 8vo, 320 pp., 24 Plates. 10s. net.

MEDICAL SERIES. No. 4.

No. XI. A COURSE OF INSTRUCTION IN OPERATIVE SURGERY in the University of Manchester. By WILLIAM THORBURN, M.D., B.S. (Lond.), F.R.C.S., Lecturer in Operative Surgery. Crown 8vo. 2s. 6d. net.

"This little book gives the junior student all that he wants, and nothing that he does not want. Its size is handy, and altogether for its purpose it is excellent."—*University Review.*

"As a working guide it is excellent."—*Edinburgh Medical Journal.*

PUBLIC HEALTH SERIES. No. 1.

No. XII. ARCHIVES OF THE PUBLIC HEALTH LABORATORY OF THE UNIVERSITY OF MANCHESTER. Edited by A. SHERIDAN DELÉPINE, M.Sc., M.B., Ch.M. Crown 4to, 450 pp. £1. 1s. net.

"The University of Manchester has taken the important and highly commendable step of commencing the publication of the archives of its

SHERRATT AND HUGHES

MANCHESTER UNIVERSITY PUBLICATIONS—*continued.*

Public Health Laboratory, and has issued, under the able and judicious editorship of Professor Sheridan Delépine, the first volume of a series that promises to be of no small interest and value alike to members of the medical profession and to those of the laity . . . Original communications bearing upon diseases which are prevalent in the districts surrounding Manchester, or dealing with food- and water-supplies, air, disposal of refuse, sterilisation and disinfection and kindred subjects, will be published in future volumes; and it is manifest that these, as they successively appear, will form a constantly increasing body of trustworthy information upon subjects which are not only of the highest interest to the profession but of supreme importance to the public."—
The Lancet.

"It is safe to say that as these volumes accumulate they will form one of the most important works of reference on questions of public health, and ought, at all events, to be in the library of every public authority."—*Manchester Guardian.*

"The volume . . . . speaks well for the activity of investigation in Manchester."—*Lancet.*

PHYSICAL SERIES. No. 1.

No. XIII. THE PHYSICAL LABORATORIES OF THE UNIVERSITY OF MANCHESTER. A record of 25 years' work. Demy 8vo, 160 pp, 10 Plates, 4 Plans. 5s. net.

This volume contains an illustrated description of the Physical, Electrical Engineering, and Electro-Chemistry Laboratories of the Manchester University, also a complete Biographical and Bibliographical Record of those who have worked in the Physics Department of the University during the past 25 years.

MEDICAL SERIES. No. 5.

No. XIV. A HANDBOOK OF LEGAL MEDICINE. By W. SELLERS, M.D. (London), of the Middle Temple and Northern Circuit, Barrister-at-law. With Illustrations. Crown 8vo. 7s. 6d. net.

"This is quite one of the best books of the kind we have come across."—*Law Times.*

MEDICAL SERIES. No. 6.

No. XV. A CATALOGUE OF THE PATHOLOGICAL MUSEUM OF THE UNIVERSITY OF MANCHESTER. Edited by J. LORRAIN SMITH, M.A., M.D. (Edin.), Professor of Pathology. Crown 4to, 1260 pp. 7s. 6d. net.

60 CHANDOS STREET, LONDON W.C.

MANCHESTER UNIVERSITY PUBLICATIONS—*continued.*
HISTORICAL SERIES. No. 4.

No. XVI. STUDIES OF ROMAN IMPERIALISM. By W. T. ARNOLD, M.A. Edited by EDWARD FIDDES, M.A., with Memoir of the Author by Mrs. HUMPHREY WARD and C. E. MONTAGUE. With a Photograuve of W. T. Arnold. Demy 8vo, 400 pp. 7s. 6d. net.

"Mrs. Humphry Ward has used all her delicate and subtle art to draw a picture of her beloved brother; and his friend Mr. Montague's account of his middle life is also remarkable for its literary excellence."—*Athenæum.*

"The memoir . . . . . tenderly and skilfully written by the 'sister and friend,' tells a story, which well deserved to be told, of a life rich in aspirations, interests, and friendships, and not without its measure of actual achievement."—*Tribune.*

"Readers of this fragment will note the writer's generally facile style, his large grasp in detail, his preference for the study of historical matters as illustrative of the progress of communities rather than as records of individual character and achievement; and will understand the loss to literature of a mind capable of such zealous, honourable, and determined effort."—*Globe.*

"This geographical sense and his feeling for politics give colour to all he wrote."—*Times.*

"The singularly interesting literary monument which in the introduction to this volume has been raised to the memory of the late William Arnold by the affection of his distinguished sister, and by the wholehearted comradeship of a fellow-worker of many years, will be welcome to the numerous friends whom he has left behind him."—*Spectator.*

"Anyone who desires a general account of the Empire under Augustus which is freshly and clearly written and based on wide reading will find it here."—*Manchester Guardian.*

"Nothing could be better than the sympathetic tribute which Mrs. Humphry Ward pays to her brother, or the analysis of his work and method by his colleague Mr. Montague. The two together have more stuff in them than many big books of recent biography."—
Westminster Gazette.

No. XVII. CALENDAR OF THE VICTORIA UNIVERSITY OF MANCHESTER. Session 1904–5. Demy 8vo, 1100 pp. 3s. net.
No. XVIII. CALENDAR OF THE VICTORIA UNIVERSITY OF MANCHESTER. Session 1905–6. Demy 8vo, 1100 pp. 3s. net.
No. XIX. CALENDAR OF THE VICTORIA UNIVERSITY OF MANCHESTER. Session 1906–7. Demy 8vo, 1100 pp. 3s. net.

MEDICAL SERIES. No. 7.

No. XX. HANDBOOK OF DISEASES OF THE HEART. By GRAHAM STEELL, M.D., F.R.C.P., Lecturer in Diseases of the Heart, and Physician to the Manchester Royal Infirmary. Crown 8vo. 400 pp., 11 plates (5 in colours), and 100 illustrations in the text. 7s. 6d. net.

SHERRATT AND HUGHES

MANCHESTER UNIVERSITY PUBLICATIONS —continued.

ECONOMIC SERIES, No. 3. (GARTSIDE REPORT, No. 2.)
No. XXI. SOME MODERN CONDITIONS AND RECENT DEVELOPMENTS IN IRON AND STEEL PRODUCTIONS IN AMERICA, being a Report to the Gartside Electors, on the results of a Tour in the U.S.A. By FRANK POPPLEWELL, B.Sc. Demy 8vo. Price 1s. net.

ECONOMIC SERIES, No. 4. (GARTSIDE REPORT, No. 3.)
No. XXII. ENGINEERING AND INDUSTRIAL CONDITIONS IN THE UNITED STATES. By FRANK FOSTER, M.Sc. Demy 8vo. Price 1s. net.

ECONOMIC SERIES, No. 5.
No. XXIII. THE RATING OF LAND VALUES. By J. D. CHORLTON, M.Sc. Demy 8vo. Price 3s. 6d. net.

ECONOMIC SERIES, No. 6. (GARTSIDE REPORT, No. 4.)
No. XXIV. DYEING IN GERMANY AND AMERICA. By SYDNEY H. HIGGINS, M.Sc. Demy 8vo. [In the press.

ECONOMIC SERIES, No. 7.
THE HOUSING PROBLEM IN ENGLAND. By ERNEST RITSON DEWSNUP, M.A. [In the press.

EDUCATIONAL SERIES. No. 1.
CONTINUATION SCHOOLS IN ENGLAND AND ELSEWHERE: Their place in the Educational System of an Industrial and Commercial State. By MICHAEL E. SADLER, M.A., LL.D., Professor of the History and Administration of Education. Demy 8vo.
This work is largely based on an enquiry made by past and present Students of the Educational Department of the University of Manchester. Chapters on Continuation Schools in the German Empire, Switzerland, Denmark, and France, have been contributed by other writers. [In the press.

HISTORICAL SERIES, No. 5.
CANON PETER CASOLA'S PILGRIMAGE TO JERUSALEM IN THE YEAR 1494. By M. NEWETT. Demy 8vo. [In the press.

HISTORICAL SERIES, No. 6.
HISTORICAL ESSAYS. Edited by T. F. TOUT, M.A., and JAMES TAIT, M.A. Demy 8vo. [In the press.

The following are in preparation and will be issued shortly :—
DISEASES OF THE EAR. By W. MILLIGAN, M.D., Lecturer on Diseases of the Ear and Nasal Surgeon to the Manchester Royal Infirmary.
DISEASES OF THE EYE. By C. E. GLASCOTT, M.D., Lecturer on Ophthalmology, and A. HILL GRIFFITH, M.D., Ophthalmic Surgeon to the Manchester Royal Infirmary.
HANDBOOK OF NERVOUS DISEASES. By JUDSON S. BURY, M.D., Lecturer on Clinical Neurology and Physician to the Manchester Royal Infirmary.

60 CHANDOS STREET, LONDON W.C.

MANCHESTER UNIVERSITY PUBLICATIONS—*continued.*

LECTURES.

GARDEN CITIES (Warburton Lecture). By RALPH NEVILLE, K.C. 6d. net.

THE BANK OF ENGLAND AND THE STATE (A Lecture). By FELIX SCHUSTER. 6d. net.

BEARING AND IMPORTANCE OF COMMERCIAL TREATIES IN THE TWENTIETH CENTURY. By Sir THOMAS BARCLAY. 6d. net.

THE SCIENCE OF LANGUAGE AND THE STUDY OF THE GREEK TESTAMENT (A Lecture). By JAMES HOPE MOULTON, M.A., Litt.D. 6d. net.

THE GENERAL MEDICAL COUNCIL: ITS POWERS AND ITS WORK (A Lecture). By DONALD MACALISTER, M.A., M.D., B.Sc., D.C.L., LL.D. 6d. net.

THE CONTRASTS IN DANTE (A Lecture). By the Hon. WILLIAM WARREN VERNON, M.A. 6d. net.

Issued from the University Press.

MELANDRA CASTLE, being the Report of the Manchester and District Branch of the Classical Association for 1905. Edited by R. S. CONWAY, Litt.D. Introduction by Rev. E. L. HICKS, M.A. Demy 8vo. Illustrated. 5s. net.

"Both the antiquarian and the student of general English history should find this volume of deep interest."—*Tribune.*

"A thoroughly creditable piece of work, carefully edited. . . . Meanwhile we wish the excavators continued success, and hope that their spirited example will be followed in other parts of the country by competent classical scholars."—Mr. G. F. Hill in the *Manchester Guardian.*

"Many admirable plans and illustrations add to the clearness of this excellently planned book on a very interesting subject."—*Daily News.*

Prof. Willamowitz Moellendorf, of Berlin, writes of the Keltic and Roman Weights:—"This is really a great result and one on which the Corpus Inscriptionum is silent."

TRANSACTIONS OF THE INTERNATIONAL UNION FOR CO-OPERATION IN SOLAR RESEARCH (Vol. I., First and Second Conferences). Demy 8vo, 260 pp. and plate. Price 7s. 6d. net.

THE BOOK OF RUTH (Unpointed Text). 6d. net.

SCENES FROM THE RUDENS OF PLAUTUS, with a Translation into English Verse. Edited by R. S. CONWAY, Litt.D., Professor of Latin in the University. 6d. net.